Your Official
America Online®
Guide to Personal
Finance and Investing

Your Official **America Online**® Guide to Personal Finance and Investing

Carol Leonetti Dannhauser
and Portia Thorburn Richardson

AOLPress

Dulles, VA

Your Official America Online® Guide to Personal Finance and Investing

Published by

AOL Press

An imprint of IDG Books Worldwide, Inc.

An International Data Group Company

919 E. Hillsdale Blvd., Suite 400

Foster City, CA 94404

www.aol.com (America Online Web site)

ISBN: 0-7645-3427-0

Printed in the United States of America

10 9 8 7 6 5 4 3 2 1

1B/SY/RS/ZZ/FC

Distributed in the United States by IDG Books Worldwide, Inc. and America Online, Inc.

For general information on IDG Books Worldwide's books in the U.S., please call our Consumer Customer Service department at 800-762-2974. For reseller information, including discounts and premium sales, please call our Reseller Customer Service department at 800-434-3422.

For information on where to purchase IDG Books Worldwide's books outside the U.S., please contact our International Sales department at 317-596-5530 or fax 317-596-5692.

Library of Congress Cataloging-in-Publication Data

Dannhauser, Carol Leonetti, 1959-

Your Official America Online Guide to Personal Finance and Investing/Carol Leonetti Dannhauser and Portia Thorburn Richardson

    p cm

  Includes index.

  ISBN 0-7645-3427-0 (alk. paper)

  1. Finance, Personal--Computer network resources. 2. Investments--Computer network resources. 3. America Online, Inc. 4. Internet (Computer Network) 5. World Wide Web. I Richardson, Portia Thorburn, 1954- II. Title.

HG179 .D333 1999

332.024'00285'4678--dc21

 is a trademark of America Online, Inc.

 is a registered trademark or trademark under exclusive license to IDG Books Worldwide, Inc. from International Data Group, Inc. in the United States and/or other countries.

Welcome to AOL Press™

AOL Press books provide timely guides to getting the most out of your online life. AOL Press was formed as part of the AOL family to create a complete series of official references for using America Online as well as the entire Internet — all designed to help you enjoy a fun, easy, and rewarding online experience.

AOL Press is an exciting partnership between two companies at the forefront of the knowledge and communications revolution — AOL and IDG Books Worldwide. AOL is committed to quality, ease of use, and value and IDG Books excels at helping people understand technology.

To meet these high standards, all our books are authored by experts with the full participation of and exhaustive review by AOL's own development, technical, managerial, and marketing staff. Together, AOL and IDG Books have implemented an ambitious publishing program to develop new publications that serve every aspect of your online life.

We hope you enjoy reading this AOL Press title and find it useful. We welcome your feedback at AOL keyword: **Contact Shop Direct** so we can keep providing information the way you want it.

AOLPress

About the Authors

Carol Leonetti Dannhauser bought her first stock with money she saved while working for minimum wage at a sweatshop during high school vacations. She is eternally grateful to a stockbroker, the father of a college mate, who made the odd-lot trade for her and waived his commission. Thank you, Charles Early.

Carol is a journalist whose work has appeared in the New York Times, Business Week, Working Woman, and on AOL, among many other publications. She has been twice nominated for Emmys by the National Association of Television Arts and Sciences, in addition to many other journalism and writing awards. This is her first book.

Carol has a master's degree in journalism from Columbia University, and two bachelor's degrees (one in journalism and one in Italian) from the University of Connecticut. She figures that if her investments turn out okay, she'll be able to send her two sons to college and have something left over. Then she'll either go traipsing through Europe, start a business with her husband, go back to school to study anthropology, or become a furniture painter. She hasn't figured out the goals part yet. Maybe she should re-read Chapter 4.

Carol has been investing online since 1992.

Portia Thorburn Richardson is a financial writer specializing in personal finance and investing.

Credits

America Online

Technical Editor
Jim Hoscheit

IDG Books Worldwide

Acquisitions Editor
Kathy Yankton

Project Editor
Paul Winters

Technical Editor
Kristen Tod

Copy Editors
Tim Borek
Marti Paul

Project Coordinator
Linda Marousek

Graphics and Production Specialists
Mario Amador
Jude Levinson
Ramses Ramirez
Victor Perez-Verala

Quality Control Specialists
Chris Weisbart
Laura Taflinger

Book Designer
Evan Deerfield

To Bill,

For investing in me

and holding

Preface

Welcome to *Your Official America Online® Guide to Personal Finance and Investing.* Our objective in this book is teaching you to save and invest responsibly.

How This Book Is Organized

This book is written to help you become an investor, offering practical, cautious financial advice and guidance. It also presents a tour of the investing resources available to you through AOL, from investor education sites to financial planning calculators and portfolio-tracking tools.

Part I: Personal Finance Primer

This first section is designed to help you get your finances in order. The chapters help you to assess your finances, reduce your debt (the single greatest impediment to your financial well being), and define your goals for saving and investing. If you're new to investing or to online investing, these steps will prepare you for the world of personal finance.

Part II: Smart Investing

As a new investor, you may not know the difference between stocks and mutual funds, or between a value strategy and a growth strategy. This section educates you about the full range of investment vehicles and strategies. It helps you determine the level of risk you are willing to assume, and then points you toward the mix of stocks and bonds that will help you safely reach your goals.

Part III: Research and Execution

After you learn about the various strategies and investment vehicles, it will be time to start building a portfolio.

These chapters introduce you to all of the tools at your disposal through AOL that can help you investigate investment opportunities. You will find out how to research investment opportunities, evaluate them in terms of your goals, and stay on top of them once you've invested in them. You will also learn how to set up a portfolio and to trade stocks online.

Part IV: Protecting Your Investments

After you have built your investment nest egg, you will need to know how to cover your assets and how to use them to help your heirs or favorite charities. Insurance and estate planning are important and often neglected considerations for those seeking stability and happiness in their personal finances.

Things change quickly on the Internet, so you might find an out-of-date detail or two in this book. AOL adds new resources regularly, and all of its partners update their sites from time to time. You may find that the screens this book directs you to look at have moved or changed. But the sites mentioned here have all been around a while and are likely to continue their presence on the Internet.

Conventions

To make this book easier to navigate, we use several different icons to indicate various points of interest that you won't want to miss:

Calls your attention to shortcuts, useful resources on AOL, and smarter ways to work.

Points out a fact or other short piece of information about personal finance worthy of further mention.

Advises you of something *not* to do.

Defines a new term that is used in the text.

Describes AOL keywords and Internet addresses.

 # Acknowledgments

Thank you to: Cynthia Marshall, for your research and your pursuit. And for encouraging my stories — in this book, and outside of it. Christina Cavoli, for your reporting, writing, tech skills, and gracious disposition, all far above and beyond the call of duty. Sandi Michaelson Warren, for your professional and personal sagacity. And for your wonderful sense of humor. Frank and Dolores Leonetti, for all your help and encouragement. Anne Kirsch and Margaret Loos Cosgrove, for responding to the call of friendship during a looming deadline and on other occasions too numerous to mention. Patricia Klein, for your energy, your empathy, and your wisdom.

Heartfelt thanks to Paul DiVito of America Online, for your confidence in this project, and to Brad Schepp, Allan Halprin, Rob Shenk, John Dyn, Mimi Hutchins, and the entire crew at AOL.

Thank you so much to Paul Winters, Kathy Yankton, and Andy Cummings at IDG Books Worldwide, Inc. for your patience, skill, and diplomacy. And to Kristen Tod, Susan Glinert, Tim Borek, Linda Marousek, Mary Jo Weis, and Melissa Stauffer for your commitment to the book's technical and editorial integrity. And to the members and experts of AOL who answered our questions . . . again and again and again. Especially to Marc Gerstein of Market Guide, Steven Cohn of Sage, Susan Pevear and Chip Norton of Standard & Poor's Personal Wealth, Bob Arnold of Business Week Online, Ted Allrich of The Online Investor, Ric Edelman of Edelman Financial Services, and Gary B. Smith of TheStreet.com.

Special thanks to Billy, Christopher, Eric, Kyle, Julie, and Alexander for your patience and understanding while your mommies were cranking out this book. And to Bill, Jeff, and Chris for your support and encouragement, in word and in deed.

America Online, IDG Books Worldwide, Inc., the author, AOL members quoted, and information providers assume no liability for any investment or personal finance decision based on information in this book.

Please invest responsibly.

— Carol Dannhauser

A book is always a team effort and the team should be recognized as much as the author. Special thanks go to Michael McLane, CFP of McLane Consulting, for his time and effort spent reviewing the chapters for accuracy and adding any helpful hints. Besides sharing his financial acumen, Michael was always cheerful and enthusiastic, which made him a joy to work with. Merrill Lynch and Co. Inc. deserves special gratitude, especially Wendell Wood Collins, vice president, Doris Meister, chairman and CEO of Merrill Lynch Trust Company, Denice Glover, investment associate, and Kevin Sheerin, vice president and financial consultant. Their financial acumen and resources really do make them a "breed apart." Thanks also go to Thomas Gaynor, Esq., and partner, Smith & Doran, and Lawrence Leaf, CPA, and Leaf, Saltzman, Manganelli, Pfeil, & Tendler for lending their estate-planning expertise. I would like to thank the creative side of the team for their efforts, tips, and technical wizardry. Included are Christina Cavoli, Julie Segal, and Fran Hawthorne; kudos for great writing, editing, and screen shots. It goes without saying that my agent, Dianne Littwin, deserves the greatest thanks for making this book happen. She's a wonderful person with a lot of integrity. I'd like to thank my mother, Mary Thorburn, who made me want to write; my sister, Emily Bolcar, for her tireless babysitting and support; and my closest friends for making me face challenges with a smile on my face. You know who you are. Finally, I could not have completed this book if it weren't for the patience and love from the people closest to me: Jessica, Anna and Casey Richardson; may you all grow up to become writers.

— Portia Thorburn Richardson

Contents at a Glance

Contents

CHAPTER

1

INTRODUCTION

A Quick Look

▶ **Embark from "Investing Central"** **page 6**

To be a successful investor, you need to research your targets; stay on top of business, market, and economic news; and execute your trades at the right time. It also helps to hear from experts and to run your strategies by peers.

There's no need to spend hours hunting down reports and analyses with TVs blaring in the background and newspapers piled at your feet. You can find all this information in one location: Keyword: **Personal Finance**. It's a launching pad to online brokers, news, tools, experts, and investment strategies.

▶ **Build Your Budget** **page 9**

Piecing together a budget certainly isn't the most scintillating part of investing and personal finance, but if you consider that a well-planned budget is the ticket to attaining those goals in life you seek, the task might not seem so burdensome after all.

For tips on getting started or fine-tuning your current budget, go to Keyword: **Money.com** and, under Money 101, check out Chapter 2: Making a Budget. Turn to the interactive instant budget maker for help reviewing your expenses and assessing your current direction.

▶ **Taking Stock** **page 11**

Which stocks are right for you? That depends on your goals and investment profile. The folks at The Motley Fool can help you narrow down the choices. Start at Keyword: **Fool** and then click News and Commentary. The Fools are never short on opinions — and they have enough tips, tools, and strategies to match.

Scroll down and look to the Daily Double for winners, the Daily Trouble for losers, and the Dueling Fools for thoughtful analysis and commentary on what makes for a successful stock.

Chapter 1

Introduction

You are about to embark on a journey, one filled with twists, thrills, excitement, and discovery. In this world where you're headed — investing and personal finance — the potential for growth is tremendous. And not just in terms of dollars in your portfolio.

When you control your finances, you gain a sense of calm and empowerment, a sense of ease and direction. With the help of this book:

► Unexpected expenses should prove less jarring (you will know how to squirrel away emergency funds).

► Debt should feel less staggering (you will know how to formulate a plan to pay it off).

- ▶ Saving for your goals should prove inspiring, not daunting (you will have an investment blueprint outlining how and when you will meet your goals).

- ▶ Investing will be straightforward, simple to understand, and exhilarating.

With the help of this book, your education will be grand. You'll understand investing from A to Z, from *asset allocation* to *zero coupon bonds*. You'll know an *index fund* (Chapter 8) from a *small-cap stock* (Chapter 6) from a *T-bill* (Chapter 7) and you'll know where, when, how, and why to buy each.

Financial Planning with AOL

Admittedly, controlling your finances and making investments takes determination and work. There is no magic route to success. Instead, you need a combination ticket: part smarts, part common sense, part self-control, and part guts. And you need a trunk full of tools.

But today the trip is easier than ever. No longer must you pore through seemingly indecipherable data to discover promising investments. No longer must you pay a broker hundreds of dollars for a piece of advice. Today, technology makes investing and personal finance simpler and the tools more accessible.

America Online helps ease the load. Consider the service an all-expenses-paid excursion on which you and like-minded travelers depart for the personal finance and investing world. AOL provides the gear, the tours, the guides, the resources, the companions, all-you-can-eat food for the brain, unlimited fun for the journey. Help abounds when you need it — as well as companions when you want to share the ride.

Close to 10 million people turn to AOL's business news, portfolio, and personal finance sections *every single day*. Why so many? Because news and tools are for the taking. Today's investor need only grab the reins and steer.

For example, ten years ago it would have cost a fortune to access stock quotes in your home. On AOL, they're delivered for free. There was a time when only Wall Streeters had direct access to things like stock analyst reports and stock-screening tools. Today, you can access these online. Your expense: a few keystrokes. The same holds for budgeting information, investing strategies, financials, and even tax advice. This book shows you where and how to find it all, as well as how to understand and best utilize the information after you track it down.

Find It Online

No need to scrutinize every newspaper to learn the latest happenings throughout the financial universe. Go to Keyword: **Business News** to access AOL's Business News Center (Figure 1-1), where the day's top stories concerning all aspects of the business world are updated continually.

Click a Department for consumer, international, technology, or economic news, or select Business Publications for news from Bloomberg, *Business Week,* the *Financial Times,* Money.com, and others.

Figure 1-1. Mergers, stock splits, bankruptcies, changing players, new products, and scandals — AOL brings you the latest buzz in the business world, 24 hours a day.

Information you need

Says Rob Shenk, Group Director of AOL Financial Services, "It's the kind of high-quality financial information that used to be available only to investment professionals — tools like stock screening, mutual fund reports and stock quotes. You get information *now*, and you get it more tailored to *your* investing interests."

Call up Keyword: **Personal Finance**, as shown in the following figure, to check it out. This is Investing Central. From here you can check stock prices (click the Quotes, Charts, News & Research link), learn what's driving the day's stock activity (click The Markets), or investigate your potential targets (Investment Research). You can share strategies with fellow AOL members (in Personal Finance Live) and order an online trade through AOL's broker-partners. It might sound overwhelming now, but don't fret — this book helps you understand how to do each of these things.

Tip

To quickly access an AOL **Keyword**, press the Control key and the letter K (Ctrl+K) simultaneously on your keyboard if you have a PC. If you have a Mac, click the apple key and the letter K (⌘+K).

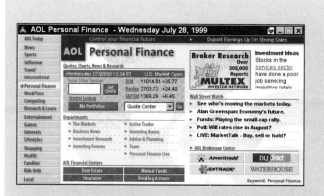

From AOL's Personal Finance screen, you can access constantly updated stock prices, mutual fund information, and market activity. You can also check the news, track down the latest investment research, or order a stock trade.

This book is your guide

In your investing and personal finance travels, you might need a translator; tips from people who have been where you're going; in-depth maps, routes, and strategies; suggestions on where to stop and rest along the way; places to have fun during your adventures; and dangerous places to avoid. This book packs them all.

Maybe you're already familiar with this world. If you speak the language of investing and money management and you know where you're headed financially, this book will show you new and interesting ways to get there, shortcuts along the route, points of interest you might have overlooked, and gems the locals know but try to keep to themselves.

If you don't know your way around, this book will be your guide. In addition to pointers, tools, and strategies, it packs expert advice from investment pros.

The experts quoted in this book are part of the AOL community, too. AOL partners who offered their time and insights to benefit smart investors eager to learn more. Although their approaches and strategies may differ, there are two things on which they agree: The best place to start saving and investing is exactly where you are now. The best time to start is right this instant.

Find It Online

The AOL community is a great place to exchange ideas. Share investing information and hear what's on the minds of top financial insiders at Keyword: **Sage Chat** to participate in daily conversations with investment experts, as in Figure 1-2. Click Missed a Chat? to read previous transcripts.

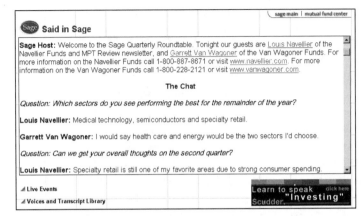

Figure 1-2. AOL's chats enable you to pose questions to financial experts, as well as discuss the answers with the experts and with each other.

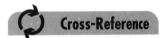

Cross-Reference

For more information on where and how to talk with other members and experts, see Chapter 15.

Get Cracking

The sooner you start saving and investing, the more you stand to gain. Don't have much of a nest egg now? Not to worry. Take the change out of your pocket and start with that. Suddenly left giddy by a recent windfall? You made a bundle on your stock options or you won Powerball? Sometimes a big gain can seem as daunting as a pile of unpaid bills. The strategies, tips, and tools in this book help you succeed whether you're starting with $100 or $100,000.

Maybe you think you have to wait before you can get serious about saving, nevermind investing. There are probably things you want now — a new car, perhaps, or living room furniture. But hear this: For every five years you postpone saving, you have to double the amount of money you save each month to end up with the same amount.

Something will always entice you from a brochure or a display window or your neighbor's driveway. Push those temptations aside until after your financial makeover. Then you can determine if they're worth your dollars.

Battle of the budget

It may not be as exciting as buying a stock that triples in price, but establishing a sound budget is the key that unlocks your investing possibilities.

If you don't know where to begin, you may want to check out the interactive budget-maker at Money.com. Go to Keyword: **Money.com**, click Investing, and then scroll down to Money 101. After you click that, select from the table of contents on the right Chapter 2, Making a Budget. The feature offers an introduction on how to create a budget, including the "Joys of Budgeting" and a section on how to list expenses.

Click the section Evaluating Them to pop up the interactive instant budget maker, a tool that helps you outline your expenses and evaluate whether they are reasonable. Answer the short series of questions about your family size and income, and click Analyze.

The next section shows average expenditures for your income. Next to the list of averages, enter the amount you usually spend. When you've finished, click Analyze to see a side-by-side comparison of your expenses to the average family's.

Are you paying more than the norm for food or entertainment? Are you getting away cheap on rent or transportation? This analysis helps illuminate areas where you might be able to make some changes.

 Cross-Reference

Want help figuring your financial goals? Turn to Chapter 4.

Your itinerary

This book can help you map out your saving and investing journey. If there are stops you're already familiar with, jump around for some new excitement. If not, enjoy the ride!

Get your financial house in order

After you finish this book, you'll know how to do everything that follows:

▶ Make a budget.

Cross-Reference

What will it take to reach two common goals: paying for college and retirement? Find out in Chapter 12.

▶ Get out of debt if you're stuck there. For help, turn to Keyword: **Financial Independence** for advice on crawling out from under debt and conquering your spending and charging habits (see Figure 1-3). Or turn to Chapter 3.

Figure 1-3. AOL provides dozens of sites that can help you map out your financial strategies — from creating the most basic budget to finding the right tax-deferred investments to refine your portfolio.

▶ Save money, even if the practice has always eluded you.

Set your goals

▶ Determine what it is you're saving for.

▶ Understand how much your goals cost and determine whether they are attainable.

▶ Determine what kinds of returns you'll need and which types of investments can meet these goals.

Outline the right types of investments for your portfolio

▶ Understand investment terminology.

▶ Understand the risks and rewards of various investments.

▶ Devise your own investment blueprint.

Detect and follow investments online that work for you

▶ Learn how to research investments and screen stocks and mutual funds like the pros do.

▶ Learn how to select a broker and trade online.

▶ Know how to stay on top of investment news and in touch with your fellow investors.

Stock answers

Need help finding the right kinds of stocks for your portfolio? The pundits at the Motley Fool will open to you their cache of humorous, down-to-earth investment resources, tools, and tutorials.

Go to Keyword: **Fool** and click News and Commentary. The Fools' opinions and advice help you separate the winners from the losers. Check out the Daily Double for a company whose stock is going great guns, or read the Daily Trouble for a stock that's shooting blanks. For many stocks, the answer isn't so obvious. Click Dueling Fools for two contrasting opinions about a company, and then vote on whether you think it's a hot prospect or a cold fish.

You can discuss all stock prospects with The Fools. Track down topics by industry categories such as healthcare or retail, and look for insight on what's promising and what's not.

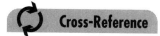

Cross-Reference

For the ins and outs of navigating your portfolios, turn to Chapter 14.

▶ Understand how to track your investments online, as in Figure 1-4, which you'll find at Keyword: **Portfolio**.

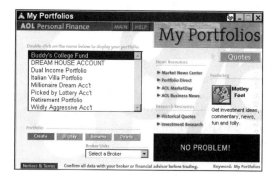

Figure 1-4. AOL's My Portfolios lets you track all of your investments — both real and imagined — throughout the trading day.

Manage your money online

▶ Understand what kinds of insurance are right for you and how to research them online. Check out Keyword: **Insurance,** and then click Auto Insurance. Next, enter your zip code where indicated under Free Auto Insurance Quotes and click Go to reach the screen in Figure 1-5.

Tip

Keyword: **Banking** takes you to AOL's Personal Finance Banking Center. Click Get Started with Online Banking: What's it all About? for a primer on banking in cyberspace.

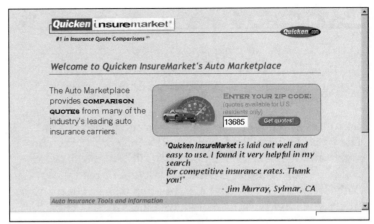

Figure 1-5. Comparing car insurance rates online gives AOL users a quick way to find the best deals — without having to endure days of research and innumerable sales pitches.

▶ Learn how to plan your estate so Uncle Sam doesn't walk away with a big chunk of your assets.

Some of these stops might seem a ways off. But you'll get there. Just take it one step at a time.

Follow the Path

This book holds your hand along the way. First, you'll learn exactly how much money flows in and out of your house so you can sock some away for savings. You designate an amount and stick to it each month while keeping the reins on your spending. You don't have to be a tightwad. Just be sensible. If you can't pay cash for something — with the exception of a house or tuition or something else that invests in your future — don't buy it.

Once your financial house is in order, you're saving for the future, and your debt's under control, you'll get to the fun part: investing for your goals. What is it you're saving for, anyway? A house, a car, or college tuition — plus a comfortable retirement? When you have specific goals, you can draw up a plan that estimates how long the ride will take and what you'll need to get there. With this plan in hand, you might pause before plopping down a big chunk of money for something that doesn't bring you any closer to your goals.

Then you can start digging. This book and AOL give you the knowledge and tools to find the right stocks, bonds and mutual funds yourself, and to buy them online. When you devise your own plan and build your own portfolio, you have a much greater chance of ending up where you want to be (assuming your plan is realistic).

That's not to say you shouldn't use a financial advisor if you read this book — good advisors appreciate knowledgeable customers and will sell you their time without trying to sell you a product. The more you know, the more you can take advantage of their expertise.

 **Find It Online**

Scouting for a financial planner? Find out the right questions to ask in your search at Keyword: **Edelman**, then scroll down to Search Ric Edelman's site. Type in **Chapter 82** and press Enter. Then select How to Find a Planner.

And another thing . . .

Before you read any further, you have to promise to acknowledge four things. Deal?

OK, here they are:

1. There are no Keys to Instant Riches, as Figure 1-6 indicates. Go to http://www.theonline investor.com and choose the 1, 2, 3 . . . Invest link. Then choose The First Step. No matter what any advertisement promises. No matter what some seminar guru evangelizes. No matter what your rich brother-in-law swears to. The only way to save and invest successfully is to devise a realistic plan that works for *you*, to thoroughly research your investments and to understand the potential risks and returns of whatever you buy.

Figure 1-6. Short of inheriting a pile of money or winning Powerball, there are no quick ways to get rich. Investors need to establish goals and have a plan to achieve financial success.

2. You are to be commended for reading this book, or any investment and personal finance book that's trying to empower you, not sell you something. Many people throw up their hands and surrender to ignorance when it comes to money matters. Way to go for taking the time and effort to figure out how to do it right!

3. Managing your finances is imperative in today's business environment. One day you can be a fat cat for a hot, hot company. The next you can be just another warm body with a pink slip in the unemployment line.

4. Finally, there's no point in working so hard on money matters if you don't work for the riches of love and friendship. Seriously, don't get so wrapped up in your "smart investing" that you ignore what's really important in life. You have to make a lot of decisions when you formulate your budget and outline your goals. Don't let greed or envy drive you. Remember that the point of investing is to make life more comfortable for you and your loved ones — not to drive a more expensive car than your neighbor.

How's Your Financial Fitness?

Take AOL partner Quicken.com's financial health quiz below to assess your trouble spots. If you want to access the quiz online, go to Keyword: **Quicken.com**, and scroll down to the bottom to find the search box. Type in Financial Fitness Quiz and click Go. When the results are displayed, select the Financial Fitness Quiz (shown in Figure 1-7).

When you take Quicken's online quiz, you will be presented ten questions, including the following. Do you know how much you spend in a year? Do you pay all your bills on time? Have you done any retirement planning? Are you doing anything to minimize the taxes you pay? Do you keep records of your financial assets? Do you understand the differences in your investment types? Are your investments diversified? Do you have a satisfactory credit rating?

You are then given four answer choices, *a* through *d*, for each question. Give yourself 10 points for each *a*, five for each *b*, one for each *c*, and condolences for each *d*.

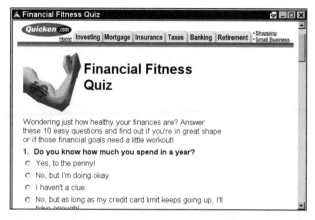

Figure 1-7. Quicken helps you assess your financial smarts and fitness and provides immediate feedback for your individual profile.

Did you reach 90 or 100? Congratulations, you're in great shape! You're going to love the tips and tools in this book, especially in the investing area. Consider yourself in decent shape if you score 50 to 80. You probably have some weak spots, though. After you get through this book, you'll be fit as a financial planner. Once you get below 50, though, it's time to step up those workouts. If you score in the 30s or below, hit the ground running to Chapter 2!

A Quick Look

▶ **Your Financial Health: Is It Time for a Checkup?**　　　**page 19**

With all the business of everyday life, it's easy to let your finances get away
from you. Even if you manage to avoid debt and to save a good chunk of
money each month, you might still be missing opportunities for growth or
stability. Quicken's 20-Minute Financial Health Checkup helps ensure that
your current financial plan is the best one for you. Go to Keyword: **Web
Center** and then click Saving & Spending under Personal Finance. Under
Tools & Stuff, click Financial Health Checkup to take the quiz.

▶ **Budgeting Ideas That Work**　　　**page 27**

Slashing expenses and hiking savings sounds great, but it's not only hard to
accomplish, it also sometimes seems downright impossible. You don't have to
go it alone — budgeting experts at TheWhiz point you in the right direction
and make cash flow manageable. Go to Keyword: **Whiz** and then click Credit
and Debt. Scroll down to the Resources section, and click Budgeting Ideas
That Work. In addition to articles about saving and spending wisely, you can
link to an online budget worksheet from the Consumer Credit Counseling
Service of Atlanta to help you assess your current budget and develop your
future financial picture.

▶ **Where Does All the Money Go?**　　　**page 31**

No matter what your income size, money has a way of slipping through your
fingers. Fortunately, there are ways to hold on to your hard-earned cash.
Quicken helps you track your spending and boost your savings. A great place
to start is Keyword: **Quicken**. Click Quicken.com and check out the Banking
tab. It's full of tools and tips, ranging from advice on how to pinch a few extra
pennies each month to how to recover from debt.

Chapter 2

Building Your Budget

An inheritance from the dearly departed, a fat trust, or a winning PowerBall ticket might be the only direct spigots to a future bathed in wealth. Most people have to dig a well first. Instead of burrowing randomly, you can follow a path to pinpoint your resources. And that path is creating a budget.

After you create a budget, you can funnel your newfound resources into savings and investments. But it's practically impossible to figure out how much you can stash away if you don't know how much you make, how much you spend, and how much is left over. There are all sorts of budgeting articles and planners via AOL, such as the one shown in Figure 2-1, found at the Better Homes and Gardens Family Money homepage. Go to Keyword: **Family Money** and then click Budgeting and Borrowing, under the Family Finances heading.

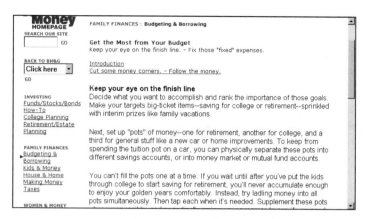

Figure 2-1. Developing a budget and meeting financial priorities are the first steps to a sound financial plan.

A Quicken checkup

Much as you're sure your financial health is sound, a quick review could reveal some weak underpinnings. Quicken's Financial Health Checkup might be just what the doctor ordered. After you invest about 20 minutes answering questions, your personal finances are analyzed, with feedback provided to help you decide if your financial well being needs some tonic.

If you don't go the Keyword: **Your Money** route, you can start at Keyword: **Quicken**, and click Quicken.com. Then, select the Banking tab, and then under the Tools heading select Financial Health Checkup.

Gather your financial records for reference before you start, so you don't have to run around looking for them, leaving open the window for distraction.

First, answer the questions about your investing, retirement, debt, and other key financial areas to help establish your individual profile. Then take the quiz. It begins with a few questions about you, such as marital status, family size, and age, and then gets into your personal goals and opinions. Obviously, the quiz makes broad generalizations, but this step helps establish your attitude towards saving, working, taxes, retirement, and risk.

Next, fill in the figures: your annual income, your net worth, debt, mortgages, and so on. Answer the queries about your health and insurance plans, educational plans, taxes, retirement, and estate planning.

Tip

To jump-start your investing, you need to draw up a "cash-flow inventory, a chronicle of what goes in and what goes out," recommends Susan Pevear, senior analyst for AOL partner Standard & Poor's Personal Wealth (Keyword: **PersonalWealth**). After you complete this inventory, Pevear says, you can create a realistic budget and spring onto the track to savings and investing.

Find It Online

How financially fit are you? Take the fitness quiz. Go to Keyword: **Your Money**, scroll down to Financial Health Checkup, and see how your finances measure up.

2

Building Your Budget

As you take the quiz, note that most financial terms are high-lighted. If you have a question on exactly what to include in "consumer debt" or "liquid net assets," for example, these terms are hyperlinked to a glossary. Just click any term and the definition will pop up.

After you complete the checkup, you get immediate tips and feedback in each area, including ways to increase your assets and decrease your expenses.

How Much Do You Spend?

If you already have a budget, or you're pretty comfortable with how much you save and spend, pat yourself on the back and take the express lane to "Pay to the Order of . . . You," later in this chapter.

You don't have a budget? You're not alone. For many people, when a paycheck seems to evaporate faster than bytes on your hard drive, it appears pointless to write down where it's all going. But if you know where it's spent, you can plug some of the leaks.

Make a paper trail

The first step in building a budget is to know where your money goes. If you don't know exactly, it's time to keep track. And that means of everything, from $3 for that cappuccino to $16 in the gas tank. For two months, note every single dime you spend. Scribbling "$60 from the ATM" doesn't count. How do you spend the $60?

Start with your daily expenses, like lunch, golf balls, and news-papers. (Okay, it sounds nit-picky, but it's only for a couple of months, and it'll be worth it when you're done.) A pocketsize notebook or electronic organizer is perfect for jotting these down. To jump-start your inventory online, try Quicken.com's Banking QuickAnswers worksheet (shown in Figure 2-2). This worksheet shows you how much you can save each month by cutting your spending. Go to Keyword: **Quicken**. Click Quicken.com. On the Quicken homepage, click the Banking tab. Next, under Four Steps for Managing Your Money, click

Get Out of the Red. Then, under QuickAnswers, click "How Much Can you Save by Reducing Your Spending?" to access the interactive worksheet, and begin filling in the blanks.

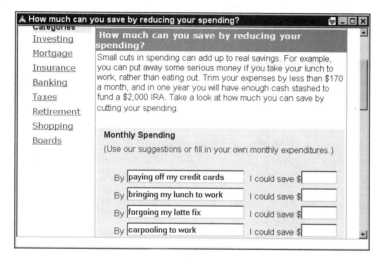

Figure 2-2. Keeping track of every expenditure enables you to see where you can cut back. Small reductions can create big possibilities, as demonstrated in this Quicken tutorial.

While you're tallying the daily purchases, you'll also need to uncover your annual spending. Do this on a number of fronts: look to credit card statements to pinpoint your plastic trail, canceled checks to chronicle your bills, bank statements for withdrawals and electronic payments, and receipts for your ATM activity.

Granted, this stage is a big pain. And it certainly won't be fun when you discover that you spend way more on CDs or break-fast-to-go or gadgets for your boat than you ever realized. And it *really* won't be fun when your spouse/partner realizes how much you spend on these items, either. But don't worry, your spouse has expenses you probably consider trivial or over-indulgent. Accept your budget chronicle as a fact-finding mission, not a finger-pointing one.

If you start to get nervous as you do this, remember: Just because you log your purchases doesn't mean you have to give them up. The exercise simply gives you a better under-standing of where your money goes so you'll have a greater awareness of the big picture.

Tip

On your two-month recovery expedition, you must be sure to trace expenses that crop up periodically, like car insurance payments, property taxes, medical expenses, vacations, and snow removal. And don't forget those miscellaneous expenses that sprout each year like dandelions: gradua-tion presents, basketball uni-forms, Mother's Day gifts.

2

Building Your Budget

Go figure

When you inventory your expenses you have to be completely honest. If you must estimate these bills, overestimate them. Otherwise, you risk being short-handed at bill time.

You can tally your expenses by hand, you can buy software with built-in budget makers, or you can do it online. If you opt for the latter, here are two options to consider. Go to Keyword: **Credit&Debt** and then select Calculators, which brings up a budget form into which you insert your figures. Or, from the Calculators page (Keyword: **Calculator**), select Budgeting, then How Much Am I Spending, and plug your numbers into the categories. The results will look something like those in Figure 2-3.

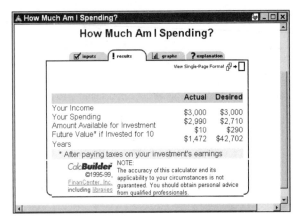

Figure 2-3. Gasp! Facing reality can be unpleasant, but making financial changes can be easier than you think.

Add up all the numbers. This is your annual total of how much you spend.

Now divide your total by 12 to get an average of how much you spend each month.

Keeping your spending in check is a lot easier to accomplish when you work off of a monthly budget. Here's why: See all those bills you listed that you pay periodically, like car insurance and vacations and taxes? You need to put money aside for them each month even though the bill isn't actually due. But more about that later.

How Much Do You Earn?

Now that you know what you spend, it's time to compare
it with what you earn. Dig up last year's tax return and track
down your income sources. For your salary, though, don't use
your Form 1099 total, because you never actually take home
that much. Instead, refer to your check stubs or direct deposit
statements and add up the amount you took home after taxes
and other deductions.

And don't include that hefty bonus you got last year when the
company made its pie-in-the-sky numbers. Instead, if a bonus is
an expected part of your pay, include the minimum you could
have reasonably expected to get. (Leave stock options out of the
picture altogether. They do not guarantee income and shouldn't
be figured into your budget. When you exercise your stock
options you can direct the proceeds right into your investments
or goals accounts. You can read more about that in Chapter 11.)

Just for fun, see how your expenditures compare to the norm
in America. Check out Money.com's tallies at Keyword:
MoneyMag, call up **http://jcgi.pathfinder.com/money/
howareyoudoing**, and follow the steps as shown in Figure 2-4.

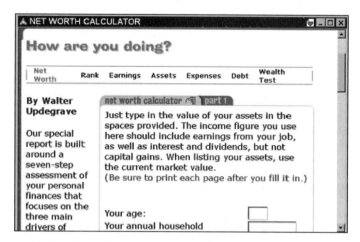

Figure 2-4. When calculating your assets, make sure to underestimate them rather
than be overly optimistic. This helps allow for taxes, deductions, and any other potential shortfalls.

Don't feel chagrined if you don't have income from all these sources. Most people just have paychecks!

Investment gains, Interest income, and Dividends will change from year to year. For the best guess, track down the figures from your most recent tax return and add any capital gains you've made so far this year.

Add up all your income and divide it by 12 to get your average monthly earnings. Again, this is more a reflection of past income, but that works to your advantage. When you create a budget, if you err on the side of having more than you expected, you'll be pleasantly surprised.

What does your picture look like?

You now have a snapshot of your monthly expenses and income. How do they compare? Most likely, your picture fits into one of these three scenarios:

- ▶ You can breathe a little more easily now, knowing your income comfortably exceeds your expenses. Congratulations! Feel free to head over to Chapter 4 or stick around and pick up some good savings and credit tips between here and there.

- ▶ Your spending and earnings are about the same. That belt feels a bit too snug around your waist. Relax. There are easy ways to move it back a notch or two without lifestyle liposuction. Take a few breaths and follow along.

- ▶ The amount you spend exceeds the amount you earn. Join the club. Government studies show Americans are increasingly spending more than they earn. Heck, every time you turn on the TV or the computer, or open your newspaper, somebody is trying to sell you something (which you probably don't need). It's no wonder you spend so much. (Feel better now?) But the pattern doesn't have to continue. And it can't if you want to be able to save and invest. If your snapshot looks like this, some cropping might be in order to attain a more pleasant picture.

Pinpoint the Problem

Now, you might not want to hear this part. When you spend more than you earn, the problem is not necessarily your income. More often than not, the problem lies in your spending. There are people who earn $27,000 a year and manage to save money, and others who earn $227,000 annually but can't seem to climb out from under their bills.

Financial success doesn't equate with an income that has a whole lot of zeros at the end. It means breathing more easily at bill time, and knowing you've invested the resources to help your children with college or other needs, and understanding that you'll be comfortable during retirement. To launch a successful investing campaign, even when bills seem to swallow your paycheck whole, you must live *below* your means.

Most people don't think they spend too much. Often, their spending rises slowly and steadily along with their income. Then one day the things they used to consider luxuries seem to be necessities. Manicures, magazines, lawn care, takeout food, DVD drives, summer camp, tropical vacations, ski outings.... The list could take up a whole chapter.

Snip, snip, snip

When your spending is beyond your means (as shown in Figure 2-5), you need to stop and think before you make another purchase. Do you realize that a week for two at Fun 'N' Frolic costs more than a fully funded IRA for you and your spouse? Maybe you don't care one way or the other, and that's fine, so long as you acknowledge and accept the trade-offs.

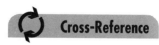

Cross-Reference

See Chapter 4 for more information on how to set and attain realistic financial goals.

Find It Online

Need to talk about your budget woes? Check the schedule for weekly chats on budgeting, credit, and debt with AOL partner TheWhiz.com. Go to Keyword: **Whiz**, select Credit & Debt, and then scroll down to the chat schedule. Another option is to enter Keyword: **Quicken** and then click Quicken.com. Once there, select the Banking tab, and then select Boards. Penny Pinching and Debt Downsizing are your best bets for debt reduction chats.

2

Building Your Budget

Figure 2-5. Once you account for all of your assets and expenses, a financial profile should begin to emerge.

If you don't have to accomplish a major overhaul to get your monthly outlay comfortably lower than your income, a few nips and tucks just might do the job. Instead of spending $5 for lunch every day, put your leftovers from dinner in a piece of Tupperware twice a week and eat them for lunch at the park. That's $500 right there. If you pay the lawn guy $25 a

Tip

Instead of going out to dinner, get takeout and a bottle of wine and spread a picnic blanket out in the park. If your saving needs are greater, make it sandwiches and sparkling water. Instead of buying the kids the latest fad, go on a scavenger hunt in the woods and see what you can construct with your newfound materials. Instead of shelling out $50 for the latest electronic gadget for your brother, frame old pictures of the two of you and tell him what you like best about him. Cash in the fancy health club membership and start walking.

Find It Online

Looking for savings tips? Go to Keyword: **Bankrate**, select Savings, and then scroll down to Archive of Savings Stories.

week to mow your grass, either do it yourself or pay your own kids to do it. Better yet, do it *with* your kids. You'll set a good example, spend some time together — and save money.

The possibilities for spending less are endless. You don't have to go without if you don't need to. Just trim, trim, trim. Go down your list of expenses and highlight those you think you can shrink.

Deep cuts

If you need a spending reduction that's four or five figures deep, it might be time to take a closer look at your lifestyle. Instead of going to exotic locales for your vacations, go camping or hiking at a state or national park. Instead of driving your late-model showpiece, trade it in for something less costly. Also, don't underestimate the effect taxes have on your income. Sit down with your accountant during her off-season and figure out a plan for how you can really cut taxes. Then make an appointment with the benefits specialist at work and ask him to explain every company benefit that could save you money.

Get the whole family together and compile budget-trimming suggestions. Remember to emphasize the benefits of spending less: reduced stress at bill time, money for a vacation or a new house or the college fund, and a comfortable retirement.

Outline Your Plan

Even if your spending equals your income and you're sailing on smooth seas right now, you might be trouble-bound — when an emergency arises, when the college bills come due, when your daughter gets married, or when retirement knocks hard at the door. Then the choppy seas could take you down.

The only way to prepare for your bills and for future events is to draw up a plot — your *budget* — that outlines your income, your expenses, and how much you will direct into savings. If you are in that first scenario — you have a comfortable amount of money left over each month — and you're happy with how much you spend and save, you don't need to do much to your budget other than review it every year to make sure you're still where you want to be.

If you're in the second or third scenario, you have to tinker with your numbers to see what it will take to get your monthly income and your monthly expenses first to balance, then to have income exceed outlay, and then to have enough left over to save. The idea is to whittle your spending down to 90 percent of your take-home income so that you can direct at least 10 percent of your income toward saving for your goals.

Take out your calendar and write out a budget month by month. Your detective work probably turned up some trends. Maybe you spend more during the holidays or in the summer or when your hobby is in full swing. Maybe you get paid more during specific times of the year. Each month devote a percentage of what you take in to match the total you came up with for monthly bills and expenses.

The amount you set aside to cover your monthly bills won't be the same as your actual expenditures that month. But you need to put aside a predetermined amount each month so that you'll accumulate enough to cover the expenses that appear sporadically. It's like the escrow some people pay with their mortgage to cover the taxes. You pay a little bit into your "escrow account" each month so that when those sporadic bills are due you have the money in there to pay it.

It might be kind of tricky at first finding a comfortable level between your monthly income and monthly expenses. You might seem to have extra money if it's been a slow month in the bills department. Or you might come up short. Maybe this is the month the car insurance bill comes in, even though you haven't saved for it yet. Eventually, though, it works out. Your monthly bills will be paid on time, you'll put aside "escrow" to pay your sporadic bills, and you'll have a savings mechanism underway.

Pay to the order of . . . you

If you want to get anywhere with your savings, you have to start, well, saving. Once a week or every month. The best way to do this is when you draw up your budget. You need to add another expense that must get paid *before* all others. And that expense is Y-O-U. You have to pay yourself just like you pay the rent, the utilities, or the grocer. But you must pay yourself first, because if you wait until everything else is paid — the takeout, the magazines, the CD-ROMs — you'll come up empty by month's end.

Find It Online

Looking for a place online to hammer down budgeting essentials? Go to Keyword: **Whiz,** select Credit and Debt, and then choose Budgeting Ideas That Work.

Definition

Escrow: Something put in care of a third party and not delivered until certain conditions are fulfilled.

2

Building Your Budget

Savings

Is there nothing left over when you match expenses to income? You're not alone. As you'll find in the article shown below, many people have limited money for saving and investing. (Find it at Keyword: **Bankrate** and then click Savings; scroll down to Archive of Savings Stories.) Notes Susan Pevear of Standard & Poor's Personal Wealth, people new to the workforce, for example, typically have little, if any, savings, and they often have college loans to boot. She says the same holds for new parents, students, new homeowners, retirees, new car owners — heck, just about everybody at one time or another has hefty loans, new expenses, or negligible savings.

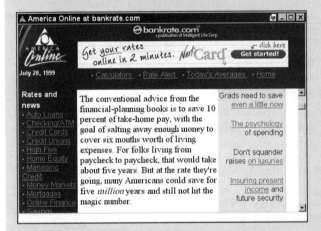

Saving 10 percent of your income is considered a fundamental part of a solid financial program, yet in 1998 the American personal savings rate hit an all-time low of -.02 percent

No amount is too little

Not to worry. Savings is within your reach. Can you spare $2 a day, Monday through Friday? Pretend you have to pay a toll (or another toll!) to get to work, or that your bus pass suddenly costs more, so you need to pay $2 more for your commute. Take that $2 and stick it in the glove compartment or in your desk. Do it each weekday. At the end of the week deposit it in the bank, in a brand-new account you swear you won't touch. This is your *goals account*. Even if you skip a few days, you end up with $500 by year's end. If you had started putting that pocket change in the stock market in 1950, you would have more than $1.6 million now (based on the stock market average annual return of about 12% since 1950)!

Okay, maybe you weren't even born then. But the point still holds. Let's up the ante a bit. Say you squirrel away $25 a week starting today, or $1,300 a year, you'll reach $1 million in 38 years, based on 12% interest. Fifty dollars a week, or $2,600 a year, gets you a cool million in a bit over 32 years. Obviously, some amounts will be easier for some people to put away than for others. Whether you put away $5, $50, or $500 each week is not the point. The point is that you're taking your money and saving it. Once you're in the habit of saving, you can inch up the amount as you go. Now, where were we? Oh yes, $100 a week — $1 million in 26 years.

Although the glove compartment approach will probably work (unless you're the type to go rummaging around in there for cigarette money), the easiest way to channel money into savings is never to handle it. Imagine (it's just pretend now) that they're having a bad year at Widgets 'R' Us where you work, and that you will be forced to take a 2% pay cut. Now (this part's for real!) take a deep breath and direct your employer to automatically deposit 2% of your check into that goals account you *swear* you won't touch, no matter how great the temptation. Once you get used to not having that money, inch your deposit up percent by percent, (dollar by dollar, if you have to) until you get to a place you feel is reasonable, yet not uncomfortable.

If Widgets 'R' Us has a great year and plops a hefty raise or bonus into your hands, pretend you never got it. Instead, take another deep breath and deposit that extra money directly into the account-you-swear-you-won't-touch.

If you set up your financial life so that saving occurs automatically, you'll be less likely to sabotage your investment plans. If you pretend the savings account doesn't exist and you don't withdraw from it, you'll be surprised at how quickly the money for your goals accumulates.

Find your comfort level

Needless to say, don't put so much money away that you can't buy food or pay the mortgage. Your budget pinpoints how much you have left over to save. Once you design it, follow it

For hundreds of great budgeting tips from AOL members, go to Keyword: **Moms Online**, and then choose Home Space, then Family Finance, and then scroll down to Saving Money or Simple Living.

Want to know what it will take for you to become a millionaire? Call up those trusty calculators at Keyword: **Calculator**, select Personal Finance, then Savings, and then What Will It Take to Become a Millionaire, and plug in the numbers appropriate to your situation.

For comprehensive savings and budget plans for life events at all ages, go to Keyword: **Budget**. Pick from calculators, tips, advice, features, and forums.

closely to make sure you stay within your limits. But don't get consumed by it. You might have to juggle the numbers a few times before you settle into something you're comfortable with. Accept that you'll probably stray every now and then. The idea isn't to become so picayune that you deprive yourself of buying a magazine. It's to rethink how to spend your money, and to focus on the greater goals of saving for emergencies and investing for your future and the future of your children.

Banking Online

There's a tool that helps tremendously with your budgeting. Online banking enables you to track your accounts, pay your bills online, or apply for a loan. No circling around the parking lot 15 times to find a space. No fumbling around for a stamp. No waiting in bank lines ten people long. No wondering how much is in your account or whether a check cleared.

Banking online works especially well if you link it with money management or personal finance software, which helps you create budgets, lets you determine when to send out your payments, and enables you to stay on top of your spending and saving. You pay your bills on time, without having to search for them in a bottomless pile. And as you pay, the software sorts billing information into categories in your budget. You can see at a glance how close you are to making your numbers, where you risk going over, and how much you have spent on what.

Advantages

The benefits of banking online are significant, especially in terms of time and money saved. Among the advantages:

- ▶ You can bank any time of the day or night from any place you can get online.
- ▶ Electronic transactions such as bill paying and other online conveniences tend to be hassle-free.
- ▶ Because online banks have lower overhead, they may offer higher interest rates and charge lower fees than traditional banks do.

Note

When you bank online, you have access to your accounts 24 hours a day. You can double-check how much you withdrew during those hasty trips to the ATM over that long weekend or how much you spent at the 7-11 with your debit card. You can download these transactions into your budgeting software, if you have it, creating a "paper" trail. You can transfer money to cover any deficits — all during halftime of *Monday Night Football*, with time left over to watch the Sunday game highlights.

Tip

Find out more about personal finance software at Keyword: **Quicken**.

> ▶ Setting up an account is easy. You can move your
> money through a wire transfer if you don't want
> to leave the house.

> ▶ You don't have to wait for checks to clear or send your
> checks out a few days ahead of time to make sure they
> get where they're going on time.

Some advantages are manifold. Consider bill paying, for example.
Many bills, such as your mortgage, your bus pass, or the cable
bill, are the same each month. When you pay your bills the old-
fashioned way, you write out the amount and your particulars,
stamp the envelope, and send it off, spending time and postage
on the same tasks month after month. When you set up your
bill-paying system online, you enter the recipient's name,
address, amount you pay, and the date on which you want to pay
it. This information stays on your computer and you don't have
to deal with it again unless the information changes.

For bills whose amounts change from month to month, all you
do online is insert the new amount. You select Enter and all
the bills get paid from your checking account while you sip
your coffee. Not only does this expedite your administrative
tasks, but also it helps you keep track of your spending.

To review electronic banking advantages online, check out the
article pictured in Figure 2-6. Go to Keyword: **Quicken,** click
Quicken.com, and select the Banking tab. Under Four Steps to
Managing Your Money, select Plug into Online Banking. Then,
choose Six Reasons You Should Bank Online.

Note

Many banks may be willing
to waive checking account
fees if you set up direct
deposit, if you're a shareholder, or if you agree to
bank only through ATM
machines.

2

Building Your Budget

Choosing a Bank

All banks do not offer the same services online. Some only let
you pay your bills or check your account balances. Others
enable you to transfer from one account to another and let
you incorporate your personal finance and online investing
software. Some let you apply for loans. Others offer free
account access but charge for automatic bill payments. Some
offer online services to augment their bricks-and-mortar operations. Others operate exclusively online.

Find It Online

Have a question about banking online? The experts at Gomez.com will give you an answer. Go to Keyword: **Gomez** and choose Ask the Expert, under Community.

Note

Internet banks don't have those stately marble columns out front. In fact, they don't even have branches or ATMs. They run lean operations, as their overhead is a tiny fraction of what traditional banks shell out for tellers, paper, postage, rent, and the like. But they must abide by the same federal regulations as their columned colleagues. Technophobes might be put off by the lack of human contact, but Internet banks — perhaps more than their traditional cousins — understand the importance of seamless transactions and customer service. You reach them by phone, e-mail, or snail mail.

Figure 2-6. Are bankers' hours becoming a relic from the past? Online banking gives you around-the-clock access to your accounts.

What should you look for in an online bank? Find out at Keyword: **Whiz** and click the Banking link at the bottom of the page. Scroll down and select "WHZ 101: Online Banking: What You Need to Know to Get Your Account Wired" (Figure 2-7). The article includes a list of features to investigate before selecting a bank.

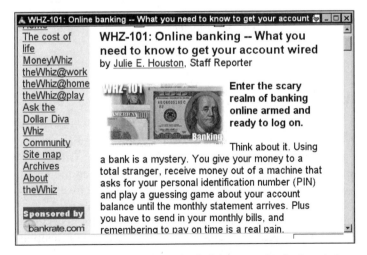

Figure 2-7. Understand what you need to look for in an online bank — before you sign up for an account.

Matching your profile

Which bank should you opt for? That depends on your customer profile. Internet commerce watchdog Gomez.com (Keyword: **Gomez**) divides online banking patrons into four categories.

▶ "The Internet Transactor" — You want your banking to be simple and automated. You want to access all your accounts online, including checking and credit card accounts. You're looking for the ability to pay bills at low cost and for tools to simplify your banking needs.

▶ "The Saver" — You're willing to maintain a high balance in your online bank account in return for high yields and low costs. You're very keen on the ability to transfer among accounts.

▶ "The Borrower" — You look to online banks as additional sources of money — for lines of credit, for a home equity loan, to extend your credit cards, to borrow money for a car. You want the lowest interest rates and easy repayment methods.

▶ "The One-Stop Shopper" — You seek convenience in the banking process — a total package of services ranging from credit cards to bill payment to checking accounts and loans. You look for easy use and lots of services.

To see which banks are recommended for each category, go to Keyword: **Gomez**, click Internet Banker Scorecard, and scroll down under View Scorecard to By Profile, listed on the right. Choose a category to see a description, as pictured in Figure 2-8.

Make a list

After you figure out your profile, you can draw up a checklist that tailors your questions to your needs. Go to the banks' online sites and find out the following:

▶ What are the rules regarding ATM use? Is there a limit to the number of free visits? How much does each visit cost and is it the same regardless of the number of visits?

▶ Do you offer bill payment online? Do I need proprietary software? Can I use any brand of personal finance or money management software? Do I have to pay more for this? How much will I pay per month?

Caution

As an extra precaution, use a different password to bank online than you use for your AOL account. And never send account information via an Instant Message.

Find It Online

How can you find the best yields for your accounts? Go to Keyword: **Bank Rate**, click Today's Averages, and then scroll down to Savings Deposits for CD and Money Market account rates.

2

Building Your Budget

Find It Online

Which banks are tops in online banking? Ask the independent scorekeepers at Gomez. Go to Keyword: **Gomez** and then, under Scorecards, choose Internet Banker Scorecard. Click Review for more information about a bank's performance and services.

Firm	Score
1. Security First Network Bank (review)	6.60
2. Wells Fargo (review)	6.16
3. Net.B@nk (review)	6.13
4. Citibank (review)	5.99
5. Huntington (review)	5.84
6. Salem Five Cents Savings Bank (review)	5.78
7. Bank One (review)	5.77
8. Bank of America (review)	5.76
9. CompuBank (review)	5.75
10. First Internet Bank of Indiana (review)	5.69
11. Ohio Savings Bank (review)	5.64
12. Crestar Bank (review)	5.49
13. BankBoston (review)	5.44
14. US Access Bank	

Gomez Internet Banker Scorecard

Internet Banker Scorecard
GomezWire
Community
Tools

View Scorecard

by category:
Overall Score
Ease of Use
Customer
Confidence
On-Site Resources
Relationship
Services
Overall Cost

or

by profile:
Internet Transactor
Saver
Borrower
One-Stop Shopper

Figure 2-8. What kind of online bank is best suited to your needs? Do you value personal attention, or prefer an automated system? Your preferences determine which bank to choose.

▶ Do I have to pay for check writing and check ordering? Is there a limit to the number of free checks I get? Will you waive it if I maintain a certain balance or sign up for direct deposit?

▶ Do you offer overdraft protection? How much does this cost me?

▶ Can I transfer money online and are the transfers credited in real time?

▶ Can I get access to my accounts 24 hours a day?

▶ Is there a minimum balance I need to maintain?

▶ What if I have questions? How do I get them resolved? Do you have real-time online tech support?

▶ Can I apply online for a loan?

With your checklist in hand, you can scope out the suspects. And scope out you must, as the differences in interest paid and earned and fees charged can amount to thousands of dollars over the life of your account.

For example, a checking account at some banks can cost hundreds of dollars a year when you take into account per-check and ATM fees. A "free" checking account isn't really free if you have to maintain a high minimum balance with money that could be generating interest for you elsewhere.

Check it twice

First, see if your bank operates online. Go to Keyword: **Find;** then, type in the name of your bank and click Search. Then, scroll through the Matching Sites to see if it has an Internet site.

If your bank doesn't have an Internet site, AOL can hook you up with a bank that offers online banking. Start at Keyword: **Bank,** as pictured in Figure 2-9, and explore AOL's five banking partners: NationsBank, BankOne, Citibank, Union Bank of California and Wells Fargo. If you'd prefer a bank closer to home, scroll down to your state under State Banking Centers and select Go. Then double-click the bank you're interested in to link directly to its Web site.

Caution

While many online banks lure you by waiving the monthly fee for bill-payment online, most will charge you for the service after the promotion period expires.

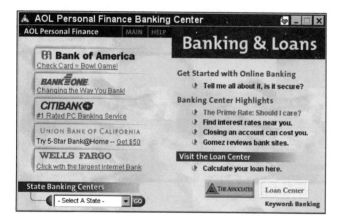

Figure 2-9. Banking online can save you time and money. You can explore the possibilities in AOL's Banking Center.

Call or e-mail the banks to find out their answers. If a bank is reluctant to assist you now, forget about getting any help when you have a more pressing problem. Better to choose another bank.

Summary

Now you know what you spend and you know how that matches up to your income. You've pinpointed your problem areas, and you've formulated a plan of attack for fixing them.

Tip

If you have any difficulty setting up banking with an AOL banking partner, call AOL's Personal Finance Channel Help Line at 1-800-771-8267 from 6 a.m. to 4 a.m. Eastern time.

And you have built your budget. You've even launched a savings plan! You understand the advantages and disadvantages of banking online, and you know how to find a bank that serves your needs.

Even after taking the pruning shears to your expenses, you might find there is still a colossal hurdle in the path between you and your investing. It's a piece of plastic no thicker than a Popsicle stick: your credit card. Sooo easy to use. Sooo bad for your financial health. But your credit card woes aren't a death sentence. Antidotes are at the ready in Chapter 3.

CHAPTER

3

CRUSHING CREDIT CARDS

▶ The Bottom Line   page 45

You may be an expert bargain hunter, but if you carry credit card debt it does-n't matter that you bought that great stereo at a fire-sale price. After adding in the interest payments on your card, the bottom line could be well above what you would have ever considered spending.

Before you make another credit card purchase, figure out how much the bill will really cost you. AOL's Financial Calculators show you how long it will take to pay off your purchases, and how much you have to ante up in interest. Go to Keyword: **Calculator**, and click Credit Cards, under the Personal Finance section. Select What Will It Take To Pay Off My Balance?. Enter the required information concerning your expenses and your credit card. Then click Results to learn how long it will take to be clear of the debt, and how much it will cost before you are through.

▶ Making a Plan   page 46

After you realize just how much you owe, you may fear you'll never be clear of your credit card obligations. But there's help around the desktop. The folks at iVillage can help launch your journey to financial freedom with an interactive debt-reduction planner.

Go to Keyword: **iVillage**, select Money, and then click Debt-Reduction Planner, under the Interactive Toolkit. (If you are not already a member, you must click Launch the Planner and then register before you can get to the screen where you enter your information.) Enter your information to create a debt-reduction plan tailored to your financial situation.

▶ Browsing for Bargains   page 48

There's no reason to hold onto a money-sucking credit card when with ease you can go online and find the lowest interest rates, the longest grace periods, and the cards with no annual fees. Start your quest at Keyword: **Bankrate;** click Credit Cards and then click Start, under Find the Best Rate for You. Answer a few questions about the type of credit card you need, click Enter, and Bankrate returns a list of the best credit card deals around that meet your requirements.

Chapter 3
Crushing Credit Cards

IN THIS CHAPTER

How Debt Undermines Investments

Make a Plan to Pay Off Debt

Find the Lowest Fees

Obtain Your Credit Report

Call for Help

Chapter 2 showed you that the best way to gain control of your finances is to stop spending what you don't have. In other words, if you don't have enough money to pay for something, then you can't buy it. And you know what *that* means ...

No More Credit Cards.

Cut those cards up. Burn them. Chop them in the blender. Run them through the mulcher. Credit cards allow you to buy things you can't afford. Then they charge you ridiculous amounts of money in interest rate penalties when you don't pay them back on time!

Why Credit Card Debt Is Bad

Not all debt is bad. Borrowing to pay for something that will be worth more in the future — like your home or a college education — is an investment. But borrowing money to buy consumables or vacations or toys is dangerous. Americans are loaded with credit card debt. It's so darned *easy* to take out the plastic when there's no money in your wallet and that sleek, new tennis racquet is tantalizing you from the display case.

But as noted in Figure 3-1, credit cards are a fast way to wind up in deep debt. To read the full article, go to Keyword: **Quicken**, click Quicken.com, and select Banking. Click Credit, and choose Take Charge of Your Cards: Seven Strategies for Managing Your Credit Cards.

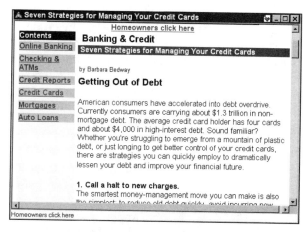

Figure 3-1. Falling victim to the call of the credit card and the burden of the resultant debt is one of the most common financial pitfalls.

Credit cards can be lethal to your bank account, serving up double-digit interest rates (an average of 18 percent) the moment your balance passes its due date. And what do credit card companies do as you build your balance higher and higher while you keep paying the minimum each month? Why, they raise your credit limit! And then they offer their congratulations! With your higher credit limit, you charge more and more, and dig yourself deeper and deeper into debt on any number of cards.

You don't get what you pay for

Caution

Earning free miles by using your credit card can appear to be a great benefit, but keep a few points in mind. Most of these cards have annual fees ranging from $40 to more than $100, the interest they charge is typically at the high end of most cards, and many put expiration dates on the miles you accrue. Make sure you understand the rules of your card so you know exactly what you're getting.

Find It Online

You can get more real-life examples at Keyword: **Whiz;** click Credit & Debt and then scroll down to Managing Credit under Resources. Under What Happens If You Don't Manage Money Wisely? click Real Life Stories to read about consumers who got in over their heads, and how they regained their footing.

There's nothing inherently wrong with credit cards. In many ways, they're ideal. They are very convenient. They provide you with a way to keep track of your spending. They are useful in an emergency. They offer help in a dispute with a vendor about merchandise, and they even let you accrue frequent-flyer miles.

If you charge an item and pay the bill by the time it's due, you don't have a problem. The problems start when you don't pay the bill in full each month. When there's a balance due, interest accrues on your new purchases the second you make them. (When there's no balance due, you have a grace period between the purchase date and the date payment is due.) Then credit cards turn evil, sucking up dollar bills at every turn. In their wake, even stellar investment returns can be reduced to a pittance.

To get an idea of the interest rates typically charged by credit card companies, as shown in Figure 3-2, go to Keyword: **Whiz**. Select Credit & Debt from the links at the bottom of the page. On the next screen, scroll down and click Credit Card Rates under the Resources heading. Under Credit Cards, click National Averages for an index of fixed and variable interest rates for gold and standard cards.

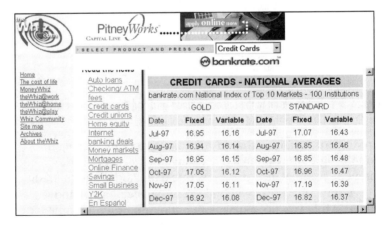

Figure 3-2. Investments that generate a higher rate of return than the interest rates on most credit cards are few and far between.

Consider this example from AOL partner and credit expert TheWhiz. Suppose you buy a nice living room set for $5,000, but you don't pay it off immediately. Suppose, also, that your credit card carries a 15 percent penalty for not paying your bill in full. If you don't charge another thing, and you pay off the debt in a year, the $5,000 furniture set costs you another $415 in interest.

But that requires hefty monthly payments of $451. Say you reduce your monthly payment to a more tolerable minimum payment of $106. You might be able to breathe more easily at bill time, but it will take you six years to pay off the loan from the credit card company! And, notes The Whiz, "you'll be forking over $2,612 in interest payments. You've just increased your purchase price by 52 percent. Did you really need the new couch that badly?"

The first approach to paying off credit card debt is to pay it all off, plain and simple. If you have the money, take it from your savings account or your investments and pay the credit card bills in full. Yes, it's painful to say good-bye to a big chunk of money that took so long to accumulate. And although you might feel more satisfied investing your money and watching it grow than directing it toward your credit card debt, it makes more sense (and more cents) to pay off bad debt.

Debt robs investment returns

Suppose you earn a robust 17 percent return on a $5,000 investment. Suppose you have a $5,000 credit card balance, too. The 15 percent interest you might pay on your card balance reduces your whopping investment return to a mere 2 percent for your financial prowess — less than what you would get on a passbook at People's First Federal Constitution and Trust. Why work to find investments that yield in the double digits only to squander your earnings by paying interest to creditors?

AOL partner and mutual fund expert Sage illustrates how paying off the plastic is crucial when it comes to smart investing. (To find the example online, go to Keyword: **Sage** and select Sage Search. Type in **First Things First** and then press Enter. Then, from the list of titles, click First Things First.)

Gung-Ho Joe, Poor Patty, and Ready Freddie all have $3,000 in credit card debt, charging 18 percent interest. Each has $200 a month to invest.

Find It Online

Feel like you're the only one who's fallen into the credit card trap? It might help you to learn about others who were there, too, who survived, and who went on to prosper.

The Whiz offers true-life, up-from-the-depths financial stories and provides a Money Makeover — a detailed analysis for resolving budget dilemmas and creating a new financial plan. Go to Keyword: **Whiz**, click Credit and Debt and then scroll down to Money Makeover, under Community. Click Makeover Stories to read archived profiles.

You can even submit your own financial profile for a possible makeover. New candidates are chosen monthly.

3

Crushing Credit Cards

Find It Online

AOL partner and financial planner Ric Edelman suggests never spending tomorrow's income today and focusing on the positive rewards (such as buying a new car or house) that result from prudent saving to help keep your debt in check. For some other tips, go to Keyword: **Edelman** and select Truth About Money and then 12 Steps to Being Debt-Free.

▶ Gung-Ho Joe puts $30 a month towards paying off his credit card and $170 a month into investments.

▶ Poor Patty puts $100 a month towards paying off her credit card and $100 a month into investments.

▶ Ready Freddie puts all $200 towards paying off his credit card, and begins investing $200 per month when his balance is paid off.

All three investors earn 10 percent a year in the market.

Table 3-1. Debt versus Investment

Ten Years Later . . .	Gung-Ho Joe	Poor Patty	Ready Freddie
Portfolio Value	$35,574	$32,650	$33,240
Debt	-$ 7,820	0	0
Net Worth	$27,754	$32,650	$33,240

For illustration purposes, this chart assumes the investors' annual rate of return is 10 percent. Varying rates of return affect the figures significantly.

Ready Freddie was able to outperform Joe and Patty by simply paying off his high interest debt first.

Take the pledge

To get your finances in order it is an absolute priority to eliminate credit card debt and swear on this book never to accumulate it again. First, repeat three times: I WILL NOT BUY ANOTHER THING WITH A CREDIT CARD IF I CAN'T PAY FOR IT IN FULL WHEN THE BILL COMES. (Go ahead, repeat it.) You really, really have to kick the credit-card habit. Otherwise you'll fall back into the trap again.

If you must pay with plastic, make it a *debit* card, which withdraws money directly from your bank or brokerage account. If the money's not there, you can't make the purchase. Or use a *charge* card, such as American Express (Keyword: **American Express**), which forces you to pay in full at the end of the month. If you insist on using a credit card for some particular reason, make sure you pay off the balance in full each month.

How much will it take?

To see exactly how much you will save in interest by paying off your debt now, check out CalcBuilder's "What will it take to pay off my balance?" calculator, shown in the Figure below. Go to Keyword: **Calculator**, and click Credit Cards under the Personal Finance section. Select What Will It Take To Pay Off My Balance? to open the tool. Enter the figures. The input page will ask you to enter your current balance, an estimate of future monthly charges and the average payment you plan to make each month, as well as the annual rate and fee your credit card company charges. If you'd like to pay off everything within a certain time frame, you can indicate that as well.

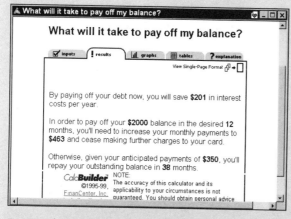

Even a modest credit card balance of $2,000 can mean hundreds of dollars lost over time to interest payments.

After you enter the information, click the Results tab to see how long it will take to pay off your cards and how much of that money will go towards interest. If you've suggested a timeframe for repayment, the calculator will indicate how much the monthly payments have to be to meet that schedule.

If you want to see charts that display how time and rate will affect your overall picture, click the Graph tab. For example, the Time Compared to Payment graph illustrates how a higher payment each month will shorten the time it takes to repay your debt.

Pay It Off

Cross-Reference

See Chapter 4 for a discussion of the importance of maintaining emergency savings.

There are ways to begin to pay off the debt you have, so you can get out of this nasty cycle. The options you choose depend on your individual situation. If you have the luxury of being able to choose between investing money you have saved and paying off the cards, pay off the cards first. That said, don't wipe out your savings. You still need an emergency cushion. There's a delicate balance here, and it's different for everybody, depending on your resources and goals.

It takes a village

Need a plan to escape from the credit quagmire? You don't have to go it alone. iVillage offers an interactive debt-reduction planner to help you get back on your feet, marching towards financial freedom.

Go to Keyword: **iVillage**, select Money, and then click Debt-Reduction Planner, under the Interactive Toolkit. To map out your plan you need to have on hand information on your debts, such as loan payment books and credit card statements. The planner helps you develop a snapshot of your overall debt, then follows with a plan to pay it off.

Click Launch the Planner to begin. (Remember, you must register as a member before you can get to the screen to enter your information.) Click Next to read through the text, or select Debt to enter your information into the planner, as pictured in Figure 3-3. After you enter each debt, click Save so the planner will keep a running tally. After you've listed your debts, click Next to view a debt summary that includes how long until you can be debt-free, and how much you will pay in interest.

The next step, Savings, illustrates how increasing your payment schedule can save you time and money. And Expenses enables you to recalculate your debts by increasing your payments and decreasing your expenditures.

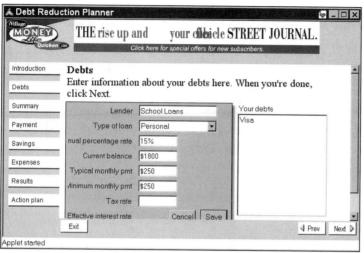

Figure 3-3. Even when your bills seem out of control, you don't have to surrender to debt. Online debt-reduction planners, like this one from iVillage, can help you design an attainable, manageable method for reducing your expenses.

For more debt-reduction tips, check out Keyword: **Your Money**, scroll down to Saving and Spending, and select Get Out of Debt under Reduce Your Debt.

Results' interactive graph allows you to change your payment amounts and expenses to see how the changes affect your timeframe and the interest you pay. Finally, Action Plan outlines what steps you should take to reach your debt-free goal, and gives a payment schedule for the next 12 months. You can print out the Action Plan by clicking the Print button.

Get a new card

If you don't have extra money to pay off the cards, first try to make your debt more manageable. To start, switch to a low-interest card if the cards you have now penalize you with double-digit interest. That will immediately reduce how much you have to pay each month and will reduce the amount of interest that accrues with each delinquent payment. Beware of advertisements you get in the mail offering cards with low rates, though. Often these are promotional rates that skyrocket after a couple of months. Read the fine print. You want permanently low rates to lessen the debt impact each month while you pay off your debt.

You can search online for credit cards with the lowest rates. Keyword: **Bankrate** is a good place to start.

3

Crushing Credit Cards

Pick a card, any card

If you went to a department store and saw the exact sweater at two different prices, which would you buy? The least expensive one, right? Why, then, opt for a credit card with a high interest rate when you can select the same card through a different credit card company at much lower rates? With tools available through AOL, you can compare rates and cards and find the best options quickly and easily. To begin your comparison shopping, go to Keyword: **Bankrate.** Click Credit Cards from the Table of Contents. At the top of the page, click Start, under Find the Best Rate for You.

The interactive tool searches for the best credit card for your specific needs, as shown in the Figure below. Begin by specifying a particular state, or leave the search to query the entire database. Next, choose your goal: the best overall deal, no annual fees, low APRs, or a long grace period. Then, specify the type of card you want: personal, business or student, among others. Finally, select a particular class of card: standard, gold, platinum or, if you have no preference, choose All Classes. Click Search to find the cards that meet your criteria.

The resulting list will include the name, rate, fee, grace period, and contact information for each credit card. Click Details if you want more information.

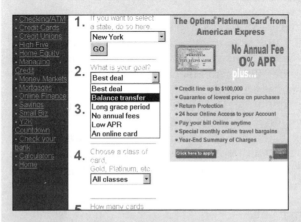

Even the slightest difference in interest rates can produce significant savings or costs.

Which card is better? The card you ultimately choose depends on how long it will take to pay off your credit card debt. If you think you can pay off the debt before the introductory rate expires, go with the lowest introductory rate. If you think it will take awhile to pay off the debt in full, go with the best overall rate.

No matter which way you go, after you get the new card, transfer as much as you can onto it from your existing cards with the highest interest. Then cut up the old dogs and, when they have zero balances, cancel the accounts!

Credit card fees

When shopping for a card, be sure to read the fee disclosure box on the credit card offer. Look out for:

▶ Transfer fees. Some credit card companies make you pay as much as 4 percent to transfer a balance.

▶ Closure fees. Some cards charge you to close your account. Others hike up the interest on your balance due even after your account is closed.

▶ Late fees. These can start accruing even if your payment is a day late. On some cards, this late fee is a license to permanently hike the rates.

▶ Annual fees. There is no sense paying for an annual fee. Shop around for the cards that don't have one, or call your credit card company and tell them you are taking your business elsewhere unless they drop the annual fee.

Keep in mind that you might have to close your open credit lines and cancel some other cards in order to qualify for lower-interest cards. The card issuers look not only at how much debt you owe, but what your potential for debt is based on the credit lines you have. To see how many credit card accounts you have, and which you haven't used in awhile, get a copy of your credit report. You can get a free credit report via Keyword: **Credit Alert**, shown in Figure 3-4. (However, to receive this free report, you must sign up for the AOL Credit Alert program. Read the details through the link at the bottom of the page.)

Tip

Bankrate's calculators can help determine the best candidate among your finalists. Go to Keyword: **Bankrate**, select Credit Cards scroll down to Calculators and click "Which card is best?" A table will appear that allows you to enter basic information like interest rate and annual fees for two different cards, and tabulates which is the best deal.

3

Crushing Credit Cards

Tip

Were you surprised to be turned down for a credit card? Did a credit check for a job or a loan yield some unpleasant, unsuspected problems? Do you even know what creditors are saying about you? Your credit record is your business. You can ensure that it is accurate and up to date.

AOL offers you an easy way to review your credit report. Go to Keyword: **Credit Alert** and click Get Your Credit Report. To get the free report, you have to sign up for the service—which tells you who's been reading your report and whether any negative information has been added. You get a free three-month trial, during which time you can cancel the subscription. (You can still keep the free report.) If you don't cancel, you have to pay—$59.95 at last count.

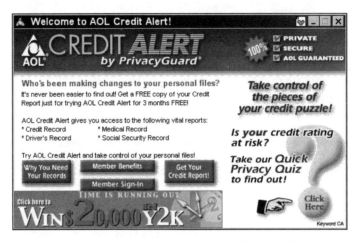

Figure 3-4. Consumers have the right to see their credit reports. Check yours periodically to make sure the figures are correct and up to date.

One plan of action

Now, a plan of attack to pay off your balances. Combine the amount you've been paying on all your cards each month and put the most you can toward the card or bill with the highest interest rate, while still meeting the minimum due on the other bills. You want to pay off the cards with the highest interest rate first. Every time you get extra money, even if it's a dollar or two, use it to pay off the bill with the highest interest.

Consider an equity loan

Here's another option. If you have equity in your home, take out a home equity loan that's no greater than the balance on the cards and use it to pay off the cards. Then immediately cut up the cards. Remember, you're not taking out the equity loan to give yourself a trip to Tahiti. You're doing it to pay off the credit cards. The interest on the equity loan will probably be much less than the credit card rate. The end result is even greater after you factor in that the interest on the equity loan is tax-deductible. But you must stop using the cards, otherwise you end up in deeper trouble.

The loan lowdown

If getting a loan still conjures up images of standing in line at the bank, hat in hand, waiting to talk to Mr. Big, it's time you took another look at banking. Today, you can avoid going to the bank altogether by applying for a loan online.

Go to Keyword: **Loan**, as pictured in Figure 3-5, to get started. The AOL Loan Center will help you calculate how much you can borrow, find information on different types of loans, and even apply for the loan online. Scroll down to Loan Questions and Answers for quick information and loan rates updated daily.

Tip

If you don't want to go the subscribe and unsubscribe route, the major credit reporting services, including Equifax, Experian, and Trans Union, will send you a report for less than $10, or for free if you've been denied credit recently. You can link to all three from the Whiz's homepage at Keyword: **Whiz**. Click the Credit & Debt link at the bottom of the page. Then on the next page, click Credit & Debt archive. Finally, scroll down to How to Fix a Shabby Credit report. This article tells you what to do if you find errors in the report. Once in there, click Part I for the links.

Figure 3-5. There's no need to work the phones and beg the bankers in order to apply for a loan. You can access calculators, compare interest rates and apply for all types of loans at Keyword: *Loan.*

The Loan Center offers information and tools for several types of loans: car, education, personal, home equity, small business, and mortgage loans. Click any of the icons for more information. Select Home Equity Loans, for example, to open up a calculator that can figure how large a loan you can obtain on your home. Enter the appraised value of your home and the mortgage you owe, among other figures, and click Results to see the value. If you don't know what a term means, scroll down for an explanation.

Find It Online

Are you ready to do what you have to do to climb out of debt? If so, Keyword: **Money.com** can lend a hand on the way up. Scroll down to Money 101, and select Step 9: Controlling Debt for a primer on how to manage debt.

3

Crushing Credit Cards

For more information about banking online, refer to Chapter 2.

Looking for tips from AOL members on how to handle debt? Go to Keyword: **Fool** and then click the Messages tab. Click message boards and then select the Managing Your Finances message board for postings on credit cards and debt.

Related calculators, such as "What will the tax savings be?" and "Should I consolidate my debt?" are available by scrolling down to the bottom of the page.

If you want to apply for a loan, click "Home equity lines featuring fixed rates" for links to banks offering online loan applications. Before you send the application, though, be sure to check out "Watch the Dangers of HELOCs (Home Equity Line of Credit)" or "How to Shop for HELOCs," both in the Home Equity section.

If you are interested in another type of loan, click it to open a similar calculator and links as described for home equity loans. Select Auto Loans, for example, to open a calculator to help you determine how much you should spend on a car, an explanation of terms, and links to sites offering further assistance.

This same strategy works, by the way, for other bad debt with high interest. Take a high-interest car loan, for example. You can take out the lower interest equity loan and use it to pay off the higher interest car loan. There is a real danger with this approach, though. You might have a lot of equity in your home today. But if the real estate market dies tomorrow and your house is suddenly worth less than the balance of your mortgage and equity loans, you or your heirs are stuck with the difference between what you owe and what your house is worth — a real problem if you or they must sell.

So pay off the equity loan as quickly as you can. When the loan is paid off, you have "found money." Take that whole chunk of money you were using to pay off your debt and redirect it into your portfolio.

As mentioned earlier, managing investments, credit and debt is a delicate balancing act. In some instances, you're better off with a loan if your savings can be used more productively elsewhere. For example, for several years many car manufacturers have offered very low financing to lure you into buying their cars. If you have a choice of plopping down $25,000 in cash to buy a car versus borrowing that money at 3 percent, take the loan. (Only if you can afford the car, though. Otherwise, get a cheaper model!) Your $25,000 in cash can generate a whole lot more than 3 percent if you invest it wisely.

Call for Help

If you're still having trouble reining in the debt after taking these measures, don't fall prey to those grandfatherly salesmen on TV who pitch debt-consolidation services. Or to so-called "debt doctors." Or to credit-repair programs. These services end up costing you a lot more money in the long run than you owe now.

Instead, call your creditors and tell them the truth: You've done all you can to pay them and you need help. From your credit report they'll see that you're in over your head. Use the B-word (bankruptcy). When the threat of bankruptcy looms, they'll often agree to a new, lower repayment schedule with lower interest. They'd rather do that than write off your debt.

If you don't have any success, contact the Consumer Credit Counseling Service, as shown in Figure 3-6. (Keyword: **Yellow Pages**, then, under Business Name, type in **Consumer Credit Counseling** and your state of residence.) The nonprofit group helps you work out a plan to repay your creditors, albeit for a monthly fee. The fee slides according to your debt and income.

Cross-Reference

Part II, "Smart Investing," outlines many ways to invest your money, along with the returns you can earn.

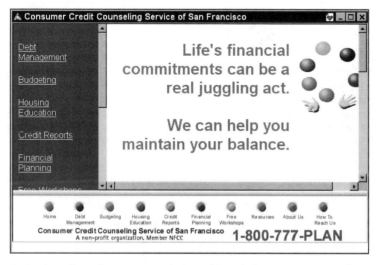

Figure 3-6. If your finances seem to be beyond control, there are many nonprofit agencies that can help you regain your footing.

Note

Because of CCCS's backing, the company will never recommend bankruptcy. Don't rule out bankruptcy as an option if you have only a few assets, a great deal of debt and limited income.

The CCCS typically goes to the credit card companies and gets your rates reduced by promising your repayment. After you get over the fact that CCCS is funded primarily by credit card companies, the very demons you have to repay, use the group's advice and work out a plan to repay that unwieldy debt.

Understand the consequences of everything you agree to: what happens if you sign up with CCCS, and what happens if you renege on the plan. Signing up with CCCS is likely to show up on your credit report as "debt restructuring," which has a negative connotation. It broadcasts to all that you couldn't pay your bills on time and had to have them reduced.

Some debt services, including CCCS, might ask you to turn over your paycheck. Don't do it. Your goal is to be able to control your finances yourself.

Chat for help

Of course, it's best to avoid debt in the first place. If you need frequent motivation, drop in on the weekly chat on credit and debt from theWhiz.com (Keyword: **Whiz**) for suggestions on how to rid yourself of debt, and get the most out of your credit (Figure 3-7).

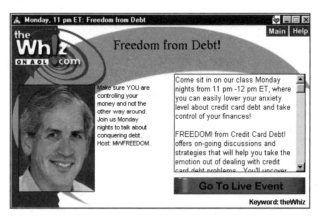

Figure 3-7. There are many sources — including online chat rooms — to turn to for advice and encouragement as you climb your way out of debt.

From the Whiz homepage, click Chat. Click the Chat Guide for a schedule of regular events. (Freedom from Debt is featured every Monday evening, for example.)

If you wish to participate in a chat, or just to eavesdrop, click Go to Live Event. You may also read the transcripts from previous events. Select Read: Live Event Guest Transcript from the subject box, and click the title you'd like to see.

Chats are divided into two sections: Stage Chats, which include only what the featured hosts or guests have to say among themselves and to the audience; and Audience Chats, where AOL members enter the conference room and participate. The chat window displays comments made in the audience to other audience members, and comments directed by audience members to the stage. To make a comment or ask a question of someone on stage, type your message in the input field at the bottom of the screen, and press Send. Any response from the stage will show up in the Stage Chat Area.

For more information on a topic or speaker, click the graphic on the top right of the screen.

Summary

Now you realize how credit cards undermine your investments and creep into your savings, and you understand why you must pay your balance in full each month. You have a plan to pay off your debt and you know how to go about finding the lowest credit card fees. You know how to obtain a copy of your credit report and how to apply for loans online. And you know where to call for help if you need it.

After you get your debt under control, you can start saving for your goals. Strategies are for the taking in Chapter 4.

A Quick Look

▶ **The Laz-E-Boy Guide to Riches** **page 59**

Is it really possible to become a millionaire? The folks at Armchair Millionaire say it is not only possible but also almost anyone can do it by following a five-step process. The "get-rich-slowly-but-surely" plan helps you in your pursuit of the big bucks goal. Go to Keyword: **Armchair Millionaire**, and click Five Steps to Financial Freedom. Enter your information to create a personalized action plan.

▶ **Forget the Slide Rule** **page 63**

Figuring returns, tax advantages, interest rates, and other intricacies of investing and financial planning can be an eye-crossing challenge. But not if you take advantage of AOL's many tools. Financial calculators make complex equations as simple as plugging in a few numbers. Why give yourself a headache when the computer will do all the work for you? Go to Keyword: **Calculator** and play with the numbers. From calculating mortgage payments and terms, to depreciating your car, to mapping out exactly how long it will take you to become a millionaire, these calculators can crunch the numbers quickly.

▶ **House-Hunting** **page 76**

You don't need to run all over town to go house hunting. You can launch your quest online. Rev up Keyword: **Real Estate** to start the search. Click House Hunting to search a database of more than a million homes. Search by state, on a map, or by entering a zip code. Plug in the type of home you're looking for, the price and the features you want, and up come homes for sale that meet your specs.

▶ **The IRS Delivers** **page 83**

It's the night of April 14th — do you know where your Schedule C form is? Did you forget to pick up the Exclusion Form for income earned abroad? Maybe you left your state tax forms at your office? Don't panic. You can download and print out anything from the IRS inventory, from forms to publications to instructions. Go to Keyword: **Taxes**, and click the desired form under Download Forms. If you want something that isn't shown, or you need your state tax forms, click More Forms.

Chapter 4

Grasping for Goals

Now you know what you earn, what you spend, and how much you can save. What are you saving for? What is it you want? What are your *goals*? You need to have goals in order to come up with a financial plan. Do you want to buy a home? Put the kids through college? Buy a Porsche? Re-do the kitchen? Have a couple of million for retirement? All of the above?

Successful financial planning and investing is goal-driven. First you figure out what you want down the road. Then you figure out how much the goal costs. Then you add up how much you can save toward the goal between today and the time you hope to reach it. Then you look at the difference between what you can save and how much the goal costs. *Then*, you figure out how you can invest your savings to try to make up the difference.

Figure 4-1. If becoming a millionaire is your goal, kick up your feet and start reading. The Armchair Millionaire can help you plan how to get there.

Find It Online

It might sound a little convoluted, but if you hang in there step-by-step, it makes a lot more sense. For example, if becoming a millionaire is your goal, you can find a five-step plan at the Armchair Millionaire. Go to Keyword: **Armchair Millionaire**. From there click Five Steps to Financial Freedom and then click Go To Tool, as shown in Figure 4-1.

Making a million

What will it take to reach your million-dollar goal? A good plan and prudent savings, say the experts at The Armchair Millionaire. Find out the slow-and-steady strategy at Keyword: **Armchair Millionaire**. First, click Five Steps to Financial Freedom to open the interactive "get-rich-slowly-but-surely" plan. Fill in the appropriate information about your savings and income, and the plan will show you what to do to reach your million-dollar goal, as well as how long it will take to get there.

In addition to providing the steps to make you a millionaire, the site offers help in investing wisely and keeping informed, especially by joining an online *investment club*. These types of clubs pool resources — typically $20 to $50 a month — of club members into one portfolio. The resources are in theory only on this site. Most of the clubs require nothing more than the contribution of ideas and interaction. The real dividends from such clubs are the educational opportunities and experience gained. To learn more about investment clubs, click The ABCs of Investing Clubs on the Armchair Millionaire homepage.

Stash emergency cash

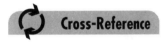 **Cross-Reference**

See Chapter 16 to learn what kinds of insurance are right for you.

The first couple of financial goals are universal. One is to pay off any credit card debt you have. You learned in Chapter 3 that it doesn't do you much good to shovel your money into investments when credit card debt burns your returns.

The second universal goal is to save enough money to cover emergencies: the water heater breaks, the garbage truck backs into your car, your employer moves to South Carolina, you slip on the ice and need pins in your back.

To figure how much you need, assume a worst-case scenario — all your household's sources of income come to a screeching halt. How much will you need to cover your expenses? While there's no perfect answer, count on at least three to six months' take-home pay as a good start. At the same time, make sure you have adequate health and disability insurance.

Now that your budget is up and functioning, direct your first savings into an emergency fund, and don't touch it ever (unless, of course, you have a real emergency. A sale at WalMart doesn't qualify). Make sure the account is *liquid*, which means you can take money out when you need it, and that it carries little or no risk. Common, risk-free, liquid accounts include savings accounts and money market funds.

You must build up your emergency fund before you put your money anywhere else. Once you reach the three- to six-months-of-expenses level, pat yourself on the back. Now you can work on that nest egg.

Outlining Your Goals

With credit card debt and emergency savings taken care of, you can get to the more exciting stuff. Why are you reading this book? What is it you want? You have to spell out something more specific than "a pile of cash." How high is that pile and what's it for? You don't necessarily have to plan out your whole life when you sketch out your financial goals. But if you outline your objectives you'll have a good idea of how much you'll need at specific points in time.

To get started on your outline, first make a wish list. Sit down and write out your top three or four goals. Think in terms of one or two short-term (five years or less), medium-term (five to 10 years), and long-term (more than 10 years) goals.

The task is easier if you're single with no dependents. Then the only person affected by your decision is you. If you have a spouse or a partner, and dependents, too, it gets a little tricky.

Sharing goals with a partner

It's not uncommon for couples to have different goals. Maybe Pat wants to retire, sell the house and use the proceeds to ride a motorcycle with sidecar across the country. Maybe Lee wants to stay in the city, go to the theater, take care of the in-laws, and live off of Social Security and a part-time job. Maybe Pat envisions Ivy League schools for the kids, but Lee figures they'll go to community college.

Pat and Lee could be headed for trouble. When couples and families don't talk about their financial goals until a decision is imminent, it's usually too late to do anything about it — the children, parents, and grandparents have their own objectives and there's not enough money to address them all.

MONEY Magazine and AOL provide an in-depth look at the financial conflicts that often erupt between spouses, and provide ways to resolve those conflicts. To find the article in Figure 4-2 as well as others like it, go to Keyword: **Advice & Planning**, click Marriage & Money, and then click Your Marriage: Is money ruining it?

It is a lot easier to work toward attaining your goals if you share the vision with your partner. But first, you and your mate should sit down *separately* and write out your goals. It's OK to fantasize here. Do you seek enough $$ to put the kids through . . . Harvard? Enough to retire and buy a yacht? Enough to unload the clunker and buy a minivan? These are *your* goals. Be subjective here.

Be honest with your partner. If you really don't want to squirrel away all your money, only to turn it over to State U for the kids' tuition, it's better to fess up now. Otherwise, if you pick goals you don't really want, you'll probably lose the motivation to attain them, or you might attain them but resent the out-

Find It Online

Keyword: **Advice & Planning** collects great resources for many common goals under Saving for School, Retire in Style, and Marriage and Money.

4

Grasping for Goals

come. Settle on the goals you can agree on, and prioritize those goals. Then agree to talk each year about the ones you can't seem to settle.

After you each make your list, go somewhere fun (not in the kitchen you want to renovate!) and share your goals with each other. Go to the beach or to a park or to the mountains, and keep the conversation positive. You're talking about dreams here, not labor negotiations.

When you draw up your list of goals, try to keep to a half-dozen items or fewer. Otherwise, the planning becomes unwieldy.

Figure 4-2. Not having a mutual investment strategy can cause a great deal of friction in a marriage. With AOL, you'll find tools that help remove the static.

Set Attainable Goals

When you have mutual goals and that trip to Tahiti tantalizes, or that sapphire sparkles, or that Harley harkens, your goals will act as buoys when the waters don't seem navigable, helping you steer toward a predetermined course. Write your goals on paper, not in stone. Then if you miss a couple of contributions toward your goals, you will not despair. The worst thing to do in saving and investing is to give up. Better to reassess your financial status and to design more realistic expectations.

Table 4-1 presents a list of some common short-, medium-, and long-term financial goals. How much will they cost you? You may have to do some research to come up with the numbers. Find out what they cost now and then tack on 3 percent a year to account for inflation.

Table 4-1. *Calculate the Costs of Your Goals*

Goal	Cost	Years From Now
Eliminate credit card debt		
Fill the emergency fund		
Buy a car		
Send the kids to college		
Put a down payment on a house		
Retire in comfort		
Buy a vacation home		
Start a new business		
Go back to school		
Quit work and volunteer		

Now you have your goals, and you know what they cost. Are they reachable in the time you can save for them?

To find out, go back to the budget you compiled in Chapter 2 to remind yourself how much you will be saving. Then, divvy up your savings as if it were a pie. Each chunk goes to a goal, with the size of the chunk relative to the goal. Work backwards and add up how much you can actually save between when the goal comes due and now. If you have to, pare down your list of goals to make sure you're left with those your income and savings will support.

Calling all calculators

You can use the savings calculator at Keyword: **Calculator**, shown below, to determine if your goals are attainable. AOL's financial calculators from CalcBuilder fall into three main categories: Lending, Investing, and Personal Finance. To answer your questions about savings, scroll down to the Savings Calculator, located under Personal Finance. From the list of questions, choose the calculator that best fits your needs.

Continued

Find It Online

How much will it cost for that remodeling plan in the future? Find out at Keyword: **Realtor.com**. Once there, click Remodel.com, under What's new. Then select Calculators and plug in the supplies you need. The calculator will estimate the cost of the job.

Cross-Reference

Want to know more about real estate goals? See "Buying a House" at the end of this chapter.

Tip

Giving to charity not only helps your fellow humans, it's tax deductible. Keep track of every mile you log in your charitable endeavors, as you can deduct 14 cents a mile for these efforts.

4

Grasping for Goals

Calling all calculators *(continued)*

For example, if you have a specific goal, and you'd like to know when you will reach it, click "What will it take to save for a car, home, etc.?" and plug in your numbers.

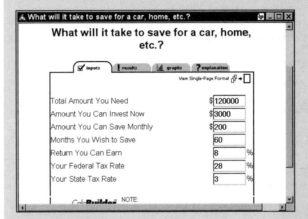

Decided your goal in life is to drive a Ferrari? With a few figures, you will know exactly when — or if — you can get behind the wheel.

It's helpful to have handy a few particulars — such as your federal and state tax rates and your current savings and income — before using the calculators. After you enter your information, the calculator will display your answers: exactly how long it will take to reach your goal, the actual amount of money it will take to make your purchase (taking into account variables such as inflation and taxes), and how additional or less savings will change the results.

Investing to Reach Your Goals

Here's a wonderful element of investing: The amount of money you're able to save does not have to equal the cost of the goal in order for the goal to be attainable. In fact, most often, your savings will not come close to what you need. That's where investing comes in.

Take sending the kids to college, for example. Say Junior loves toddling through the house building things at every turn. He balances blocks, he stacks stones, he piles pots and pans into tremendous towers. You just know he's going to study architecture. With visions of a Harvard diploma on his office wall, mosey over to the College Board (Keyword: **College Board**) to check out the pricetag on this diploma. From the homepage, click search for colleges. From the welcome screen, click continue, then choose the "search by name" option. Type Harvard in the search box and then click the "search by name" button. When the results return, click the "see college info" button. Scroll down the page to see that you'll pay $23,618 a year for tuition. And that's today's price. Without room and board. (Don't forget to add in about 5 percent a year for anticipated price hikes between now and then.)

... That was your time to gasp.

Now, go back to that pie and figure out how much you can amass between now and freshman orientation. Obviously, this will be an estimate. Take the college fund pie chunk and multiply it times the number of years until Junior graduates from high school. Compare this to the cost. Kudos to you if you can save all you need. If you're like most people, though, your savings will fall short of your goals. Far short. But many people can attain their goals anyway because of what they *do* with their savings — *how they invest it* — to make up the difference.

AOL offers a collection of resources, tips, and tools to help meet specific goals, like the one from *The Wall Street Journal's SmartMoney Magazine* shown in Figure 4-3. To get to the article, type in **http://www.smartmoney.com.** Click Planning, then select College Planning from the list of contents. Scroll down to Investing for College and click How Will You Get There.

You can explore the articles offering tips on designing portfolios for college, learning about financial aid, and what to do if you've waited until the last minute to save.

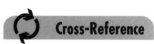

Cross-Reference

In the next chapter, you'll learn what to look for in an investment to meet a particular goal; and in Chapter 12, you'll learn exactly how to invest to pay for college. For now, understand how investments *can* make up the difference between your savings and how much a goal costs.

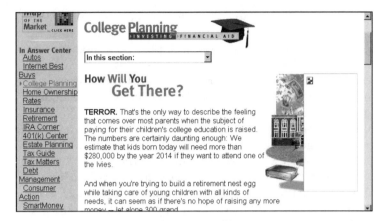

Figure 4-3. With the proper planning, it is possible to conquer tuition terror.

Investing for long-term goals

Whether or not your goal is attainable will depend on how much your investments *return*. Does return matter all that much? Indeed it does. Take a look at Junior's college fund prospects. Your chances of having enough money to pay Harvard tuition depend significantly on the return you get on your college fund investments.

There's a great tool on AOL for figuring out how much your investments need to return over time to meet your goal. Go to http://quicken.aol.com/saving/. Click Savings Calculator, then on Annual Yield, because that is what you're trying to determine when you're looking for return. Then plug in the numbers appropriate to your situation. (See Figure 4-4.)

Suppose college starts 16 years from now. You figure it will cost you $100,000. You have $4,000 now, and you can add $150 a month in savings to the college fund. This gets you to a total of $32,800 between now and then. What kind of a return will you need to get you to $100,000?

Plug these numbers into the calculator and check *annual yield*:

Opening Balance	$4,000
Monthly Savings	$150
Number of Years	16
Annual Yield (Return)	
Ending Balance	$100,000

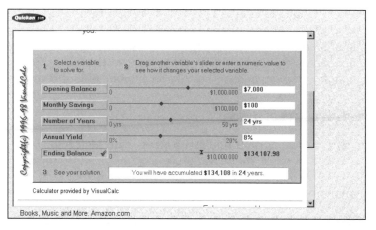

Figure 4-4. Even the best plans are subject to change. Quicken's Savings Calculator allows you to see how a change in one factor can affect your long-term goals.

The calculator will show you that you need at least a 10.908 percent annual yield, or return, on the money you save between now and then to reach your goal. The stock market has returned an average of 12.5 percent annually for the last 40 years. Congratulations! This goal seems doable. Play with the numbers a bit on this tool and see how the return on your investments tremendously affects how quickly — or if — you can reach your goal.

Investing for shorter-term goals

Timetable and return have a crucial relationship that's explored in depth in the next chapter. For now, take a look at how one affects the other. For example, suppose Junior has an older brother you think is destined for college. Change one little variable in the formula — Number of Years — and watch that return figure soar. If Junior's older brother is seven, you have 11 years until tuition time. Input into the calculator the same amount for everything but Number of Years, and look at the difference.

Opening Balance	$4,000
Monthly Savings	$150
Number of Years	11
Annual Yield (Return)	*19.28%*
Ending Balance	$100,000

4

Grasping for Goals

Cross-Reference

Don't fret about it now. There are plenty of options in the "Saving for College" section of Chapter 12.

Find It Online

For an online primer, check out Keyword: **Personal Finance** and click Investing Basics. Under Becoming an Investor, click Step 8 — Long Term Success, as shown in Figure 4-5.

Yikes. It's hard to count on a 19.28 percent return on an investment without perching precariously on a limb. You might need to make some adjustments with this goal: either pump up the monthly savings, try to start with a higher figure, or aim for a less expensive college for Junior's older brother.

Return, meet risk

So all you have to do is find investments with high returns to meet your goals, right? Not quite. High returns also mean high risks, something you can't afford to take if your goal is imminent.

Will you have to take risks to achieve the results you seek? Are you comfortable with these risks, or do you need to revise your goals according to your income? Which investments should you choose to reach your goals in the time you have? All these questions figure into your investment blueprint, which you will design in the next chapter, when you shape your investment strategy.

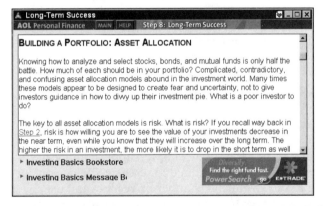

Figure 4-5. Simply plunking all your money into the vehicle with the highest potential return is a high-stakes bet. The time constraints and nature of every investor's goals determine where money is best directed.

There are many other factors that might arise when pursuing a goal. You can read about saving and investing for college and retirement in Chapter 12. Here's a look at another common goal: buying a house.

Buying a House

So, you want to buy a house. This is a common goal for many investors. So many factors figure into this tremendous outlay of cash. Are you ready to make the commitment? To help you decide, you should be able to answer 'yes' to the following statements:

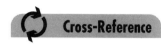

Cross-Reference

To review ways to obtain your credit report, see Chapter 3.

> ► You'll be staying put in your new home for at least five years. (Due to the heavy costs up front, you're apt to lose a lot of money unless you stick around this long.)

> ► Your financial house is in order and your credit history is clean.

> ► You can afford mortgage payments without compromising your financial health.

> ► You can afford the other costs that go with home ownership, like utilities, repairs, insurance, property taxes, and others.

> ► Your income will remain steady or will increase, even if children come into the picture.

> ► You're ready to do your homework to find a good mortgage.

> ► You have enough money to make a down payment without wiping out your reserves.

> ► You can afford the hidden fees that come with buying a house: a credit check ($50-$75), appraisal ($150-$300), home inspection ($200-$350), title insurance (up to 2 percent of the home's cost), property taxes, attorney's fees ($750 to $1,000), points, the movers (even if it's a rental truck and pizza for your buddies), paint, curtains, rugs, appliances, hoses, rakes and shovels, a lawnmower, and whatever else you don't have in your old digs.

Compared to renting, owning a home has tremendous benefits. Among the advantages, your mortgage payment stays the same each month, while renters risk annual rent hikes. Your payments stop when you pay off the loan, whereas renters pay forever. Your mortgage buys you more of the house you live in, while rent never gains the renter any equity. If your home rises in value, you get to keep the profits when you sell. Much of your monthly mortgage payment is tax deductible.

4

Grasping for Goals

Buyer's quiz

Is the time right for you to become a homeowner? There are lots of places to pursue this question. For example, financial planner Ric Edelman's buyer's quiz can help you determine whether or not you're ready to buy. Go to Keyword: **Edelman**, then click search Ric Edelman's site, then enter "10 questions" then click Chapter 56 – How to Buy Your First Home.

In addition, you can turn to the article shown in the Figure below for further discussion. Go to Keyword: **Real Estate,** and click Resources. Under the heading Information, click Motley Fool: Find A House, and then select Ready for a Home?

Are you ready to make the American dream come true? Find out if the time is right to own your own home.

While it might make sense for you to own your own home, having enough money to make the purchase is another story altogether. Most likely you'll have to borrow an awful lot of cash from a financial institution to be able to realize your dream.

Mastering the mortgage process

Getting a mortgage can be frustrating and anxious. But there are many ways to expedite the proceedings and relieve the anguish. Foremost among them, you can understand the mortgage process.

First, understand that a mortgage is one of the most reasonable loans you can get. This is because the lender gets built-in collateral — your house — which typically appreciates over the time of the mortgage. Lenders want to give you a mortgage, because your income proves you can pay them back, and you're motivated to do so because you don't want to lose the roof over your head. If you should stumble or fall, and you can't pay up, the lender can take that collateral right out from under you.

The amount of a mortgage you can get depends on a few factors: your income, your assets, your debts and the interest rate on the mortgage. There's a formula that spells out how much you can qualify for.

To figure how much they will loan you, most lenders require that your monthly mortgage payment (including mortgage principal and interest, taxes, homeowner's insurance, and private mortgage insurance) be *28 percent or less* of your monthly income.

So, first, you figure out your income: your gross pay, your moonlighting money, your investment dividends, your retirement income and your alimony and child support. Suppose you and your spouse earn $84,000 combined. Divide this by 12 and you get $7,000 a month. Take 28 percent of $7,000 and you get $1,960 for a monthly payment.

Don't go rushing off to the lender yet. This is where qualification takes a tricky turn.

Most lenders also require that your mortgage payment *plus your other monthly debt payments* total *less than 36 percent* of your income. That means if your income is $84,000, you can't pay any more than $2,520 a month for mortgage plus other debt payments. This isn't to shoot a hole in your mortgage possibilities. It's for your own protection. So now you need to review your debt, which you examined in the last

Find It Online

For an online primer on the whole process of buying a home, from finding a Realtor to securing a mortgage, go to Keyword: **Real Estate**, then click Resources, and scroll all the way down under TheWhiz.com to Home, Home on the Web.

Note

If you want to apply for a mortgage to buy a retirement home, try to apply for it while you're still working, as getting a mortgage is extremely dependent upon your income.

Note

When calculating your debt payments, you don't have to include any debt that will be paid off within the next 10 months.

Cross-Reference

Turn to Chapter 7 for everything you need to know about Treasury rates.

Find It Online

To examine the advantages and disadvantages of both mortgage types, as pictured in Figure 4-6, go to Keyword: **Bankrate,** click Mortgages, and scroll down to The Basics, under All About Mortgages. Scroll down again and choose The Basics: Part I, and select Adjustable vs. Fixed.

chapter. Add up your payments and come up with a monthly figure. Now, add this to how much your mortgage payment is likely to be.

No need to pick up the phone book and do the voice mail limbo to find current interest rates in order to figure out the payments. You can find the going rates at Keyword: **Bankrate.** Then, under Today's Averages, click 30-Year Fixed. Once here, you'll see rates including the 30-year fixed rate, the 15-year fixed rate and the one year ARM (which is the adjustable rate mortgage). Under All About Mortgages, click Compare the Cost to see how these rates compare.

For a $100,000 loan, for example, you might see:

Type of Mortgage	Rate	Monthly Payment
30-year fixed	7.85%	$723.33
15-year fixed	7.45%	$924.17
1 year ARM	6.43%	$627.47

You typically have two options, a *fixed rate*, a higher interest rate that never changes for the life of the loan; and a *variable rate*, a lower interest rate that changes with the Treasury rate. While the terms of a variable rate mortgage differ from one to the next, typically, the rate can rise or fall no more than 2 percent a year with a lifetime cap of an additional 6 percent.

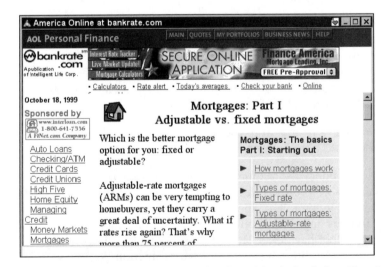

Figure 4-6. Make sure you understand the benefits and drawbacks of adjustable and fixed mortgages before you choose a lender.

Suppose the fixed rate is 8 percent for 30 years and the variable figure is 6.5 percent for 30 years. How much would your monthly payments be? To find out, call up the mortgage calculator at Keyword: **Bankrate**. Select Calculators. Then, under Mortgage Calculators, select Should You Get a Fixed or Adjustable Rate Mortgage. Fill in the variables to see the best and worst case scenarios of how much you might pay over the life of the mortgage.

Once you have a ballpark monthly mortgage payment, and you know your monthly income and your monthly debt payments, you can figure out how much you will qualify for. To do this, you can turn to yet another online calculator. This time, go to Keyword: **Quicken**, then select the Mortgage tab. Click the Let's Get Started tab and then Home Affordability under the Tools header in the left-hand column. The link takes you to the Home Affordability calculator, pictured in Figure 4-7.

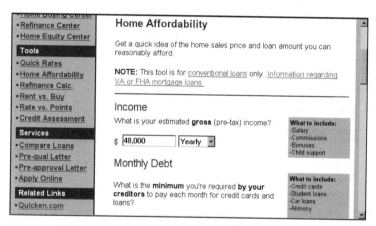

Figure 4-7. Before you set your heart on your dream house, get a realistic idea about how much you can afford, based on your income, debt, and savings.

Fill in your income; your minimum monthly debt payments, such as credit card payments and car loans; and the amount you can put down for a down payment. Then click Calculate! The calculator uses current national interest rates averages to come up with a low and a high estimate of how much of a mortgage you might qualify for.

Once you understand how much you're likely to qualify for, you can start shopping for a house.

Finding a House

Before you begin searching for your new home, it helps to make a list of the items you're looking for. Include in your list your price range, the location (near schools? recreation? your job? your family or friends? medical services?), the style of house you like, number and types of rooms, amenities, such as a fireplace, pool, garage, deck, security system, etc.

For help on what else to consider when house hunting, turn to Keyword: **Whiz**. Click Renting & Real Estate, among the links at the bottom of the page. And select WHZ 101: Buying a House: A play in 3 acts. Click Preparing a List, shown on the left of the screen (Figure 4-8).

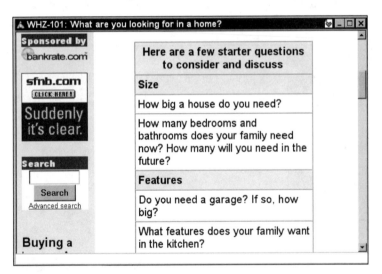

Figure 4-8. You can refine your house hunt by deciding what you want in a home — before you go looking.

Once you're done with your inventory, print it out so you can bring it with you as you look. This helps you keep the details manageable.

Next, start your search. Most buyers rely on a real estate agent to help them. An agent should have a thorough understanding of a geographic area, should understand what is a reasonable and an unreasonable offer, and should know how to present that offer to the seller. In addition, she should be able to connect you to all those people who inevitably become part of the buying process — the home inspector, the appraiser, the mortgage company rep, the bankers, the lawyer, the zoning commissioners, and anybody else who might traipse through your potential palace before the deal is done.

Finding a realtor

You can search for an agent online at Keyword: **Realtor.com**. Click the Find a Realtor QuickTool, as pictured in Figure 4-9. Then either click a state on the map or, if you know exactly where you want to look, enter the city and state, and click Continue. Select Yellow Pages if you want to see the Realtor's specialty, Web page and contact information, or click White Pages, select the locale you're looking in and select either Find Realtors or Find Offices.

Note

Note that the agent technically represents the seller, even though you enlisted her services. Her fee comes out of the sale price. (Agents typically split 6 percent of the sales price, half to the agent working with you and half to the seller's agent.) But it's in her best interest to sell you what you're looking for, so you'll recommend her to others and you'll use her again when you want to sell your house.

Caution

You won't save any money by not using a real estate agent to buy a house. The seller pays 6 percent to his agent, regardless of what you do. His agent typically splits the fee with your agent. If you don't have an agent, his agent keeps the entire amount.

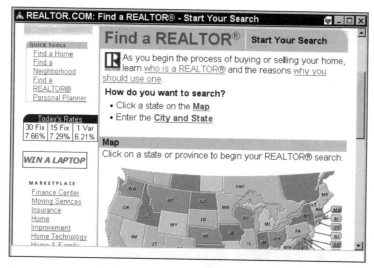

Figure 4-9. No need to listen to one sales pitch after the next to find a real estate agent to help you find a new home. Narrow the field by conducting your preliminary search online.

Once you settle on an agent you feel comfortable with, take your list and together start looking.

House-hunting online

In addition to getting help from an agent, you can launch
your house search online. Start your search at Keyword:
RealEstate, then click Find A Home under the QuickTools
header to search a database of more than a million homes.
Click your state on the map. Next, select an area either by
clicking the map, clicking the corresponding link below
the map, typing in the name of the city or town or entering a zip code. If you are looking in a particular area, scroll
down to the town and click Continue. You may need to
click through several screens to specify the area you are
looking for. Next, plug in the type of home you're looking
for, as shown in the Figure below, and click Continue.

AOL can help point you to houses for sale in a specified area. You'll be able to
see details including floor plans, pictures, prices, and specifications.

You can refine your search for the number of bedrooms,
baths, and square footage you seek. You will also need to
input a price range. Note that you should include prices
about 15 percent above and below your target price to be
sure to include all houses that might meet your criteria.

Next, click Search and see what turns up. As you review
the prospects, click Save This Listing if there's a home that
interests you, or make note of the MLS number. (MLS
refers to the Multiple Listing Service, a database of all

homes on the market to which all agents have access.)
Note the amount below Estimated Payment Calculator.
This tells you approximately how much your monthly
mortgage payments would be for a 30-year mortgage,
based on 20 percent down and the current interest rate
average.

Find It Online

For suggestions on how to
negotiate a price, go to
Keyword: **Moneymag**,
then select Real Estate, then,
under In This Lesson, click
Closing the Deal.

Making the bid

Once you find a house you like, you need to make an offer
on it. How close a bid should you make to the sale price?
That depends on a couple of factors: whether the market in
the area is hot or cold, and how other homes have sold in the
area. In the process of your house hunting, try to find the last
three homes that sold in the neighborhood. What was the difference between the list price and final price? Ask your real
estate agent to find this out for you.

If the ultimate sales price was an average of 6 percent below
the list price, for example, you can offer 8 or 10 percent
below the list price, and then negotiate from there. But if the
market was so hot that houses typically sold for the list price,
don't try to lowball the price. You risk losing the house.

You might be able to negotiate other features into the deal
to make the price more palatable. If the owners are leaving
town, for example, they might be willing to throw in all the
appliances or some of the furnishings, even if they can't lower
the price. In a slow market, there's room for maneuverability.
But in a hot market, you might have to offer the list price on
the spot. That's why doing your homework ahead of time is
so important.

Obtaining a Mortgage

Once your offer is accepted, it's time to get the mortgage.
Hopefully you have done your preliminary work and know
how much you can qualify for. You have to get into the

4

Grasping for Goals

Caution

If your down payment is less than 20 percent, you'll probably have to pay private mortgage insurance, which ranges from a half percent to 1.25 percent of the total loan, due at the closing, in addition to annual PMI costs which are built into the mortgage payment.

Note

You can't borrow money to meet your down payment, but you can use money that has been given to you.

nitty-gritty now. Be ready to provide check stubs, tax returns, bank statements, and the story of your life. Have your down payment at the ready.

Go back to Keyword: **Bankrate.com** again to remind yourself of the average interest rates, then start shopping for the best deal that works for you. You can apply for a mortgage online at Keyword: **Mortgage**, then click Let's Get Started, as pictured in Figure 4-10, to start your comparison shopping with Quicken.com. Or you can check with your bank or credit union to see how their packages compare.

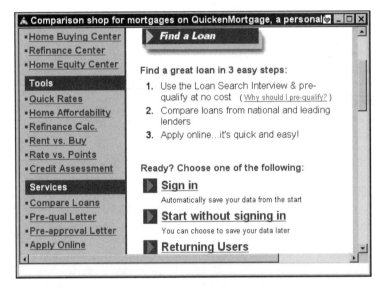

Figure 4-10. A house might be the biggest purchase you'll ever make. Shopping around for the best mortgage deal can make a huge difference in the ultimate pricetag.

If you don't qualify for the amount you need, there are a couple of ways you might be able to obtain a larger loan. Many lenders will approve a bigger mortgage if you can come up with a down payment that exceeds 20 percent of the price of the home.

You can reduce your monthly payments (and therefore qualify for a bigger loan) if you pay *points* (also known as the *loan discount cost*), which lower the interest rate. One point equals 1 percent of your loan. Typically, your lender will agree to lower your interest rate one percent in return for three points. So if you're looking to borrow $150,000 but you can't afford the 8 percent monthly payments, you can probably get that interest rate reduced to 7 percent if you pay 3 points up front, or 3 percent of the total, which is $4,500.

Once you get your mortgage and close the deal, pick up your keys and pat yourself on the back for attaining this challenging goal. And give yourself extra congratulations. You may not realize it, but you've accomplished another common goal with your home purchase — reducing your tax bite.

Filing Taxes Online

Owning a home is part of a good tax strategy, in addition to being a practical goal. When you own a home you can deduct mortgage interest (and interest on home equity loans) from your taxes.

To estimate how much you save on taxes with a mortgage, go to Keyword: **Calculator.** Under Lending, select Mortgage Calculators, and then click How Much Can I Save in Taxes? to open the tool pictured in Figure 4-11. Fill in the information regarding your mortgage and tax rates, and then click Results to see a tally of how a mortgage might affect your tax burden.

Find It Online

You can find many more real estate tips and tools at Keyword: **Moneymag**, then click Real Estate. Scroll down and select Picking a Team, under In This Lesson.

Note

Because points are technically interest, they are tax-deductible in the year you pay them.

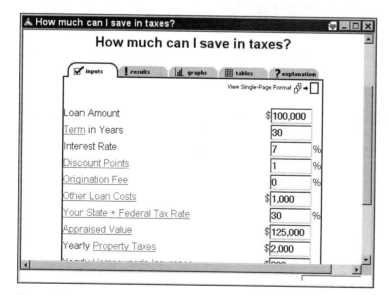

Figure 4-11. Does going into debt to buy a home really save you money in taxes? Let AOL's mortgage calculator do the math to help you find out.

To fully take advantage of the opportunity your newfound tax savings presents, go a step further with your tax management, and file your taxes online.

You're not alone if you prefer to steer clear of the IRS and anything having to do with taxes. But if you spend a little bit of time and energy up front learning about taxes you can save much time, much energy — and many dollars — as a result.

AOL offers a variety of resources to help you in your quest, from explaining the ABCs of taxes to offering advice on tax-sheltered investments to information on filing online. Begin at Keyword: **Taxes** (see Figure 4-12) for links to tax primers, tax forms, the IRS Web site and more.

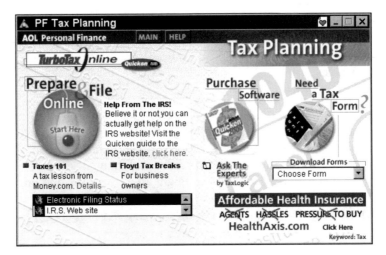

Figure 4-12. AOL provides a launching pad for understanding taxes and filing your returns.

Some 25 million taxpayers submit their tax returns electronically through the IRS' e-file option. Why so many? A number of reasons, including:

▶ Time savings. Often, when you file a tax return you must fill in the same information again and again on various forms. But when you file online, the software retains the information and inputs it throughout the return.

▶ Electronic filing greatly improves accuracy, says the IRS. The error rate for electronic returns is less than one percent, compared to the error rate for paper returns, which hovers between 20 and 21 percent.

▶ You get a refund in a hurry — the time is slashed in half if you file electronically versus filing with paper. The wait shrinks even further when you opt for Direct Deposit, which sends your refund to your bank account.

▶ Filing online expedites an otherwise tedious — perhaps even overwhelming — task. After you set things up the first year, subsequent filings are a relative breeze.

The software recalls your information so you don't need to input it all over again, year after year. You just change the annual variables, like income and interest income and your deductions. Many programs even flag items that might raise concern: figures that seem extraordinary compared to the norm, responses on your return that don't make sense with each other and numbers that clash with previous returns.

In addition to easing the tax filing burden, many tax software programs work together with your budgeting and banking software to help you set up your own accounting system so you can automatically keep track of your tax-deductible expenditures.

Electronic filing

There are two e-file options available: submission by an authorized tax preparer; or submission with a personal computer, modem, and authorized tax-preparation software. You can refer to the article in Figure 4-13 for an overview of the filing options. Go to Keyword: **Whiz**, click the Taxes link at the bottom of the page, and select the title "WHZ 101: Tax filing options."

If you choose the latter option, you complete your return on your computer and then you send in the return via your modem. If you don't want to send it in over the phone lines, you can print out and mail in a response sheet that prints only the numbers the IRS is looking for without that dictionary-sized package full of forms you would normally have to sendin.

Tip

AOL offers a fast, easy, way to get tax software. Go to Keyword: **Turbo Tax** to access software offered through the Quicken Store. Click Web Turbo Tax to download the software to file your taxes electronically. Note that you have to pay for this software.

4

Definition

Electronic Return Originator, or ERO: The person or company responsible for transmitting a tax return to the IRS electronically. An ERO filing on someone's behalf must have a signed Form 8453, authorizing the electronic transmission of the tax return.

Caution

Be careful of a tax preparer who guarantees your "refund" in just a few days. That deal is more likely a Refund Anticipation Loan (RAL), which is simply a short-term advance against the anticipated refund, and which will cost you additional fees and interest. Make sure you know what you are paying for, and whether getting a refund back quickly is worth sacrificing part of the refund to interest payments or fees.

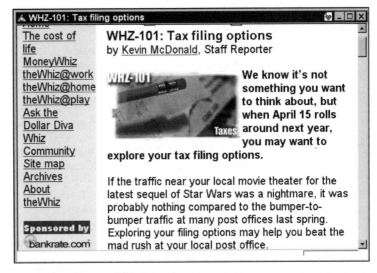

Figure 4-13. Planning on spending another April 15th at the post office? Maybe it's time to investigate other options for filing your taxes.

E-File for state taxes

Here's an added incentive to e-filing: In certain states you can file federal and state returns electronically at the same time! The electronic filing software places your federal and state return data in separate packets. These packets are transmitted to the IRS, which then forwards the appropriate data to the participant state. The state receives and processes the electronic return.

The Federal/state e-file is available in 35 states plus the District of Columbia. For a list of participating states, as shown in Figure 4-14, go to **http://www.irs.gov.** Scroll down and select Electronic Services, then select Federal/State *e-file* For Taxpayers. Scroll down and click Can all Federal and state income tax returns be filed using this option? Or, call the IRS at 1-800-829-1040 or call your state tax administration office.

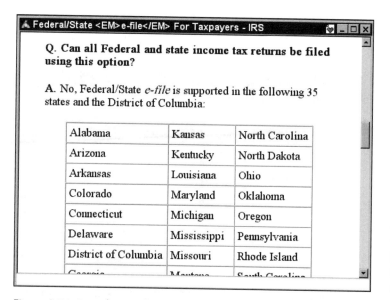

Q. **Can all Federal and state income tax returns be filed using this option?**

A. No, Federal/State *e-file* is supported in the following 35 states and the District of Columbia:

Alabama	Kansas	North Carolina
Arizona	Kentucky	North Dakota
Arkansas	Louisiana	Ohio
Colorado	Maryland	Oklahoma
Connecticut	Michigan	Oregon
Delaware	Mississippi	Pennsylvania
District of Columbia	Missouri	Rhode Island

Figure 4-14. Depending on where you live, you may be able to file your federal and state taxes in one step, using the online e-file option.

Forms, forms, and more forms

If you're not ready to file online, you can still turn to AOL for help during tax time. Download and print state and Federal tax forms, or order them by mail, at Keyword: **Taxes.** Click the icon on the right for downloading forms.

The most commonly requested forms are listed. If the form you need isn't among them, click More Forms, as pictured in the Figure below. A more detailed list will appear which includes links to States. If the form you want still isn't listed, or if you want the publication and instructions that accompany the form, try **http://www.irs.gov.** Scroll down and click Forms and Publications to access every weapon in the IRS arsenal.

Continued

Find It Online

If you'd like to file your taxes electronically, the IRS provides a list of approved e-file providers and tax preparation software. Find the list at Keyword: **Taxes,** and select IRS Web Site from the subject box. Click Electronic Services at the bottom of the page, then scroll down again to the bottom of the first column for links to help you get started e-filing.

To locate an accountant offering e-filing in your area, choose Search for an Authorized IRS E-File Provider. To find IRS-authorized software, click Online Filing Companies.

Note

If you owe the IRS money, you can have the funds withdrawn from your checking account using Direct Debit. Include your bank routing information and account number on Form 1040 when you file electronically. You can designate the exact date (up to and including April 15) that you want the payment withdrawn from your checking or savings account.

Tip

Because tax forms and publications are so content-heavy, they cannot be simply downloaded. You must use Adobe Acrobat software, a program that translates large Web pages into a useable format that your computer can read. If you don't have Adobe Acrobat, you can download it from AOL for free. Click Get Acrobat First in the Download Forms subject box and your computer will download the software. Once Adobe Acrobat is ready, select the IRS form you wish to download.

Tip

If you're reading this section on April 14th, you might appreciate the Running Behind? links in the More Forms site. The Last Chance icon is a direct link to the form you need to file an extension with the IRS.

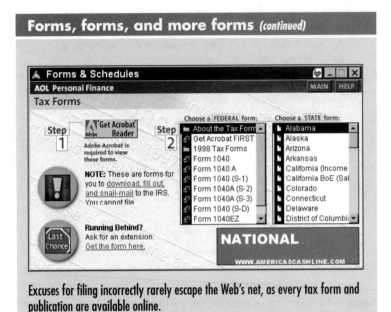

Excuses for filing incorrectly rarely escape the Web's net, as every tax form and publication are available online.

Going Solo versus Getting Help

Just because you file your taxes online doesn't mean you don't need an accountant. Filing is administrative. Accounting is a skill. If your taxes are relatively simple, you may not need to spend money to have someone else do them for you. But what, exactly, constitutes simple taxes? You could be missing out on opportunities to save, due to your unawareness of some arcane tax law.

Your taxes are based on the income you receive for the year, everything from your salary or contract income to interest, dividends, and capital gains on investments, inheritance money, gambling earnings, even certain gifts and prizes. Once you add up your earnings and come up with your gross income, you can take certain expenditures out, and the result is your *adjusted gross income*, or *AGI*. Once you establish your AGI, you subtract other exemptions. The final figure is your *taxable income*. The lower your taxable income, the less you have to pay in taxes.

With all this deducting and adding and itemizing, planning and forethought can make a tremendous impact on the bottom line. This book is peppered with tax tips and tax savings strategies. You can research additional strategies to slash your taxes at Keyword: **Whiz.** Click the Taxes link at the bottom of the page. Then select WHZ 101: Avoiding Taxes. *Legally*, as in Figure 4-15.

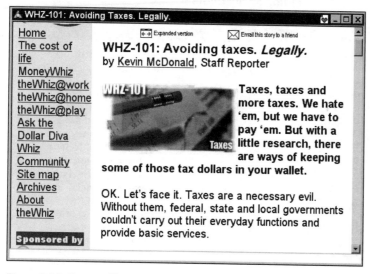

Figure 4-15. Your tax obligation? To pay exactly what you owe, and not a penny more.

To help you decide if you'd be better served by doing your tax return alone versus using an accountant, take Money.com's interactive quiz. Go to Keyword: **Moneymag**, and click Taxes. Then click the Go button, next to the title "Do You Need an Accountant or Are You OK Going Solo?" Then fill in the 20-question, multiple-choice quiz to assess your tax savvy. Click Check It when you're done to see your score. Based on your score you'll see if you should be sharpening your pencils and getting down to business, or stuffing your paperwork in a folder to hand to a trained professional.

Even if you do end up filing your tax return by yourself, it is often more efficient, both in terms of time and money saved, to consult a tax professional before you file. You probably pay at least tens of thousands of dollars in taxes. It is worth spending a couple of hours and a couple of hundred dollars to make sure you are reducing your tax bill where you can.

Sit down with your accountant and assess the prior year's tax return to help you make changes for the upcoming return. (Needless to say, don't wait until spring to make this appointment.) See the article pictured in Figure 4-16 to help you decide when you should consider hiring an accountant, as well as tips for selecting someone you can trust. Go to Keyword: **Whiz**, and select Taxes. Scroll down to the title WHZ 101: Finding an accountant.

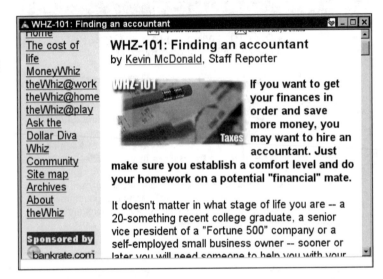

Figure 4-16. With your money and your reputation at stake, it's a good idea to research the qualifications of any accountant before you hire her.

Without an accountant peeking over your shoulder you might be tempted to stretch the interpretation of the tax laws. This little indiscretion can result in those nice men from the IRS knocking on your door and demanding to see your files. An audit is nothing to fear if you do what you're supposed to do — obey the tax laws, keep your receipts and make sure you have good records to back up your claims. But even if you're within the letter of the law, some items on your return might raise a red flag. These include

▶ Not enough income to support your deductions

▶ Investment returns that are lower than a savings account rate

▶ Unreported income

▶ Profit from a business or profession that's below the norm

▶ A refund that seems too big for your gross income and exemptions

▶ An expense item that is 5 percent or more of your total expenses

▶ An expense item that costs tens of thousands of dollars

▶ Excessive charitable contributions

You'll find many tax suggestions beginning in the next chapter and appearing throughout this book.

Find It Online

Still, as the *MONEY Magazine* article pictured in Figure 4-17 states, don't let the fear of an audit keep you from taking deserved tax breaks. To read the full story, go to Keyword: **Money. com**. Scroll down to Money 101 along the left-hand side, and select Lesson 19: Taxes. Click Much-dreaded audits.

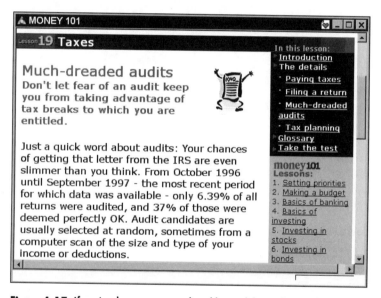

Figure 4-17. If you've done your research and kept solid records, you should have nothing to fear from an audit.

Summary

Wow, that was a lot of information you learned. You're well on your way to achieving one of your goals: being a smart investor.

You know to save for emergencies, you have outlined your goals and you know what they cost. You know how the power of returns can turn your dreams into reality, and you know how to calculate what your returns need to be to meet your goals.

If buying a house is a goal of yours, you know where to find and how to use online tools to help you search for a real estate agent, a house and a mortgage. And you also know how to file your taxes online.

Coming up next, methods of turning your goals into realities, in Chapter 5.

A Quick Look

A few small steps for the beginner, a giant step towards investing.

Eager to join the investing fray, but worried your lack of experience could get you into trouble? The Mutual Fund Masters at AOL partner Sage offer a fast way to get up to speed with their 8-step program. Written in easy-to-read language and in a short, to-the-point format, the topics take novice investors from the basics of mutual funds, to creating a diversified portfolio, to dollar-cost averaging. After shoring up on the facts, a multiple-choice final exam tests your newfound knowledge before sending you out to fight the good fight. Go to Keyword: **Sage School**, and click Sage's 8-Step Program to begin.

How far out on a limb are you comfortable climbing?

Do you like to gamble, or do you prefer to play things safe? Your tolerance for risk greatly affects how you structure your portfolio. If you've got the time and the nerves to take big risks, an aggressive strategy might suit you. If you're retired and concerned with protecting what you have, you're better off with a conservative portfolio.

To get a feel for your own take on risk, try Sage's Risk Quiz. Go to Keyword: **Sage**, click Sage Search, type in **Risk Quiz**, and press Enter. Double-click Determine Your Investment Style from the list of articles. At the end of the article, click Determine Your Investment Style again to being the quiz.

Learn from the experts at Standard & Poor's Online Learning Center

Want straight answers from seasoned pros? Go directly to Standard & Poor's Learning Center. This financial giant offers the lowdown on investing, from stock basics to advanced financial strategies. Features include the Learning Curve, a series of articles that analyze and explain current economic activity in layman's terms; Taxing Matters, an ongoing advice column on the ins and outs of managing your taxes; and for the new investor, the Basics of Smart Investing and Retirement Tutorials. Go to Keyword: **Personal Wealth**, scroll down the S&P homepage to the Departments box and click Learning Center.

Chapter 5

Shaping Your
Investment Strategy

Talk to a purveyor of practically any investment vehicle and he is certain to try to convince you that his strategy is best.

Sorry. No plan is guaranteed to beat the market and land you that villa with the vineyard. But there is a plan that works great — the one that encompasses *your* timeframe, *your* goals, *your* willingness to do your homework, tolerant of the risks *you* want to take and within *your* reach.

While some investors might make do — even do very nicely — scattering their assets haphazardly, the most successful investors plan ahead. They know that having an investment strategy is like listening to the weather report before getting dressed. It allows you to embark in your travels better prepared for the journey.

Invest in homework

AOL packs a posse full of partners willing to help with the preparation. Start at Keyword: **Investing Basics**, shown in Figure 5-1, and launch your strategy building from there. AOL Personal Finance provides this step-by-step introduction to investing for beginners or for those who are rethinking their investment strategies. The experts don't always agree on the best way to do things, but there is one thing on which they concur: designing a successful investment strategy has less to do with grasping for meteoric rates of return than with creating a sound game plan based on your goals.

Tip

Herein we provide the Consummate Strategy: There Is No Consummate Strategy.

Note

You have already made one smart investment decision: getting this book.

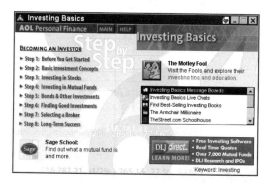

Figure 5-1. AOL provides a wide range of tools to help the beginner develop an investment strategy.

Research and education are imperative when it comes to financial fitness. Don't be so eager to invest that you skip your homework. Investing information is so plentiful, organized and easy to reach on AOL that it takes a lot of the work out of homework. If you put in your time up front, you save yourself from scrambling when you hit a bump in the road. In shaky times, you will take comfort knowing your investment choices were wise ones based on solid research and planning.

Do's and don'ts

Crucial to this strategic planning is avoiding costly errors. AOL packs a trove of tools, as shown in Figure 5-2. Reach this screen at Keyword: **Quotes**. From here you can look up a symbol for a stock, get a quote, read relevant news items on the stock, obtain research reports or read message boards, or you can jump to your own personalized portfolio.

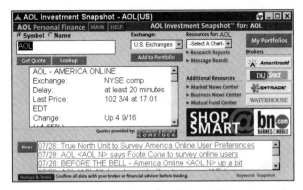

Figure 5-2. Now matter how hot the stock tip, never act on blind faith; research your prospects with the quick and easy tools available on AOL.

With that in mind, heed these do's and don'ts.

▶ Don't invest in anything you don't understand. Investments abound, leaving no reason to put your money into any investment that is beyond your full understanding. Trying to get rich quickly can make you poor just as fast.

▶ Do be well aware of an investment's risks, historic returns and conditions that affect its performance before you sink any money into it.

▶ Don't put all your eggs in one basket. Any basket, no matter how seemingly sturdy or strong, can break carrying an inappropriate load.

▶ Do diversify your holdings so that when one basket is weighed down, another lessens the load.

▶ Don't underestimate or overestimate the power of stocks. Over the long haul, stocks are the only investment to outperform all other investment vehicles — making them imperative for long-term strategies.

5

▶ Do be aware of their swings, however. From 1968 to 1978, the S&P 500 index produced (drumroll, please) only 3.85 percent. Yikes! But from 1988 to 1998, they turned in 13.6 percent. One look at 1998's market shivers — when stocks sunk 500 points one day in August and jumped 300 points a couple of days later, shows you how volatile they are.

▶ Don't be tempted by commodity futures, options trading or margin trading unless you have extra sacks of money lying around the house that you don't mind tossing out the window.

▶ Do find sensible vehicles in which to invest.

▶ Don't put a second mortgage on the house and buy Widgets 'R' Us stock just because your Aunt Mary's brother-in-law says he heard the company is about to sign a big deal with Intel.

▶ Do buy stock based on your own research.

▶ Don't change your investments as frequently as you wash your clothes. Unless you make your living as a daytrader — which is entirely different from investing — the cost of transactions, capital gains taxes, paperwork, Excedrin and Mylanta will neutralize your gains.

▶ Do map out a strategy, find solid holdings — and stick to them.

Investment Basics

In order to map out a solid investment strategy you need a good understanding of what you can invest your savings in. Investment vehicles fall into two categories: *debt* and *equity*.

Things like bonds and savings accounts are in the *debt* category. Why? A savings account is nothing more than a loan to an institution, like a bank or credit union. The bank invests the money you loan it in order to make more interest than it's paying you. A bond is a loan to a company or government. The company or government uses the money to buy something it needs and repays you and other lenders with interest.

 Definition

commodity futures: Contracts that force the holder to buy or sell a certain number of commodities at a predetermined price by a certain date.

option: A security that gives you the right to buy or sell a certain number of shares of a stock at a certain price for a certain time limit. If you don't exercise the option before it expires, you lose all the money you paid for the option.

margin: The equity you deposit with your broker as collateral against money you borrow from him to buy more securities.

 Find It Online

Looking for a compendium of investing elements? Head over to Keyword: **Investing Basics**.

Find It Online

Learning about investing is like going to boot camp. For basic training, march on over to Keyword: **The Street**, then pick Full TSC site, then scroll all the way down to Basics for primers on mutual funds, bonds, taxes, and other investment matters.

Cross-Reference

For the nuts and bolts of investing in stocks, see Chapter 6.

Equity conveys ownership. When you own stocks, for example, you have equity — or part ownership — in a company. When your company performs well, the stock typically commands a higher price. If the company performs badly, your stock price will most likely tumble. On the whole, equities produce much greater returns over time than do debts, but equities are much more volatile. Typically, small or international company stocks are more volatile than the stocks of large, American companies.

Where to stash your cash

When you devise an investment strategy, it's worth examining where fellow savers park their money. There's a myriad of possibilities, including under the mattress, savings accounts, checking accounts, certificates of deposit, money market funds, stocks, mutual funds, bonds (corporate, municipal, Treasury, Savings), insurance products/annuities, real estate, retirement vehicles such as IRAs, SEPs, Keoghs, 401(k)s, 403(b)s, and others.

Each parking place has its advantages and disadvantages. Let's examine them. You could stuff your money under the mattress for "safekeeping." But the mattress method actually isn't so safe. In fact, if you hide your money, you might as well be slipping the bills under the sill and out the window. Why? *Inflation.* Inflation essentially means your dollar will buy less tomorrow than it buys today. It siphons about 3 percent a year from your pile. If you stashed $10,000 under a rock in the yard, inflation would essentially eat away about $2,500 worth of buying power after 10 years.

In fact, inflation and taxes negate the earnings of a bank account, as demonstrated by the table in Figure 5-3. Find this information at Keyword: **Edelman**, then double-click The Truth About Money Online, click Part 1: Introduction to Financial Planning, and then Chapter 2: The Story of Taxes and Inflation. It maintains your investments must earn more than 8 percent to beat the effects of inflation and taxes.

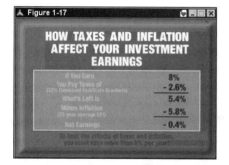

Figure 5-3. Without a sound savings and investment strategy, the evil twins inflation and taxes can eat away at your hard-earned pennies.

Cash

Putting your money in vehicles like savings and checking accounts or CDs and money markets carries low risk, but generates meager returns of about 2 to 4 percent, sometimes even less, depending on maturities and other factors. Still, these vehicles and a handful of government bonds are the only ones on which you can rely if you absolutely must have your money within a short period of time. The Federal Deposit Insurance Corporation insures cash in the bank to $100,000.

Stocks

When a company first opens its doors to public ownership, it issues a certain number of shares. As the company becomes more valuable, its stock should too. Stocks can return higher rewards — yet carry much higher risks — than other investments. Historically, stocks represent the best vehicle for long-term appreciation, about 12 percent since 1940. But because they're so unpredictable, they're a bad bet for any short-term goal.

Find It Online

For the online lowdown on stock basics, go straight to the experts at Motley Fool, Keyword: **Fool**, scroll all the way down and click on Fool's School. Then click Investing Basics for a crash course n taking on the market, delivered in a straight-shooting, light-hearted tone.

Other Fool's School tutorials include "How to Value Stocks," a guide to evaluating companies and making sense of the Byzantine prospectus financials before purchasing stocks, strategies for tax time and tutorials on forming an investment club.

What would school be without fun with your buddies? Fribbles, the Motley Fool's forum for free speech, wit, education, and amusement, are offered up by the best "Foolish pundits on the planet;" in other words, by online investors just like you. To read the daily entry, go to the Quick Find search box at the top of the page and select The Fribble, under Personal Finance. From there you can browse previous fribbles, or submit your own observations.

Mutual funds

⟳ Cross-Reference

For the finer points of mutual funds, see Chapter 8.

Remember when everybody in the office contributed $5 apiece and together you bought reams of PowerBall tickets? This is similar to a mutual fund, where investors with similar goals and interests pool their money to buy stocks, bonds or assets that the mutual fund manager believes will meet your mutual goals. (Hopefully your manager has done her homework, however, making your chances of faring well much greater than winning PowerBall.) Mutual funds are assembled according to goals (such as growth or income) or holdings (such as technology or health care stocks). The ones you select depend on your portfolio needs, as shown in Figure 5-4. Go to Keyword: **Sage**, then navigate to the area on Portfolio Strategies. From here you can find ratings of different fund families, or advice on index funds, bonds, and retirement strategies.

Figure 5-4. Mutual funds play an important role in a well-diversified portfolio.

Mutual funds represent an easy way for you to zero in on a particular investment need or to diversify across a wide range of asset categories, without poring over the minutiae of each holding. Keep in mind, however, that "easy" does not necessarily mean "successful." While many mutual funds report stellar achievements, the vast majority underperform the Standard & Poor's 500.

Bonds

As previously mentioned, bonds are loans governments and corporations obtain to pay for extraordinary needs. In return for the loan, most of these entities promise to repay the lender a fixed amount of interest for the life of the loan, then to

Go to school

To get the online basics of mutual funds, go to Keyword: **Sage**, click Sage School, and then select Sage's 8-Step Program.

If mutual funds leave you a bit baffled, Sage's tutorial is a great way to get up to speed without investing something no one has enough of: time. Start with Step 1: What is a Mutual Fund? The introduction offers up a few basic terms and concepts, and leads directly to Step 2: Types of Funds, a review of the different fund categories and the kinds of investors who find those categories appealing.

Step 3, Before you Invest, is another admonishment to get rid of all your credit card debt before even considering investing elsewhere. Step 4, How Much Risk?, helps you find the level of risk and stability that is appropriate to you.

Step 5, Fees and Loads, offers more vocabulary lessons to help explain the costs Mutual Funds carry. Step 6, Selecting a Fund, leads you through a flowchart of questions to ask when purchasing a fund. The last two steps, Building a Portfolio and Dollar Cost Averaging, teach you about diversifying to reduce risk and creating a steady plan of investing for long-term returns.

After brushing up on Funds, try taking the Final Exam to

return the principal at maturity. For this reason bonds are termed *fixed-income* securities. Other entities sell bonds at a discount to their face value, and pay the face value at maturity.

The return on bonds typically exceeds that of cash vehicles like CDs and money markets, and in some instances the interest is tax-exempt. Bonds offer a healthy degree of safety, stability, and reliable income to your portfolio (except for high-yield junk bonds, which are extremely risky). Beware of interest rates, the bond's silent enemy. When interest rates rise, long-term, fixed-income bonds, whose interest rates were set when the bond was issued, become less attractive because higher interest can be gained elsewhere.

Cross-Reference

For the lowdown on bonds, turn to Chapter 7.

Find It Online

For an interesting counterpoint, AOL partner Ric Edelman offers 11 reasons why you're better off in equities than real estate at Keyword: **Edelman**, then scroll down to The New Rules of Money, and select Mortgages, Home Ownership and Real Estate.

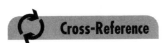

Cross-Reference

To review the ins and outs of buying a home, turn to Chapter 4.

Real estate

Real estate can be very lucrative over the long haul, although it might be difficult to sell for a profit in a short period of time if the market is saturated. Still, many consider it a worthwhile component of a long-term investment strategy.

You can find active markets online, beginning at Keyword: **Real Estate**, shown in Figure 5-5. From here, you can get help or information on Selling, Renting, Moving, and Mortgages. You can look up current listings for homes as well as the latest mortgage rates.

Figure 5-5. Online resources make it easier than ever to learn about almost any real estate market in the world.

Insurance/annuities

An annuity is a contract with a life insurance company that pays you benefits in return for your premium payments. The insurance company invests your premiums, and the return accumulates tax-deferred until you retire. Annuities are worth exploring once you contribute the maximum to other tax-deferred retirement plans such as IRAs and 401(k) plans.

IRAs, Roth IRAs, SEPs, Keoghs, 401(k)s, and so on

These retirement plans allow you to invest money in the above-mentioned vehicles, and your returns are tax-deferred. If you qualify for an IRA, you can deduct your contributions up front. Roth IRAs differ from IRAs in that Roth IRAs offer no tax advantage up front on contributions, but their returns are totally exempt from federal taxes under certain income guidelines when used for retirement, a first house, or education. Keoghs and SEPs are for self-employed people, and employers sponsor 401(k)s. These retirement plans are an integral component of any investment strategy

Find It Online

Keyword: **Insurance** gives you the online dish on annuities.

Cross-Reference

For more information on insurance and annuities, see Chapter 16.

Your First Investment: A Retirement Plan

Unless you have an imminent financial need that you outlined in your goals, the first move of your investment strategy must be to take full advantage of retirement plans, even if your retirement isn't until 40 years from now. Disregarding retirement savings plans is like finding gold nuggets in your backyard and tossing them in with the gravel in the driveway. Why? Most employers subsidize these plans. Many companies will add to your contribution, and some actually match it!

To find out how your much money you should put away to invest for your retirement, go to Keyword: **Calculator**, then select Retirement. Plug your numbers into the "How much can I invest before taxes each year?" form, shown in Figure 5-6. Then click the results tab. For more information on the results, click the explanation tab.

Cross-Reference

Everything you ever wanted to know about retirement planning is in the retirement section of Chapter 12.

Find It Online

Looking for tips to boost your 401(k) performance? Go to Keyword: **401k**, then choose Your 401(k): Supercharge It for tips from Money.com

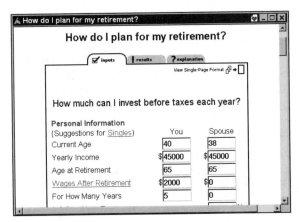

Figure 5-6. Don't fret over the calculations: AOL's calculator can help you figure out what your financial picture will look like when you retire.

401(k) plans

Plans such as 401(k)s are an investor's dream for so many reasons. They safeguard your money from Uncle Sam's grasp until you withdraw it; the amount you contribute is subtracted from your salary before you pay taxes; they hide your money in an investment vehicle before it ever reaches your cash-eating wallet; they make your employer give you more money; with your money relatively untouchable it compounds like mushrooms after a spring rain, without that tax vacuum sucking out the profits; because you have to pay a penalty if you withdraw the money before you retire, you have a compelling reason to keep the money safe-guarded unless you absolutely, positively need it.

401(k) plans allow you to invest a certain percentage of your salary, with a $10,000 cap, before taxes. Here's how it works:

Suppose you and your spouse earn $70,000 a year combined, and neither of you contributes to your retirement plan. If you're in the 31 percent tax bracket you will pay $21,700 in taxes on your earnings, leaving you a net income of $48,300.

Now, say you contribute 10 percent of your joint salary, or $7,000, to your 401(k). You will pay less in taxes — $19,530 — because your income is lower — $63,000. This nets you $43,470 after taxes. It has cost you only $4,830, ($48,300 minus $43,470), in take-home income to invest $7,000.

If your company adds a percentage of what you contribute, which most do, you will more than make up the money missing from your paycheck, once you consider the return on your investment. Say the company kicks in 25 percent of what you contribute, or $1,750. Now it has cost you $4,830 in take-home income to invest $8,750!

Here's how the numbers break down:

Table 5-1. *Look at the Numbers*

No 401(k) contribution

Your salary	$70,000
Your contribution	0
Net before taxes	$70,000
Taxes paid	$21,700
Total take-home	$48,300
Total invested	0
Net	*$48,300*

10% 401(k) contribution with partial company match

Your salary	$70,000
Your contribution	$7,000
Net before taxes	$63,000
Taxes paid	$19,530
Total take-home	$43,470
Company 25% match	$1,750
Total invested	$8,750
Net	*$52,220*

After ten years at 10 percent interest, your one-time contribution of $7,000 (plus your employer's 25 percent match) will reach *$23,686.* If you both make that same contribution each year, at the end of 10 years you'll have *$173,051*! And after 20 years you'll reach *$617,877* — of which you will have contributed only $96,600 after taxes. And that just reflects federal tax savings.

Sculpting Your Strategy

Cross-Reference

For a closer look at exactly what to put in your portfolio, refer to Chapter 11.

How you invest the money in your 401(k) or retirement vehicle becomes the cornerstone of your long-term investment strategy. The tricky part is choosing the assets in which to invest.

For a general discussion on how to measure and assess investments, stay right here. For the particulars, turn to the stocks, bonds and mutual funds chapters, and then to Chapter 11 and 12. Some online research can help. For example, try the 401(k) Center shown in Figure 5-7. You can reach it at Keyword: **http://www.SmartMoney.com** and then clicking the Planning tab. From there, choose 401(k) Center from the list of links in the gray section to the left.

From the first page, "Making the Most of Your 401(k)," you move on to lessons such as "Asset Allocation" or "5 Things You Should Know About Your 401(k)." You can also find rankings of the best 401(k)s or your own personal or company's plan.

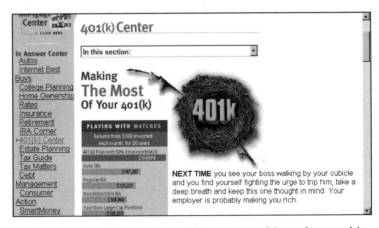

Figure 5-7. Your 401(k) investment can be the most powerful part of your portfolio. But it is easy to be overwhelmed by the choices. A bit of online research can help clear the fog.

Deciding which vehicles to invest in — whether inside of a retirement account or out — depends on several key factors. Pay them heed, as these factors chisel the shape of your entire investment strategy.

When you design your investment strategy you must assess your tolerance for *risk*, your *timeline* and your *return needs*.

Risk

Let's start with risk. Risk refers to an investment's volatility. How likely are its actual returns to deviate from their historical average? Degrees of risk range from negligible or low (in vehicles such as savings accounts and government bonds, to stratospheric (in vehicles such as commodities and options). Investments with high risks can reap higher rewards. But be forewarned: they can also suffer tremendous losses fast, even if they might recoup those losses and generate later gains.

The greatest risk

What's one of the greatest risks? Not saving at all, as the article shown below indicates. Go to Keyword: **iVillage** for a collection of articles, geared toward women, on investing and saving money. Scroll down the left-hand list of links, and under the heading Channels, choose MoneyLife. Again, scroll down the left-hand list of links and choose Investing under the Departments heading. Choose any of the links under Your Portfolio, Stocks, Bonds, Mutual Funds, or Strategies for a current article with timely advice. To find the article shown below, click the Article Archives link from any current article. Then scroll down the list until you find "Developing Risk Tolerance with Marlene Jupiter."

Continued

"It's hard for people to know how risk-averse they are until they lose money," reports Susan Pevear of AOL partner Standard & Poor's Personal Wealth (Keyword: **Personal Wealth**). The stock market's sudden freefall in the summer of 1998 was a jolt of reality. Giddy investors had coasted through most of the 1990s riding the market's wave, with barely a bump. Suddenly there was a confluence of bad turns. Financial queasiness in Asia, then in Brazil. Institutional investors housecleaning. Hedge-fund managers trying to cover their bets. "The magnitude of that drop was a rude awakening for many people," Pevear says. "But it carried a message: Volatility is here to stay, gang."

The greatest risk *(continued)*

Investment always carries risk, but saving unwisely or, worse, not saving at all can be the highest risk of all, as this iVillage site explains.

So many things contribute to an investment's risk. Market performance and sentiment, interest-rate changes, political changes, currency fluctuations, world events. It's a wonder anybody has the courage to invest at all. Perhaps it's because they understand the risks of *not* investing:

▶ Inflation will siphon your money out of your "safe" accounts and you will outlive your savings.

▶ Interest rates will wreak havoc on the bond funds you've depended on for income from year to year.

▶ The once lofty CD rates that paid the bills every month will shrink to a pittance.

Then there is the other extreme. Ignoring risk. It's been a good 10 years since that Black Monday in October 1987, when the market crashed 25 percent on one day. Some investors are still reeling from that. Think about it. You're planning to retire. The big day is coming up. Suddenly the money you're expecting to live off for the rest of your life drops 25 percent. Or you're saving up for a down payment on a house, counting heavily on anticipated money from your company stock options. Your options are nearly vested and then the bottom falls out of the market.

Relatively new investors high on the market's surges over the past 10 years might feel a false sense of security. But in investing, those who are the least prepared suffer the worst.

Risk tolerance

The first question you need to ask yourself when assessing your risk tolerance is whether the goal you're saving for is coming sooner as opposed to later. The sooner you need the money (for those short-term goals you outlined in Chapter 4), the more stable and conservative your investments must be, as you won't have time to recover if they stumble.

If you need money on an ongoing basis and you rely on income-oriented investments to generate that money, your investments need to be relatively conservative and carry relatively low risk, as you can't afford to gamble with the grocery money. If your goal is 10 years off (those long-term goals), your investments can be growth-oriented, aggressive and carry higher risk, because they have a longer time to recover from nosedives and international crises.

To test your stomach for risk, imagine that you put a big chunk of money into an investment and it shrinks by half overnight. Can this really happen? Certainly. You can gauge the probability of it happening by examining data that chronicles the investment's history. When the holding had a bad year — or a bad five years — how bad was bad?

Dips and crashes underscore the need to be comfortable with the risk you're undertaking, lest you flee when your investments are suddenly teetering on shaky ground. The worst time to run from stocks is during a tailspin, for you crash into a throng and there's no room to maneuver. Everybody else is in a panic, too, trying to unload whatever they have and forcing them to sell for prices lower than they should. Better to understand the risks inherent with your

Find It Online

For historic returns on AOL, see Keyword: **Investment Research**, plug in the symbol of the holding you're investigating and select All Report Types for a comprehensive look at the past and present, and forecasts for the future.

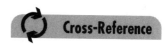

Cross-Reference

For an in-depth guide to stock research, see Chapter 9.

Risk tolerance quiz

How risk-tolerant are you? Are you willing to risk it all for the big payoff, or do you value your bird in the hand more than the flock in the bush? To test your limits, check out the Sage Risk Quiz.

To take the quiz, go to Keyword: **Sage**. Click Sage Search, type **Risk Quiz**, and then press Enter. Double-click "Determine Your Investment Style" from the list of articles given.

The feature opens with "Nallilaters and Monkey Bars," a lighthearted explanation on what risk means, and the most common types of risk tolerance among investors: Conservative, Moderate, or Aggressive (or, as the article explains, just how high you are willing to climb on those monkey bars).

At the end of the article, click "Quiz Yourself" for a self-test guide that helps you determine your investment style, and offers up a portfolio model that is most appropriate for you.

The quiz's questions, such as "How do you feel about fluctuations in your portfolio?", "Can you handle a sudden big drop?", and "Are you attracted to fixed-income vehicles?", extend five answers from which to choose. You pick the one that best reflects who you are as an investor. Keep track of the numbers you choose. At the end of the quiz, add up your answers to find out what they reveal about you.

Maybe you're deemed conservative and primarily interested in protecting your money, or maybe you rate very aggressive and willing to weather extreme financial swings for the possibility of big gains. Whatever your profile, Sage presents a model portfolio to suit your needs, outlining the best combination of investments to represent your risk tolerance.

investments, so you can watch from higher ground when panic strikes your fellow investors. You can rest better knowing you have taken precautions to weather the storm.

Diversification

Certain kinds of risk can be avoided altogether by *diversifying* across assets. For example, if you invest in only one stock, and the company's profits spiral downward for quarters on end, so, too, does 100 percent of your portfolio. But if you hold stakes in 10 unrelated securities, the decline of the dog will be cushioned by the strengths of the stalwarts. Even though the risk of the one stock remains the same, the risk to your portfolio is reduced significantly because you spread out your vulnerability across holdings from unrelated areas. To find a good cross-section, sift through information on the many thousands of stocks available at Keyword: **Company Research**, shown in Figure 5-8. To Search for Research Reports, simply type in the company name or ticker symbol, select the specific type of report you would like to see (or leave the selection at All Report Types), and then click Search.

Figure 5-8. An abundance of information on companies around the globe is available online, giving you a financial edge from the comfort of your desk.

As Figure 5-9 points out, to achieve a good balance, smart investors diversify. Diversifying means spreading out your money among different investment categories — bonds, stocks, mutual funds, real estate — to try to temper the swings of the market. Diversification helps alleviate shock to the whole portfolio when one area is bleeding. It buys you time. When your portfolio is diversified, you can rely on other holdings for stability while your struggling investment heals. That's why a good investment strategy encompasses many holdings: a mix of stocks in small, large, foreign and American companies; bonds (corporate, municipal and foreign), cash, and real estate, held either individually, through mutual funds, or both. To read "How to divide your investment pie," shown in Figure 5-9, type in Keyword: **Whiz**. From among the links in the bar along the top of the page, choose Investing. Scroll down the page to Money Whiz Investing Basics, and click Divide your investment pie.

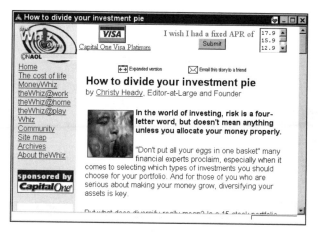

Figure 5-9. Lower your risk by keeping a colorful portfolio — a bit of stocks, a dab of mutual funds — rather than allowing all your money to rise and fall on one investment.

Note

"Whenever I sit with anyone, the first thing I ask is, what's their time horizon? How many years till you need the money?" Susan Pevear says. "It's absolutely essential."

Your Timeline

Assessing your risk tolerance and understanding the need to diversify is a springboard to developing a strategy. Next comes determining your timeline, which is the schedule of your needs over your lifetime. Your timeline starts the second you begin saving for a goal and ends when you plan to remove your money to pay for that goal. The longer your timeline — in other words, the longer you can keep your money invested without needing it — the higher you can allow the risk to be, and the greater the potential returns.

For example, if your goal is a year or two away, you will rely on a completely different plan than if your goal is 15 years down the road. When your needs are short-term you invest in something extremely stable and dependable, so you can hang onto what you accumulate. Your tolerance for risk is low, because you can't afford to lose principal. So even though these vehicles generate low return, you go for them, because you need to be safe.

While planning for almost any goal, don't forget to jump online for some help. If you're planning a wedding, for example, you might benefit from some tips and advice pictured in Figure 5-10.

Looking for the best savings rates around? Go to Keyword: **Bankrate**, then select Savings to compare the best savings, CD and money market rates.

For the highest-yielding money market funds, go to Keyword: **Bankrate**, then pick Savings and scroll down to Money Markets. Choose High Yield MMAs and Start.

Go to Keyword: **Your Money**, click Marriage and Money, and then scroll down to "Big Day Budgeter" in the features box.

Figure 5-10. Knowing what you are saving for and when you will spend it — your daughter's wedding, for example — will dictate much of your financial strategy.

Short-term savings

When you're saving for the short-term, forget about stocks, due to their propensity for volatility. In fact, even those stock mavens at the Motley Fool warn against stocks and stock-based mutual funds if you will be reliant upon the money within three to five years.

When your investments need to be liquid in three to five years or less, you have to stick to the following boring-but-stable vehicles:

Simple, low-risk vehicles for short-term goals:

▶ Savings Account — Common at banks and credit unions, a savings account typically returns about 2 or 3 percent interest.

▶ Certificate of Deposit (CD) — Yields interest that's a tad higher than a savings account in return for your promise to keep the money at the financial institution for a pre-determined period of time. The longer the period, the higher interest rate the bank will pay you in return. You risk paying a penalty if you withdraw your CD before the maturity date. Typical return: 3 to 5 percent depending on the length of the CD.

▶ Money Market Fund — This type of mutual fund invests in very short-term bonds and is available through your bank or brokerage. Its average yield of 3 to 4 percent is a bit more than a savings account, and a bit less than a CD, depending on the maturity. A money market fund carries low risk and, unlike a CD, is liquid, which means you can cash it in at any time without penalty. For this reason, it's Pevear of Standard & Poor's favorite vehicle for short-term goals.

▶ Treasury Bills — These government-sponsored bonds come in three-, six-, and 12-month maturities. Denominations begin at $10,000 and are sold at a discount, representing interest of about 4½ to 5 percent. You can buy the bills directly from the Federal Reserve, by mail or online at **http://www.TreasuryDirect.gov**, as Figure 5-11 indicates. You can also get them from a broker, but then you have to pay a commission.

At TreasuryDirect, you can get information from the list of Resources, buy Savings Bonds, T-Bills, State and Local Government Bonds, or find out more information on the Public Debt.

Note

"If it's a case of 'I definitely need the money' versus 'I might need the money,' it's worth looking into T-notes. If you don't need all of it, put 50 percent in fixed vehicles and the other half in equities, depending on your income streams and other factors," Pevear says.

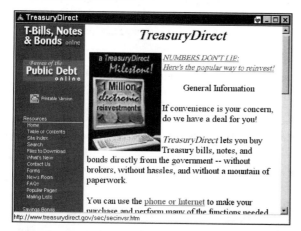

Figure 5-11. Not only does the Internet provide a quick, easy way to purchase Treasury bills but also it allows investors to avoid brokerage fees.

Tip

Want a quick estimate for how long it will take to double your money? Call upon the *Rule of 72*. Divide 72 by the interest rate the investment returns to come up with the estimated time. For example, if your investment produces 8 percent a year, divide 72 by 8, and you get 9. So it would take you about 9 years to double an investment that earns 8 percent a year.

Cross-Reference

For a close look at stocks, turn to Chapter 6.

Intermediate-term

If you won't be cracking open that egg until five to ten years down the road, you can open up your portfolio to a greater mix of investments. But the mix is dependent on a whole host of factors, primarily how closely wed are the goal and the deadline, and how much of a cushion you have with your other investments in the event the one you've targeted for the goal is stumbling. If you have to start paying the tuition bill for college in six years and you don't have extra money to spare, you have to be more careful with your investments than if you're saving for an exotic cruise that you could postpone if you had to.

Intermediate-term goals present the greatest investment challenge. The temptation is great to rely on small-cap stocks or hot sectors like Internet stocks to boost potential returns. Especially in a healthy market. But this health can decline seemingly overnight. If there is flexibility in your plans, don't rule out blue chips or an index fund altogether, because you want to keep your investments growing. But if your goal is inflexible, err on the side of being too conservative.

Treasury Notes, whose maturities run up to seven years, are sold at a discount from their face value. Read all about them in Chapter 7.

With an intermediate timeline, definitely stay away from individual junk bonds, international stocks and micro-caps.

Long-term

Here you're looking at investments for goals at least ten years down the road. First, have a realistic picture of what you're aiming for, and don't rely on sky-high returns to get there. As you learned in Chapter 4, you don't necessarily have to. A one-time investment doubles in ten years with just a 7.1 percent return, as long as you let the interest compound.

Still, many opportunities exist to improve that return. Most experts turn to stocks and stock-oriented mutual funds for the greatest and most efficient growth over the long term. Granted, stocks are more volatile than other vehicles, but they are the only investment whose returns have outpaced inflation since the beginning of the 1800s.

Return needs

As you learned in the last chapter, once you figure out how much your goals cost and how much you can save between now and when the goal is due, you deduce what your return has to be in order to meet your goal. Suppose you can save up $10,000 for a certain goal three years down the road that costs about $13,000. What does your investment have to yield to get you there? (It's 8.775 percent.)

With visions of double-digit returns dancing in your head, it's easy to be lulled into a stupor when you drop your savings into some of these vehicles. But a look back to that same history provides a reality check. A 25 percent drop in 1987, a 40 percent freefall in 1972, an 80 percent travesty in 1929. Make sure your goals really are long-term — at least seven years away — when you're depending on stocks, so you have enough time to recover.

Note

Notes AOL partner The Motley Fool at Keyword: **Fool**, "From 1946 to 1992, an investor would have earned a total return of 15,981 percent in stocks versus 847.2 percent in short-term bonds — almost 20 times as much. That's quite a gap for a difference of only 6.5 percent per year. That is the power of a higher rate of return if you hold over a long period of time — even periodic drops of 20 percent or greater are swallowed whole."

Your Investment Blueprint

Now that you know how risk, return and your timeline are inter-related, you can outline your investment strategy. In your investing explorations you will undoubtedly encounter models of "ideal" scenarios that mandate how much to invest where, promising double-digit returns and happily-ever-after retirements.

But alas, the world is not ideal. Nor is there an ideal strategy. You have to create your own. With so many investments out there, how do you decide what to put where? How do you target assets within your portfolio? How *do* you diversify and still remain true to your risks, timeline and needs? You have to design an Investment Blueprint. To help you along, AOL

Find It Online

Want to talk about your stock strategy with beginners? Join your brethren at Sage Chats for Beginners, Keyword: **Sage**. Next choose Sage School. Then scroll down to Beginner Chat Schedule.

Caution

Don't follow somebody else's blueprint for success. Only you know your needs and risk tolerance.

provides a step-by-step guide to becoming an investor. Go to Keyword: **Investing Basics**. Then choose Step 2: Basic Investment Concepts to find out more on Planning and Setting Goals. (See Figure 5-12.)

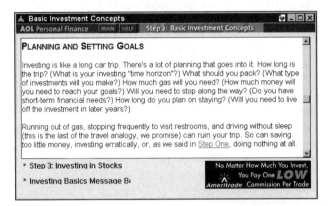

Figure 5-12. No matter how many get-rich-quick schemes you hear about, the truth is there are no simple shortcuts. The smart investor has to make hard decisions about long-term plans and goals.

Your blueprint is like a highlighted map that outlines your trip and destination. The routes you ultimately take boil down to where you want to be at a certain point in time and what risks you're willing to take en route. No route is the only correct way to go. A dozen different travelers might formulate a dozen different strategies to get from Connecticut to California. While they might ultimately arrive at the same destination, they will encounter different decisions, scenery, strategies, pitfalls and highlights along the way. They might take the Interstate, stopping at established landmarks touted in a guide. Or they might do their own exploring, traveling the back roads, uncovering gems of their own.

Just as an educated traveler considers a trove of maps, guides, signs, directions, hunches and suggestions in deciding where to stop during her travels, so does the educated investor. What is her timeframe? What can she afford to spend or lose? What does she risk in a particular place? What does she gain in return? What stops are really worth her while? What's her traveling style?

Maybe she barrels away at 85 mph, throwing caution to the wind so she can reach her destination in a hurry. Maybe she barely breaks 55 mph, happy with the knowledge that — eventually — she'll most likely end up where she needs to be. In either case, when the weather turns ugly or the road gets a little bumpy she turns to her map for a safer, slower route.

But she always has that map. It's just like this with an investment blueprint. It's your highlighted map to meeting your goals. Your blueprint spells out:

▶ Your investment goals

▶ The investments you're targeting to meet each goal

▶ The additional deposits you need to make to arrive where you're headed on time

▶ The minimum returns you need in order to meet your goals

▶ The length of time you will commit to each investment

▶ What you plan to do with the investment after each goal is met

▶ An alternative plan, in the event an investment or market sours

You design this blueprint. It must suit your taste in architecture, not some current fad or prefab. It must be structurally sound; diversified; solid enough to reduce risk brought on by inflation, market swings, interest-rate changes or the need to cash out at an inopportune time.

As you design your blueprint, make sure you know where your resources are, so you can determine if you need to trade in, trade up, or save for faster or more efficient wheels for the trip.

Now, take your list of goals, your budget and your list of resources and make a great big blueprint. It should include the goals, their cost, how many years until they're here, how you plan to save for them, and how you plan to invest the money to attain the total you need.

Revisit your blueprint as your investment timeframe, risk aversion, goals and means change. In essence, as your lifestyle changes, so too should the design of your blueprint.

Find It Online

For pointers on what to consider when designing your strategy, go to Keyword: **Personal Wealth** for Standard & Poor's The Learning Center.

Cross-Reference

Obviously, this is just a sketch. For the nuts and bolts of what you actually put into your portfolio, see Chapter 11.

Summary

Hopefully by now you're well on your way to nailing down your Investment Strategy. You've done your homework and learned the dos and don'ts of investing.

▶ You've learned the Basics of Investing, including the various vehicles in which to invest.

▶ You learned the importance of formulating a retirement investment plan as your first investment. And you learned the ins and outs of 401(k)s.

▶ You then began to formulate your own individual strategy, gauging your risk tolerance, and learning how to limit risk with diversification.

▶ You then moved forward with your strategy by making a timeline, measuring the length of time until you reach your goals, deciding which investments will help you meet short-, medium-, and long-term goals, and calculating the returns you need to achieve (balanced, of course, by the amount of risk you are willing to face).

▶ Finally, you learned how to make an investment blueprint that meets your needs.

Beginning with the next chapter, you will investigate in depth the various investment vehicles. Chapter 6 tells you all you need to know about Stocks.

CHAPTER

THE SKINNY ON STOCKS

A Quick Look

▶ **Looking for Mr. Good Stock**   **page 127**

With stocks of more than 10,000 companies traded on the exchanges, how do you pick a winner? Should you follow gut instinct, heed the word around the water cooler, or try to make sense of the dizzying collection of investment terms and numbers?

Go with the terms and numbers. There's no need to feel daunted. *Fools* make finances fun. Go to Keyword: **Fool**, and click Fool's School for articles, links, tips, and tools about the basics of investing in stocks from The Motley Fool.

▶ **Final Exam**   **page 134**

Think you've mastered stock basics? There's one more test before you open your wallet: Take the stocks quiz at Money.com.

Start at Keyword: **Money.com**, then scroll down to Money 101 in the table of contents on the left. Click Chapter 5: Investing in Stocks, for the 15-question, multiple choice test. After you choose the answers you think are right, hit Submit. Your score will appear — as well as the right answers to each question you missed.

▶ **Join the Party**   **page 138**

Owning stock isn't a privilege reserved for the rich and famous. Anyone with a few dollars can enter the fray. For a crash course to get you up to speed on the basics of selecting and purchasing stocks, head for stocks school online at TheStreet.com.

Go to Keyword: **TSC**, click Full TSC site, then select Basics. Scroll down and click Stocks Class: From the Bottom Up. Go ahead — talk out loud and chew all the gum you want.

Chapter 6

The Skinny on Stocks

Millions of Americans own stocks, either outright or through mutual funds. And it's no wonder why. Stocks have turned in the greatest yield on the dollar over history. In fact, only stocks have outpaced inflation over time.

You've read in earlier chapters exactly what a stock is — an ownership interest in a corporation. That interest is backed by a claim on the company's assets and earnings. But you can't buy stock in just any company. In fact, most companies in America are privately owned. The coffee shop on the corner. The factory on the other end of town. Your favorite dry cleaner. You buy their goods or services and their owners keep the profits.

But there are also publicly owned companies, more than 10,000, in fact. They come as big as Coca-Cola and McDonald's and General Electric and as small as the latest dot-com start-up that began in your cousin's garage. They might have had private funding at first, maybe from the founder's rich uncles or from a venture capital firm, but eventually they decided to *go public* — to relinquish part ownership and sell shares of their company to the public in order to generate funding for their enterprise.

For an online refresher course on stocks, check out SmartMoney University's Investing 101. Go to Keyword: **http://www.smartmoney.com** and click SmartMoney University. Click Investing 101 and select Stocks from the list on the left (see Figure 6-1).

Figure 6-1. As American as apple pie: Owning stock is a direct way for you to have a stake in a company — and in the economy.

Who Owns Stock?

Anybody can own stock in public companies. When you buy stock, you get a piece, or a *share* of the business. When somebody buys the company's goods and services, you and the other owners — the *stockholders* — get a piece of the profits. As you sit home with the remote in your hand, you might be entitled to proceeds from McDonalds or Coca Cola, from the electric company that powers your PC, and from the company that made your keyboard, depending on which stocks you own.

As part owner, you get a say in who runs the company. From your kitchen table you can vote for who sits on the *board of directors* — the people who hire the CEO, who set the company's direction, and who decide how the company will spend the money it makes. You get one vote for each share you own, so the more shares you own, the bigger your claim in the business.

You also suffer the consequences when the company isn't as profitable as you — or analysts — expected it would be. If business takes a turn for the worse, the price of your shares may fall. If the company goes bankrupt, your stock can end up like the flower of a dandelion: vibrant and attractive one day, dried up and blowing in the wind not long after. That is the greatest risk of investing in stocks. Unlike with most other investment vehicles, what you invest in stocks could be gone overnight. It rarely happens, but it could.

Why Invest in Stocks?

Why concern yourself with the headaches of a company you barely know when it's hard enough sometimes to keep track of what's going on under your own roof?

Payback.

The *Standard & Poor's 500*, a collection of 500 large, multinational company stocks, has returned about 12 percent a year since 1950. And from 1993 through 1998, that return has surged to about 23 percent a year! It's hard to beat that kind of return.

See Figure 6-2 for a chart of the S&P index's climb upward. Go to Keyword: **http://www.smartmoney.com**. Then click SmartMoney University and select Investing 101. Under the heading Why It Works, select "The Odds Are in Your Favor," to review the chart.

The market has had banner years with returns as high as 65 percent. But there's a flip side of that coin. In 1987, for example, the Dow Jones Industrial Average sunk about 36 percent. Still, over time, the good has outweighed the bad. As a group, stocks perform like most waistlines: they expand with age.

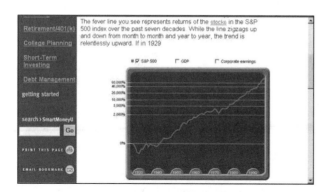

Figure 6-2. This chart of the S&P 500 Index, considered a broad measure of the stock market overall, shows returns over the past 70 years. A few stumbles and jigs notwithstanding, the returns move markedly upward over time.

Profiting from stocks

When you invest in stocks, you can make money in a couple of different ways, through *dividends*, *capital appreciation,* or a combination of both.

For a quick lesson online on the difference between capital gains and dividends, see Standard & Poor's investing primer, shown in Figure 6-3. Start with Keyword: **Personal Wealth**, then scroll down and click the Learning Center. Under Tutorials, select The Basics of Smart Investing. Then, select Stocks from the Table of Contents on the left. Choose Ways to Profit from the Table of Contents on the left to review the article.

Definition

Standard & Poor's 500: a collection of 500 widely held stocks, including, at last count, 374 industrial, 74 financial, 41 utility, and 11 transportation stocks.

Definition

When you tune in to the news of the day you will no doubt hear or read reference to the *Dow Jones Industrial Average.* The DJIA is the average daily movement in the prices of 30 actively traded blue-chip stocks.

6

The Skinny on Stocks

Figure 6-3. There are two ways to profit from stocks — and they are not mutually exclusive.

Tip

Want to compare dividends, or determine how a stock's dividend compares to the yield on another investment? Find the *dividend yield*. To do this, divide the stock's annual dividend by the current price per share. For example, if the stock's annual dividend is $1 per share and the stock costs $20, the dividend yield is 5 percent. If you want to find this yield figure online, go to Keyword: **Quotes**, plug in the stock symbol, and look under Yield in the Snapshot.

Definition

bull market: The extended rise of the stock market over time. To be *bullish* is to believe stocks will continue to rise, or to maintain a positive outlook on the economy.

bear market: A significant decline in the stock market for an extended period of time. To be *bearish* is to believe stocks are set to fall. While financial analysts don't agree on what constitutes a bear market, many agree that a decline of 20 percent or more over three months or longer is one sure indicator.

Dividends are a percentage of the company's profits, divvied up and sent to you, the shareholder. The board of directors decides whether or not the company will pay dividends and, if it will, how much it will pay per share. Then the company sends you a check quarterly or twice a year.

Many companies don't pay dividends. They figure stockholders will be better served if the companies roll profits back into the business to fuel growth. Why would you invest in a stock that doesn't pay a dividend compared to one that offers a 5 percent yield? Because you're betting that the difference in price between when you buy the stock and when you sell it will more than make up for the dividends. That's *capital appreciation* — an increase in the price of your shares, minus your transaction costs.

Say you buy 100 shares of Widgets 'R' Us for $50 apiece, then you sell them for $65 apiece. Your capital appreciation is $1,500 minus whatever it cost you to buy and sell the stock. You pay taxes on this appreciation.

Dividends have been overshadowed by capital appreciation during the bull run of the 1990s, as many individual investors seem more interested in catching a ride on the double-digit growth train than in picking up a couple of percent each year in dividends. But that trend will change when the stock market levels out, which will inevitably happen. Despite the market's roller coaster ride through history, dividends have provided a stabilizer. In fact, their yield accounts for almost half of the market's annual double-digit returns over time.

Appreciating capital growth

There are a couple of conventional methods of pursuing capital appreciation. One is to buy stocks you think are priced below what they're worth and to hold onto them until they're going for a price you determine is fair. Then you either sell them and make your profit, or you hold onto them if you think they will continue to appreciate. (At some point, though, you have to sell, or you never make any money.)

Another way to pursue capital appreciation is to buy a stock whose company's profit potential is so good you believe the stock price will skyrocket. Then you unload the stock before the price drops. Interestingly, stocks with the most capital appreciation in recent years have been those whose futures hold promise but whose profits remain at bay.

These two methods notwithstanding, most good stocks appreciate in price over time. The key is to wait out the unstable periods, instead of selling and running for cover as soon as the thunder starts.

It's very difficult to judge where a stock is headed sometimes. Even when a good company has a decent year, public sentiment, or a bad economy, or being in an industry that's not doing so well, can pull it down. Even in a healthy stock market, stocks in good companies can have bad years.

 **Cross-Reference**

To learn how to evaluate a stock's price, see Chapter 9.

6

The Skinny on Stocks

Fool's School

How can you tell the difference among the good, the bad and the ugly stocks? Ask the Fools. They'll help you determine what factors make for attractive stocks. Start at Keyword: **Fool**, then prepare yourself for merriment among the money meisters. Click School and then select The 13 Steps to Investing for stock basics.

Want to set up an online trading account? Before you sign up, click Open a Discount Brokerage Account for the lowdown on what to look for. Looking for the ideal place to park your first investment? Select Index Funds. Want to track down financial information? Find out how at Read Financial Info. Looking for hidden gems throughout the site? Click Get Fully Foolish. If you want to talk with other stock jocks, click the Messages tab at the top of the page.

You can also link to related stock items, such as How to Value Stocks, shown in the Figure below.

Continued

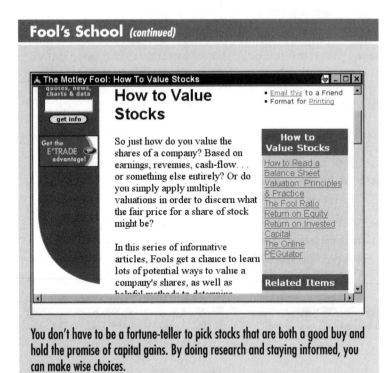

Fool's School *(continued)*

You don't have to be a fortune-teller to pick stocks that are both a good buy and hold the promise of capital gains. By doing research and staying informed, you can make wise choices.

A solid stock is judged so based on its history. But nobody can accurately predict where a stock is headed. Regardless of the destination, the journey will be fraught with risk.

Risk

Get those fishing rods ready. Risk opens a whole can of worms! When you invest in stocks, you face market risk, economic risk, liquidity risk, industry risk, and management risk, to name a few. Often, they're all related.

Here's an example. It's a beautiful day, the sun is shining, stocks are surging on the news of great earnings by Big Blue (IBM). Your tech stocks are climbing, too, holding Big Blue's hand on the way up. How wonderful that the market works that way, you think. When a company reports stellar earnings, especially if the report comes as a surprise, everybody seems to benefit, particularly companies in the same industry. The financials on *your* stocks may not have changed, but overall optimism in the market and in their industry has lifted their value.

It is another day. Anticipating a continuation of the climb, you sit back, take a sip of your coffee and check your portfolio (Keyword: **Portfolio**), certain everything will still be on the rise. And then you see the stock prices: down, down, down. There are a couple of possibilities here. Could be *market risk* — everything's crashing everywhere, so you're going down, too. You check the market news (Keyword: **MNC**) to find out what's going on. Seems the consumer price index came out in the morning and it reports a steep rise in prices. Higher prices could mean an economy growing too fast. And that smells of inflation. Waving the flag of *economic risk*, many stockholders are retreating, selling fast in an attempt to grab the gains they've reaped, or bailing before their losses mount too deep.

You, of course, are hunkered down, as your portfolio is structured to weather such storms. Maybe you've read the article shown in Figure 6-4 about sitting tight when the market trips. Find it at Keyword: **Family Money**, then select How To, under Investing. Scroll through the articles and select What to Do When the Stock Market Stumbles.

Cross-Reference

How can you stay abreast of market happenings? See Chapter 15 for details.

6

The Skinny on Stocks

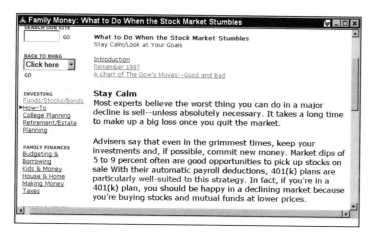

Figure 6-4. If you're investing for a long-term goal, a little stock market tumble shouldn't get you too riled. Historically, the stock market has provided the best average returns of any investment.

Neighbor Niles, however, is bailing fast. The tuition deadline is tomorrow and he needs to sell his stocks to get the cash. As usual, he let greed get in the way of good sense, and didn't sell a couple of years ago, when he should have. Now he has fallen prey to *liquidity risk* — the possibility that he won't be able to sell his stocks for a "fair" price. It's not only a fast-falling market that precipitates liquidity risk. Sometimes an inactive market can trigger the same result. If there aren't enough buyers around, and you need to unload your stock in a hurry, you might have to settle for a cheaper price than what the stock would fetch in a healthy market.

While your stock is likely to suffer as a result of some blunder by the executives at the top (*management risk*), more often than not, the change in a stock's day-to-day price has much more to do with what's happening in the market than in the value of the company itself. Just look at all the dot-com stocks, those Internet-related issues whose prices tend to rise and fall as one breath, regardless of what's going on at the time at a particular company. Even if your company is solid, with nothing new to report, it is likely to sag if one of its big brothers stumbles. That's *industry risk* — the possibility your company's stock price will fall because of some trauma that befalls other companies in the same industry.

As shown in the article in Figure 6-5, the reproach or worship of an industry can doom or resuscitate a company's stock. For up-to-date commentary on stocks and industries, go to Keyword: **Quicken**, and select Quicken.com. Click the Investing tab, and then click the News link beneath the tabs. Under the News heading on the left side of the page, click the Commentary link for a selection of articles by a group of Market Mavens. Daily commentary is offered up by Tom Calandra of CBS MarketWatch, with weekly articles by Herb Greenberg and Jim Cramer of The Street.Com. They offer a take on what's going right and what's going wrong in the current market picture.

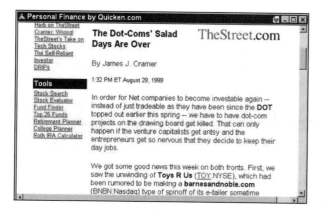

Figure 6-5. Even a growing and glowing company can take a hit if its industry gets nailed in the media.

Limiting risk

Can you avoid the risks of stocks? No, but you can limit your exposure to them in several ways:

▶ Avoid having to sell in a fire sale. Instead, expect drops and take advantage of them by buying. Make your commitments to stocks long-term commitments. Understand that short-term transactions are speculative because they don't provide enough time for the stocks to correct themselves if there's trouble.

▶ Don't buy anything without doing your research. Instead, make a plan that addresses all possible scenarios so you won't panic when the market experiences fits and starts.

▶ Diversify your holdings across types of stock and industries so when one type gets slammed, your entire portfolio will not feel the reverberations.

Types of Stocks

There are all kinds of stocks, and they differ in a range of ways. Different stocks fill distinct needs. Large, conservative stocks pay you a dividend. Moderate stocks offer dividend and growth. Aggressive stocks can supply you with — or cost you — a lot of money very quickly.

Caution

Don't invest in stocks with money you might need in five years or less. If the stock market sinks you might not have enough time to recover before you need to pull your money out.

Cross-Reference

How should you diversify? Get the lowdown in Chapters 5 and 11.

6

The Skinny on Stocks

The pundits at the Motley Fool consider investing in small stocks part of their basic strategy, as shown in Figure 6-6. Find their recommendations at Keyword: **Fool**; click Fool's School, and under The 13 Steps to Investing, select Step 11 to learn about investing in small stocks.

Figure 6-6. If you're investing for higher gains, small-cap stocks can rack them up.

The object when investing in equities is to link a stock's characteristics with your investment needs. Here is an explanation of some terms you'll come across in your exploration of these characteristics.

▶ *Blue-chip* stocks: Sort of a Who's Who of solid, big companies, except that there's no book listing what is a blue-chip and what isn't. The description is far from definitive. Blue-chips have a history of healthy earnings, reliable dividends, slow and steady growth and higher-end pricetags. *Large-cap*, blue-chip stocks historically represent a healthy, steady place to put your money for long-term goals of 10 years or more. They are considered conservative as equities go.

▶ *Cyclical* stocks: These are a barometer of the economy because their company sales are extremely sensitive to economic conditions. When the economy is strong, cyclicals thrive. But when economic conditions sag, and interest or inflation rates rise, these companies pay the price. For example, the fortunes of automobile makers typically ebb and flow with the health of the economy. Demand for their products doesn't go away; it just gets delayed a bit until people feel they have money to pay for the products. The same holds for homebuilders and steelmakers and computer manufacturers and for many other companies that manufacture consumer goods.

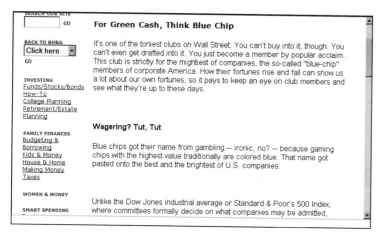

For Green Cash, Think Blue Chip

It's one of the toniest clubs on Wall Street. You can't buy into it, though. You can't even get drafted into it. You just become a member by popular acclaim. This club is strictly for the mightiest of companies, the so-called "blue-chip" members of corporate America. How their fortunes rise and fall can show us a lot about our own fortunes, so it pays to keep an eye on club members and see what they're up to these days.

Wagering? Tut, Tut

Blue chips got their name from gambling -- ironic, no? -- because gaming chips with the highest value traditionally are colored blue. That name got pasted onto the best and the brightest of U.S. companies.

Unlike the Dow Jones industrial average or Standard & Poor's 500 Index, where committees formally decide on what companies may be admitted,

If you want to explore further how blue-chip stocks came about and why they are an important indicator of current economic health, go to Keyword: **Family Money**, and select Money 101, under Tips, Tools and Info. Scroll down and select the article For Green Cash, Think Blue Chip, as pictured in Figure 6-7.

Figure 6-7. Blue chips may not necessarily be the biggest winners on Wall Street, but they often set the trend for the rest of the market.

market capitalization: The number of outstanding shares in a company times the price of the stock. Different analysts make the cut-offs at different numbers, but here's one interpretation: *micro-caps,* $300 million or less; *small-caps,* $300 million to $1 billion; *mid-caps,* $1 billion to $3 billion; *large-caps,* $3 billion and above.

▶ *Defensive* stocks: The opposite of cyclicals. Their fortunes remain steady and reliable regardless of the economy, because their wares are an everyday staple and withstand economic woes. For example, pharmaceuticals and utilities are among defensive stocks because people will always get sick, and turn on their lights, generating demand for these industries' products regardless of the economy.

▶ *Seasonal* stocks: As the name indicates, these companies fare differently with the seasons. Retailers' and toy makers' fortunes are often tied to holiday sales, for example.

▶ *Growth stocks:* These companies experience speedy acceleration in revenues or earnings, and are expected to continue growing at a quick pace. Typically they offer low or no dividends. The aim of the growth stock is capital appreciation. Growth stocks have typically been small-cap or micro-cap stocks, but in the past couple of years large technology companies have also generated strong growth.

6

The Skinny on Stocks

Find It Online

For more on Cyclical stocks, go to Keyword: **Quicken**, then choose Quicken.com. Select the Investing tab, then click the Basics link under Departments in the left column. Under Inside Basics on the left side, click The Investment FAQ. Then scroll down to the Stocks heading and select Cyclicals.

Tip

Because many growth- and aggressive-growth stocks are small- or micro-cap, they might be overlooked by financial institutions and can prove very rewarding to the patient investor, yet lethal to the overanxious one. Their returns tend to outweigh the risks for investors with a very long timeframe, deep pockets or a solid understanding of how these stocks work.

Cross-Reference

See Chapter 9 to further explore the benefits and drawbacks of owning various types of stocks.

▶ *Aggressive-growth* stocks: These don't offer dividends or reliability; they lure you with their promises. High-growth companies bulldoze their revenues and profits (if they have any) back into the business to position themselves for the future. They attract aggressive investors who are not dependent upon dividends for income, aren't dissuaded by high prices and accept the possibility that they might lose a big chunk of their investment, in return for what might be exponential growth down the road. The price of stocks in these companies can be particularly volatile. The same traders quick to pick up a stock for high returns are often just as quick to unload it when the price starts to sink.

Test your knowledge

Before you begin looking at individual companies, you need to have an idea of which kinds of stocks are right grasps for growth? Or are you better off with a more conservative income stock? To review the choices online, go to Keyword: **Money.com**. Scroll down to Money 101 on the left and select Investing in Stocks. Then click the chapter heading Different Strokes, where you can review the advantages and disadvantages of various types of stocks.

While you're at Money 101 you can shore up your vocabulary by checking out the stocks primer. From the table of contents again, click Chapter 5, "Investing in Stocks." Then click the Glossary feature for an A-Z listing of 2,500 financial terms.

The same Money 101 chapter offers the Top Ten Things you should know before investing in stocks, an overview of the stock market and the myths that surround it. Other topics include how to allocate your assets based on your individual investor profile, how to identify bargain stocks and how to place a trade.

When you think you've mastered the topic, click Take the Test for an interactive, 15-question quiz. Submit the results, then your score appears. Money.com is a tough grader — you need a 70 or better to pass. Don't worry, though. After you finish the test you'll get the right answers to the questions you missed.

▶ *Income* stocks: These stocks pay generous dividends
on a regular basis. Their companies are stable and profits are reliable. The companies, such as utilities, often
have painfully slow growth rates because they have a
limited customer base, but those customers aren't
likely to disappear. The companies plow their profits
into dividends. Income stocks attract investors such as
retirees who want steady income from their holdings.
The investors sacrifice capital appreciation for that
steady check, but the potential exists for a little growth
over time, making the stocks more appealing to some
investors than other income-producers, such as bonds.

▶ *Growth and income* stocks: These represent companies
in the middle of the road — appreciating, but with less of
a propensity for volatility than pure growth stocks. They
have a good track record of profits and should produce
moderate growth in the future. In addition, these stocks
grant a percent or two or three in dividends. They attract
investors who are willing to accept moderate volatility,
but are reluctant to throw caution to the wind. These
investors' returns might not jump off the charts, but
neither will their blood-pressure rates.

▶ *Value* stocks: Think stocks on sale. Value stocks represent
companies whose stock prices should be higher, based
on the company's financials, but for one reason or
another they're temporarily in the doghouse. Often the
company is rebuilding from a setback, leaving investors
wary. Maybe it's a temporary earnings reversal or a product rollout that gets delayed. The value investor perceives
the problem as temporary, though, and believes the
stocks will climb above their current, on-sale price.

Which type of stock is right for you? That depends on your
goals and portfolio. None of these stocks is a "smarter" investment than the others. In fact, as you've learned, the best
strategy encompasses a combination of stocks selected
to meet your needs.

For help figuring it all out online, check out Keyword:
Personal Wealth. Select the Learning Center, and click
Basics of Smart Investing, under Tutorials. Select Stocks
from the table of contents, and choose Selecting Stocks
for a series of articles on how to choose between Value
and Growth stocks, as shown in Figure 6-8.

Caution

Occasionally, stocks that pay
a high dividend do so only
because the company is in big
trouble. If the company's performance continues to lag, it
might not have enough money
to continue paying dividends.
Be sure to evaluate a stock's
health by checking out its
ratios in Chapter 9.

Cross-Reference

You'll learn how to custom-
build your stock portfolio in
Chapter 11.

6

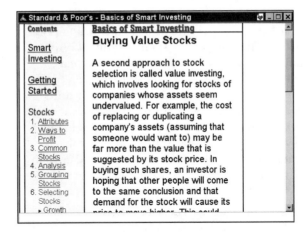

Figure 6-8. Value stocks may be diamonds in the rough — capable companies whose assets seem undervalued and whose stock price is in the deep-discount bin.

Scrutinize the Candidates

In your efforts to decide which stocks to buy, you need to operate as a business buyer would. Scrutinize the operation, examine its expenses, and determine its potential for growth. Judge if the potential returns warrant your investment. Don't let public sentiment rule your decision, but keep in mind how much this sentiment affects the price of your company.

How do you scrutinize the candidates? You can't just pack your laptop, go knocking on the door of Gigantic Monopoly, Inc., and say to the receptionist: "I'm considering purchasing some stock. I need to see your financials now, please. And when can the CEO spare an hour or two? By the way, how much are you spending on this basket of fancy fruit? Do all employees really need to have free gourmet coffee. I'm concerned about the bottom line..." She's likely to call over those two nice security guards to escort you to the door.

You *can* study a company inside out — from the outside in. Public companies file reams of material with the Securities and Exchange Commission, and that information is analyzed, charted, examined, and regurgitated by hundreds of investing companies. AOL provides you with your own personal reference room to inspect these findings. (And you can eat, make noise, and drink coffee while you're researching!) Start with Keyword: **Investment Research** for a direct line to all the resources you need. You need to examine the information, determine whether you have a solid candidate, determine if the price is reasonable, and leave compelled by something that tells you this company is worth *your* investment.

After you've brushed up on a bit of the lingo, even the nearest newspaper's financial section can offer a quick look into a company's fortune, as explained in Figure 6-9. Go to Keyword: **Family Money**, select How To, under Investing, and click How to Read Stock Tables for a step-by-step guide on how to decipher the small print in the business section.

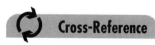

Cross-Reference

Head over to Chapter 9 for an in-depth exploration of Keyword: **Investment Research**, the launching pad from which you can learn everything you need to know about evaluating a company, its stock and its stock price.

6

The Skinny on Stocks

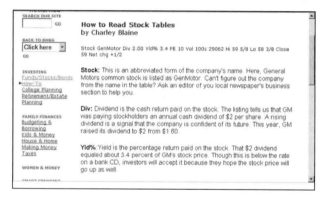

Figure 6-9. That blur of numbers in the newspaper will give you the scoop on how a stock is faring, after you know how to crack the code.

Stock price

What makes a good buy? That provokes the greatest disparity among investors. Remember, each time you buy a stock, somebody else has decided it's time to get rid of it! There's no hard and fast rule on stock price. Price moves on the short term on news, fear, cheerleading, rumors, spending, analyst reports, meetings of economic policy makers. Over time, though, it's usually a company's products, earnings, management, and the kind of business it's in that shape where the price goes.

Sometimes a good stock tumbles when the market is rising. Sometimes a feeble stock rises when the market falls. Stock *traders* try to benefit from these daily moves. They look to profit from the market's machinations, and aren't apt to hold a stock for long. *Investors*, on the other hand, regard the

For a primer on how to evaluate stocks, check out The Street.Com's Stocks Class: From the Bottom Up. Go to Keyword: **TSC**, click Full TSC site, then select Basics. Scroll down to the Stocks class, then click How to Get Started at Stock Picking.

This guides investors through the process of researching and evaluating companies. Chapter Two, "The ABCs of Charts," helps you sort out graphics and charts to launch your stock analysis. Other chapters discuss IPOs, stock splits and share buybacks among other topics for new and seasoned investors.

To talk about all this stuff, click Community, on the left. Find out when the experts are scheduled to talk, refer to their comments in the Chat Archive or find out what other TSCers have to say on The Street's Message Boards.

moves as transitory. They look to past, present and future earnings to drive their buying and selling decisions and tend to stick with stocks even through unpleasant periods. Neither is a "better" way to buy and sell, but they are extremely different motivations and require different strategies.

Sometimes when stock price catapults to new highs, many companies fear their stock will appear too costly to consumers. The company's board of directors might then call for a stock *split*, a decision to divide each share of stock into more shares. The board might vote to award two stocks for each one you already have, or they might give you three for every two you have. If you had 100 shares of Widgets 'R' Us priced at $80 apiece, after a 2 to 1 split you would have 200, priced at $40 apiece.

A company could also declare a *reverse split*. If the company believes its stock price has fallen so low that it's in the picked-over clearance bin, the board of directors might boost the price by combining a certain number of shares into one. For example, Widgets 'R' Us might declare a reverse 2 to 1 split. If you own 100 shares of Widgets 'R' Us, worth $10 each, after the reverse split you would have 50 shares worth $20 each.

Which companies plan to split their stocks? Find out at Keyword: **Online Investor**, then, under Stocks, click Splits (see Figure 6-10).

```
OLI - upcoming splits listed by pay date                         _ □ ×
OLI  The Online Investor                        OLI Main        Help
Stock Splits: upcoming splits listed by pay date

                          Stock    Announce    Record
Company Name              Split    Date        Date
        Splits announced in the past week are in RED.
       * Asterisk indicates options are traded on the stock

Gateway Computer (GTW)   2 for 1   8/09        8/20       9/07 *
Applied Micro Cir.(AMCC) 2 for 1   8/03        9/02       9/09 *
Innodata (INOD)          3 for 1   8/18        8/30       9/09
Tribune Co. (TRB)        2 for 1   7/27        8/19       9/09 *
4Kids Entertainme(KIDE)  2 for 1   8/12        9/01       9/13
First Bancorp (FBNC)     3 for 2   8/18        8/30       9/13
Semtech (SMTC)           2 for 1   8/24        8/30       9/14 *
▶ Understanding Stock Splits and Dividends      Investor's Business Daily
▶ Doing The Stock Split Math                     FREE TRIAL    Click
▶ Reverse Splits...and why they're bad news                  keyword: OLI
```

Figure 6-10. A two-for-one special should be good news, right? Stock splits may have a positive, negative, or neutral effect on your holdings, depending on the split.

How Stocks Trade

If a stock is like a brick in a company, and the company is already built, how do you get a piece of it? You can buy it from an owner who wants out. Maybe this owner bought her stocks years ago and has now made a pile of money. She wants to sell and build a retirement home with her profits. Or maybe she is in a panic because the stock is sinking. You think it's a solid company, though, so you scoop up the stocks she previously held, happy to get them at a low price.

At Money 101, shown in Figure 6-11, you can learn all about how stocks are traded and exchanged. Go to Keyword: **Money.com** and select Investing in Stocks under Money 101, then choose Placing a Trade.

Figure 6-11. In most cases, to purchase stock you must buy it from someone who wants to sell it.

You can also own stocks indirectly, through a mutual fund. A mutual fund manager buys stocks and assembles them in funds designed to meet certain objectives. You buy the funds that suit your needs.

The place where you trade with other stockholders is called an *exchange*. You place your order with a broker to buy, and the seller places her order with a broker to sell, and your brokers get together on the exchange and make the deal.

Tip

What do active traders look for in a stock? Ask them at Keyword: **Traders**, then click The Trader's Lounge. Chat in The Shark Tank with other AOL members about trading opportunities as they unfold, and head to The Trader's Lounge to chat at length about any market topics.

Note

The company's earnings haven't changed during this move, so your holdings aren't worth any more on a split. But the stock *appears* more affordable, generating more interest among potential buyers.

Cross-Reference

For more about IPOs in this book, see Chapters 10 and 13.

Cross-Reference

You'll learn more about mutual funds in Chapter 8.

The exchange doesn't set the price and doesn't buy or sell, it is simply the place where your broker and her broker do business together.

Exchanges

There are two types of exchanges. On a *listed* exchange, *specialists* are responsible for trading all the shares of a certain stock. These specialists match buyers with sellers, and ensure the transactions occur in an orderly and upright manner. The specialist charges the buyer a fee for this service.

The New York Stock Exchange is probably the best known of the listed exchanges. The NYSE swaps stocks of more than 2,000 companies, plus bonds and assorted other vehicles. There's also the American Stock Exchange, which is composed of regional exchanges.

Then there is the *over the counter* market, the other type of exchange. The NASDAQ is the best known here. Some 5,000 stocks trade on the NASDAQ, and several thousand more trade on the NASDAQ Small Cap and the OTC Bulletin Board. These exchanges don't require brokers to be present on the trading floor. In fact, there is no trading floor. The NASDAQ and the like conduct business electronically. The brokers, called *market makers*, complete your transaction. They buy and sell with *you*, as opposed to brokering the trade between you and another investor.

Legend

In your investing travels you might need a map legend, a key for deciphering the *stock snapshot*. This indispensable picture, found at Keyword: **Quotes**, helps you navigate the numbers behind the going stock price. See Figure 6-12 for an example. If you're a trader, you'll probably look at these numbers at least daily. If your commitments are long-term you might not look at the numbers as often, but you will certainly need to understand their meaning. Each of these terms is explored more fully in Chapter 9.

Note

Everyone needs a broker to trade. Even when you order your own trades online a licensed broker needs to execute that trade.

Cross-Reference

For the ins and outs of fees and brokers and trading, see Chapter 13.

Definition

ticker symbol: the code of letters used to abbreviate a company's name on an exchange.

Find It Online

To look up the ticker symbol of a particular stock or fund go to Keyword: **Quotes**, select Name, then type in the name of the company and press Lookup. The symbol will appear in the quote box.

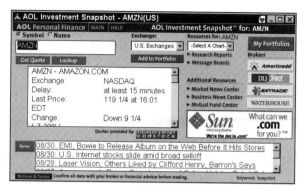

Figure 6-12. AOL's Investment Snapshot offers a quick way to assess the current value of a stock during the trading day.

Here's an example, a hypothetical quote from Widgets 'R' Us.

WRU	Widgets 'R' Us Inc.
Exchange	NYSE comp
Delay	at least 15 minutes
Last	128¾ at 13:32
Change	Up 1¼
High	129⅜ at 12:22
Low	127⅞ at 10:11
Open	127⅞
Previous Close	127½ on 10/27
Volume	1,333,767
30-Day Avg. Volume	2,468,000
Shares Outstanding	532,235,000
Market Cap	$68,525,256,250
52-Week High	132½
52-Week Low	78.13
Beta	0.83
Yield	1.00%
P/E Ratio	15.51
EPS	8.30
Currency Units	U.S. Dollars

Note

There are more than two dozen classes and levels of stock. You can find a list of them all, as well as their ticker symbols, at the Motley Fool's stock code FAQ at Keyword: **Fool**. From the Quick Find pull-down menu, choose Site Index, under Info/Help. Next, under F, click Fool FAQ, then choose Stock Symbol Codes

6

The Skinny on Stocks

Here's what the terms in this snapshot mean:

Exchange: Indicates where the stock trades. In this case, the NYSE, which is the New York Stock Exchange. Other likely spots would be the AMEX (American Stock Exchange) or the NASDAQ (National Association of Securities Dealers).

Delay: The time that has elapsed since the quote was captured from the exchange.

Last: The price at which one share of stock last traded, and the time it traded.

Change: How much the price has moved since the market closed the previous trading day.

High: The highest price paid for a share of this stock so far this day, and the time it was paid.

Low: The lowest price paid for a share of stock so far this day, and the time it was paid.

Open: The price of the stock when the market opened on this day.

Previous Close: The price of the stock at the end of trading the previous day.

Volume: The number of shares traded so far today. A significant swing in volume compared to the monthly average often foreshadows or accompanies company news.

30-Day Avg. Volume: The average number of shares traded each day over the past 30 trading days. Here's some perspective: The average daily volume for stocks, according to AOL partner Market Guide's database, is about 200,000. Small-caps trade about 100,000 shares a day. Large caps trade about 1.6 million shares a day, and many gigantic stocks trade well over 5 million shares a day.

Shares Outstanding: The number of shares held by the public. (Companies retain a great big chunk for themselves.)

Market Cap: Shares outstanding times last price. (Value of company overall.)

52-Week High: The most that has been paid for a share of this stock in the past 52 weeks of trading.

52-Week Low: The least that has been paid for a share of this stock in the past 52 weeks of trading.

Beta: Beta measures a stock's volatility — how often it went up and down over the past year compared with others in the market. Like WRU, stocks with a beta of one or below are considered to carry a *low beta*. Beta below one means the stock price goes down less than others when the market is down. If the beta is higher than one, it means the stock price rises by a higher percentage than others when the market is up. After you determine your stock's beta, you can compare it to others in its industry, its sector and its index. The S&P always has a beta of 1.00.

If your Widgets 'R' Us stock has a beta of 0.83, your stock goes up and down 83 percent as much as the market. That points to stability. But it could also mean your stock underperforms the S&P 500 when the market's on the rise. The good thing is it falls more softly when the market's on the plunge.

Growth stocks typically have high beta values. Income stocks typically have low betas. How much you should pay attention to beta depends on your investing preferences. Some investors look for stocks that have a beta lower than one when they think the market is going down and, if they think the market's on the rise, they look for targets with a beta higher than one. For all investors, it's worth examining how your target's beta matches up to others in the same sector and industry.

Yield: The amount of money returned on your investment via dividends. The annual dividend rate shown in the snapshot is a percentage of the price of the stock, so your WRU stock would pay $1.28 per share if the dividends were declared at this price (0.01 times 128 equals 1.28). For companies that don't yield dividends, the space next to yield would be blank.

P/E Ratio: Stands for *price-to-earnings ratio*, which is the price of one share of stock divided by the company's earnings of the past four quarters. Many investors love to compare P/Es. You know the ones, always talking about how their P/Es are lower than 10 or 15 or 35 or whatever. (And saying it in a way that intimates their lawn is greener than yours.) As you know by now, while there might be a chemical recipe for green grass, there is no magic formula for growing money!

Definition

sector: a grouping of industries that represents a segment of the economy

industry: the line of business along which similar companies operate

Note

Dividends are important in stock analysis because they represent direct cash flows to investors and cannot be manipulated by accounting techniques.

6

The Skinny on Stocks

Back to P/Es. They are important in judging a stock's merit, but in different ways to different people. In the old days, some analysts used them to estimate the number of years it would take to recoup your investment if the company stayed its course. In other words, if you invested in Widgets 'R' Us it would take you 15-plus years to recoup the money you invested there. But these kinds of measuring sticks are out of date today, as many companies have P/Es of 80, 90, 100, or more — exorbitant compared to years past, when a P/E higher than 25 sent up red flags. These days, many people are willing to pay for tremendous growth potential tomorrow in spite of fledgling earnings today. If there's no P/E listed in the snapshot, it means your company has no earnings yet, which is not uncommon among the dot-coms of the world. When a company has no earnings, investors buy into what they believe is the company or industry's potential.

Some investors even choose a stock *because* of its high P/Es, believing the numbers are a sign of the optimism Wall Street is showing for the company. Not all investors, though. Some investors think it's preposterous to pay anything for a stock with no earnings. These are completely different interpretations of the same ratio! And neither is the right or wrong answer. It's all a matter of what *you're* looking for in a stock.

EPS: Stands for *earnings per share*. The amount of money the company earned in the 12 months before the last quarter, divided by the number of shares of stock in the company, or how many dollars the company earned for each share held by you and fellow stockholders. Charting a company's EPS will tell you if earnings are growing each quarter, as they should be in a healthy company, and if they are growing by a greater percentage each quarter. If you can't decide between two very similar companies, put their EPSs side by side to examine their earnings growth. Keep in mind that large companies have a tougher time increasing their earnings growth each quarter than small companies do.

Currency Units: Denomination of currency in which the given security trades and is quoted.

You'll get the inside scoop on these research terms and the ways to evaluate them at Keyword: **Investment Research** (see Figure 6-13). The full tour of Investment Research is up ahead in Chapter 9.

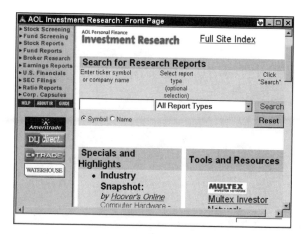

Figure 6-13. AOL's Investment Research site is a good place to ferret out which stocks are winners and which ones to avoid.

Summary

You now know who invests in stocks, and the motivation behind these investments. While you learned of the stock market's appreciation over time, you also learned to be wary of stocks' risks.

You know which types of stocks are apt to behave in what way, you know where to turn to research stocks, and you understand the terminology behind the numbers. You also learned how stocks trade.

Now that you're all pumped up to find hot stocks, it's time to meet their even-tempered cousin.

Up next, bonds — the ballast when stocks rock your boat.

A Quick Look

▶ **Checking Out the Models**   **page 153**

Feel like you're in a foreign land when it comes to dealing with bonds? Sage makes the trip easy. From translating bond-speak to helping you come up with the right mix for your portfolio Sage packs the perfect suitcase. Start at Keyword: **Sage Models** and then click Investing in Bonds.

Up comes The Sage Income Investor, your ticket to Bond World. Hear what experts in the bond business have to say, find the top-rated bond funds and refer to the bond glossary to help keep you straight on the terms. Follow the links if you want to learn more.

▶ **Investing With Uncle Sam**   **page 159**

If you have a savings bond or two tucked away, you're not alone. Close to 55 million investors support Uncle Sam by buying his bonds. If you're not quite sure what they're worth, whether or not they're still earning interest or what they'll total in the future you don't have to crunch the numbers or call your accountant to find out. The fastest way to do it is online.

Have the Savings Bond Wizard do the calculations for you at Keyword: **http://www.treasurydirect.gov;** click Savings Bond Wizard. Download the Wizard and enter your numbers.

▶ **Bring On the Bonds . . . But Which Ones?**   **page 161**

So you've decided to diversify and incorporate a steady fixed-income vehicle into your portfolio. Bonds seem like a natural choice, and with your decision made, you are ready to buy. But which bond is best? Should you go for a tax-deferred option, a long-term payoff, or a steady, no-frills standby?

To figure out which bonds offer the best return and the best fit for you, go to Keyword: **Calculator**, scroll down to Bond Calculators, and click Which Bond is Better? By plugging in a few particulars of different bonds, you can get an immediate readout of which bond delivers the highest after-tax returns.

Chapter 7

The Fix on Bonds

So your brother asks you to loan him $100,000 to open the barbershop of his dreams? He agrees to pay you back a set amount each month, with interest to boot. Just about everybody needs a loan now and then — probably even you — to go to school, or to buy a house or car. Even credit cards are loans — but we won't talk about those because you gave them up chapters ago, right?

Introducing Bonds

Your brother had the right idea when he hit you up for the money. When corporations and governments find themselves strapped for cash, or when they need money to pay for extraordinary expenses, they borrow from the public. Maybe Conglomerate Corp. wants to buy another company. Maybe Boomtown has to build a school. Maybe Uncle Sam needs to build subsidized housing. The entities, called issuers, borrow money for a specific period of time from financial institutions, called *underwriters*, and the loans they take are called *bonds*. The underwriters, in turn, sell the bonds to you.

The borrowers pledge to return the principal to the underwriter (who then turns it over to you) when the loan comes due; and promises to repay interest on a predetermined schedule each year. The interest the borrower pays is set by the prevailing interest rates at the time the bond is issued as well as by the viability of the issuer.

Income and investment stability

Bonds are called *fixed-income* investments because you receive the same interest payment every year. Even if stock markets are plunging, governments are falling, currency is bouncing all over the place, your check arrives like clockwork, seemingly immune to the turmoil. That's why bonds are a popular income investment — you know how much money you'll be paid, and when to expect the check. Such a low-risk investment is perfect for some investors. To find out if bonds are right for you, read on in this chapter. If you're online, you can refer to the article in Figure 7-1. Go to Keyword: **http://www.Smartmoney.com**, click the Bonds tab, and select The One Bond Strategy You Need Now.

Bonds are an integral component of many portfolios. Generally, bonds:

- ▶ Add diversification to your portfolio
- ▶ Sometimes offer tax-free yields
- ▶ Can be sold
- ▶ Are less volatile than stock

Find It Online

Have a question for AOL members about fixed-income investing? Find out what they have to say at Keyword: **Sage Models**. In the features box, click Investing in Bonds and then choose Fixed Income Message Board.

7

The Fix on Bonds

Figure 7-1. Although they lack the glamorous sudden-wealth potential of stocks, most bonds provide stable, low-risk income and help diversify a portfolio.

▶ Are repaid before stockholders are if the issuer goes bankrupt

▶ Are a great option for capital preservation for short-term goals

Since the Great Depression, the return on bonds has barely surpassed the inflation rate, although in the last five to 10 years long-term bond and bond-mutual-fund yields have far outpaced inflation.

Choosing a Bond

You're probably counting on bonds for some diversification or stability. Look back at your Investment Blueprint to figure out how much you want to invest in bonds. Are you looking to them to fill a particular income need? How much do you seek over what time period? Now, take a look at the options bonds afford you. Two become clear: some bonds work for your low-risk, stable investments. Others meet your riskier high-yield desires. Which are right for you? The answer lies in the bonds' features.

Why bonds?

Explore Buying Bonds: A Primer (shown in the Figure below) at Keyword: **TSC** and then click Full TSC Site. Click Investing Basics and then scroll down to Buying Bonds: A Primer. This walks you through an introduction of bond basics and outlines strategies for introducing bonds to your portfolio.

Cross-Reference

Review Chapter 5 for your Investment Blueprint and investing goals.

Bonds gained respect during the harrowing stock market dips in 1998, underscoring the importance of having a balanced portfolio.

7

The Fix on Bonds

BondSpeak

There are all sorts of features to consider when you buy a bond. These include maturity, redemption features, interest rate, credit rating, yield, price, and tax features. To help in your pursuit, yet another term-tutorial is in order.

▶ *Par value* or *face value*: The amount the issuer borrowed from you and promises to repay when the bond matures. Par value for most bonds is $1,000 per bond. You can buy a bond above or below par value while the bond is out in the market to take advantage of market conditions. (More about that later in this chapter, under Bond Prices.)

Definition

term: The length of time until maturity.

▶ *Coupon:* The interest that the debtor will pay you each year. The *coupon rate* is a percentage of the par value. In other words, if the par value of the bond is $1,000 and the debtor agrees to an 8 percent coupon rate, the debtor will pay you an $80 coupon in annual interest. (More often than not, the issuer will pay you $40 every six months.) A *zero-coupon* bond, as the name implies, doesn't pay a coupon. Instead, you buy the bond at a discount and you're paid in full when the bond *matures* (see below).

▶ *Maturity date:* The date on which the debtor promises to repay your principal. This is also when interest payments end. The maturity date can be anywhere from one day to 30 years down the road. *Short-term notes* mature in four years or less; *medium-term notes* mature in five to 12 years and *long-term bonds* mature in 12 or more years.

▶ *Call:* An announcement that the borrower plans to return your principal before the bond's maturity date. Typically, bonds are called when interest rates drop significantly and the issuer wants to refinance his debt. Corporate and municipal bonds stipulate whether or not they can be called when they are issued. Federal bonds cannot be called. If a bond is callable, there will be a call date that stipulates when the issuer can redeem the bond. Make sure you know for sure whether or not a bond is callable when you purchase it, especially if you are buying it secondhand. That's because you will lose anything you paid above its face value when it's called, as well as your steady stream of income.

▶ *Put:* A license to allow the investor to force the issuer to repurchase the bonds at a particular point in time.

▶ *Current yield:* The annual interest payment divided by the bond's current price.

▶ *Yield to maturity:* The interest payments you will receive between now and maturity, plus the amount you gain or lose if you bought the bond above or below its par value.

Sage advice

Municipal bonds, Treasury bonds, junk bonds, callable bonds . . . Your head spinning yet? Like many new investing topics the world of bonds seems to speak its own language. Your initial entry into this new land might make you wish you'd brought a pocket translator.

Fortunately, the experts at Sage are on hand to provide the interpreting. Go to Keyword: **Sage Models** and then click Investing in Bonds in the Feature box. The Sage Income Investor screen pops up, fills you in on what's new in the Bond world, offers up expert opinions, and points you to sites for learning more.

Searching for a top-rated bond fund? Check out Top Ten Bond Funds for a list of star performers, or click All Star Bond Funds for a series of articles on the best of the lot. Basics on Bonds and Fixed Income Articles offer a steady diet of education and advice for the investor new to bonds.

You can find the Sage Bond Glossary, shown in the Figure below, by entering Keyword: **Sage Models** and then click Investing in Bonds in the Feature box. At the Income Investor screen, scroll down to Bond Glossary.

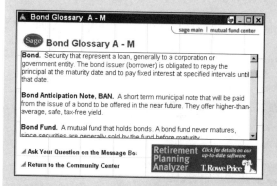

Financial lingo can make you feel like you are in a foreign country. Sage and other sites offer glossaries to help you translate.

Note

Calculating current yield: Suppose a bond has a par value of $1,000 and a coupon rate, or yield, of 7 percent. If you buy the bond for $1,000 and your interest rate is 7 percent, your current yield is also 7 percent (70/1000). But suppose you don't buy the bond when it is issued. Instead, you buy it in the secondary market, after it was issued (more about that later). You will either have to pay a premium for the bond or you will get it at a discount, depending on the market interest rates at the time. How will you know how this difference affects yield? You have to calculate the current yield — the interest payment divided by the current price. Say you buy the bond at $900, and the interest payment is $70 (which is a 7 percent rate). Your current yield will equal 7.77 percent — the interest payment ($70) divided by the current price ($900).

7

The Fix on Bonds

Bond Risks

With the promise of getting back your principal and receiving regular interest payments twice a year, bonds offer great stability, right?

Well, yes and no.

Inflation risk

In addition to that regular income stream, there's a shadow, and it's a dark one. The economy can wreak havoc on the real strength of your returns. When inflation creeps up and interest rates rise, what happens to your bond yield? Absolutely nothing. It stays the same. You don't benefit even as all other interest rates and prices around you are going up, up, up. That's one risk of bonds, and it's called *inflation risk*.

And there's no sense in trying to sell your bond when interest rates are rising. Who would want to pay as much for your bond with its lower interest payments as for a new bond paying current interest rates? No one would. When interest rates rise, lower-yielding bonds become less attractive, so the price you can sell them for is lower than what you paid.

Some bond funds pay particular heed to heading off inflation risk. To find out which do, go to Keyword: **Sage Models**, click Investing in Bonds, and then click Fixed Income Articles, as shown in Figure 7-2.

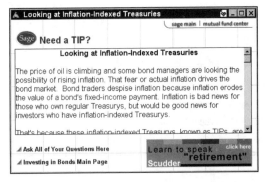

Figure 7-2. Beware the specter of inflation; it can wipe out the profits you may be earning from bonds. Some bond funds specifically seek to avoid this danger.

At the other end of the spectrum, however, when interest rates fall, you're holding a bond that yields more than the new issues. If you want to sell it, you can probably get more than you paid for it.

Regardless of interest rates, you will get the bond's face value if you hold it to maturity . . . unless the bond gets called.

Call risk

When interest rates fall, everybody runs out and refinances their mortgage to take advantage of lower rates. Well, sometimes bond issuers do the same thing. If interest rates fall, they call, or redeem, their bonds at face value so they can issue new ones and pay less interest on them. You get stuck having to cash in your bond before you thought you had to. If you get a new one the interest you generate is lower than what you were just earning. This is called *call risk* — the chance that your corporate or municipal bond issuer will call the bond before it matures. Callable bonds generally pay slightly higher interest rates than comparable bonds that are not callable to compensate for this risk.

For a primer on call risk, see Standard & Poor's Basics of Smart Investing, at Keyword: **Personal Wealth**. Click the Home tab to the left of the page and then scroll down to Departments. Click The Learning Center. Then click Basics of Smart Investing. Scroll down and click Fixed Income Securities. Again scroll down and click Types of Bonds located to the left of the page.

The article shown in Figure 7-3 explains callable bonds.

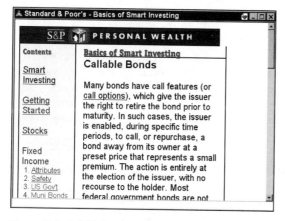

Figure 7-3. Callable bonds can be reclaimed during times of low interest rates, an action that benefits the borrower but leaves the investor out in the cold.

Credit risk

There's a third risk bondholders face, which is that the bond issuer won't be able to meet its payments. This is called *credit risk*. There's nary a chance of that with U.S. Treasuries, but with corporate bonds, and even with municipal bonds, it is a possibility. If the debtor runs out of money, it can't pay you back. While bondholders get to line up in front of stockholders to collect their money from a bankrupt entity, there is no guarantee there will be enough money to pay you back.

Types of Bonds

There are four types of bonds: those issued by the U.S. government, those from state and local governments, those from corporations, and those from foreign entities. Their yields directly correlate to their risk of default.

U.S. government bonds

Often referred to as Treasuries because they are sold by the Department of the Treasury, these are the safest bonds of all. They're backed by a promise of repayment by the United States government, and the promise is backed by the government's power to collect taxes. Treasuries range in maturity from 90 days to 30 years. The longer the maturity, the higher the interest yield. The following are types of U.S. bonds:

▶ *Treasury bills*, or T-bills, mature in either 13 weeks, 26 weeks, or a year. They come in denominations of $10,000 and are sold at a discount from their face value. In other words, you don't get any interest payments. Instead, the price you pay is $10,000 minus the interest the bond yields, which has been hovering around 5 percent. Then when the T-bills mature, you get $10,000 back. The interest on Treasuries is exempt from state and local taxes, but you have to pay federal taxes on it. T-bills are popular among people with imminent goals, like a tuition bill or a wedding, who want to preserve the capital they're investing yet still earn more interest than they would get from a CD or passbook.

▶ *Treasury notes*, or *T-notes*, mature in two to 10 years. The minimum you can invest is $1,000 for five- and 10-year notes and $5,000 for two- and three-year notes. The government pays you twice a year a fixed interest rate, which has been hovering between 5 percent and 6 percent a year. Because of the low-risk nature of these bonds, Treasury notes are a favorite investment of retirees and people with intermediate-term goals who don't want to endanger their principal.

▶ *Treasury bonds*, or *long bonds*, carry the longest terms, from 10 to 30 years. You can buy these in denominations of $1,000. As with Treasury notes, the government repays you interest twice a year. Interest rates on Treasury bonds are the highest of the Treasuries, recently above 6 percent, and these rates are set at auction (see Buying and Trading Bonds, later in this chapter). Although Treasury bonds might seem to be the most stable investment of all because of their long maturity, in fact, this longer maturity exposes you to greater interest rate risk than you would face with the Treasury bond's cousins. In addition, studies have shown that due to inflation, long bonds actually yield *less* over time to buy-and-hold investors than Treasuries with intermediate maturities (see Figure 7-4).

Find It Online

What are T-bills, T-notes, and Treasury bonds yielding? Their "Fixed Income" designation notwithstanding, the yields can vary day to day, depending on the market and interest rates.

Before purchasing or selling bonds, find out how they are faring in the market. Go to Keyword: **Market News Center** and click Bonds & Money. A chart tracks the progress of the Treasury bond, or *long bond*, 1-year T-bills, 2-year notes, and 10-year bonds during the course of the business day.

In the Features box, click U.S. Yield Curve to find out the current yields. The maturation date, current price and yield, and previous price and yield are shown, giving you quick access to any ups and downs.

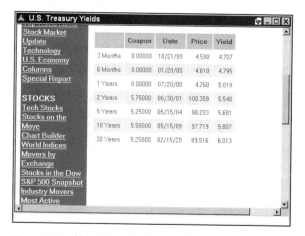

Figure 7-4. Although long bonds carry a higher yield, intermediate bonds often prove the more profitable investment.

Tip

You can buy just the interest-bearing coupons of Treasury bonds, too. These are called *Treasury strips*, and you buy them either from your discount broker or right from the government (learn how later in this chapter) at a discount from their face value.

Note

Note that the bonds can't be in the child's name in order to qualify for the exemption. They need to be in the name of a participant who was at least 24 years old when he bought the bonds.

▶ *Inflation-indexed Treasuries*, like regular Treasuries, the interest rate on these is set at auction and remains fixed for the life of the bond. But with inflation-indexed securities, the principal amount is adjusted to reflect inflation. (The Consumer Price Index is used to measure the inflation rate.) Your semiannual interest payments are based on this adjusted principal, and when the principal is repaid to you at maturity, the amount you get will either be par value, or the amount adjusted to reflect inflation, whichever is greater.

Other types of government bonds

▶ *U.S. savings bonds* are also sold by the Treasury, but for some unknown reason they're not included in the "Treasuries" category. For many investors — close to 55 million people at last count — savings bonds represent the easiest way to invest savings.

Savings bonds range in value from $50 to $10,000. They're sold for half their face value. The bond reaches that face value in 17 years. It then continues paying interest for 13 more years. When you cash in savings bonds you pay federal taxes on the interest, but not state or local tax. Federal tax is waived altogether if you're paying for college and your combined household income is less than $79,650. Portions are waived when you earn up to $109,650 combined.

Another type of savings bond, the Series HH bond, is available in denominations of $500, $1,000, $5000, and $10,000. These reach face value in ten years and continue to generate interest ten years after that. You can convert many of your EE bonds into HH bonds. With HH bonds, the government deposits interest payments directly into your bank account every six months.

▶ *Mortgage-backed bonds.* Several government agencies issue bonds and repay the debt using money collected from mortgages. The Federal National Mortgage Association (also known as Fannie Mae), the Government National Mortgage Association (also known as Ginnie Mae), and the Federal Home Loan Mortgage Corporation (also known as Freddie Mac) all sponsor government-assisted loans, and they give investors a stake in these loans through bonds.

Only Ginnie Mae backs up her bonds with a U.S. government guarantee. The others are backed by their federal agency. All three of these mortgage-backed bonds yield about one percent more than Treasuries with similar maturities. The upside: these bonds pay interest monthly. The downside: the interest is taxable, and the bonds come with a hefty price tag of about $25,000. Because these types of bonds are extremely susceptible to interest-rate fluctuations, their volatility can wreak havoc in bond funds that carry them.

Buy bonds online

Remember that savings bond Aunt Ida sent you for your birthday when you were a kid (and hoping for new Hot Wheels)? It probably seemed unexciting at the time, but if it's been collecting moss in your file cabinet all these years, you might be surprised at just what old Aunt Ida's gift has amounted to. Or maybe you're in Aunt Ida's shoes now, and you want to send something a bit longer-lasting to your little nieces and nephews than the latest action figure. You can send the little ones a bond to invest in their future.

There's a fast way to do both. To figure the worth of your savings bond inventory, or to calculate what they'll be worth in the future, call up the U.S. government's Savings Bond Wizard, a nifty piece of software that does all the calculating for you. Go to Keyword: **http://www. treasurydirect.gov**, then scroll down to Savings Bonds, and click Savings Bond Wizard. Download the Wizard, then enter your numbers.

If you want to buy savings bonds online, click Forms, under Resources, and then click Savings Bonds Forms Ordering.

Wondering if savings bonds are a good investment for you? From the same Treasury Direct site, under Savings Bonds, click Savings Bond Calculators and then click the Tax Advantages Calculator, shown in the Figure below. Plug in your tax bracket and a few other numbers and the calculator determines the results.

Continued

Tip

If that $25,000 a chunk initial investment is too steep for you, but you like the tax-savings, opt for muni-bond mutual funds.

Find It Online

For the latest national muni bond yields, go to Keyword: **MNC**, click Bonds & Money, and then scroll down to Muni Bond Yields.

Buy bonds online *(continued)*

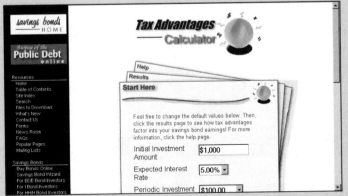

U.S. savings bonds are a popular way of saving. Although yields can be modest, the tax advantages can make them more attractive than some investments.

Municipal bonds

These state and local bonds are often referred to as *munis* (derived from municipalities). When the mayor of Moontown doesn't want to hike taxes to pay for the new elementary school, she might ask the town council to approve a bond package. The town borrows money from the public to pay for the schools, and repays it slowly, with interest. Typically, large financial institutions loan the town the money, and the underwriters parcel out the loans.

Munis mature anywhere from a year to 35 or 40 years down the road and cost about $25,000 apiece. From 1993 to 1998, those with the lengthier maturities yielded about 5 percent, a shade less than what Treasuries and corporate bonds paid.

But this return can be deceiving, for the interest on municipal bonds is exempt from federal taxes. And if the bonds are issued by the state or municipality in which you live, they are also exempt from state taxes (except in a handful of states, which tax their muni bonds). The result is interest that's triple tax-free!

On paper, yields on municipal bonds are less than those of taxable bonds of equal maturity and quality. But because of the tax implications, they might end up netting you more. You have to consider what insiders refer to as the *TEY*, or *Taxable Equivalent Yield*. Say your municipal bond yields 5 percent, and you're in the 39.6 percent tax bracket. To figure out your after-tax yield, divide the yield (in this case, 5 percent, or 0.05) by 1.0 minus your tax rate (0.396). This is 0.05/(1.0-0.396) or 0.05/0.604, which equals 0.0827, or 8.27 percent. So a municipal bond yielding 5 percent nets you the same as a taxable investment yielding 8.27 percent.

Munis are the bonds of choice for investors in high tax brackets. Because they are tax-free, there is no point putting munis in your IRA or 401(k); they should be in the taxable portion of your portfolio. If you sell them for more than your purchase price, though, you will still have to pay capital-gains taxes.

Check out The Street.com, at (Keyword: **TSC**), to explore the advantages of municipal bonds. Click Full TSC Site, and then click Investing Basics. Scroll down and click Buying Bonds: A Primer, then select A Special Focus on Muni Bonds (see Figure 7-5).

Find It Online

How do your muni bond yields stack up to the yields of other bonds? If you don't want to do the figuring, let AOL handle the math at Keyword: **Calculator**. Under Bond Calculators, scroll down to Which Bond is Better. This interactive tool allows you to compare two bonds side by side to see which is the better investment option. For example, you might enter a low-yield municipal bond and contrast it with a high-flying corporate bond to see which yields more over the long term.

Plug in the information for the two bonds and then click Results to see how they compare. If you don't know what to enter for any underlined term, click the term and a box will pop up with an explanation. The results show what to expect before and after taxes if you hold your bond to maturity, or if you sell early. Seeing the two choices together can help steer your investment decision.

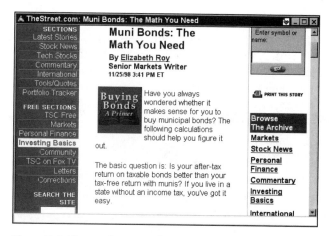

Figure 7-5. The tax advantages of investing in municipal bonds often outweigh the seemingly inferior yields.

There are three types of municipal bonds:

▶ *General obligation bonds*, or GOs, which are backed by the entity that issues the bond (the town, state, or county, for example).

▶ *Revenue bonds*, which are backed not by the government but by revenues generated by specific institutions, projects or agencies. (For example, a coliseum or stadium authority might use its revenues to repay the bond that generated the funds to build it).

▶ *Industrial development bonds* (IDBs), which are used to finance facilities like airports and piers that will be leased out. The idea is to use low financing to lure developers into a geographical area. Once the buildings are leased, the lease money repays the bonds that financed construction. Beware of the tax implications, however. Investors in some municipal bond funds that invest in "private" activities like building airports have to pay the alternative minimum tax on their interest.

Muni risks

"Municipals are also considered (with Treasuries) high quality because they are backed by the full faith and credit of a state," says Standard & Poor's Norton. But they're not a given, he cautions. Though it's rare, municipalities can fall on hard times and go bankrupt, too. There's one other risk: There might not always be a buyer if you need to unload your munis fast.

To explore the reliability of munis, go to Keyword: **Edelman** and click The Truth About Money Online. You must then choose The Truth About Money Online from the scroll down menu. Select Part 3, Fixed Income Investing, and then go to Chapter 9 (see Figure 7-6).

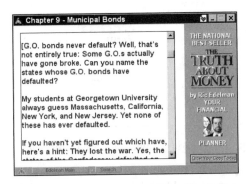

Figure 7-6. A comforting aspect of muni bonds: their security, says financial planner Ric Edelman in "The Truth About Money."

Corporate bonds

When a company needs money to grow — maybe to take over Widgets 'R' Us, or to buy a business that augments its current operations, or to finance a new division — it looks to the public for a great big loan. The interest it repays is a bit higher than interest on government bonds, because corporations know that they are considered riskier investments than the government, and they want to attract lenders. Realistically, though, the rate of default by large, well-established corporations is extremely slim.

Investing in a corporation's bonds is less risky than investing in its stocks for a couple of reasons:

 **Find It Online**

Want to know which companies are issuing bonds this week? Go to Keyword: **Personal Wealth**, click the Site Map and, under Bonds, select Credit Week focus.

▶ When a bond is floated, the interest rate and the repayment schedule are set and not subject to market fluctuations.

▶ A bond is a legal obligation by the company. The amount of the return is not subject to the whims of the company's board of directors, as stock dividends are.

▶ If the company goes belly up, bondholders are first in line to be paid as creditors. If you hold *secured bonds*, which are backed by a specific asset of the issuer — equipment, for example — you get paid first. If you hold *unsecured bonds*, which are backed by the good faith of the company and get a hair more interest, you're second in line. Both types of bondholders get back at least some of their investments before common stockholders ever get a penny.

Although corporate bonds yield higher interest than government bonds, this interest — paid twice a year — is subject to local, state and federal taxes.

Foreign bonds

Foreign bonds are loans to corporations and governments outside of the United States. As bonds go, these are pretty risky (though they're less risky than foreign stocks) because they can be affected by factors other than the borrower's ability to repay the debt. Foreign bonds are sensitive to political, economic, and currency fluctuations. You can track these fluctuations by going to Keyword: **WorldlyInvestor** and clicking

7

The Fix on Bonds

Quotes and Rankings. Click Global Indices to eyeball the international financial indices (see Figure 7-7). They can offer an interesting entrée into foreign markets, which is appealing in terms of portfolio diversification.

Note

Buying and selling foreign bonds can be extremely confusing and difficult to execute for individuals. Individuals shouldn't even attempt it. "The reason is that you'll have to deal with a foreign broker and use research from a foreign agency," Norton says. Then you'll have to deal with currency translations and fluctuations. Even a far greater risk, in Norton's opinion, is the liquidity risk, "the risk that there is not an actively traded market for these markets, either buying or selling." You might end up with a bunch of foreign bonds that no one wants when you need to get rid of them.

"If you're interested in foreign bonds, do it via international bond funds," Norton recommends. "Let the portfolio manager take care of the complexities of international fixed-income purchases." You get to deal in dollars, and your risk is dispersed, as the fund spreads out the risk over many holdings.

Figure 7-7. As demonstrated by the Hong Kong financial index, investing in foreign economies can be extremely volatile, making foreign bond funds a risky venture.

Zero-coupon bonds

Zeros offer no annual yield. Instead, these bonds — which can be munis, corporates, or government — are sold for a fraction of their par value. When the bonds come due, you get back your principal plus interest, which equals the face value of the bonds. You can learn more about zero-coupon bonds by going to Keyword: **Sage Models** and clicking on Investing in Bonds. Click on Fixed Income Articles, and scroll down to "Zero-Coupon Bonds, By Sage Basics," as shown in Figure 7-8.

Because they pay no coupon (you get your interest in the form of a discount from the purchase price), you have no interest to reinvest. You still have to pay taxes on this phantom interest, however. In the meantime, the bond "reinvests" the interest for you at the interest rate the bond carries to arrive at the par value. Zero-coupon bonds aren't for people looking for income. Instead, they are an easy way to lock in a goal a number of years down the road.

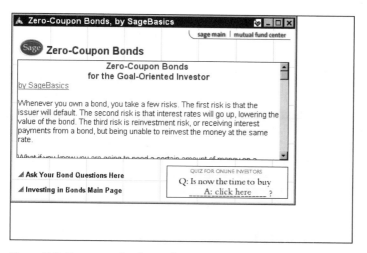

Figure 7-8. Zero-coupon bonds provide a secure investment for long-term goals.

Junk bonds

The type of corporate bond many bond ratings agencies (more about them in a minute) deem unworthy of investment is the high-yield bond. These carry an extremely high potential for default. High-yield bonds (also called junk bonds, because when they crash they're worthless) often finance company takeovers by other companies with little in the bank to begin with. Junk bonds seemed to be all the rage in the 1980s, when companies used megaloans to buy each other out. Although the news about them may have simmered down, their interest is boiling. More than $100 billion is currently invested in high-yield bond funds.

When issuers of junk bonds promise to repay the loan, they offer little more than their name and high hopes. They agree to high interest payments in return for your belief (and your cash) in their sometimes speculative ventures. Even if the interest payments materialize initially, it is not uncommon for the bond issuer to later default, with you kissing your capital good-bye.

Ratings

All bonds are rated, or graded, by a handful of investing houses such as Moody's and Standard & Poor's. They assess the bond's risk potential, financial stability and ability to repay you, and

Find It Online

For current international bond yields, go to Keyword: **Bonds** and then click International. Chart the international movers on the left and follow their news on the right.

Note

"The lower the rating and the higher the yield, the less likely the company is to continue to make timely interest and principal payments," Norton says. He recommends that investors avoid buying individual high-yield bonds, and instead rely on mutual funds for their high-yield fantasies. Individual junk bonds have "a massive liquidity problem," he says. "It's easier to let fund managers handle these. As institutional investors, they have far greater economies of scale when dealing with the market than individual investors." In a mutual fund, if the junk-bond issuer defaults, the remaining viable companies in the fund cushion the blow.

7

The Fix on Bonds

report this in the bond's prospectus. They then monitor the issuer's health over the life of the bond.

You can find information on S&P's Ratings Services at Keyword: **http://www.standardandpoors.com/ratings**. (See figure 7-9) To find out a bond's rating online, scroll down to Ratings inquiries and click Send a Request By E-mail. You may request up to four ratings inquiries per e-mail per day. Fill out your vitals first, then provide the vitals for the rating you are requesting: the CUSIP number (a nine-digit number assigned to every security), issue name, series, and maturity date. After you enter the information, hit Submit. S&P will provide an answer within two business days.

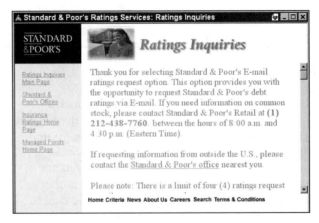

Figure 7-9. Standard & Poor's and Moody's are among the top financial institutions providing bond ratings.

Typically, bonds are rated from *secure*, the highest rating, to *below investment grade*, or *speculative*, the lowest. Different rating agencies use different number or letter grades, as well as different rating systems. Typically, the higher the grade, the safer the investing house believes the bond to be. ("AAA" is the highest rating given by companies S&P, Fitch IBCA, and Duff & Phelps Credit Rating Co. "Aaa" is Moody's highest rating.) Treasuries always get a high grade, and all other types of bonds vary depending on the viability of the debtor. BBB ratings and above are bonds of investment grade. Anything rated BB or below is considered speculative. To really understand what a grade means, you need to refer to the individual rating agency's guidelines.

Bond Prices

Many investors buy a bond, put it in the safe deposit box, and don't think about it for ten years, or whatever the time until maturity. But bonds are negotiable, which means you can buy and sell them at any time, so long as there is a party on the other end who wants them. When you re-sell your bond you probably won't get what you paid for it. You could get more — or less.

You might want to resell your bonds, or buy someone else's bonds secondhand, for a couple of reasons:

- ▶ Maybe you suddenly need money, and the only place you can get it is from the bond you're holding.

- ▶ Maybe your bond pays higher interest than the market's going rate. You decide to sell the bond for more than you paid for it to pick up some capital gains.

- ▶ Maybe you want to buy a bond that was issued a few years before because it has positive tax implications for you. For example, it was issued in your state and its interest is tax-free. The only way you can get it is to buy it secondhand from somebody else who bought it from the issuer.

The price you pay to buy or sell depends on a host of variables, with interest rates foremost among them. When interest rates rise, the value of existing bonds falls. Say interest rates rise and you suddenly find yourself desperately needing that principal you loaned. So you have to sell your bond. But nobody will want your bond that pays maybe 5 percent, when they can buy a newly issued bond with the same par value that pays 5½ percent interest, a rate that reflects the current market. So you have to reduce your sales price to provide for your buyer the same return as a newly issued bond. This is called *selling at a discount*.

To learn more about the difference interest rates make on bond yields and coupon rates, go to Keyword: **Investment Basics** and click Step 5: Bonds and Other Investments. Scroll down to Why Bond Yields Can Differ from Coupon Rates to find the article in Figure 7-10.

Find It Online

What is a reasonable price to pay for a bond you're eyeing? Find out at Keyword: **SageSchool**. Scroll down to The Income Investor, then Calculators for Income Investors, and then click What Price Should I Pay? Finally, begin plugging the amounts of your variables into the calculator.

Find It Online

For the latest news and discussion on how interest rates are affecting the market, go to Keyword: **Interest Rates**. For a look at current rates, go to Keyword: **MNC**, click Bonds & Money, click U.S. Treasury Yields, then, under Rates and Bonds, select Key Rates.

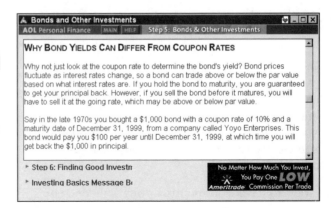

Figure 7-10. When you purchase a bond, the outcome seems like a sure thing, but changing interest rates can make selling your bonds a time-sensitive issue.

The longer a bond's maturity and the lower the coupon, the farther the price will drop as interest rates rise, because the ramifications are longer. So long-term bonds stand the greatest risk. That's why they pay higher rewards to begin with. The risk that you will have to lower the bond's price to attract buyers when you want to sell doesn't affect you if you hold your bonds to maturity.

Now, when interest rates fall, your bonds become more attractive, because their annual interest exceeds what the market is currently paying for newly issued bonds. This time, if you want to sell the bonds, you can raise your price because you will be offering investors higher annual interest than they could earn on newly issued bonds. This is called *selling at a premium*.

Here again, if you hold your bond to maturity, the falling rates do not affect your return. Depending on the spread between current interest rates and the interest your bond pays, you just might want to sell to take advantage of your gains — in spite of your pledge to hang onto the bonds. If interest rates fall just one percent, your 25-year zero coupon bond, for example, would earn more than 20 percent over newly issued bonds by the time it matures.

Changes in interest rates can significantly affect your whole bond portfolio, particularly when you are locked into long maturities. The risk that interest rates will change and, as a result, your bond's price would have to change is called *interest-rate risk*. If you hold a bond to its maturity, these price fluctuations don't affect you much. You still get the same principal back, as well as the interest you were promised. But many people, in spite of their intentions, find themselves having to sell bonds for one reason or another.

Buying and Trading Bonds

So you're ready to buy a bond. This is a bit trickier than buying a stock or mutual fund. You don't have to buy a bond right from the issuer. In fact, most investors can't even get in on the issuer's direct offering. Bond underwriters bid against each other to see who gets to buy all the bonds from the issuing agency. The high bidder then sells its inventory through brokers.

You buy it through your broker or underwriter in the secondary market. (Call or e-mail your broker to find out if she trades bonds.) If you buy a bond from your brokerage's inventory, you don't pay a commission, but you pay a built-in markup. If your broker has to go out into the market to get your bond, you might have to pay transaction costs and commissions as well. Commissions and markups vary according to the type of bond you're buying. And, for reasons that remain a mystery, unless you insist on knowing, no one will tell you what that markup is.

You can find out how brokers compare when it comes to trading bonds. To hold up the bond-trading services of top online brokerages, as shown in Figure 7-11, go to Keyword: **TSC**, then click Full TSC Site. Click Basics, TSC's Guide to Bonds Online, and then How the Biggest Online Brokers Stack Up. When finished, click the back button. If you want to gauge the markups, click All Aboard the Bond Express database for bond dealers' inventories and the prices they're charging.

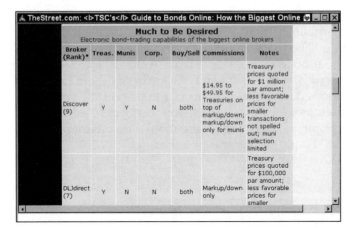

Figure 7-11. Investors must go through a brokerage for most bond transactions. As brokerage fees and commissions are usually built into the prices of bonds, make sure to ask questions about what's included.

Selling your bonds can be a bit tricky, too. Bonds are not as easily traded as stocks, plus you have to use a broker and her commission is completely dependent upon the bond's liquidity. Outside of Treasury securities, trying to sell anything worth less than $20,000 takes work, and brokerages will charge you for their effort. Even if a buyer can be found, he might not be willing to pay your price. Don't agree to sell your bond until you know how it stands to fare on the market. You can buy Treasuries from a broker for an extra cost, or you can buy directly from your uncle in the business — at no extra cost.

Treasury direct

The Bureau of the Public Debt's Treasury Direct program enables investors to purchase Treasury notes, bills and bonds directly from Uncle Sam, without a broker (see Figure 7-12). You can apply by phone (at 202-874-4000), or from Keyword: **http://www.treasurydirect.gov**. You tell the bureau how many securities you want to buy and their maturities, and then you make a *tender*, or a bid. Individual investors typically offer a *noncompetitive bid*, which means they will pay the market price determined at the most recent Treasury auction. Commercial investors usually offer a competitive bid, which must fall within the price range determined at the auction in order to be accepted.

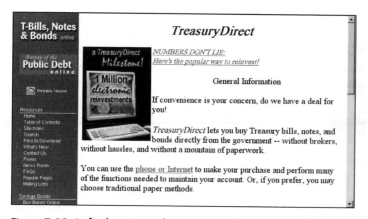

Figure 7-12. By far the easiest and most economical way to invest in Treasuries is online.

To get started, go to Keyword: **http://www.treasurydirect .gov** and then click FAQs under Resources. This introductory list of questions explains the features of the Web site and Treasury technicalities. To apply, click Forms under Resources and then Securities Forms — TreasuryDirect. You can get the forms by snail mail or you can download them. Just click the ones you need. If you want auction information, click Auction Information under T-Bills, Notes and Bonds.

With Treasury Direct, you can directly deposit payments and reinvest your interest into your Treasury Direct account. When your interest is paid or your note matures, the government pays you back electronically, directly into your account. If you want to sell your Treasuries, you can use the bureau's Sell Direct program. The government will act as your broker, deducting a $34 transaction fee from your account.

Individual bonds versus bond-based mutual funds

Time for the D-word again. To keep the bond section of your portfolio stable, you must — you guessed it — diversify. The best strategy is to spread your bond portfolio among Treasuries, municipals and corporate bonds.

In your attempt to diversify, you might be tempted to bypass individual bonds altogether and go right to bond-based mutual funds, but these aren't always the best option. In fact, depending on the type of bonds held, these can be even *more* volatile

Get the full monte on mutual funds in Chapter 8.

than individual bonds. (See, for example, *The Wall Street Journal's* SmartMoney discussion on bonds versus bond funds [see Figure 7-13]. Go to Keyword: **http://www. smartmoney.com**, click Bonds, scroll all the way down to Resources, and then click Bonds vs. Bond Funds.)

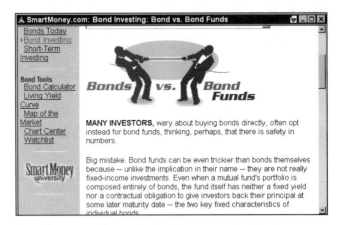

Figure 7-13. Depending on the bond, investing in bond funds can sometimes be riskier than investing in individual bonds.

Unlike bonds, bond funds do not promise a fixed income and they — by no means — are under any obligation to return your principal. An individual bond's risk decreases the longer you hold it. But a bond fund manager trades bonds constantly, making his fund respond more like equities than bonds.

Still, unless you have wads of money to buy lots of individual bonds and hold them to maturity, bond funds might be the way to go for certain types of bonds. The funds do have advantages: they offer diversification not available through individual bonds, so they spread out your risk; they are more liquid than individual bonds; and they pay dividends monthly, versus twice a year for individual bonds.

Whether you should opt for a bond or a bond fund really depends on a couple of things: how much you have to invest, your tax status, and the kinds of bonds you're interested in. For a convenient comparison, go to Keyword: **Vanguard.** Click the Education, Planning & Advice tab at the top, and then click Forms & Brochures. Scroll down and click Plain Talk Library. Again, scroll down, click Plain Talk: Bond Fund

Investing, and then click the Read Online link. Figure 1 in this article provides a quick comparison of bonds and bond funds (see Figure 7-14).

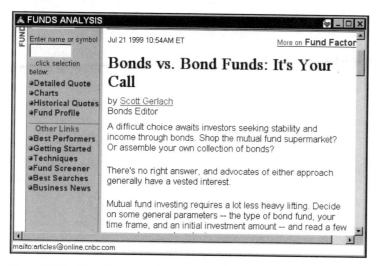

Figure 7-14. Although many analysts recommend purchasing individual bonds, bond mutual funds can offer some advantages, including professional management.

If you have less than $100,000 and you want tax-free income, for example, you're probably better off with a municipal bond fund. Good muni funds let you in for about a tenth of the $25,000 you need for an individual muni.

The same holds for corporate and mortgage-backed bonds. If you're set on investing in these, you're better off going with bond funds. And if it's high-yield, junk bonds you're interested in, junk-bond funds are by far the safer choice over individual junk bonds. If one bond defaults, its plunge in the fund is cushioned by the other holdings.

If you want Treasuries, though, stick with buying them commission-free from Treasury Direct. There's no point in paying a broker $50 or more for something you can get right from your Uncle at cost. The only time buying from Treasury Direct could be a problem is if you're looking to pick up a long bond quickly, as sometimes only a handful of long bond auctions occur per year.

Note

Because Treasuries are safe, clear-cut, and easy to buy, it seems foolish to invest in expense-laden government bond mutual funds that concentrate on Treasuries. Because there is no real risk of them defaulting, the only thing the mutual fund manager can do to attempt to outperform them is to try to time the market and guess the direction of interest rates. Short of a crystal ball, the manager can't do that any better than you can. Why pay if you don't have to?

7

The Fix on Bonds

Laddering

One easy way to limit your risk and guarantee your income is to spread out the bonds' maturities. Many investors accomplish this by *laddering*.

Start by buying equal amounts of Treasuries with one-, three-, five-, seven- and nine-year maturities. This gives your portfolio an average maturity of five years (1+3+5+7+9=25/5=5). When your first batch comes due in a year, buy the same dollar amount of new ten-year notes. Now your portfolio has an average maturity of six years. A year later your two-year notes will mature. Sell these and buy more 10-year notes. If you continue to buy ten-year notes each time a batch matures, your portfolio will always maintain an average maturity of five to six years.

If rates rise shortly after you buy your bonds there's no reason to sweat. As soon as the next batch comes due, you can buy some new bonds and lock in the new rates. If the rates drop, you can take solace knowing you have locked in higher rates for the next few years.

Keyword: **http://www.smartmoney.com** offers online advice on laddering (see the Figure); click the Planning tab, then click Retirement in the Table of Contents on the left. Scroll down to Laddering Your Bonds under How Should I Invest my Savings?

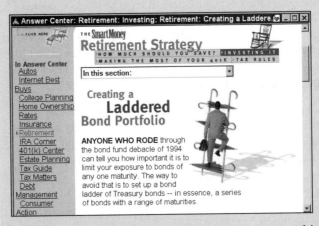

By staggering the maturity dates of your bonds, you protect your portfolio from being walloped by a sudden change in interest rates.

Be aware that although bonds represent a relatively safe component of your portfolio, you shouldn't rely on them as your sole investment vehicle. Bonds offer no potential for growth, and they fall prey to high inflation rates. If you're locked into a long maturity and inflation is creeping up, the real value of that principal you loaned Uncle Sam or Gigantic Monopoly Inc. will fall fast, shattering your stability.

Summary

There now, bonds aren't so daunting after all. Now you can talk BondSpeak, you understand the risks of these so-called stable investments and you know a Treasury strip from a zero-coupon bond.

You've learned why bond prices change in the aftermarket and how to buy and sell your bonds.

Now that you know all about stocks and bonds, it's time to look at the vehicles that carry them both: mutual funds, coming up in the following chapter.

7

The Fix on Bonds

A Quick Look

▶ **Sage Advice** **page 181**

Looking for a great launching point to start your mutual fund explorations? Start at Keyword: **Sage**. The all-things-mutual-funds site offers information about almost every aspect of investing in mutual funds. You can get lists of the top performing funds, understand how economic trends will impact your funds, find a sound investment strategy to fatten up your retirement portfolio and learn much more. Check for current articles, strategies, tips, and guest speakers. Or go to Keyword: **Sage School** for a thorough education in the ABCs of mutual funds.

▶ **Fund Fact-Finding** **page 187**

There's no need to guess how a fund compares to its peers or to take your neighbor's word for it when mountains of information can show you how the fund stacks up. Go to Keyword: **Morningstar**, enter the mutual fund's symbol or name, and click Search. Select AOL Investment Snapshot for a quick look at the fund, or click Mutual Fund Reports for in-depth financials, including past performance, risk and volatility, holdings, management, returns, and more.

▶ **Funds, Funds, Everywhere** **page 203**

With more than 10,000 mutual funds out there, picking a winner might seem dizzying. Never fear — fund-screening tools can set the whole matter straight. The tools take any investor, from novice to skilled, through a series of easy-to-answer questions and variables to find funds that match a portfolio's needs. Go to Keyword: **Mutual Funds** to access the AOL Mutual Fund Center, and click Fund Screening. Then pick your route — easy or customized — to start your search.

Chapter 8
Mutual Funds

By now you know you have to tailor your investments to fit your goals. To be safe and smart, you need to invest in a cross-section of equities to take advantage of growing markets. And you need to rely on the stalwarts during volatile market swings.

In other words, you have to own pieces of companies large and small, national and international. And you need a safe haven during the inevitable times these companies' stocks tumble. So you have to own bonds, too. And real estate. And . . .

Is there no end to this list? Seems like you just pulled yourself out of debt a couple of chapters ago? Where will you come up with all the money for all these investments?

Indeed, you might need a mountain of money to purchase all these vehicles separately. You would certainly need an enormous amount of time to research them all. But you don't have to own all the vehicles outright to make sure they're part of your fleet. You simply need a part of them. You can accomplish this very easily and relatively inexpensively, with mutual funds.

A mutual fund is like a gigantic garage that holds many different vehicles. In this case, the vehicles include stocks, bonds, real estate, cash, gold, commodities, mortgages, options, and others. A mutual fund manager buys anywhere from a dozen to more than 3,000 of these vehicles and combines them into one fund, and that fund pursues a certain objective — maybe to generate growth or to yield handsome dividends. The manager pays for the assets with money you and fellow investors pool, giving you all pieces of the assets in just one fund.

To review ways to pull yourself out of debt, see Chapter 3.

For more information on 401(k)s, including which investments to choose for them, see the retirement section of Chapter 12.

Advantages of Mutual Funds

Some 77 million Americans invest in mutual funds — more than 10,500 funds, worth more than $5 trillion — in fact. Some 50 years ago, the number of funds nationwide totaled less than 100.

Triggered by the upsurge of 401(k)s (the tax-deferred retirement plans to which many employees and employers contribute), investors are socking money into mutual funds at record levels — more than $700 billion in 1998 alone. Why? You can participate in and profit from many different markets without spending the time or mastering the expertise needed to single out winners and losers.

And you don't need a bundle of money to start. Many mutual funds let you buy in with less than $100, a pittance compared to the thousands of dollars many brokerages require of you in order to open an account. If you have more to stash in the nest, mutual funds welcome $25,000 as easily as they do $25.

8

Mutual Funds

Cross-Reference

To learn how to select exactly what's right for your portfolio, see Chapter 11.

Unlocking the door

If you do your homework, you can find solid mutual funds with reasonable fees and low monthly minimum deposits. Start at Keyword: **Mutual Funds** (see the Figure below). The site is a springboard to AOL's best mutual funds information and tools. Start with the Features section, which offers different articles each day to help you master mutual funds. Mutual Fund basics, for example, might offer ways to minimize taxes, plan for retirement, or pick various funds. Archives brings up recent features and past articles by subject.

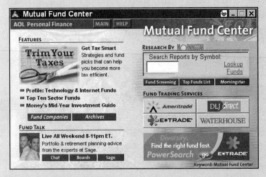

AOL's Mutual Fund Center is a springboard for mutual funds information online, including news, advice, research, and commentary.

Another reason mutual funds are so popular is that without towers of money, you'd be hard pressed to attain the diversification mutual funds can offer. One fund can hold thousands of assets. To put together a balanced portfolio, you can rely on one simple balanced fund to do the work for you, or you can invest in a dozen or more funds that nail the targets you want to hit.

Mutual funds and risk

Mutual funds inherently reduce the risks you face with individual securities because funds spread that risk among hundreds or thousands of securities. In a mutual fund, if one stock flops, there's barely a ripple in the pond. But if you own the stock that flops, and if it's among your primary holdings, the ripple could become a tidal wave, with you clinging for life.

Still, you have to be particular when you select a mutual fund. You can't buy one just because you found it in a list of top performers that you came across in a magazine at the dentist's office. Similarly, you have to close your eyes to fancy TV commercials promising you a retirement of basking in the sun as your grandchildren adore you from the pier. No such guarantees exist. Even with mutual funds, there are risks. When a whole sector plunges and it's one reflected in your fund, or when the entire market gasps for air, mutual funds feel the pain.

When you buy a mutual fund, you don't have to scrutinize each company stock, compare bond yields, and know the latest yen-to-dollar exchange in order to invest successfully. Fund managers do the work for you. The fund manager acts as your very own money administrator, examining industry reports, listening to analysts, studying the market, assessing risk. He or she then takes your money and buys and sells assets with the fund's stated objectives in mind.

Chat with Experts

Sage's site is a hub in AOL's mutual funds world. Look to Daily Features for articles about trends in the financial world and how they affect your mutual fund portfolio. Listen in on chats and question and answer sessions with financial experts and fund gurus. Under Departments, click Live Events to see the daily schedule of guest speakers and topics. You can exchange information with other AOL members in the chat rooms, or, if you are new to the chat room scene, you can ease into the discussions in the chat room for beginners. If you've missed a chat, you can turn to the transcript archive at Sage Voices, a department that allows you to search for past guest speakers and read their pearls of wisdom, as in the Figure below.

Other sections include the message boards, where you can solicit opinions or offer your own, and the portfolio planning department and retirement center, both stocked with advice for using mutual funds to get the most out of your portfolio.

Continued

8

Mutual Funds

Note

"Mutual funds are easy to use," says Stephen Cohn, co-founder of the mutual-fund site Sage (Keyword: **Sage**), an AOL partner. "They're attractive for any type of investor. You put money into a mutual fund and have it professionally managed for you. You don't have to make those difficult investment decisions. Day-to-day decisions are left up to the manager."

Chat with Experts *(continued)*

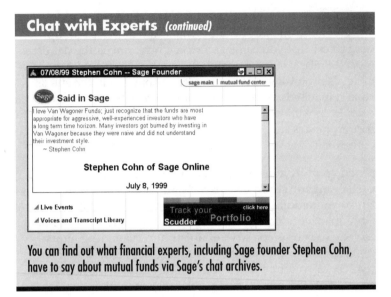

You can find out what financial experts, including Sage founder Stephen Cohn, have to say about mutual funds via Sage's chat archives.

If the fund's holdings perform well and the manager reacts wisely, the fund's assets grow and your shares are worth more. In addition, you might get rewarded with interest, dividends, or capital gains. If the manager responds poorly or the assets are in a tailspin, your shares can be worth less. Still, you rarely suffer to the extent you would if one company in which you owned stocks or bonds were to take a nosedive.

Suppose your selection was a wise one and your mutual fund shares rise, or you get a big check from the fund's capital gains. Try not to touch these returns, if possible. Instead, roll them right back into the fund. If you need your mutual fund money fast, you can cash in with the mutual fund family at any time. Investors in mutual funds are not at the mercy of a buyer, as mutual funds are liquid. This is a big advantage over stocks that might be hard to unload for a decent price when popularity or performance start to plummet.

Use funds to diversify

Just as you diversify individual holdings in your portfolio, you need to do the same with mutual funds. The reason to diversify is to take advantage of — and protect yourself from — fluctuations in the market. If equities are getting walloped, maybe bonds are holding strong. Blue chips could be mediocre, while micro-caps are multiplying. U.S. companies might be in the doldrums, while emerging markets are sprouting like mold on week-old strawberries.

How can you make the most of the diversification offered by mutual funds? How many, and which ones, should you own? There is no standard formula. What is right for some investors might not necessarily be right for you. Keep in mind your ideal portfolio, goals, risk tolerance, timeframe, and asset allocation, then pick those funds that zero in on your needs. You have to select those mutual funds whose assets match your investment blueprint so that you don't carry too much of one fund type, and not enough of another.

The goal is to end up with a diversified portfolio of funds representing stocks and bonds from home and abroad, whose risks and returns meet your goals. Whether you focus on growth, income or value, or opt for micro-cap or blue chips depends on your goals. Same holds for your international exposure. You can look to emerging markets if you're aggressive, developed countries if less so. Same goes for bond funds. You can pick up a high-yield fund if you're aggressive and a municipal-bond fund to protect you from taxes. This is simplifying, of course. There are thousands of funds from which to choose. The key is in selecting those that target your goals, without duplicating your efforts by tallying up more and more funds.

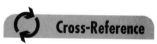

Cross-Reference

For a refresher on determining your investment goals, see Chapter 4.

Find It Online

To get start looking, turn to Keyword: **Quicken**, and click Quicken.com. Under Top Features, click Pick Top Funds to go to the Mutual Fund Finder, as in Figure 8-1. From here, you can search for top performing funds, select funds based on your own criteria, or let the Fund Finder show you some of the most popular screening methods.

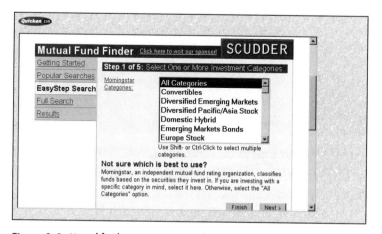

Figure 8-1. Mutual funds come in so many shapes and sizes that trying to pick one can be overwhelming. Fund finders, such as this one on Quicken.com, can help narrow your search.

8

Mutual Funds

Avoid the dogs

All mutual funds are not alike. Even among those with similar types of assets, many outshine their peers. Others can't seem to find luster even when there's incredible growth and profit-making all around them. With literally thousands of funds in existence you need to be able to single out the truly stellar performers from the mediocre.

Advertisements, Neighbor Niles, financial advisors — all boast about some fund's remarkable earnings. But no one seems to talk about the dogs. Yet many do exist, and frankly, it's difficult to imagine why these funds are even in business, when so many tools exist to help investors find solid funds that match their needs.

Sadly, many people act on sales pitches rather than doing their homework. And that's unfortunate, as unearthing a solid mutual fund takes a lot less work than mining for other investment gems. One excavation tool that helps ease the load is SmartMoney.com's Fund Analyzer, shown in Figure 8-2.

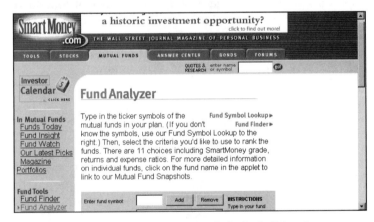

Figure 8-2. No need to rely on a sales pitch to find a fund. All the information you need to analyze any mutual fund's performance is available online.

SmartMoney.com's analyzer will show you several funds at one time, side by side, so you can see how that fund Neighbor Niles is always bragging about really measures up to its peers. Go to **http://www.smartmoney.com**, and click the Mutual Funds tab. Click Fund Analyzer, under Fund Tools on the left. If you know the symbol of the Mutual Fund you'd like to research, type it in. Otherwise, click Fund Symbol Lookup to track down the symbol by the fund's name.

Once you've entered the symbol you have several viewing choices. The drop-down box underneath the symbol defaults to *SmartMoney Grade*, an overall letter grade from A to F, based on factors such as performance, stability, and returns. You can also view such information as Risk/Volatility; 1-, 3-, or 5-year returns and sales charges. Click the drop-down arrow and select the rating you'd like to see. The chart will update automatically.

After you review a fund, it is helpful to include other funds you are considering to see how they rate side by side. Again, enter the new fund's symbol, and click Add. The chart will automatically adjust to show where in the ratings the new fund falls. For example, if you list several funds and click Smart Money Grade, you will see what grade each fund receives, from glowing A+ to a hands-off D-.

During your scouting, if you'd like to review all the information about a particular fund, double-click the fund's name in the chart, and a detailed Fund Snapshot will appear, showing everything from the fund's philosophy to detailed financials and major holdings.

The important thing is to compare a fund to others like it, and check their *total return*, which is how much the fund returned, minus fees and expenses, for the period indicated. This is the ultimate measure of how well they perform. If you hold up a list of *all* funds by return, and go for the highest payer, you risk volatile consequences. These are often the ones that typically have moonshot returns and double-digit losses the next. Instead, look for quality, consistently. The key to that consistency is a good manager.

Tip

Want to know what fund managers in the trenches are thinking? Managers from hundreds of funds chat with AOL members live each day. Get the schedule, and transcripts of past conversations, at Keyword: **Mutual Funds**, then select Chat.

Types of Funds

There's no shortage of types of funds to choose from. In fact, there are dozens of fund classifications. Often, their names reflect either the types of securities held in the fund, or the fund's goals. About half of all mutual funds today are stock-oriented, and more than half of those are in retirement accounts.

About a third of all funds are bond funds. The rest are either money-market funds or a combination of all three.

For a complete list of fund classifications go to Keyword: **Morningstar**, then select Fund Screening, then Fund Definitions, for 44 classifications, as in Figure 8-3.

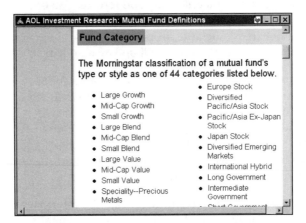

Figure 8-3. There's a mutual fund to fit every need. Morningstar lists all possible categories.

Bond funds

Also known as fixed-income funds, bond funds try to generate a reliable stream of income for investors. They're popular with the retired set, who rely on their nest egg to supply them with income to pay the bills. The majority of bond funds are low risk because of the vehicles — bonds — in which they invest. If a bond fund should happen to include a bond that's defaulted on, the losses are cushioned by the reliability of the other bonds. The result is a subtle reduction in the fund's yield, as opposed to the drastic consequences an investor suffers if one bond they hold is defaulted on.

To peek into the window of a bond fund's risks, look up its *average maturity* in the prospectus or in a fund report. Funds with longer maturities typically return more but suffer stronger consequences when interest rates rise. The longer the fund's average maturity, the more interest rates will affect it.

Developing the snapshot

The details in Morningstar's fund reports help you discover a fund's underpinnings. Go to Keyword: **Morningstar** then plug in the fund's symbol. If you don't know the symbol, click Name and type in the fund's name. Even if you only know part of the name, or the Fund's parent company, a list will pop up and allow you to choose the correct fund.

Once you type in the fund's symbol, you can either click Mutual Fund Reports or select the AOL Investment Snapshot.

Clicking the AOL Investment Snapshot gives you a quick, easy look at the fund: its current net asset value, the NAV from the previous day, and the high and low prices over the past 52 weeks. If the fund has been in the news recently, stories about it will be listed below the snapshot, under news. Click the headline to read the text.

Mutual Fund Reports tell you how much the fund costs to operate, give you insight into the fund's management, and tell you the minimum you need to invest if you want in (see the Figure below). You can also learn the annual returns, holdings, ratings, and asset allocation. Click Nuts and Bolts for fees, expenses, management, and fund history and purchase information.

Definition

Net asset value, or NAV, is the price of a share of the fund. To determine this share price, divide the total net assets of the fund by the number of shares outstanding.

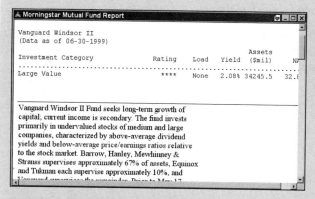

Access the current facts and figures for any mutual fund with Morningstar's Mutual Fund Reports.

Ratings and Risk shows you how volatile the stock is, and Total Returns shows you financial information including past annual returns and trailing returns.

8

Mutual Funds

See Chapter 7 for the ins and outs of bonds as income instruments.

Don't keep municipal bond funds in your 401(k) if you don't have to, as you waste the tax benefits. Keep your equity-oriented holdings there instead.

There are about half a dozen types of bond-based mutual funds, named for the types of bonds the fund invests in. For example, *government security funds* invest in vehicles backed by the U.S. government. These include Treasury bills, bonds, and notes and carry low risks. While it's easy to set up these funds, and you collect your checks more frequently than you would by investing in Treasuries, the majority of government security funds fail to yield what Treasuries themselves yield. Average returns of a government bond fund: 1 year: 2.5 percent; 3 years: 5.95 percent; 5 years: 6.34 percent; 10 years: 7 percent.

Municipal bond funds

These invest in bonds issued by municipalities. While the yield on these funds is typically a bit lower than what federal or corporate bond funds yield, it is not subject to federal income tax. If you invest in a fund that offers only bonds issued by the state in which you live, or issued by a municipality in your state, the interest income generated by the fund is free from *federal*, *state*, and *local* taxes!

For this reason, municipal bond funds are popular with all types of investors who want a relatively low-risk method of generating tax-free income over the moderate to long-term. Average returns of a municipal bond fund: 1 year: 1.58 percent; 3 years: 5.53 percent; 5 years: 5.97 percent; 10 years: 6.64 percent.

Corporate bond funds

These invest in bonds issued by corporations. They yield a bit more than government bond funds because they carry a slightly higher risk. Even with this slightly higher risk, though, funds that invest in high-grade corporate bonds are extremely reliable. They're popular with investors who want to make sure bonds are represented in their portfolio. Average returns of a corporate bond fund: 1 year: 2.27 percent; 3 years: 6.22 percent; 5 years: 6.75 percent; 10 years: 7.41 percent.

World bond funds

These afford you international exposure with less of a risk than you would suffer if you bought individual international bonds or international equities. You still fall prey to international economic conditions, however. These types of funds are for moderate investors looking for bond safety as well as international exposure, without the risks of international equities. Average returns of a world bond fund: 1 year: -1.28 percent; 3 years: 4.58 percent; 5 years: 6.6 percent; 10 years: 10.69 percent.

Find It Online

Figure 8-4. Many international funds offer great potential, but carry high risk. Make sure to do your research before you select a foreign fund.

For help selecting a top international fund, try Keyword: **Sage**. Select Sage's Top Ten Fund Picks at the bottom of the screen and click Go. Different fund categories are featured weekly. To see global or international funds, scroll down and select the fund under Other Top Ten Information and click Go, as in Figure 8-4.

High-yield bond funds

High-yield bond funds fall under the corporate bonds umbrella, too, but their characteristics must not be confused with their risk-averse brethren. High-yield bond funds do not carry investment-grade bonds. Managers of these funds invest in precariously perched businesses desperate for cash. When purchased individually, high-yield bonds — also called junk bonds — are considered extremely speculative. Collectively, though, that risk is tempered a bit in a fund. The yield generated by junk bonds certainly makes these funds an appealing way to generate cash. But keep in mind they're really only for aggressive investors who aren't dependent upon the money in the fund. Average returns of a high-yield bond fund: 1 year: -1.79 percent; 3 years: 7.62 percent; 5 years: 8.54 percent; 10 years: 9.25 percent.

Caution

When you're looking into mutual funds, don't confuse the extremely risky *high-yield* bond funds with their risk-averse corporate cousins, *high-grade* bond funds.

Bond funds are typically classified by types of holdings and length of maturity, and include: long, short, and intermediate government funds; long, short, intermediate, and ultra-short-term corporate bond funds; high-yield; multisector; international; short-, intermediate-, and long-term national munis; and long-, short-, and intermediate-term single state munis.

Equity funds

Find It Online

You can get the top perform-ers by going to Keyword: **Mutuals Funds**, and clicking Top Funds List. Morningstar shows the top performers for the past five years, listed by Fund categories such as Large-Cap or Small-Cap funds, as in Figure 8-5.

Cross-Reference

See Chapter 6 to review the different kinds of stocks.

Stock funds are as diverse as the tens of thousands of companies whose stocks they hold. Some target their holdings according to market capitalization, others specialize in particular sectors. Some mimic the indexes of the market, others look for growth or value. Some offer a combination of both. Stock funds are a great way to invest in stocks when you don't have a lot of money or time. They're great even if you have plenty of both, but you'd rather spend that money and time on other things. You simply start your homework by picking types of funds whose objectives match yours, and go from there.

Figure 8-5. Sometimes it seems there are more stock funds than actual stocks. Morningstar corrals information about them all and provides lists of the top perform-ers in all categories.

Aggressive growth funds

These invest in stocks that fund managers believe have the potential to soar. Many aggressive growth funds concentrate on firms within sectors such as technology, bio-technology or healthcare. Others use options and futures to corral profits. Don't look to growth funds for income. Their promise is capi-tal appreciation and their managers typically snatch whatever gains the funds garner and reinvest them.

In a healthy economy and market, aggressive growth funds tend to be hot, sometimes out-returning the S&P 500. When the market turns cold, however, their returns tend to slide further than the market in general. It tends to take awhile for growth funds to recuperate. But when they do recover, investors tend to be rewarded handsomely. Aggressive growth funds are best suited to aggressive investors with long-term goals of capital appreciation. Average returns of an aggressive growth fund: 1 year: 18.46 percent; 3 years: 15.4 percent; 5 years: 20.15 percent; 10 years: 14.54 percent.

Growth funds

These carry stocks with quite a range. They can include everything from blue chips to recently snagged IPOs. Sometimes there are even some bonds and cash mixed in for stability. The goal of these funds is capital appreciation, and there's a fair amount of caution tossed to the wind to generate that growth.

Growth funds are an ideal allocation in the long-term portion of anyone's portfolio, particularly in your retirement funds. The percentage you maintain, though, depends on your risk tolerance and capital preservation needs. Average returns of a growth fund: 1 year: 16.99 percent; 3 years: 21.18 percent; 5 years: 22.02 percent; 10 years: 15.97 percent

You can read discussions such as the one in Figure 8-6 on blue chip growth stocks at Keyword: **Sage**, then select Sage's Top Ten Fund Picks and Go.

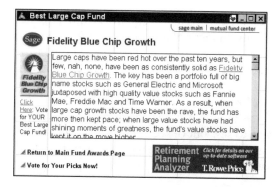

Figure 8-6. AOL members and experts contribute their recommendations on the best funds; more food for thought when you're searching for funds.

Value funds

These have a different orientation than growth funds, but a similar goal. Value funds contain stocks, too, but their managers try to hunt for bargains. The objective is to buy stocks on the cheap, then unload them when the price moves back up, pocketing the profit. Value and growth funds are thought

Tip

Which are the best aggressive growth funds according to AOL members? Find out at Keyword: **Sage Fund Awards** for the Top 10 AOL Member Picks.

Find It Online

Are you better off with a value fund? Find out what the experts have to say at Keyword: **Sage**, then click Portfolio Strategies, then Portfolio Focus Archive, then scroll down to Dedication to Value.

to move in opposite circles. But that dichotomy has been less pronounced in recent years. Value funds are popular with moderate investors who already have a heavy orientation on growth and are looking to keep checks and balances in place in their portfolio. Average returns of a value fund: 1 year: 4.48 percent; 3 years: 15.99 percent; 5 years: 17.54 percent; 10 years: 13.37 percent.

Blended funds

In spite of their seemingly polar orientations, growth and value funds are not mutually exclusive. In fact, *because* of these orientations, they make a good pair. Managers of blended or balanced funds assemble a collection of growth and value holdings. They try to pick up bargains where they can, and look for rising stars at the same time. The point is to grab profits where they find them. Many conservative investors with a long-term horizon look to these for some equity presence in their portfolios. Average returns of a blended fund. 1 year: 11.79 percent; 3 years: 19.66 percent; 5 years: 20.55 percent; 10 years: 14.64 percent.

Sector funds

These try to realize gains by focusing on equities within a particular industry. Some focus on technology, others on the financial industry, others in health care or biotechnology. Sector funds are one way to take advantages of trends in the market. When a sector is strong, so too should be the investor's returns. But when a sector has big losses, there is nothing in the fund to cushion your fall. Nearly all sector funds charge a front-end load. It's probably best to stay out of sector investing unless you are extremely familiar with the industry and can anticipate and stomach its volatility.

Sage's Top Ten Fund Picks, shown in Figure 8-7, can be a place to familiarize yourself with the funds. Go to Keyword: **Sage**, then pick Sage's Top Ten Fund Picks, then under Other Top Ten Information, pick Sector Funds, and Go. Average returns of a sector fund: 1 year: 15.02 percent; 3 years: 12.51 percent; 5 years: 14.57 percent; 10 years: 11.4 percent.

Figure 8-7. Sage offers advice on selecting the best sector funds, and offers up a list of the top 10 sector funds around.

International equity funds

These carry the potential for eye-popping returns. Emerging markets funds and foreign stock funds grant managers the chance to uncover big winners in obscure countries. Investors get the opportunity to diversify internationally without traipsing the globe, calculator in hand. Global stock funds can include United States assets in the mix.

They're for aggressive investors who are already covered at home and who are willing to lose a lot in an attempt to make a lot. All international equity funds are largely dependent on currency exchanges and political strength and should only be considered with a keen understanding of the high risk involved. Returns swing like a pendulum, but on average, they return: 1 year: 13.61 percent; 3 years: 6.95 percent; 5 years: 7.84 percent; 10 years: 8.8 percent

Index funds

These reflect the movement and health of a particular representation of the stock market. They mirror everything from the S&P 500 to Internet stocks. They simply invest in a companies that compose the particular index, and stick with those stocks unless the computer-triggered programs order them to sell when a company slips from the list. The minimal trading results in low expenses. As a result, index funds tend to be among the best buys of all mutual funds.

Tip

Feeling a bit lost in mutual fund land? Can't find out exactly what you need? Don't want to wait for an answer on some message board? Tired of waiting for someone in the know to enter a chat room? Try Page a Sage for help. You can communicate directly with Sage employees and other Sage experts, using AOL's Instant Messenger service. Go to Keyword: **SageSchool**, and in the features box, scroll down to Page a Sage. Click a name, and if the Sage is available, he or she can help you with your questions on the spot.

8

Mutual Funds

Find It Online

To get a quote of how indexes are faring on the day, go to Keyword: **MNC**, then choose Chart Intra-Day Stock Prices, Indices and select the index you're looking for. Chart-o-Matic will display the quote at the top of the graph, as in Figure 8-8.

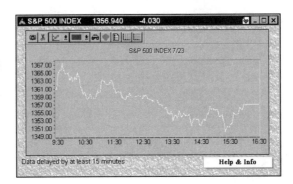

Figure 8-8. You can buy a mutual fund to imitate the performance of indexes like the S&P 500.

If you want to have something in your portfolio whose return equals that of the S&P 500 — a healthy, easy-maintenance, high-growth, very profitable, long-term strategy, by the way — simply put the equities' share of your portfolio money into an S&P index fund. When you think about it, most investment returns fall short of the S&P anyway. Why not just invest in the S&P 500 to begin with?

Index funds are an ideal place to plant your stakes in the market while you fiddle with individual stocks and other holdings. Average returns of the S&P 500 index: 1 year: 22.76 percent; 3 years: 29.10 percent; 5 years: 27.85 percent; 10 years: 18.77 percent. The swings over the past 10 years were quite significant, however, ranging from — 3.12 in 1990 to 37.53 in 1995.

For the NASDAQ composite index, returns averaged: 1 year: 41.77 percent; 3 years: 31.36 percent; 5 years: 30.64 percent; 10 years: 19.96 percent. These swings were more severe, from — 17.81 in 1990 to 56.85 in 1991.

Money-market funds

These offer a safe haven for short-term investors trying to eke out a bit more interest than their credit union or bank pays for a savings account, without the hassle or liquidity concerns of a CD. Money-market funds earn interest by trading very short-term bonds such as Treasury bills. They're a great place to stash that emergency fund of yours. They're out of sight and, hopefully, out of mind, so you won't be tempted to take the eggs from the nest unless you absolutely must. About a quarter of all mutual fund money is parked in money market funds. The historical average return of a money market fund is about 3 percent.

You can find top-ranked money market funds at Keyword:
Bankrate, then click Money Markets, on the left, as in Figure 8-9.

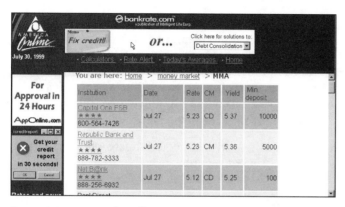

Figure 8-9. Money markets allow you to earn decent interest rates without having to tie up your money.

Balanced funds

These try to do your balancing for you — a little bit of this, a little bit of that — to try to give you the ideal portfolio-in-a-fund. Balanced funds, also called growth and income funds, invest in stocks, bonds and cash, in an attempt to provide you with slow and steady long-term growth as well as some risk protection and some returns. Managers fiddle with the allocation of each segment according to market conditions, but they try to keep the overall fund balanced proportionately. The goal is to generate solid returns and steady income when the market is healthy, and to soften the blows in bad years. For this reason, they are popular with moderate investors looking for long-term growth. Average returns of balanced funds: 1 year: 9.34 percent; 3 years: 15.08 percent; 5 years: 15.5 percent; 10 years: 12.03 percent

Asset-allocation funds

These are a type of balanced fund. But instead of following a mandate to keep their positions balanced, some managers tend to aggressively shift assets according to current and projected market conditions. They spread investments among cash, bonds, stocks, gold, currency — anything they believe will fare well.

The only way to figure out the characteristics of a particular asset-allocation fund is to scrutinize its assets.

Money market funds are the best place to park your emergency money.

For Sage's take on the top performers in all these categories, go to Keyword: **Sage**, then scroll down to Sage's Top 10 Fund picks.

Beware of nomenclature. Some managers of asset allocation funds really are more like market timers, who switch assets from one segment to the next to try to divine where the market's going. There's no way to predict where the market's going. So before you buy into these, study the assets the fund holds to make sure they are more balanced funds than market timers.

8

Mutual Funds

Finding the Right Funds

As explained at the beginning of this chapter, you choose funds whose holdings and objectives match the types of investments you outlined in your blueprint. But you want the *good* funds in these categories, not the dogs. Mutual funds share a characteristic with baseball teams, soufflés and actors: past performance doesn't guarantee future results. But it certainly is a good indicator.

To try to glean how a fund is expected to fare, check out its returns and management records.

The manager

Every fund has a manager. In theory, he is so good at what he does that all you have to do is go golfing and count your dollars. But in reality, it doesn't always work that way. Even when the market's on cruise control, some managers hit a slump. And when the market's turning somersaults, well, that's the true test of a manager's mettle. The chance that your manager will under-perform his peers, lose his golden touch and bomb, even while everybody else is racking up golden gains, is a real possibility and is called management risk. It's important to measure a manager's response against others in similar types of funds, especially during a bear market.

Figure 8-10. Check out who's hot and who's not with Sage. While you're there, cast your ballot for the best fund managers.

One thing to look for is how long a manager has been with a fund. The longer she's been on board, the more certain she will be of the fund's objectives and the more likely she will stay the course during turbulent times. Her tenure is included in the prospectus and in many fund-screening tools.

If the manager leaves, it doesn't mean you have to get out of the fund. But you do need to pay closer attention, to make sure the newcomer has the same strategies as his predecessor. If he's making big changes, make sure they remain in line with your objectives, and be prepared for the big tax consequences and transaction costs that his trades might generate. If he consistently increases the size of the fund, or if its performance begins to lag compared to others in the same category, it might be time for you to find a new fund.

Cracking the prospectus

How do you find out things like management records, fund size, fees, holdings and objectives? The *prospectus* is the key to cracking the code. The SEC requires all mutual funds to list their fees and returns in the prospectus. It also includes dividend and gains dates, performance, sales procedures, expenses and financials. The prospectus provides you with data on annual returns for the past 10 years, if the fund is that old. Typically it chronicles for you how a $1,000-investment would have fared over one, three and five years. It graphs the fund's charges on that $1,000 investment, as well as its returns.

There's no need to go hunting for phone numbers, addresses, and stamps to gather all the prospectuses of your potential candidates. AOL can direct you right to prospectus central.

Go to Keyword: **Edgar** (see Figure 8-11), then plug in the mutual fund's ticker symbol, under Detailed, scroll down to PROSP and Search.

Once you've accessed the prospectus, the first thing you do is confirm that the fund's objectives match yours. Scroll through the first couple of pages of the summary. What is the fund's goal? Growth? Current yields? Capital preservation? The goal will be spelled out.

Tip

How will you know when a manager leaves? And who's coming on board to take her place? How can you discover loose underpinnings in your favorite fund? Subscribe to Sage's free daily e-mail mutual fund newsletter *The Sage Tribune* at Keyword: **Sage**, then choose Sage Voices, then Newsletter Archive and Subscribe.

Note

In order for the manager to keep a firm grasp on the reins, it helps if the fund isn't too big. Some funds carry $25 *billion* in assets. This might be OK for a corporate bond fund, in that it helps diffuse risk and reduces shareholder costs, or for a government bond fund. But when assets of an actively managed stock fund, especially a small cap, start climbing beyond $500 million, managers have a difficult time moving big blocks of stock without affecting price. When assets fall below $50 million, the same manager doesn't have the money muscle behind the fund to keep up with institutional investors.

Note

What's the ultimate figure you're checking for in a mutual fund prospectus? Total return: how much the fund returned after fees and expenses.

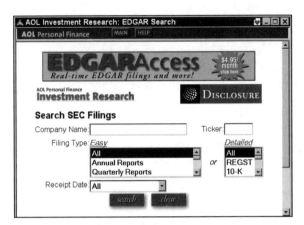

Figure 8-11. Finding financial information on funds and companies is a cinch with search engines like Edgar.

If it's what you're looking for, check out how — or if — the fund realizes these objectives. The prospectus spells out the fund's buying policy, listing the means the fund manager can employ to achieve her objectives. Note that these methods might include selling short and buying warrants, methods you might not be comfortable with. The prospectus enumerates the fund's assets, and lists special risk factors. While reviewing all this information might seem tedious, in fact it's like searching for treasure with a map in your hand!

The better you know what's in a fund, the better you can match it exactly to your needs. Once you confirm that the fund's objectives match yours, and that the assets are those you would like to invest in, scrutinize the fee and expense tables.

Just how much will this fund cost you, anyway?

The Price Tag

Front-end loads. Back-end loads. No loads. Is there no end to this loaded issue? Sometimes it seems that way. More than half of all funds charge *loads*, or sales commissions. Yet study upon study prove there is no correlation between loads and returns. Loads are for investors who don't want to lift a finger researching funds. You leave the decision on what to buy to your broker, who chooses the fund for you and slices off a piece of your investment as a commission for herself. (That's the essence of a load. It's explained in further detail in a minute.)

Expenses are the albatross of mutual funds. Even if you opt for a no-load fund, all kinds of fees slowly and silently suck the air out of the returns. Stacks of studies have shown expenses to be the most powerful factor affecting how much return a fund generates. When you're doing your comparison shopping, you need to look at the price tag.

Find It Online

To learn online how fund fees break down, check out SmartMoney.com, as in Figure 8-12. Go to **http://www. SmartMoney.com**. Click the Mutual Funds tab, and click Fund Fee Analyzer, under Fund Tools.

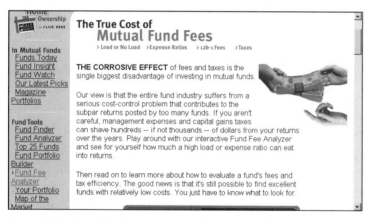

Figure 8-12. Mutual funds: easy to use, good for your portfolio. So what's the catch? Hidden fees and expenses. Make sure you understand the fees associated with a fund before you choose it.

Language lessons

This isn't as simple as it might seem, though. Fees seem clandestine in the mutual fund world, masquerading as marketing materials, management costs, asset turnover, annual meeting charges. . . . All these expenses and more add up to a hefty bite out of the assets, dampening a hot return. How can you nail down the price tag? A dogged pursuit of the fine print and yet another language lesson straightens it all out.

Portfolio turnover

This tells you how often the fund manager buys or sells holdings. It is determined by dividing the number of either purchases or sales (whichever is lower) by the fund's worth on the average month. A fund with 100 percent turnover means assets were

Tip

If you like a fund that has a front-end load, but you refuse to pay ridiculous fees, call up the fund administrators and ask if they would consider waiving the load if you buy the fund yourself, without going through a broker.

held, on average, for a year. If turnover is 200 percent, assets were held about half a year; 400 percent means they were held about three months, and so on. Portfolio turnover for stock funds averages around 80 percent, and bond funds are about 100 percent.

Funds with high stock turnover generate high operating costs and expenses. Funds that don't require much management, like index funds, boast lower costs. While portfolio turnover doesn't tell you how a fund will perform, it is a window into how much you might expect to pay, especially in taxes. When fund managers crank out the buys and sells, trying to take advantage of the market to up your profits, they are also racking up transaction costs and capital gains. Funds don't pay taxes on these gains, though. They distribute the profits and gains back to you. So you pay taxes on the gains the year the fund generates them, whether or not you take any money out of your fund.

Front-end load

Suppose you start dreaming about that retirement villa again. You go to the broker prepared to invest $5,000 in a small cap growth fund. For her sound advice and help picking "the right fund," your broker will immediately lop off a front-end load from the top of your $5,000, and put the rest in the fund.

When you buy a mutual fund from a broker, and you pay that broker a commission, the commission is called a front-end load, and your shares are called *Class A* shares. Front-end loads pay for advice and someone else's footwork. How much gets shaved? It depends. Front-end loads can range up to *8.5 percent* of the amount you invest! If the front-end load on the fund you end up with is 5 percent, your broker will snag $250 right off the bat, reducing your deposit to $4,750.

Back-end load

Mutual fund companies don't like it when you take your money back. Some discourage this practice by charging you a *back-end load*, or *deferred load*, when you sell your shares back. These funds, also called *Class B shares* tack on up to *7.25 percent* when you redeem your shares! The money goes to the broker doing the selling.

Typically with Class B shares, though, the load is reduced each year you're in the fund, and after maybe half a dozen years there's no load at all. The shares can then become Class A shares, for which there's no redemption fee. A *redemption fee* is similar to a back-end load in that it is assessed when you cash in your shares. But this fee, up to 2 percent, goes to the fund family and not to the broker making the sale.

Level load

Funds with a level load entice you by charging less up front than Class A shares, and less when you withdraw than Class B shares. But be forewarned: these level loads, called *Class C shares*, carry hefty annual expenses that flatten your returns.

No-load

These funds don't charge anything up front and don't charge upon redemption. They do, however, charge management fees and up to 0.25 percent in 12b-1 fees (see below). Hmmm. They don't charge, but they do charge.... It sounds confusing because it is!

12b-1 fee

Funds use this fee to pay for advertising and marketing so they can recruit more investors. The fee can equal up to 1 percent, or .25 percent for a no-load, of fund assets each year. You pay 12b-1 fees each year but you might not realize it, as they're subtracted annually before the fund distributes its returns. Many front-end load funds don't charge 12b-1 fees, as they have brokers — and not TV stations or publications — advertising for them.

Management fee

You have to pay the mutual fund manager something for toiling for you. She and her analysts and colleagues receive a management fee of about 1 percent of the fund's assets for their efforts. This fee also gets deducted from your returns.

The expense ratio

If there is a key to unlocking the true cost of all funds, it is the expense ratio. Shareholders pay all the aforementioned costs and fees, as well as the company's operating expenses —

Note

Typically, back-end load shares carry a 12b-1 fee (see below).

Note

There's a difference between loads and fees. A load is a sales commission on the fund. Even if you don't pay a commission (as with a no-load) there can still be many fees associated with the fund.

Caution

In a sneaky ploy to convince you their funds are appealing because they carry a low load, many fund companies have taken to shrinking their front-end load — but hiking their 12b-1 fees — which they swipe from the kitty each year before paying out profits. The net result is higher expenses and lower returns.

8

Mutual Funds

Note

Says Sage's Stephen Cohn, "On an average growth stock mutual fund, for example, an expense ratio above 1.5 percent is outrageous. To us, if there's an expense ratio above 1.5 percent we wouldn't invest in that fund. In fact, we like to see it below 1 percent."

Find It Online

You can find the expense ratio in the financial highlights or per share data section of the prospectus or in the mutual fund reports. To do this via AOL, go to Keyword: **Morningstar**. Select Mutual Fund Reports and type in the fund's symbol, and click Search. Select Mutual Fund Reports again and look for expense ratio, as in Figure 8-13.

Note

Loads are not included in the expense ratio and add to your cost. When you have similarly performing funds in your list of finalists, get rid of the ones with the loads and examine the expense ratios of the remainders.

office space, salaries, equipment, shareholder, and transaction costs, the cost of the toll-free customer service, the printed prospectuses, support services. . . . These all add up to the expense ratio.

The ratio is technically the percentage of assets deducted from the fund each year to operate it. These include advisors' fees, the 12b-1 and the administrative costs. You don't pay these expenses directly — they are simply deducted from assets.

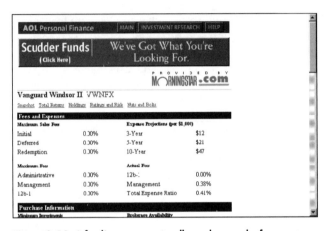

Figure 8-13. A fund's expense ratio tells you how much of your returns are really going to expenses.

When digging for funds, you need to sift through a lot of dirt to find the gems. Many partners will help you with all this sifting. One in particular, AOL partner Morningstar, comes to the task, shovels and screens in hand.

Screening Mutual Funds

With the many thousands of mutual funds available, the temptation is great to just throw in the towel and let a banker or broker or your colleague in the next cubicle pick funds for you. But the task is made easy when you use a simple tool: The mutual fund screen.

Fund screens help you sort the possibilities according to criteria important to you. They help you narrow your lists by singling out funds that meet your objectives. They rank the results according to your wishes. You can pare down these lists further and further to come up with the winners.

To start, crank up the mutual fund screening tool at Keyword: **Mutual Funds**, then select Fund Screening. If you're new to fund screening or to mutual funds in general, click Step-By-Step Screening, then choose Find Funds, to find a match for you. As you answer the questions, the screening tool will slowly narrow down the options. Note that each area in the screening tool has been addressed in this chapter.

Step-by-step screening

First up, minimum initial investment. How much can you spend? Slide the arrow on the graph to the correct spot and then click Next.

Next, click the category of fund you're searching for. To help you pinpoint exactly the kind of assets you seek, click More Detail. You can choose several options, if you'd like. Then click Next.

Now you need to specify price. Are you looking for a Load or No Load fund? Select No Opinion if you're indifferent. Note that during the screening process you can click the terminology for an explanation of anything that's unclear.

Next, select the size fund you had in mind, or choose No Opinion if size isn't important to you. Then click Next again.

Now you have to specify the tenure of the manager, and of the fund. Slide the rulers to the reflect the number of years you're looking for.

Next you indicate whether it's important to you that the fund be sold by a broker, as opposed to directly from the fund company.

Now you need to specify a minimum Morningstar Rating.

Now you can sort the results, by performance, by expense ratio, or by Morningstar rating. Up come all funds that meet your qualifications. To see how these funds match up against one another, click Compare With Another Fund, and click the funds you want to match up.

Cross-Reference

To help you determine exactly how much you should invest in a fund, refer to Chapter 11.

Definition

Morningstar Star Rating: a fund's return score minus its risk score. A fund gets 5 stars if it's in the top 10 percent of its category, 4 stars if it's in the next 22.5 percent, 3 stars if its in the middle 35 percent, 2 stars if it's in the bottom 22.5 percent, and 1 star if it's in the lowest 10 percent. Star ratings are calculated each month.

8

Mutual Funds

If you want to see a particular feature displayed when your list of candidates comes up, click the Show box next to the feature.

Standard deviation: measures the range of a fund's performance, which indicates volatility. The greater the standard deviation, the greater a fund's volatility.

If you want to change any items without erasing your previous inputs, click the Back button on the toolbar. If you want to clear the slate and start over, click Reset Form.

For the ins and outs of closed end funds, go to Keyword: **Mutual Funds**, then select Archives, then click Wide World of Closed-end Funds.

Custom screening

If you want to handpick the finalists, click Custom Fund Screening on the fund screening page.

Select the category you want to make your priority, and click its circle under Sort.

First you need to pick the Fund Category. You have about 50 possibilities here, including the fund types reviewed earlier in this chapter. If you don't want to eliminate any possibilities, leave it on the Not Selected default.

Next, select the number of Morningstar stars you're searching for. Then type in a family name, if you're limiting your search to a particular fund family. After that, select the amount of fund assets. Then, indicate your load preferences. Next you can choose a standard deviation. (If you don't know a term, click Help, then select Mutual Fund Definitions.) Then click a minimum investment. Pick the manager's tenure, then specify a year-to-date return.

You can also input low or high values for the 1, 3, 5 and 10-year returns. Then click Screen Funds to come up with your final list of candidates.

Buying Mutual Funds

Now that you know what you want to buy, there are a couple of places to do your shopping, depending on the type of fund. There are two categories of mutual funds:

▶ Open-end funds, which constantly acquire new assets with money from shareholders. You can get these through your broker or the mutual fund company; and

▶ Closed-end funds, which raise money by selling a fixed-number of shares up front, and then these shares trade at a discount or a premium on the stock exchanges. You trade for them as you would a stock.

When you invest in an open-end mutual fund, you're buying a piece of the total assets the fund holds. You don't buy a number of shares per se. You invest a dollar amount, and the company figures out how many shares this gets you. If the fund has $300 million in total assets, for example, and there are 20 million shares, each share is worth $15. If you invest $1500 in the fund, you get 100 shares.

The price of each share, or the net asset value, goes up and down each day, as the value of the assets changes. The figure is published at the end of the business day. To find a fund's NAV, go to Keyword: **Quotes**, type in the fund's ticker symbol, and up comes its snapshot.

After all your work, there's no sense going to a broker to buy a fund. You'd have to pay her a sales commission. Pick up a no-load fund straight from the mutual fund company, or find out if your discount broker will sell it to you fee-free.

For ease of deposits, withdrawals and transfers, and reduced paperwork, you can probably get all the funds you need from one company. For information on a mutual fund company's offerings, check out its Web site. For the real low-down, though, talk to investors who have had dealings with it.

When you fill out a mutual fund application with a fund family, you'll have to tell the company the name of your fund selection; whether you want an individual (just for you), joint (for you and somebody else) or trust account (which you direct on someone else's behalf); whether you want to write checks against this account; if you want to deposit money into the fund from your bank account or paycheck (This is a very convenient option, and a way to insure your regular commitment to investing in the fund.) Then you need to send in the check.

Smart investors direct a steady stream of money into their funds on a weekly or monthly basis, right out of their paycheck or bank account. This is a great way to purchase mutual funds, as it takes the guesswork out of when to buy. If the market happens to be strong, you're sure to get in on a piece of the action. If your fund has a bad quarter, and the shares decrease in value, your deposit buys more shares for a cheaper price. They'll be worth more when the market picks up.

Cross-Reference

For more about the Snapshot, see Chapter 9.

Tip

To learn which brokers will sell you a fund, go to Keyword: **Morningstar**, type in the ticker symbol, and select Mutual Fund Reports. Then click Nuts and Bolts and check under Brokerage Availability, under Purchase Information.

Find It Online

You can find thousands of messages about mutual fund companies at Keyword: **Mutual Funds**, then, under Sage Message Boards, scroll down to the name of the company and click it for investors' commentary on more than 100 companies.

Note

If there is a minimum investment that you can't meet, some funds will waive the minimum if you participate in an automatic investment program.

8

Mutual Funds

Caution

There is a great temptation to fund-hop every quarter based on returns. But many studies indicate that the investor who sticks with a fund outperforms the fund-jumpers in the same class.

Tip

Most funds distribute their capital gains toward the end of the year. If you own the fund, you pay taxes on these gains, whether or not you were in long enough to benefit from them. Call the fund company before you invest in the fund and find out when the fund will make its distributions. This way, you can weigh the tax implications of waiting versus getting in now.

When to Sell

When should you sell a mutual fund? There are a couple of scenarios. Perhaps you bought it because you liked the manager. She had a great record, and you liked her style. And then she left. Maybe you want to follow her to her new fund. If so, make sure it has the right objectives for your portfolio.

Perhaps your fund has a new manager who blows in with a new style and different objectives, changing the holdings so much that the fund has a whole different collection of assets. Maybe they carry a greater risk than you care to carry. Maybe they represent an industry you already have covered in another fund. If so, it could be time to sell.

Perhaps your fund consistently underperforms the others in its class. Once four quarters pass and others in its class have outperformed your fund each quarter, you might have to suck it up, admit you made a mistake, and rid of it.

Summary

Congratulations! You've learned the advantages and disadvantages of mutual funds, the types of funds there are and how you can find the right funds for you.

You know how to find a fund's prospectus, and how to navigate it. You know a *back-end load* from a *12-b* and you know what all those financial terms really mean.

Finally, you learned how to screen for funds that will work for you.

Next in Chapter 9, you'll learn how to dig for stocks that meet your needs.

CHAPTER

MINING FOR GOLD

A Quick Look

▶ **Grasping the Big Picture** **page 218**

Hearing some buzz about a hot stock pick? Before you hit that "execute trade" button, make sure you first check the company out. Begin with an easy to read company summary at Keyword: **Hoovers**. Enter the ticker symbol and select Company Overview for a quick but comprehensive look at the company. Find out what it does and who is in charge. Read financial highlights and other key figures, and check out recent headline stories about the company. Links in the overview pave the way to more detailed information about every aspect of the company. Note: to obtain some information about companies, you may be required to register and choose a password.

▶ **A Direct Line to Uncle Sam** **page 222**

All public companies are required to report extensive financial information with the Securities and Exchange Commission, and the public has a right to access all of this information. You can go online to check out all reports filed with the SEC and immediately receive the most current data. Keyword: **Edgar** brings you directly to the SEC database. Type in the ticker symbol for the company, and select the particular reports you want to review, or select All to see a list of everything on file. You may search for past reports, or limit the list to current information only.

▶ **Access the Analysts** **page 224**

Even after you've dutifully read every bit of company literature, financial data, and every news article available on your target, you still might feel unsure. For a second (and third, and fourth) opinion, read what financial analysts and brokers are saying about the stock. You can gather this information with ease at Keyword: **Multex**. You have to register to use the site, but it doesn't cost anything. After you sign up, enter the company's ticker symbol in the Search box, and click Research. A list of reports on the company appears, offering the perspective of major brokerage firms and analysts as to how the stock is valued. Many of these reports are free, and some are available for purchase from brokers. Note: You must have "cookies" enabled on your browser in order to register and login.

▶ **Great Expectations** **page 228**

Even if a company is turning a tidy profit, if it was expected to do better the stock price can take a tumble. How do you find out what great things are expected from a stock? Turn to Keyword: **Estimates** to access Zack's Investment Research. Enter the company's ticker symbol, hit enter, and select Earnings Estimates for a look at what Wall Street is predicting.

Chapter 9

Mining for Gold

Search the Internet for stock tips and you're likely to come up with more advice than Warren Buffet has dollars. If the Internet doesn't catch you, then yesterday's news might, with tales of a hot little stock that quadrupled while you slept.

When the stock market soars and every investor around you is boasting his score, you might be tempted to rush out and spend the wedding gift money on 500 shares of that stock on the cover of yesterday's business page. Guess what? Thousands of people already beat you to it, potentially pushing your profits as far away as your silver anniversary.

When it comes to stocks, there's only one way to find a gem. And that's to dig for it.

There are many ways to mine the mountains of available information, and different investors will take different routes to arrive at their decisions. Regardless of your tack, if your research is thorough, you'll be able to differentiate the gems from the rhinestones. Otherwise, if you grab haphazardly, scooping up the first thing that glitters or taking somebody else's picked over goods, you're left with baubles.

If you don't want to dig for and scrutinize stocks on your own it doesn't mean you won't be able to profit from them. Just admit to yourself up front that you won't do the work. Then, for a fraction of the effort, go unearth a good mutual fund, where the manager does the digging and examining of stocks for you. Know, though, that with a mutual fund, you're reliant upon selections that serve someone else's needs. When you pick stocks yourself, you end up with exactly those that meet your requirements.

If you're ready to do the work yourself, you're in the right place. AOL is Research Central when it comes to researching stocks. Keyword: **Investment Research,** pictured in Figure 9-1, calls up all manner of excavating tools: company overviews, analysts' reports, earnings estimates, financial ratios, stock screening tools, even reports filed with the Securities and Exchange Commission. This chapter is your guide to them all.

Cross-Reference

How do you find a good mutual fund? Find out in Chapter 8.

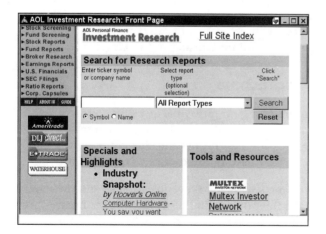

Figure 9-1. No matter how good the buzz sounds, you need to do some research before plunking down your money on a stock.

What's Your Philosophy?

Cross-Reference

To review the kinds of stocks, see Chapter 6.

Note

Investors who look to make money quickly on a stock and then to unload it just as fast are not true growth investors. They are better referred to as traders.

Note

Keep in mind that every type of investor should seek some growth, otherwise their assets actually shrink in the shadow of inflation.

When you start prospecting for great stocks, you need to bring a treasure map. What kinds of stocks are you on the lookout for? Maybe you want a half-dozen large-, medium-, and small-cap stocks in diversified businesses for your rainy day fund. Maybe you're looking for aggressive growers for your long-term goals. Maybe you want high-yielders to support you in retirement. Perhaps it's a cross-section of the above.

Whatever the case, you need a list of potential candidates so you can choose wisely. You find these candidates by ferreting them out according to your objectives — typically, in one of three ways:

Investing for growth

If you're investing for growth, you try to find high-quality companies whose sales or earnings are growing — or will grow — by leaps and bounds. If this potential is realized, then stock price should appreciate significantly, too, which is the aim of the growth investor. True growth investors look at the potential for growth over time, excited by the prospect of new products in new industries.

True growth investors often examine the rate at which the company is growing as the most important factor for whether or not they'll buy it. They study revenue, income, and cash flow to find a company growing at a faster rate than its peers. (All these terms are explored further in this chapter.)

Investing for income

The parallel to investing for growth is investing for income. There's a tradeoff between the two. Companies in major growth mode suck up their profits and shovel them back into the company, so they have more resources to build with.

But many companies with solid revenue streams and slow and steady sales take their profits and distribute them to shareholders in the form of dividends. This is what the *income* investor looks for — a paycheck, in the form of dividends.

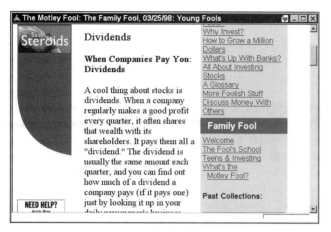

Figure 9-2. Typically, income investors seek stocks offering dividends, while those interested in growth focus on stocks with potential for capital gains.

Typically, high dividends come from businesses such as utility companies, which have a given customer base and little opportunity for growth. Beware, though — some companies are in such trouble that the only way they can woo investors is with a high yield. Make sure you understand why the income from a potential stock is much higher than that of its peers before you buy the stock.

To see how a stock's income measures up, compare its yield to the average yield in the industry and sector.

If yield seems a bit high, you might have uncovered a needle in a haystack. Or, your company could be out of favor on Wall Street, as yield can be a barometer of investor sentiment. Suppose a stock has historically yielded about 1.2 percent of its price, and the industry has carried a similar yield. But at the time of your research, yield is up past 2 percent, a huge difference over the industry. That's often a clue to one of two scenarios: either your target is in trouble and is dumping money into dividends to remain attractive to investors, or Wall Street doesn't like your target relative to others in the same industry, and has squashed the stock price.

Investing for value

If you are a *value* investor, you try to find stocks priced at a discount to what you believe they're inherently worth. But this can be a tricky quest. Who doesn't want to buy stocks at

Find It Online

To read online the advantages of profiting through dividends, go to Keyword: **Fool**, and choose Search from the Quick Find pull-down menu. Type in **Dividends**, and click Submit Search. Then scroll down and click The Motley Fool: The Family Fool, 3/25/98: Young Fools article on dividends, pictured in Figure 9-2.

Cross-Reference

To explore dividends more fully, see Chapter 6 and Chapter 10.

Find It Online

To compare a stock against the parent industry's average yield, go to Keyword: **Market Guide.** Enter the company's ticker symbol, hit enter, select Stock Report, then select Ratio Comparison. Scroll down to the Dividends table to compare the company's yield to its overall industry and sector.

Find It Online

How can you identify bargains the way legendary billionaire Warren Buffet does? Go through the short course at Keyword: **Money Mag**, scroll all the way down on the left to Money 101, select Investing in Stocks, and then click Identifying Bargains.

a discount to what they're worth? Every investor (except for short-sellers, who you'll read about in Chapter 10), buys a stock they believe will be worth more tomorrow than what they paid for it today. This makes the theory of investing for value a difficult one to follow.

True value investors look to buy stocks that are a bargain relative to their *intrinsic* worth — how much the company would probably sell for today in a reasonable market. Most often these are stock stalwarts that have hit a jag. Investors tend to ignore these iron horses when the market is running. But while value stocks tend to lag during bull markets, they often fare better during tumultuous or sagging markets.

Setting Your Strategy

After you know what types of investments you're looking for, you can hammer out your analysis strategy. Try to do this before you start digging, so you maintain a consistency when evaluating one company's stock to the next.

Stock analysis follows a number of different approaches:

▶ Examining historical trading patterns

▶ Examining the company itself

▶ Examining the company's numbers

▶ Developing your own plan

Technical analysis

Technical analysis examines historical patterns in stock sales and uses sophisticated charts and algorithms to trigger when to buy and sell, regardless of a company's financials. Investors who use technical analysis believe charts of the market help predict whether or not the market for a stock can go higher. AOL partners Decision Point (Keyword: **DP**) and The Shark Attack (Keyword: **Shark Attack**) point you to specific chart formations and information they believe will predict certain price movements.

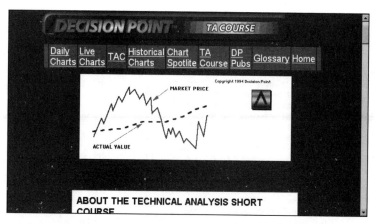

Figure 9-3. Technical analysis focuses on trends and patterns in trading instead of a company's financials.

Technical analysis is best left to chartists and software. The bulk of this chapter will help you research information open for interpretation: the fundamental health of the company and the strength or weakness of its numbers, on its own and compared to its peers.

When you're done working through all the information you will be able to make an investment decision based on the quality of a company, the direction in which it's headed and the reasonableness of its stock price.

Fundamental analysis

Fundamental analysis, as the name implies, examines the company's fundamentals: How good is management? How competitive is the market for its products? Is the company in a healthy industry? Do its financials warrant your buying the stock? The point of fundamental analysis is to examine a company's underlying viability. You can read about it online in the article pictured in Figure 9-4. Find it at Keyword: **Personal Wealth**, then click the Learning Center, and select Basics of Smart Investing, under Tutorials. Then click Stocks, and select topic four, Analysis.

A very subjective approach, fundamental analysis involves assessing a company's strategy, leadership and strength to determine how much its stock is worth. There is no inherent formula for doing this, but there are ways to measure performance among companies.

Find It Online

If you're interested in technical analysis, Decision Point offers a huge collection of free technical analysis material online. To get started, go to Keyword: **DP**, and scroll down to Technical Analysis Short Course for a primer on how to select stocks using this type of research, as pictured in Figure 9-3.

Decision Point also offers tools that allow you to track a company's progress using charts. Possibilities range from a minute-to-minute update of current activity to historical charts going as far back as 1926. For a daily update of stock activity, click Daily Charts and Reports or Live Reports. If you'd like an overview of past performance, click Historical Charts.

Note

It helps to go online while you're exploring this chapter so you can call up the sites and walk through the steps referred to in the text.

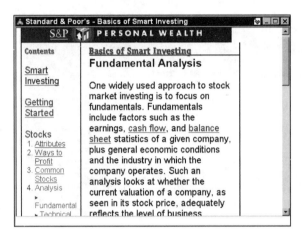

Figure 9-4. By using the same method to analyze various companies, a potential investor can make valid comparisons between stocks.

Quantitative analysis

For one, there's quantitative analysis. Instead of focusing on the touchy-feely fundamental analysis of a company, such as management and goals, quantitative analysts get right to the numbers. They believe that the right proportion of the right ingredients makes for a great pie, whether or not you're familiar with the pie. Quantitative analysts use the ratios examined later in this chapter, which you can find at Keyword: **Investment Research**.

Sizing Up the Candidates

When you start stock shopping, you can and should do what any prospective business buyer does — scrutinize your target from top to bottom before making a purchase. In other words, examine the numbers and the management and the potential for profits.

Unfortunately, many people spend more time examining the features of a new television set before buying it than they do a new stock. But there's no reason for that. With all the investment information available online, you can readily examine not only what's on the surface of a stock but also what's in the guts of the company.

Capturing the components

Unlike with a TV, figuring out the components of a stock requires no special training. You just need to know what to look for and do a little exploring. You'll want to examine your target's management and organization to determine its goals, products, profits, and prospects for the future. You can find this information from the companies themselves.

You don't have to fly out to Oshkosh to examine that paper plant you're thinking about investing in. You can go online and unearth filing cabinets' worth of information that illuminates the majority of public companies.

Most publicly traded companies have Internet sites. To track them down, go to Keyword: **Stocks**, choose Name, type in the company's name, and select Lookup. When the stock symbol and the snapshot appear, select Research Reports on the right of the screen, then choose Company Overviews for a summary like the one pictured in Figure 9-5.

Figure 9-5. Researching target companies is easier than ever, thanks to the abundance of information companies and investment sites put online.

A Quick Overview

At Company Overviews, AOL partner Hoover's (Keyword: **Hoovers**) delivers the goods. Up comes the company's name, address and phone number, and a direct link to its Web site. Before you follow the link, take a look at Hoover's overview. The synopsis will give you some perspective when you later swim through the company-supplied superlatives.

The overview gives a quick, no-nonsense description of the company from an objective point of view. It lists key numbers, such as previous year's sales, net income, and number of employees, as well the company's main competitors. It also highlights key officers, subsidiaries, divisions, and affiliates.

You can follow links for comprehensive coverage of every aspect of the company, from an in-depth profile, to annual financial statements for the past three years.

Be sure to read recent news stories (as shown in the Figure below) that mention the company, at the bottom of the Overviews page. Oddly enough, many investors tend to overlook current news in their research, as much stock research focuses on past performance. You don't want to become so hyper-focused on the numbers that you miss a trend that's emerging right before your eyes. So take a quick look at the news stories before you get too deep in your digging.

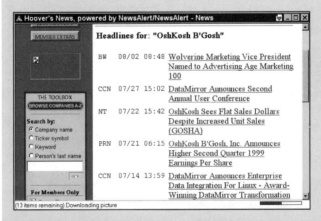

Financial figures provide insight into the health of a target, but don't overlook news about the company when you do your research.

Next, follow the link on the Overviews page to the company's Web site. Surf around a bit. What type of industry is the company in? Where is the company headed? Look up product lines and philosophy. Give yourself a general familiarity with the company. Next, head to the link to investor relations.

Ask your target's investor relations representative to send you the latest annual report, annual and quarterly financial documents (called the *10-K* and *10-Q*), press releases, and analysts' reports, and ask to be put on the e-mail list for updates. This is probably the easiest way to all this information. The tidy package you get in the mail often serves as a springboard for what to pursue further online.

Reading the annual report

You've already explored the company overview, so you have a general idea of the corporation's business. Now that you have this package of information before you, you can learn *exactly* what the company does. The glossy annual reports provide a good, albeit subjective, synopsis of where and how the company does business.

Cross-Reference

For the ins and outs of the exchanges, see Chapters 6 and 13.

Find It Online

Want to learn online how to read the annual report? Go to Keyword: **Fool**, click School, and then click Step 8: Read Financial Info.

Find It Online

You can find annual reports online at Hoover's Company Overview. Start at Keyword: **Hoover's**, then enter the company's ticker symbol. Select the Company Overview report, and scroll down in the Table of Contents on the right to For Investors, under Key Resources. Click Annual Report for the company's latest report, as pictured in Figure 9-6.

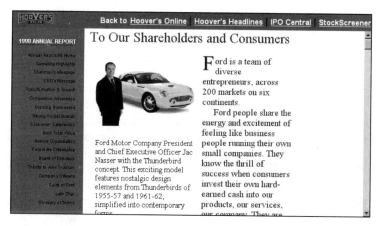

Figure 9-6. You can't blame a company for trying to look good to potential investors. Although you can count on facts and figures to be accurate, expect a bit of self-promotion as well.

Look beyond the deifying bios of top executives to determine management trends and plans. Bypass the best-thing-since-sliced-bread descriptions of the products and the glorious

Cross-Reference

How will you know exactly what to put in your portfolio? See Chapter 11.

Tip

Looking for a direct connection to a company's financials? Go to Keyword: **Financials**, plug in the ticker symbol, and choose U.S. Financial Statements. Then click Search. Then click U.S. Financial Statements again. Up come the annual balance sheet, income statement, and cash flow statement.

photos of the products in order to discern how they fare compared with competitors in their industry.

After you know exactly what the company does, determine whether the industry and products are what your portfolio needs, or whether they're redundant with something you already own.

Evaluating the Numbers

All this preliminary exploration should eliminate a lot of candidates. Now you need to tackle the numbers. If you conclude that the company, management, and products are strong and in line with your needs, you'll have to determine whether or not you think the stock is worth the current asking price.

You start with the *financials*, the statements that tell how much the company is spending and earning. All public companies must make their financials available to anyone interested. The figures help you understand the company's current health, and they help you anticipate in which direction the company is headed.

Financials help you get past the glitz and gloss of an annual report or the appeal of a TV commercial. Numbers can expose a company's strengths and weaknesses. Because there is no "right" or "wrong" number, there is no formula to plug them into to come up with a "good" or "bad" stock. Each number is relative to the other information in the report.

You can use numbers as a scorecard, though, to chronicle how the company has fared historically, how it is currently operating, and how the company is poised for the future. You can also use the financials to help compare the company with others in a similar business.

What's in the financials?

Basically, there are four types of statements included with the company's financials. The *income statement* (also called the *profit and loss* or *P and L*) tells you how much the company earned during the reporting period, what costs or expenses it incurred, and the difference between the two, called the *net profit* or *loss*. Often the report contains three years' of income statements to help you gauge how the company is faring. A healthy company's earnings will increase each year. Look closely at *sales revenues* and *cost of goods sold* to help you locate trends in the operations. Gross profit margin shows the profitability margin. Ideally, this margin will stay the same or increase.

The *balance sheet* chronicles assets, liabilities, and equity. It's a snapshot of the company's financial situation at a given point at the end of the reporting period. It tells you where the company is at the moment, but has few indicators to tell you where the company is headed. (For example, see the balance sheet pictured in Figure 9-7.)

Find It Online

How will you know if a company's financials make it worth pursuing? Learn how to dissect the numbers at the interactive financial statement tutorial at TheStreet.com. Start at Keyword: **TheStreet**, then select Basics. Scroll all the way down to The Basics of Financial Statements for the Interactive Balance Sheet and Interactive Income Statement, and walk step-by-step through Sample Company's balance sheet and income statement.

▲ US Financials

Annual Balance Sheet (000$)

ASSETS

Fiscal Year Ending	12/31/98	12/31/97	12/31/96
Cash	79,000	75,000	104,000
Mkrtable Securities	NA	NA	NA
Receivables	7,891,000	6,744,000	6,408,000
Inventories	3,269,000	2,792,000	2,676,000
Raw Materials	NA	NA	NA
Work In Progress	NA	NA	NA
Finished Goods	NA	NA	NA
Notes Receivable	NA	NA	NA
Other Current Assets	1,236,000	1,155,000	964,000
Total Current Assets	**12,475,000**	**10,766,000**	**10,152,000**
Prop, Plant & Equip	2,366,000	2,377,000	2,256,000
Accumulated Dep	NA	NA	NA
Net Prop & Equip	2,366,000	2,377,000	2,256,000

Figure 9-7. Publicly traded companies must disclose certain financial information. Take advantage of the availability of this information when you research your targets.

The *position statement*, also known as *sources and uses of cash*, helps you understand where a company got its money from, and where it spent that money.

Tip

Looking for folders' worth of information on what you can glean from financial statements? Go to Keyword: **Fool**, and click the Messages tab. Then click Investors' Roundtable. Select Show me more, then choose Reading Financial Statements.

Help from Uncle Sam

You'll find financials in the annual report, but sometimes you can get a better perspective on them from additional resources outside of the company. A great place to start is at the top: The U.S. Securities and Exchange Commission. The SEC compiles thousands of business and financial files on just about every public American company. This information is free to all. Often, all this supporting information can help you unravel what's in the financials.

The SEC Online

SEC filings have always been public information, but getting your hands on them was a time-consuming process. That was before the Internet. Now the information is readily available and updated daily.

Keyword: **Edgar** brings you right to the SEC database.

Enter the name or ticker symbol for your target. If you are searching for a particular report, such as the company's annual report, employee benefit plan, or a 10-K or 10-Q report, select it from the Filing Type list. Or simply select All to review everything the company has on file.

There are two types of filing categories listed: Easy and Detailed. Easy offers a list of report titles such as "Annual Report" or "IPO Filings," while the Detailed category lists reports by their official names, like "10-K" and "10-Q." If you are not sure of the official name of the report you wish to review, click Easy for a table of all available reports.

You may also dictate a time frame for the reports, ranging from Older Than One Year, to Yesterday. Again, you can choose All to review everything in the database. Hit enter to begin your search.

Edgar retrieves a list of SEC reports, as shown in the Figure, and indicates the type of report, its date and length. Click the title to review a report.

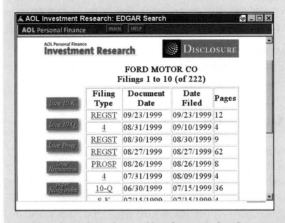

SEC filings have always been public information, but the Internet has made accessing such documents quick and easy.

There are a couple of documents that you should examine. First the *10-K*, which all companies file with the SEC each year. This document contains information you'll find in an annual report, such as addresses and directors, products and financials. But there's much, much more. In fact, the 10-K is chockfull of revelations.

For example, instead of just total revenues, you may get a breakdown of sales by region. You can use these numbers to discover if one product is carrying the load while the other products are lagging. You'll get the lowdown on insider ownership information, from where the execs went to college to the amount of company stocks they own. (Obviously, the more stock they own, the greater their financial interest in the company's fate, and the more in line their motivations will be with yours.)

Study the 10-K. Compare numbers in the balance sheets. Look at the financial statements for a snapshot of the company's financial health. For example, to determine where the company gets its money and how it spends it, review the cash flow statement. Are sales growing or shrinking? Is growth continuing at a steady rate among all the company's divisions? If the company is still in the foundling stage, does it have enough cash to sustain its growth until profits eventually materialize? To fully understand these numbers, see the *Financial Strength Ratios* section at the end of this chapter.

Companies provide a good deal of this information quarterly, as well, via the *10-Q*, which is another document you should examine. Because it's more recent than the 10-K, if you're really hot on a stock, or you suspect your favorite is beginning to wane, scrutinize the 10-Q to see if all the numbers are on track with where you think they should be before you buy or sell.

 Find It Online

Looking for a quick way to find out how much of the company insiders control? Go to Keyword: **Market Guide**, plug in the ticker symbol, select Stock Reports, then Enter. Then, scroll all the way down below Earnings Per Share to Equities, and Insiders Own.

Accessing the Analysts

If you're not comfortable navigating through this financial information, look to the people who scrutinize financials every day: the investment analysts. They work for brokerages doing exactly what you're trying to do: assess the financial health and future of the company. Analysts are assigned to follow particular companies. They examine the numbers, talk

Tip

What are the analysts' top picks of the week? Find out at Keyword: **Online Investor** and select Top Rated for the most-recommended stocks each week.

with the head honchos and examine entire industries to come up with *analyst reports*, which include earnings estimates, price targets, company goals, and other forecasts and predictions that assess the viability and strength of the company.

They also rate the stock with pronouncements such as "Strong Buy," "Buy," and "Hold." But because they rarely tell you to sell — they work for firms that could be involved in financing the companies — there's no sense getting wedded to the ratings. Read the report, then do your own assessment of a stock's price and worth based on your interpretation of the available information.

Finding analysts' reports is simple online. Go to Keyword: **Investment Research**, plug in your target's stock symbol, and select Broker Research. Up comes AOL partner Multex's annals of the analysts, as pictured in Figure 9-8. Plug in the ticker symbol again and hit Research. Up come analysts' reports of your target.

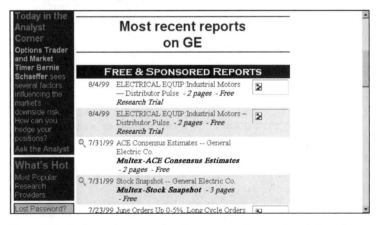

Figure 9-8. As always, the experts have lots to say, and you can benefit from their studied opinions while researching your stocks.

Analyst Reports

No matter how much time you've spent familiarizing yourself with a target, it is always worth learning what experts have to say about it as well. Multex is the gateway to opinions and analysis from financial experts and brokers.

Go to Keyword: **Multex** to open the site. Most of the resources are free, but you have to register first to use them. The process is quick and painless — click the Free Registration button and fill in the necessary information. Note: Cookies must be enabled on your browser in order to register and login.

The Multex homepage offers daily ideas, reports, and highlights about what is happening in the financial world. To get analyst reports about a particular stock, enter the company's ticker symbol in the Search box, and then click Research. A list of reports appears, many of which are free; some are available for purchase from brokerages.

To read a report, click its title. Many of these reports are quite lengthy, and you might have to view them using the Adobe Acrobat Program. If you don't have this program on your computer, don't worry. You can download it for free from the Multex site. Just click the link for Adobe Acrobat Viewer.

If you want to read an overview of different analysts' opinions, look for the report entitled Multex-Ace Consensus Estimates, as pictured in the Figure below. This free report gathers information from many sources to provide investors with a quick overview of analysts' estimations of the company.

ANALYSTS' CONSENSUS: Buy						(As of 7/31/99)
	No. of Ratings	% of Total	One Month Prior	Three Mos. Prior	National	Regional	Non-Broker
Buy	5	25	7	7	3	2	0
Buy/Hold	10	50	12	12	4	6	0
Hold	0	0	1	3	0	0	0
Weak Hold	0	0	0	0	0	0	0
Sell	0	0	0	0	0	0	0
No Opinion	5	25	5	4	1	3	1
Total	20	100	25	26	8	11	1

Average Qualitative Opinion = 1.00

Consensus Breakdown		Buy	=	>= 1.00
By National Firms	Buy	Buy/Hold	=	>=. 75 and < 1.00
By Regional Firms	Buy/Hold	Hold	=	>=.35 and < .75
By Nonbroker	None	Weak Hold	=	>= 0 and < .35
		Sell	=	< 0

This Report is derived from Multex ACE, the premier Wall Street Analyst Consensus Estimates and Recommendations Database with 3,500 Contributing Analysts covering 7,500 public companies. A glossary of terms and abbreviations used in this report is available at http://www.multex.com/mdg/glossary99.htm

After you've gathered background on a company, you don't have to decipher all the information alone. Financial experts are available online to give advice.

Estimated earnings per share

Find It Online

To see how your target's EPS compares to others in its sector and industry, go to Keyword: **Zacks**. Enter the ticker symbol for the company and hit enter. Select Earnings Estimates, and scroll down to Calendarized Comparative Analysis to see how your company compares to the average industry and sector figures, as well as the overall S&P 500.

Note

Even if a company breaks its all time earnings records — but Wall Street guessed those earnings would be higher — the market might react negatively. Similarly, when earnings per share exceed analysts' expectations — even if earnings are below what they have reached in the past — stock price could increase.

One of the most important things you need to look at in the analyst report is the *estimated earnings per share* — how much the analysts believe the company will earn divided by the number of shares of stock in the company. This helps you determine whether the company is on track to keep up its pace, or whether the analysts believe some part of the business will drag down how much is generated for those shares you own.

While these are just projections, they're very useful in helping to gauge if a company is primed for growth or if it's sitting stagnant. Analysts project EPS for the coming quarter, year, and in years to come. They also project earnings within the sector and the industry.

Investors and analysts who follow a particular company expect the company to perform as its history indicates, and in line with analysts' projections.

Often, analysts' expectations are what fuel hikes and drops in stock price. How the company's stock fares in the marketplace after the company releases its earnings can often have more to do with how its earnings compare to analysts' estimates than with the company's actual earnings growth or losses. A positive earnings report can still result in a downward spiral in stock price if the earnings didn't meet analysts' expectations.

Many stocks in recent years — Internet-related stocks in particular — have had soaring prices that are more a reflection of what the public believes is the company's *potential* for earnings than its current earnings. This can wreak havoc with investors' psyches. A company can report stunning revenue growth of 75 percent over the previous year, but if analysts were expecting 85 percent, the stock will most likely tumble — and probably pull down other technology stocks with it.

In this day and age, earnings estimates can be more powerful than actual earnings, in terms of how they affect a stock's price. You can explore this further online at the Motley Fool article shown in Figure 9-9. To reach it, go to Keyword: **Fool** and select Daily Trouble from the Quick Find drop-down list. Click Archives, and then the August link. Then click on priceline.com and you will see Figure 9-9.

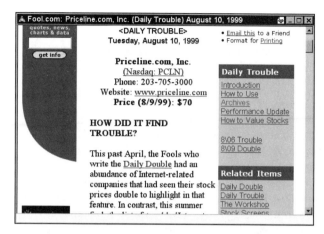

Figure 9-9. Strong profits aren't always enough. In the above example, this Internet company turned in good financial figures, but inflated expectations caused a serious drop in stock price.

So you need to know these expectations. No need, however, to drive to your broker and lean across her mahogany desk as she scans the brokerage house report for the numbers. AOL has tools that provide these estimates online. Go to Keyword: **Earnings**. This takes you to Zacks Investment Research. Plug in your symbol and up comes the earnings consensus of analysts, how the company has fared in the past compared to earnings estimates, and whether or not there have been any recent revisions to the estimates. An example is shown in Figure 9-10.

▲ Summary of Brokerage EPS Estimates and Recommendations

Company Estimate Profile

buy	buy/hold	hold	hold/sell	sell
	1.70			
7	11	2	0	0

Current consensus recommendation of 20 brokers.

	QTR Sep-99	QTR Dec-99	FY Dec-99	FY Dec-00
CURRENT MEAN EPS ESTIMATE	0.80	0.92	3.21	3.66
Number of Brokers	11	9	22	22
Year Ago EPS	0.69	0.80	2.80	3.21
Report Date	10/08/1999	1/20/2000	1/20/2000	1/20/2001

Figure 9-10. Although past performance is important, the future should be of great concern to a potential investor. EPS estimates offer a reasonable hypothesis of what to expect from a company in the coming year.

Find It Online

Profits are good, employee morale is great, and current sales are booming. So why did your company's stock take a tumble?

Because stock prices are often based on earnings expectations, if these predictions are not met stock prices can fall, even if the financials reveal a profitable quarter.

So you need to take into account the earnings estimates. Turn to Keyword: **Estimates** for a look at what Wall Street predicts for a particular company. Enter the company's ticker symbol, hit enter, and select Earnings Estimates.

AOL partner Zacks Investment Research brings you to the estimates and rates the company on a scale of strong buy to strong sell. Zacks provides a summary of brokerage EPS estimates and recommendations for the next quarter and the next year. It also brings up a history of the estimates, showing how they have evolved over the past three months.

You also get comparative EPS values for the industry and sector to which the company belongs, giving you a yardstick for comparison.

If there have been revisions, you need to discover why. Snoop around Keyword: **Company News**. If you still can't explain it, call the company's investor relations department for an explanation (albeit with the company spin on it).

Gauging growth

Now see how these earnings estimates help you assess growth. Your target may be a behemoth in its industry, but if it doesn't have increased sales, its earnings, cash flow, and dividends cannot increase, leaving it — and maybe your portfolio — to stagnate. How your target's earnings estimates compare to others in its sector is a crucial indicator because they help you identify a standard. Your target might be growing at 5 percent each quarter, making it appear very desirable, but if its brethren in the sector are raking in 10 percent gains every three months, your company has a problem.

To evaluate the sales growth of your target versus others in its industry, go to Keyword: **Market Guide**, plug in the ticker symbol, and click Search. Then select Stock Reports again. Then click Ratio Comparison. Now, look down to the Growth Rates chart. If your target's sales are growing faster than those of its peers, your target may be commanding a greater share of the market. And if earnings are growing faster than sales, that means your company is making more per sell, boosting profit margins.

Stock price

You need to examine not only company growth but stock price growth as well. First, find out how stock price has changed over time. Sometimes it's easiest to reference this with a chart.

Relative strength

A stock's price means little if you have nothing to compare it with. You need to compare the growth of your target's stock price with that of other stocks in the same sector or industry. This helps you figure out your target's *relative price strength*. To measure your target's price to a market index of similar stocks over time — weekly, monthly, or annually:

A Look at History

For a quick look at how your target's price has moved over time, go to Keyword: **Stocks**, and type in your target's symbol or name. From the box that says Select a Chart, click Charting Main, and click Enter. (You can also access this site at Keyword: **Charts**.)

Up comes Historical Quotes. Here you can tailor-make a chart that chronicles how a stock has performed during a certain time period, as shown in the figure. Plug in the stock symbol again, and select one of the pre-set time periods, or select Custom to specify your own time period. Hit the graph button to create a chart based on your timeline, or hit the Quotes button to see the information in table form.

Tip

Online Investor (Keyword: **Online Investor**) publishes a calendar of earnings announcements, and summarizes the fallout after earnings reports are released. Go to Keyword: **OLI** and click Earnings, in the Calendar category.

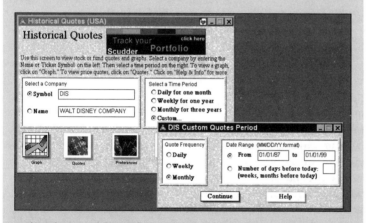

Tracking the ups and downs of a company over a period of time may help you determine the best time of year to purchase a stock.

1. Divide the price of your target at the end of a given time period by the price at the beginning of the period.
2. Take this quotient and compare it with the market index price at the end of the period divided by the market index price at the beginning of the period.

Now you can see which is stronger.

See Chapter 14 for a list of ticker symbols for common indices. Get the historical prices by date as you did just a couple of pages ago at Keyword: **Charts**.

Many investors insist that a company's earnings growth rate exceed its P/E. In addition, in an ideal scenario for a growth stock, EPS growth is more accelerated than dividend growth and than sales growth. All three should grow each year, and that growth rate should be higher each year.

For example, if you're trying to determine how the strength of your Widgets 'R' Us stock measures up to the strength of the market in general for a six-month-period, figure the formula. Suppose your stock cost $42 on February 1. On August 1 it sold for $45. Divide 45 by 42 and you get 1.07 — a 10.7 percent hike — for your relative strength.

Now look at the index quote for your target's market. Suppose it was 38.07 on August 1 and 31.07 on February 1. Divide 38.07 by 31.07 and you get 1.225 — a 12.25 percent hike.

At 10.7 percent, your stock performed quite well, but it under-performed the market against which you measured it, which turned in a 12.25 percent increase. It could be that market momentum was the only reason your stock was on the fly. Your stock's price should stand on its own strength. Even if it increased, if it didn't keep pace with the index that measures similar types of stocks, it was an underperformer.

Use the relative price strength together with the growth rate and other ratios, such as P/E, to best assess your stock's performance.

P/E, or Promising Expectations

You learned about P/E (a company's stock price divided by its earnings) in the Legend in Chapter 6. And you know how analysts and investors use it very differently. In a sense P/E measures expectation. The higher the P/E, the higher the public expects earnings to fly. For an online review of P/E, you can turn to the article pictured in Figure 9-11. Find it at Keyword: **Fool**; click The Fool's School. Under the How To... heading, click Value Stocks. Then select the topic Valuation: Principles and Practice, and then choose Earnings Valuation. Scroll through the article.

New companies that come flying out of the blocks cannot be expected to repeat tremendous growth every year. While their numbers appear strong the first couple of years, they will probably not be able to sustain sky-high growth rates. Yet they might still be considered solid growth investments.

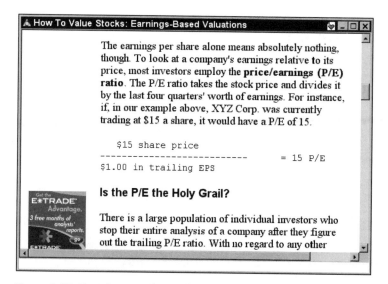

Figure 9-11. The P/E ratio is often used as a sort of price tag for a stock, allowing the investor to compare how the price of one stock measures up against another.

Financial Ratios

Now, to help you decide if you like your target's numbers, compare them to the numbers of other companies. Analysts often rely on such comparisons to evaluate the worthiness of a stock. They concentrate on four areas: growth (which you've just explored), *valuation*, *financial strength*, and *profitability*.

There is an easy way for you to measure these, through Market Guide's Ratio Reports, which you learned of earlier in the chapter. Go to **Market Guide**, plug in your ticker symbol, and select Comparison, as shown in Figure 9-12. The charts reflect the financial heart and soul of the company. They compare your target with its peers in the industry, in its sector of industries and against the S&P 500. While ratios represent an excellent way to compare one company to the next, there are no magic numbers that automatically deem your target a winner. You must combine the ratios with other information you gather in your research to judge the stock.

Tip

If figuring the growth rate is as tedious to you as weeding, the folks at the Motley Fool can help. Their PEGulator calculates the PEG—the P/E divided by the annual forecasted earnings growth rate—for you. Go to Keyword: **Fool**, scroll down to Electronic Fool, and then click PEGulator. Download the tool, then plug in the P/E, EPS, estimated earnings and a couple of other items and *voila*, up pops the Price-to-Earnings-to-Growth ratio. (For stocks that pay a dividend, figure the PEGY: (price/earnings) divided by (projected growth rate + dividend yield).)

Note

Keep in mind that all these research tools are helpful not only for examining your potential acquisitions, but are worth taking a look at each year for the stocks you currently own.

Figure 9-12. Is a company outperforming its peers or barely keeping up? Ratio comparisons show if your target is leading or trailing the rest of the pack.

Valuation ratios

Valuation ratios help you assess whether your target is expensive or inexpensive based on a host of factors, including a company's growth, financial strength, and profitability.

You've already learned about the P/E ratio. Now look on the ratio charts to compare your target's P/E to other P/Es in the same industry and sector, and to the S&P 500. If the P/E ratio for your target is less than the P/E for these others, your target's stock is selling *at a discount valuation* compared with its brethren. If it's higher than the averages, it means your fellow investors think the company will grow faster than its peers. Of course, you have to make sure that earnings — not just market hype — support that assumption.

Price-to-sales

What if there are no earnings? When companies don't pay dividends and when they don't have P/Es there seems to be no standard way to measure whether or not you're getting the stock for a "fair" price. You can look to the *price-to-sales ratio* for some help deciding, though. PSR compares your target's stock price with the company's real sales.

Find its definition online, as shown in Figure 9-13, at Keyword: **Investment Research**. Click the Help button and then select How to Screen Stocks.

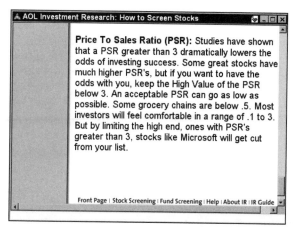

Figure 9-13. According to conventional wisdom, a stock is attractive if its PSR hovers around 1.

It seems like an odd measurement to look at, something that measures companies with no earnings and no dividends. How could such a company possibly be valuable? Because of sky-high sales and growth rates, which often indicate a rosy future.

Investors used to look for a PSR below 3, preferably 1 or below. But with today's dot-coms and their high-flying siblings, some PSRs seem ludicrously high. Still, if people are buying the stock, they believe the price isn't too high. You must decide if you think sales are growing quickly enough to warrant the price.

To check sales, go to Keyword: **Market Guide**, plug in your stock symbol and select Stock Reports, and scroll down below Growth Rates, to Sales. This tells you the percentage that sales have increased or decreased quarterly or annually. The numbers reveal if sales match the hype about the companies.

Price-to-free cash flow

Here's another ratio that investors should evaluate, especially for more traditional companies, those that have outgrown their hyper growth phase and have stabilized into established corporations. Price-to-free cash flow represents the amount of money left over after the company pays for capital expenses and dividends. This money fuels future growth. Find price-to-free cash flow in the Market Guide reports, under Valuation Ratios.

Note

Whether you're investing for growth or income, compare dividend growth to earnings growth. The Dividend 5-Year Growth rate is in the Dividends table of Market Guide's ratio reports and the 5-Year EPS rate is in the Growth Rates table. If dividend growth exceeds earnings growth, your target could be dumping so much of its profits into dividends it has limited money it can use to grow.

Note

Many dot-com high flyers, as well as companies in major growth mode, don't have any profits, so net profit margin might actually be a negative for them.

Price-to-book value

This ratio measures price-per-share divided by everything the company owns minus its debts and liabilities — in other words, what shareholders would receive if the company were liquidated. Stick to comparisons within industry on this one, as price-to-book varies tremendously from one industry to the next. (Service providers, for example, have a much higher price-to-book than manufacturers.)

Income ratios

If you plan to rely on your holdings for income, you need to check other valuation ratios to see how your target company measures up. Start with the *payout ratio*, in the Market Guide reports in the Dividends table. This reflects the percentage of earnings the company returned to shareholders in the form of dividends in the past year. The *lower* the ratio, the better, because it means the company was able to pay you and still plow profits back into the business. With a lower payout ratio, the company has a cushion to fall back on in hard times without having to cut dividends.

Payout ratios, too, vary significantly from industry to industry. For a fair assessment of your target's payout ratio, compare it with others within its industry.

Next, check the *Dividend 5-Year Growth Rate*. Has the dividend grown? Ideally, it has, at a rate that exceeds inflation. Otherwise, your dividend carries less purchasing power than you might be counting on.

Profitability ratios

Profitability ratios show you how much money the company is making, and how this compares to the company's peers. Look especially at *net profit margin*. This tells you how much of each sales dollar the company kept after expenses and taxes. The higher the number, the better off the company is.

Check your target's net profit margin against that of its peers to really gauge its strength. Keep to comparisons within industry, though, as costs — and therefore profits — differ wildly from one industry to the next. Computer companies might rack up 20 percent margins, while grocery stores make do with a percent or two

Financial strength ratios

Earlier in this chapter you explored a company's assets and liabilities in its 10-K or annual report. You can now determine how strong these numbers are by turning to the *financial strength ratios*. The stronger a company is financially, the better able it is to ride out turbulent business or market conditions.

The *current ratio* measures cash on hand plus cash projected for the next year, against liabilities projected for the next year. Ideally, assets equal or exceed liabilities, so this figure should be 1.00 or above, preferably 1.5 or above. While there's no need to head for high ground if the number is less than 1.0, the target bears closer scrutiny. The company might have to raise money fast if liabilities start encroaching on working capital and endangering current projects.

Debt-to-equity

This ratio represents how much debt the company carries divided by shareholder dollars. Many Internet and other growth-oriented companies borrow a lot of money in a short period of time in order to expand quickly. The hope is that their revenues will eventually catch up. But the greater the company's debt, the greater the risk to you, the shareholder.

When you divide debt by the amount of shareholders' equity, ideally you should come up with a very low number, preferably less than 1.0. When debt-to-equity climbs above 2.0, your company has an awful lot of interest to pay on its debt, and those payments eat away at profits.

Management effectiveness

Even having the world's best product won't guarantee a company's financial success. The company needs to have masters at the helm. A number of ratios reflect management's prowess, foremost among them, *return on equity*.

 **Find It Online**

Want to review all this stock terminology while you're online? Go to Keyword: **Investment Research**, click Help, and choose Stock Term Definitions.

Return-on-equity

How much does the company actually generate for every dollar shareholders invest? The *return-on-equity ratio* will tell you. ROE indicates how well management uses your dollars, reflecting a combination of business performance and financial acumen. An above-average ROE usually implies steady growth, a firm foothold in its industry and solid management. Maximizing your return on equity is your goal in investing. A strong company should demonstrate a solid record of at least a 20 percent return on shareholder dollars over several years.

With ROE, you *can* compare apples to oranges, as the goal of every company, regardless of the kind of business it's in, is to maximize return on equity. Examine your target's one-year and five-year ROE averages against the market as a whole. (You can find them in the Market Guide reports, in the Management Effectiveness table.) See whether your target caught fire during the hot streaks and held up during the downturns. To learn online about valuing stocks using the ROE ratio, go to Keyword: **Fool**, click The Fool's School and select How to Value Stocks. Scroll down and choose Return on Equity, as pictured in Figure 9-14.

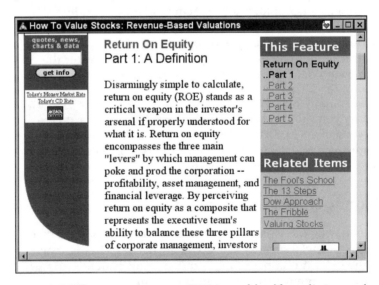

Figure 9-14. The return on equity ratio (ROE) is a useful tool for evaluating a stock. ROE takes into account profitability, asset management, and financial leverage.

Stock Screening

After you know what you're prospecting for, there's an easy way to dig without scrutinizing every piece of financial data in existence: AOL's Stock Screening tool does some of the mining.

Stock screens quickly and efficiently analyze massive amounts of data according to your parameters. You enter values to narrow the field of prospects from the 10,000 or so publicly traded stocks in AOL's database, and the electronic excavator combs through financial data and retrieves only those stocks whose numbers meet your requirements.

First, you have to figure out what those requirements are. Maybe you've decided on stocks that represent a particular sector. Maybe you want stocks that only cost a certain amount of money. Maybe you're looking for cost *and* a particular P/E ratio.

For example, let's say you think buying Internet-related stocks is like prospecting for oil in the backyard — a tremendous outlay with nary a chance of success. You refuse to pay exorbitant prices on the promise of future growth. You could screen out such pricey stocks immediately by focusing on the Price/Earnings ratio. On the screening tool, enter the highest P/E ratio you will tolerate, say 35, and leave the low value blank. That immediately cuts out all stocks you think are too over-priced for your tastes.

If you don't judge a stock by its P/E, you leave those boxes empty.

Your own objectives

It doesn't do you much good to look for attributes someone else suggests. To really make screens effective, you need clearly defined objectives that reflect *your* risk, return, and overall investment philosophy. If you're looking for stocks that generate high dividends, for example, your criteria will not include factors that screen for growth-oriented companies.

After you know what you're looking for, plug the variables into the screening program. You can get to it via Keyword:

Tip

While there is no magic recipe for picking winners, one combination seems to set the stage for success. If your target's return on equity exceeds the average of its peers, its price-to-book is lower than its peers, and its debt-to-equity is in the same ballpark, you have probably discovered an undervalued, or inexpensive, stock.

Stock Screening, as pictured in Figure 9-15, or you can go through your by now favorite page, Keyword: **Investment Research**. Once there, input the variables, click Screen Stocks, and the program sorts through millions of pieces of information to find results according to your priorities.

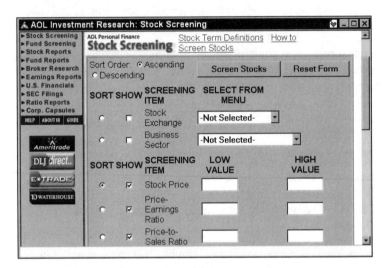

Figure 9-15. AOL's stock screening tool can help you sift through the many thousands of choices to find stocks that meet your criteria.

The key is knowing ahead of time what you're looking for, so that you plug in the right variables. Keep your objectives clear and narrow. If your objective is "Picking a winner", then a screen will not turn up answers. If "Finding a high-yielding stock compared to others in its industry" is your objective, then a screen will help.

How screens work

Screens work by comparing a company's numbers against some other numbers. When setting up your screens, stick to criteria you understand well and try not to use criteria that contradict each other. Say you're screening for stocks that generate above average income. You wouldn't screen for high earnings growth at the same time. Companies that are growing fast and furious don't have the money to shell out to shareholders. Therefore, your criteria for high growth would cancel out most of the high-yielders.

To best understand this tool it helps to be online, at Keyword: **Stock Screening**, while you explore the following information.

First off, note that you don't have to fill in every box. Say, for example, you're only interested in stocks that cost no more than $15 with a (what you deem) reasonable P/E. To fill in the Stock Price boxes, leave the low value blank and put in $15 for the high value. For P/E, leave the low value blank and maybe input 20 for the high value. Then hit Screen Stocks and away it screens.

Tip

Click Back on the toolbar to narrow your focus so you don't erase the parameters you just used.

You probably end up with more than 5,000 hits. Before you begin to analyze the results you might realize you have too many speculative cheapos. You can easily go back and fine-tune your parameters. Hit Back on the toolbar and input $5 for the Stock Price's low value, then screen again. Now you've cut the number in half. Change it to 6 and you whittle it down further. Maybe you don't want tiny companies. You put in 500 for a low value under Market Cap and now you've slashed the results, as shown in Figure 9-16. This continuous fine-tuning helps you narrow your focus.

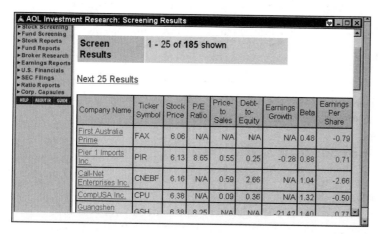

Figure 9-16. Fine-tune your variables to narrow the list of companies meeting your criteria. In this example, minimum stock price and market capitalization figures trimmed the list from thousands of candidates to fewer than 200.

Now, for the details. Your first selection is Sort Order. You have to pick one of the variables as the most important factor when determining Sort Order. Say you're interested in the highest yielders. Click the circle next to Dividend Yield and input your other values. When the stocks that fit your wish list

Note

If you'd like an online explanation for a variable, click Stock Term Definitions at the top of the Screening page to access a glossary of terms used in the screening tool, as pictured in Figure 9-17.

Cross-Reference

For more information on stock exchanges, turn to Chapter 13.

come up, they will be ranked according to Dividend Yield, in addition to meeting all your other parameters. If you want the *best* choice to appear first, select *descending* order. If you want the *lowest* of the qualifiers first, select *ascending* order.

If you want to see all the variables when the list comes up, make sure to click the Show box next to each variable before you select Screen Stocks. If you don't need to see a variable, leave the Show box next to it blank.

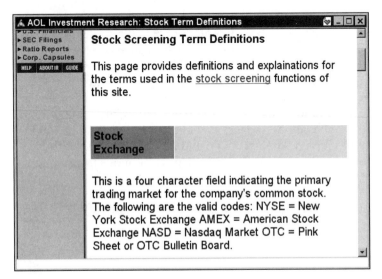

Figure 9-17. Forget what a particular variable means? All terms in the stock screener tool are explained in the glossary.

Choose your variables

You can narrow your choices by *Sector* and *Stock Exchange*, or you can opt for the default choice — Not Selected — for these two items if they aren't important to your search. Business sectors include: basic materials, capital goods, conglomerates, consumer cyclical, consumer/non-cyclical, energy, financial, health care, services, technology, transportation, utilities. Exchanges include the NYSE, AMEX, NASDAQ, and OTC.

First up, *Stock Price*. How much do you want to spend? If you don't really have a figure, but you want to weed out the really high-flyers and the penny stocks, input high and low variables. If you're looking in a particular price range, put values with a narrow spread in the boxes. Maybe Grandma gave you $1000 for graduating from college and you're looking for something around $20 a share. You might type in $17 for a low value and $23 for a high value, and whittle it down from there. Maybe you don't care how much the stock costs because you're basing your search on other requirements. In this case, leave both boxes blank. If you do want to see how much the stock costs after you run the screen, click the Show box.

Price-Earnings (P/E) Ratio is next. Depending on what type of investor you are, this area is either very important or irrelevant to you. If you don't live and die by P/E leave the boxes blank. If you think it's ludicrous to buy a stock with a P/E higher than 35 or whatever, then input this maximum number in the high value box.

Up next is *Price-to-Sales Ratio (PSR)*. As you learned earlier, this ratio is often used to gauge companies without earnings or dividends. Sales is the engine driving their growth. How much are you paying for this cash flow? If you're hunting for stocks under a particular PSR, input the high value. If not, leave both boxes blank.

Then there's *Debt-to-Equity*. This reflects total debt for the most recent fiscal quarter, divided by shareholders' equity for the same period. How leveraged are your targets? Again, whether or not you fill in these values depends on your personal investing preferences. But it's a good idea to click the Show box whether or not you input the values so you can see exactly how leveraged your targets are.

Next comes *Market Capitalization*. Market cap is the price per share multiplied by the number of outstanding shares. Are you looking for a small, medium, or large company? If you have a preference, input the values (in millions). For example, if you only want big companies, input a Low Value of at least 1,000. (It's in millions of dollars, so that would be $1 billion.) If you're looking for small or micro-caps, input a few hundred million for the High Value. If you don't want to limit your choices by market cap, leave both boxes empty.

After this is *Earnings Growth*. This measures the growth rate of EPS over the past three years. Many fast-growing companies don't even have earnings yet, so you may not want to include any values here.

Next is *Dividend Yield*. If you're looking for income investments, you'll want to pay close attention to this figure. Maybe

Note

If you don't know what to include for these values, you can refer to the sample screens at the end of this section.

Try to limit your list to about 30 possibilities before you launch your next round of investigation. Otherwise your research becomes unwieldy.

you want to find stocks that match or better a particular bond you're considering. If there is a minimum yield you seek, input that number in the Low Value box. If you don't care about dividends, leave both boxes blank.

Then comes *beta*. How risky are you willing to go vs. the S&P 500, which always has a beta of one? Even if you don't have any particular limitations, check that Show box again so you can at least see how volatile your targets tend to be.

Book Value is next. It's total shareholder's equity, minus preferred stock.

Then there's *Return on Equity*. How much return was generated for every dollar invested by stockholders in the company. The tool measures this over the five most recent quarters. The numbers you enter here are dependent upon your goals.

Next is *Shares Outstanding*: How many shares out there, or the number of people with whom you'll be sharing the pie.

Then comes *Earnings per Share*: These boxes perhaps best reflect your agenda. They measure how much earnings the targets generated per share over the past year. Remember that many of the fastest climbers in the market don't even have earnings. Leave the boxes blank if EPS is not one of the screening variables important to your search. But check that Show button.

Screen your selections

After you fill in the blanks, hit the Screen Stocks button on the top or bottom of the page to come up with your results. To further refine your selection click the Back button, change the values and hit Screen Stocks again. To screen based on different variables, hit the Reset Form button on the top or bottom of the screen and get a whole new slate.

Remember, the best way to use the screening tool is to consider it just that — a tool, not a sure-fire guarantee for instant success.

It's lots of fun plugging in your ideal scenarios on the screening tool and seeing what companies turn up. Screening is also helpful when you're shopping for something in particular. Maybe your portfolio could use something from the health or utilities sectors. Maybe you'd like something that smacks of high growth. Maybe your needs are changing and it's time to look for income as opposed to growth.

Try a sampling

The point of screening stocks is to simplify your search. If you need some help narrowing your parameters, Marc Gerstein, a director with AOL partner Market Guide, offers some suggestions to help you look for growth, income or value stocks.

That said, the first thing Gerstein notes is that there will always be exceptions to these suggestions! "The whole point of a stock screen is to make a manageable list," he says, "not to come up with instant winners."

Income screens

Business sector: to save yourself a lot of time, select NYSE for the exchange, and utilities for the business sector, as shown in the Figure. If you don't come up with what you need, change business sector to "Not Selected" and run the screen again.

Make sure that after you get your list of likely suspects, you subject the companies to the investment research you know to conduct before you actually buy anything.

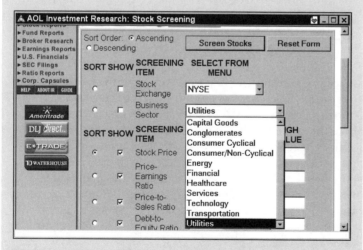

If you're looking for income stocks, you can select "utilities" as the business sector to save yourself some time.

Continued

Try a sampling *(continued)*

Price: If you're looking for income you probably don't want penny stocks. Save yourself time and put a low value of $10.

P/E: Leave blank.

P/S: Leave blank.

D/E: Leave it blank when you're running the utilities screen. When you're running the business sector "Not Selected" screen, leave the low value blank and input 1 for the high value.

Market Cap: Leave the high value blank and put in 1,000 million (which is 1 billion) for the low value. You won't get a small cap, but if a company with a $250 million market cap yields 6 percent there's something suspicious going on anyway.

Earnings Growth: Leave blank.

Dividend Yield: Start with 2.5 for the "Not Selected" screen's low value, because that's about average. For the utilities screen, jump it up to 5 for a low value.

Beta: Leave the low value blank and put the high value at 1.1.

Book value, ROE, shares outstanding and EPS: Leave blank.

After you run this the first time, you might want to "do a little trial and error," Gerstein says, to reduce your number of prospects. For the "Not Selected" screen, maybe you hike the price to $20. To get a little pickier, maybe reduce your debt to equity to 0.75. Maybe kick up the yield to 3 for a low value. You're at the point now where it's a matter of personal taste. Maybe you reduce the beta to 0.9. For the Utility screen, maybe you adjust the beta to a low value of 1 and leave a blank market cap to see what you come up with. It's a matter of tweaking the numbers to reflect your taste.

Growth screens

Stock Exchange and Business sector: Leave these blank, as growth stocks are found all over the place. (Unless you're looking to fill a particular need, in which case you might choose NASDAQ or Technology or whatever it is you're looking for.)

Price, P/E, P/S: Leave blank.

D/E: Start with a high value of 1, as oftentimes debt constrains growth. You might want to come back and change this though, depending on what your screen turns up.

Market Cap: Leave blank.

Earnings Growth: 20 for the low value (as shown in the Figure).

When screening for growth stocks, don't limit your search to a particular stock exchange or business sector, and make sure to input a minimum value in the earnings growth box.

Dividend Yield: Leave blank the low value, and put in a high value of 3.

Beta: 1.2 for the low value, as you want a little action if you're a growth investor.

Book value: Leave blank.

Continued

Try a sampling *(continued)*

ROE: Put in a low value of 15, but be prepared to change this if you don't get what you need.

Shares Outstanding and EPS: Leave blank.

You might feel you have too many candidates after you make the first pass. One way to narrow the field is to put in a P/E no greater than Earnings Growth — 20 in this instance. That narrows the field. Now you can hike up that ROE a bit — to 18 — and reduce Dividend Yield to 2. That fine-tunes your list even more. If it's still too big, pull P/E down to 15 and raise Earnings Growth to 25.

Keep in mind this screen would eliminate the pricey Amazon.coms of the world. If you don't give a care about price and are only looking for growth potential you could leave P/E blank and change the Price-to-Sales high value to 2.4, raise Earnings Growth to 30, and leave Yield blank.

Here's a kind of wacky approach that will change your growth-prospects list significantly. Instead of making your Price-to-Sales high value 2.4, make this the low value. This will reflect stocks whose prices are up, up, up — a sign of popularity among investors, but which, by most measures, indicates stocks that are way overpriced.

Value screens

Stock exchange and business sector: Leave these blank.

Price: Leave blank.

P/E: 15 for the high value.

P/S: 2 for the high value, (2.4 is average).

D/E: Leave blank.

Market Cap: Leave blank.

Earnings Growth: 10 for the low value.

Dividend Yield: A low value of 2. This is below average, so you might want to change this as you tweak your variables.

Beta: 1.2 for the high value, but this is another you might want to select by trial and error.

Book value: Leave blank.

ROE: A low value of 15, because you're looking for a nice, profitable company (shown in the Figure below).

A typical value screen might limit the ROE to no less than 15, to ensure the resulting companies are profitable.

Shares Outstanding and EPS: Leave blank.

If you want to refine the group from this point, change Shares Outstanding to a low of 20 million.

For value investors in particular it is important to scrutinize the candidates your screen turns up. "The value people shouldn't be discouraged if the first two or three look like dogs. You haven't made a mistake and you haven't screwed up your screens," Gerstein says. "Every time you do a screen based on value you're likely to get 20 of 30 companies headed for problems — chances are there are some real dogs. You really have to judge them stock by stock. You have to feel the trouble is temporary and they will come out of it. You have to buy it with your eyes open."

Summary

That was the hardest chewing you'll do in this book. You figured what kind of research you want to pursue, learned how and where to gather resources, and you know how to size up your candidates.

You can dissect the financials and tell an income statement from a balance sheet. You know where to track down analyst reports and what to look for after you find them. You've mastered the alphabet soup of investment research, from EPS to P/E to ROE, and you know how these ratios can affect your target.

You also learned to screen stocks, using variables to help you find exactly what you're looking for.

Coming up next, strategies you can employ now that you know how to find what you're looking for.

10

STRATEGIES TO PUT
STOCK IN

A Quick Look

▶ **A Thousand Words**   **page 255**

Sometimes a picture is worth a thousand words. It sure seems much easier to look at a chart to get a feel for a company's or an index's past performance than to try to analyze years' worth of financial figures.

You can chart different stocks and indexes, and compare them to past performance at Keyword: **Bloomberg**, then select Markets. From table of contents on the left, click Chart Builder under the Stocks heading, and plug in the name(s) of the stocks or indexes you'd like to see graphed. You can even choose the time frame you'd like to view.

▶ **Quicken's Picks**   **page 260**

Looking for a promising small cap? Want to know which stocks are on an upward trend and which are in the middle of a slide south?

Quicken shows you which stocks are most (and least) promising in every category. Go to Keyword: **Quicken.com**. Select the Investing tab and then click Stocks. In the pull-down list under Tickers to Watch, select the category you'd like to review.

▶ **Valuable Finds**   **page 275**

You know it's time to sell when your stocks are overvalued. For an online primer on when a stock is past its prime, ask the Fools for help.

To learn how to appraise stocks go to Keyword: **Motley Fool**, click The Fool's School, and then select Value Stocks under the How To. . . heading. Start with Valuation: Principles and Practice to shore up on the key indicators that help you determine when it's time to sell.

Chapter 10

Strategies to Put Stock In

You understand stocks, you know what types you're looking for to fill your portfolio, and you know how to research them. But successful investing in stocks takes more work than just finding them. It takes a trading strategy.

Herein lies The Secret Strategy to Successful Stock Investing: Buy them when they're low, sell them when they're high.

OK, everybody knows this. But why is it so hard to execute? Because few people can muster the fortitude to cut loose their winners, believing they will only continue to go up. Fewer still can collect the courage to buy when everything's down, believing they need to wait for the clouds to lift before making their purchase. But if you wade in the murky waters between the two, you'll never end up with a winning portfolio. You need to jump when the time is right.

For an online primer on strategies for a winning portfolio, look to the article in Figure 10-1. You can find it at Keyword: **Quicken.com**. Click the Investments tab and then choose Basics from the left-hand list to open the article.

Figure 10-1. Buy low, sell high. Timing is everything in the stock market, and there are ways to improve your odds.

This chapter will help you buy and sell stock on your terms. It will help give you a greater understanding of when and what to buy and sell, as well as different methods of buying and selling. Use the research tools you learned in the last chapter to determine when stocks are priced low, and buy them. Determine when they're high, and sell them — even if your actions fly in the face of general market sentiment. Then consider the stock strategies in this chapter to help you formulate a plan for building your portfolio, which is the subject of Chapter 11.

Active versus passive investing

One of the cornerstones of investing in stocks is deciding whether to actively select them or to rely on a formula to make the choices for you. That is the essence of *active* and *passive investing*.

To review your goals see Chapter 4.

In active investing a person does their research and decides what and when to buy and sell. That person can be you or the manager of the mutual fund you choose. No matter. Somebody *actively chooses* which stocks to buy and sell. Active investing takes a good deal of time and research on the part of the decision-maker.

In passive investing, no person decides what and when to buy and sell. Instead, those decisions are dictated by a formula and are executed either by you or by a computer. Passive investing takes a few minutes to set up, and a few more once or twice a year to make sure the investments are still in keeping with your goals.

Should you turn to active or passive investments? That decision depends on how much time you want to devote to research, what your return expectations are, how involved you want to get in your trading.

Many investors rely on a combination of active and passive strategies when choosing their investments. Here are some popular tacks.

Passive Investment Strategies

Some of the most common passive strategies are the easiest to execute, as well. Investing in index funds, for example.

Index funds

Want to match the return of the Standard & Poor's 500 — a healthy 12.5 percent a year since 1950? You don't have to call your broker and put in buy orders for every listed company. There is a simple way to enjoy the same return as the S&P 500. And that's to put your money in an index mutual fund that reflects these holdings. As you read in the mutual funds chapter, index funds pattern what the market does as a whole and are a tidy, buckled-in way to ride the market roller coaster.

Index funds are among the most popular passive investments. One reason is because they don't fall prey to a manager's whims, as their activity is computer-driven to mimic how the individual stocks in the index fare during the market day.

Another is because they allow you to concentrate your investment in a particular area without doing much homework — you simply pick the field you want represented.

Index funds aren't limited to the S&P 500. Different types of index funds reflect different registers of holdings. Some, like the Russell 2000 pattern only small-caps, others, like the NASDAQ 100, include only NASDAQ stocks. Some reflect mid-caps. Others pattern international stocks. Some emulate particular sectors or industries, like the Dow Jones Transportation Index or the Dow Jones Utilities Index.

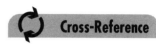

Cross-Reference

For a list of about two dozen popular indexes and their ticker symbols, see Chapter 14.

Index funds online

There are hundreds of index funds. To review a comprehensive list online and see how they fare over the short- and long-term, go to Keyword: **Bloomberg.com**, then click Mutual Funds. Scroll down to Funds by Sector, select Index funds and click Go.

To examine just the S&P 500, as pictured in the Figure below, select Markets from the top row of the Bloomberg homepage. Scroll down the table of contents on the left to the Stock section, and select S&P 500 Snapshot for a look at how this index is performing for the day and over the past year. This site also offers a list of the top 10 and 10 worst performing stocks in the S&P 500 for the current trading day.

From that same table of contents, click Chart Builder, under Stocks, to chart the activity for the indexes or stocks you're interested in. Enter the ticker symbol for a stock or a market, select the time frame you wish to view, and click Get Chart. You may also select several stocks and markets to create a comparison graph; simply enter the information for the items you wish to see and again click Get Chart.

Continued

Index funds online *(continued)*

	S&P 500 Snapshot

S&P 500 Snapshot
Wed, 11 Aug 1999, 11:23am EDT

Lookup symbol

NEWS
Top Financial
News
Top World News
Stock Market
Update
Technology
U.S. Economy
Columns
Special Report

STOCKS
Tech Stocks
Stocks on the
Move
Chart Builder
World Indices
Movers by
Exchange

The Standard & Poor's 500 Index is a capitalization-weighted index of 500 stocks. The index is designed to measure performance of the broad domestic economy through changes in the aggregate market value of 500 stocks representing all major industries. The index was developed with a base level of 10 for the 1941-43 base period.

Current	Change	% Change	Last Update
1285.50	4.07	+.32	11:12:

Index funds, which mirror market indexes such as the S&P 500, have given investors some of the best returns in recent years.

Bloomberg also offers many other tools and tips for getting the most out of the stock market. Stocks on the Move, for example, is a continually updated list of stocks in the U.S. market that are climbing, accompanied by mini-profiles and charts showing the year's growth. If you're looking for global financial indicators, click World Indices for a look at what is happening in financial markets worldwide. You can also scrutinize Regional Indices, Industry Movers, or Movers by Exchange to focus on information relevant to your portfolio.

Although index funds exist for different sectors and different-sized companies, allowing you to diversify your stocks with ease, be aware that some underperform other mutual funds with similar assets. The best of the lot is the S&P 500 index fund (available through almost all fund families), which outperforms the vast majority of all mutual funds and all index funds.

To read about index funds online, go to Keyword: **Mutual Funds**, click Archives, then select Index Funds, to find articles such as the one in Figure 10-2, which compares various funds with each other.

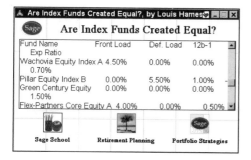

Figure 10-2. Index funds are a popular investment, but make sure to do your homework when selecting one. The differences in fees among funds can vary significantly.

S&P index funds are an easy, research-free investment with a consistent history. If you had invested $10,000 in an S&P index fund 25 years ago, and let your returns compound, you'd have almost $224,000 by now.

Dow Dividend Approach

The *Dow Dividend Approach* is another very popular passive investing strategy. Many investors would be happy with an annual 12.5 percent return generated by an S&P index fund. But maybe you want the blue-chip section of your portfolio to try to surpass those S&P returns. For this goal, many investors turn to The Dow Dividend Approach, which is also called the *Dogs of the Dow*, or the *Dow 10*, or the *High Yield 10*.

This strategy is based on the Dow Jones Industrial Average, a chronicle of the performance of 30 American megacompanies (like General Electric and Disney) that is used as an indication of how stocks are faring overall.

For an online overview of the Dow Dividend Approach, go to the Motley Fool's Fool's School (see Figure 10-3), at Keyword: **Fool**. Click School from among the top toolbar links, and then click Step 7: Dow Approach under The 13 Steps to Investing Foolishly.

There are a couple of variations of the Dow Dividend Approach strategy. The most popular is to buy the 10 highest-yielding Dow Jones Industrial Average stocks and, a year later, replace those that are no longer the highest yielders with the new high yielders. The Dow 10 strategy has delivered about a 17.7 percent average return each year for the past 25 years.

Figure 10-3. Want to try to outperform the returns of an S&P 500 index fund? Using the Dow Dividend method may give your portfolio an edge.

This is how it works:

1. Get a list of the 30 stocks included in the Dow Jones Industrial Average. There's a list of the current components in Chapter 6. You can find one online by going to Keyword: **Fool,** and clicking Dow Investing, under the School heading in the Quick Find box. The current Dow companies are listed in the column on the right. (See Figure 10-4).

2. Then calculate the annual dividend yield for each stock (which is the annual dollar dividend divided by the stock price).

3. Then list by stock price. These numbers can all be found at Keyword: **Fool.** Scroll down and click Fool's School. On the next screen, scroll down and select Dow Investing below the Foolish Investing Styles heading.

4. Rank the stocks by yield, with the highest yielder on top. If there's a tie, the one with the lower price goes first.

5. Now take the money you have allocated for purchasing blue chip stocks and buy equal dollar amounts of the top 10 yielders on the list. If you're working with $10,000, for example, buy $1,000 worth of each stock.

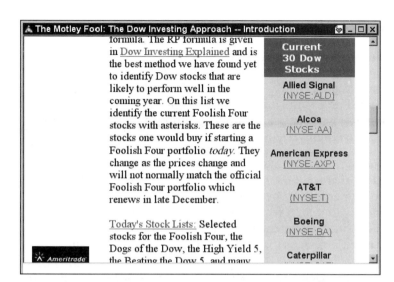

Definition

Yield — the annual dividend divided by the stock price.

10

Strategies to Put Stock In

Figure 10-4. It may seem larger than life, but the Dow Jones Industrial Average is made up of only 30 American conglomerates. But these companies often reflect the overall health of the economy.

> **6.** A year later, review the list, sell whatever's not in the top 10, and replace them with those that are.

Sound simple? It is. If you had invested $10,000 in this way 25 years ago, you would have more than $600,000 today.

Another variation of the Dow Dividend Approach, more narrow in scope, hikes that return even further. Take your list of 10, and then look at their stock prices and buy the five least expensive on the list. In the past 25 years, this strategy has bettered the Dow 10 by more than 2 percent a year. Had you invested $10,000 in this way 25 years ago, your investment would now be worth more than $1 million.

Active Investment Strategies

For the active investments you choose yourself, some strategies stand a greater chance of success than others. The following are among them:

Buying the small caps

Cross-Reference

You learned about market capitalization in Chapter 6. It refers to a company's number of outstanding shares, multiplied by the price of the stock. While the parameters change depending on which analysts you ask, you can use these as ballpark figures: micro-caps range up to $300 million, small-caps range from $300 million to $1 billion; mid-caps go from $1 billion to $3 billion; and large-caps total $3 billion and above.

Numerous studies show the biggest gains to be had are in small cap stocks. Markets tend to neglect micro and small caps. Analysts barely pay them any mind, journalists have bigger fish to fry, and institutions and mutual funds can't get in a big way without risking liquidity problems (there might not be enough buyers around to unload them).

But many individual investors love them. If you buy a stock for $10 a share and the price moves up just a dollar you're already up 10 percent. If you buy a profitable small cap that you like, stick with it for a while and wait for the rest of the market to catch on, your potential for higher returns will be greater than it is for large-caps that everybody already knows about.

Small-cap growth

Quicken.com offers a promising list of small-cap growth stocks (see the Figure below). Go to Keyword: **Quicken** and click Quicken.com. Select Investing, click Stocks, and in the pull-down list under Tickers to Watch, select Small-Cap Growth. A list of picks will show the company ticker symbol, the Price-to-Book, P/E, and Price-to-Sales ratios, as well as the stock's current price.

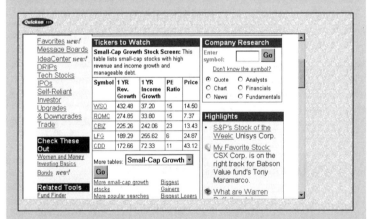

Small-cap stocks often yield hidden treasure. Neglected by analysts and unattractive to mutual funds, small-caps can produce large profits.

You can also see top-performing large-cap stocks by selecting that category from the pull-down menu. From here you can call up the day's biggest winners, losers, and heaviest movers. You can even create your own searches based on factors such as company description, valuation, growth rate, price and financial strength. Select Create Your Own Search and enter the information for the stocks you'd like to review.

For example, you can choose to see only computer companies listed in the S&P 500 with a P/E ratio between 10 and 35 and a stock price between $15 and $85. If you do not care about a particular variable, simply leave the default value as "any." When finished, click Show Results to review the list of stocks that match your criteria.

If you want more information about a listed stock, click the ticker symbol to open Quicken's investment overview of the company, including recent headline stories. From the overview you can investigate every aspect of the company, from SEC filings to analysts' estimates and financial statements. Select Rate & Discuss to find out what other stockholders are saying about the company, or to post a comment yourself.

The downside is, smaller caps tend to be more risky. As fewer people know about them, their prices might remain stagnant for a time. Also, they could be hard to unload when you need to get rid of them.

Buying the forlorn

It's not a pretty sight when a solid stock gets beaten up by a market that's overreacting to news. But it could be a great buying opportunity. The tricky part is determining whether the market truly overreacted or whether the stock was too overpriced to begin with. Wait a bit to assess the fallout, then make your move.

Buying "story" stocks

These make the climb due to a positive story: a new product like a hot drug, a new market or a new partnership. When Amazon.com first debuted, for example, it was a prime case of a story stock (see Figure 10-5. You can access similar profiles at Keyword: **Hoover's**, then type in the ticker symbol and choose Company Overviews).

Figure 10-5. At the right place and time, a company's stock can be very attractive to investors. For example, the initial success of Amazon.com stock was due, in part, to a surge of interest in Internet-related stocks.

Granted, when you invest in a story stock you won't be the only one in the know, but if you work quickly to assess the implications of the story, you can move in when the price is still reasonable. If you wait too long, it's probably best not to make the buy, as high expectations will already be incorporated into the price.

Buying the trend

When a stock's price is on the climb, and its growth is greater than the market's, many momentum investors jump on board. But if you're only buying on momentum, you have to be quick to jump off when the price starts to flatten out. Go back to your methods of assessing growth in the last chapter — when you compared your target's stock price growth to that of other companies in similar industries and to the market as a whole — and make sure you're aware ahead of time when you might be jumping off.

Buying the earnings estimate news

Some studies have shown that active investors see significant near-term results when they buy immediately after a consensus of analysts makes large, upward revisions in earnings estimates. Obviously, if the earnings forecasts are improved, the company is expected to fare better, so an upward movement in price isn't peculiar. But in many instances, the price hikes tend to persist for some time following the revisions, often up to a year after. The graph in Figure 10-6 shows a one-year price line for Caterpillar Inc., including an uptick in price following a bright forecast.

Cross-Reference

To hone the skills you need to help you determine when to buy and when to sell a stock based on momentum, review Chapter 9.

Tip

For earnings estimates, go to Keyword: **Earnings** and plug in your stock's ticker symbol. For a reminder of whose estimates are due out when, go to the Earnings Calendar at Keyword: **Online Investor** and click Earnings.

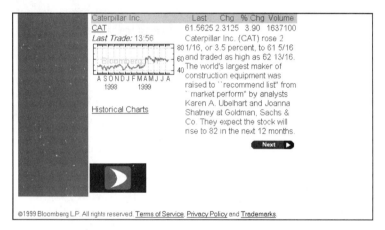

Figure 10-6. Many investors recognize an opportunity when analysts upgrade their earnings expectations for a particular stock.

Buying the initial public offering

Good luck on this front. While numerous studies have shown that getting in on an IPO at the initial offering price is extremely lucrative, the hard part is getting in.

For an online overview, visit IPO Central, shown in Figure 10-7. Type Keyword: **IPO**, and scroll down to The ABCs of IPOs. Click More to access the four-part series, *Beginner's Guide to IPOs*, dedicated to exploring the risks and debunking the myths of IPOs.

To learn which IPOs are coming up, go to Keyword: **Online Investor** and, under Calendars, click IPOs.

Figure 10-7. Just when you thought you were getting a handle on stocks, along comes another twist in the roller coaster ride: initial public offerings.

Here's how an IPO works. A privately owned company decides to go public to generate capital. A financial institution assesses the company's value and sets an initial share price. Many people who work for the company going public can buy in on this initial offering as part of the "Friends and Family" provision of the IPO process.

Financial institutions get first crack at the shares the second they're released to the "public." They scoop up what they want, then everybody else — like you — can get in on the stock. What often happens is that as soon as the shares begin to trade after their initial purchase and subsequent sales by the financial institutions, the shares get gobbled up by your online investing brethren, who let the stock rise a little, make a quick profit, then spit the stock back out again.

Recently, IPOs have caught fire on the first day of trading, only to get stomped out by day's end (see Figure 10-8). Depending on where your trade falls in the pecking order, you risk getting burned badly. You might put in an order to buy at the market rate, believing you'll be paying the initial offering price, and by the time your order comes up, the going price has quadrupled. Before you try to invest in an IPO, make sure you explore the possibilities with your broker.

underwriter, or location. GO▶▶	Biggest First-Day Jumps			
POWER SEARCH	**Company Name**	**Offer Price**	**Close Price**	**Percent Change**
	Ariba, Inc.	$23	$90	291%
Hoover's Online:	eToys Inc.	$20	$76.56	283%
Search by:	Redback Networks Inc.	$23	$84.13	266%
⦿ Company name	Log On America, Inc.	$10	$35	250%
○ Ticker symbol	Copper Mountain Networks, Inc.	$21	$68.44	226%
○ Keyword	TheStreet.com, Inc.	$19	$60	216%
○ Person's last name	Marimba, Inc	$20	$60.56	203%
	Juniper Networks, Inc.	$34	$97.88	188%
GO▶▶	GlobeSpan Semiconductor Inc.	$15	$42.31	182%
For Members Only	Mpath Interactive, Inc.	$18	$50.63	181%
POWER TOOL ★	Biggest First-Day Drops			
Find sales leads,	**Company Name**	**Offer Price**	**Close Price**	**Percent Change**
business contacts,	Streamline.com, Inc.	$10	$7.63	-23.7%
investment ideas,	ZipLink, Inc.	$14	$12.38	-11.6%
and vital	CONSOL Energy Inc.	$16	$14.25	-10.9%
competitive				

Figure 10-8. Initial public offerings can be exciting and often make headlines, but beware: for every IPO that makes a fortune the first day, there is another that takes it on the chin.

↻ **Cross-Reference**

To get a thorough understanding of the IPO trading process see Chapter 13. As that chapter suggests, if you do want to buy, put a price limit on your order to control your costs.

10

Strategies to Put Stock In

Dividend Reinvestment Plans

There's another way to buy, and this is directly from the company whose stock you already own. More than 900 companies, mostly blue-chip and rather conservative companies that pay dividends, offer Dividend Reinvestment Plans, also known as DRIPs or DRPs.

DRIPs let you the shareholder buy additional shares from the company at little or no cost, most often by reinvesting your dividend money. Some plans allow you to buy shares outright, without paying commissions to a broker. Others offer you a combination of the two options. You don't need thousands of dollars to take advantage of a DRIP, either. Many companies let you enroll in the program even if you own only one share.

Companies offer DRIPs so they can increase the number of shares held by long-term investors, thus stabilizing their shareholder base. DRIPs also provide a method for companies to raise capital without having to turn to lenders.

DRIPs are particularly appealing to investors who buy a stock and treat it like a family member — holding on year after year, sticking with it in good times and in bad. The plans are cheap and convenient — an ideal way to accumulate shares little by little over time.

For a good online primer of how DRIPs work, visit the Motley Fool (see Figure 10-9) at Keyword: **Fool**. From the Quick Find pull-down list, scroll down and select DRP Investing under the Fool's School heading.

If you don't rely on dividends for your income, or if you know you'll be holding a particular stock over the long term, DRIPs are a great way to put your dividends to good use, rather than sticking them in a money market until you figure out what to do with them.

Some online brokerages will let you reinvest your dividends at no cost, but they don't let you send in cash outright to buy more stocks without a commission.

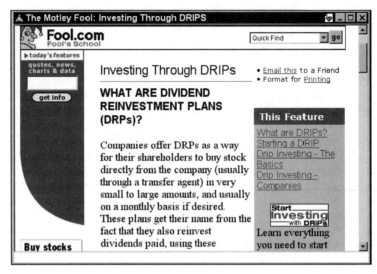

Figure 10-9. DRIPs can't be called exciting and won't provide sudden riches, but for the long-term investor, they offer stock accumulation with almost no overhead costs or fees.

DRIPs are wonderful for people who otherwise couldn't afford to buy stocks. (If you have to pay a $25 commission each time you buy one share of $25-stock, the cost becomes prohibitive.) If you participate in a number of DRIPs you can easily diversify without spending a lot of money.

Different companies offer different features in their DRIP plans. Among the features, some allow you to reinvest just a portion of your dividends and receive the rest in cash. A few allow you to send in a check each month — as little as $10 at a time — to put in your DRIP kitty. Others let you automatically invest regularly through your checking account or via payroll deduction. When your stash reaches the stock's market price, you get another share — no commission paid. And some let you set up your DRIP account as an IRA.

About 300 or so companies will sell you their stocks outright, even if you don't yet own a share. Some of these companies even offer discounts of up to 10 percent on the share price.

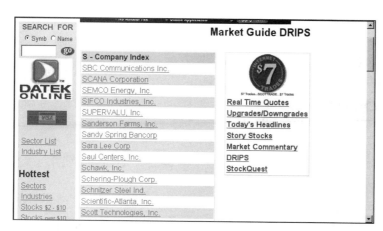

Figure 10-10. You can find out at a glance from Market Guide which companies offer DRIPs.

You can enroll in a DRIP program either through the company itself or via a transfer agent, such as a bank. Many larger companies use transfer agents to handle the processing.

Being in a DRIP is easy after it gets going, but it involves a ton of paperwork to set up. First, you have to have at least one share of stock, and it has to be registered in your name, not in the name of the brokerage house through which you bought it. If you don't have the stock certificate, you will have to request one from the broker, which might carry a small charge.

Next, you have to enroll in the program. Contact the company's DRIP administrator to request a dividend reinvestment enrollment form. Also ask for a prospectus because each plan will have its own specific requirements. For example, eligibility requirements, plan options, fees, dates, procedures outlining when your buys and sells can be made, and what can be done with your stock certificates all vary widely from company to company. Even though the process is very cumbersome, stick with it, as DRIPs are a great, affordable way to buy stocks in a company you want to hang onto for the long-term.

You can find contact information at Keyword: **http://www. marketguide.com**, then click DRIPs, click the name of your company and scroll down for contact information (see Figure 10-11).

Find It Online

No need to spend hours playing phone tag with the investor relations people in order to find out which companies offer DRIPs and what features are in the plans. You can learn all the details online simply by going to Keyword: **http://www. Market Guide.com** and clicking DRIPS (see Figure 10-10) in the contents box on the right.

10

Strategies to Put Stock In

Tip

If you don't own one share of stock but you want to enlist in a DRIP program—without the administrative hassles—you can sign up with a company that will buy the first share for you. Find out which companies your online investing brethren like on the Motley Fool's DRIPs message board at Keyword: Fool. From there, select the Messages tab, then Investors' Roundtable, and then scroll down to Drip Investing—companies and Drip Investing—The Basics.

Note

Buying additional stocks outright is really called the Option Cash Purchase Plan, but many people call it a DRIP.

Figure 10-11. Details, fees, and reinvestment opportunities for DRIPs vary by company, so be sure to check out each plan before investing.

Optional cash plans

When you enroll in a DRIP program, some companies allow you to add cash to buy more shares, many with minimum and maximum cash investment levels.

If you want to sell your shares, you have to either have the stock transferred to a broker first, or place your sell order in writing with the DRIP administrator. Whether you want to purchase outright or sell your shares, the stock administrator can only execute these trades on specific dates following your request. This makes it a bit of a hassle to sell the shares, especially for online investors, who are used to being able to execute trades in an instant.

There is a hidden danger to DRIPs. They tend to make you want to stick with the stock because you went through the whole rigmarole of setting up the DRIP. Buying and holding is a good thing, as long as your company is solid. But don't let DRIPs entice you into buying stock in a company you would otherwise avoid. And don't be afraid to unload the stock if it's no longer serving your purposes.

Smart Selling

Remember when you bought your stock? It might have felt like your first crush. You believed you'd found a winner. You rushed online to order the trade, certain that a look at your portfolio later that day or that week or that month would underscore your investing prowess. And then ...

Maybe the stock did so well that you're reading this book from the villa you bought with the proceeds. Good for you: You sold and locked in your profits.

But there's that other scenario — when your sure winner turns out to be less than stellar. In fact, now that it's not shining so brightly, your star is revealed for what it really is: hot air.

So it's time to sell. How sad. You might feel defeated. You might feel that all your research was for naught. Or you might just realize that sometimes dogs, no matter how furry and lovable and appealing, are still dogs.

Caution

Be aware that the dividends you reinvest are taxed as ordinary income.

Find It Online

AOL has a good primer on When to Sell (see Figure 10-12). You can read it at Keyword: **Investment Basics;** select Step Eight: Long Term Success to open up the Motley Fool Guide to Becoming an Investor, and scroll down to When to Sell?

10

Strategies to Put Stock In

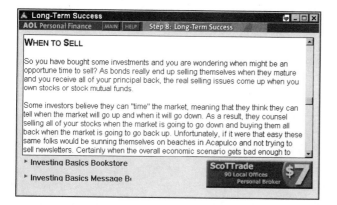

FIG 10-12. You need to keep an eye on how your stocks are performing to know when they no longer suit your portfolio.

There are a couple of reasons to sell a stock:

▶ When the company changes in a way you didn't anticipate, and it's a change you don't like.

▶ When the stock isn't worth its price and you don't expect the price to recover.

▶ When the stock hasn't moved much in the years since you bought it.

▶ When the stock has become so expensive you don't see it going anywhere but down.

▶ When you want to lock in some profits.

▶ When it's such a winner that it's taken over a chunk of your portfolio — more than 10 percent or so — and you need to trim it back and redistribute the proceeds so you're not overly reliant upon it.

When you bought the stock, you understood the company's business. When that business changes dramatically — for example, if the company suddenly changes product lines or management in a way that's not to your liking, or when it is unable to change with its industry — your investment suffers. There's no sense in holding on out of stubbornness, or in waiting until the stock price rebounds to what you paid. Your investment could go the way of the typewriter. In the meantime, while you're waiting for a rebound, opportunities to buy pass you by.

The best way to recognize it's time to sell is not to set a predetermined loss target. It's to examine the same things you studied when you decided to buy (see Figure 10-13). Put your buying process in reverse. Evaluate the financials to determine how the company is faring in its line of work. Explore the numbers. Examine that alphabet soup of indicators: the P/E, the PSR, the profit margins, the ROE, the PEG.

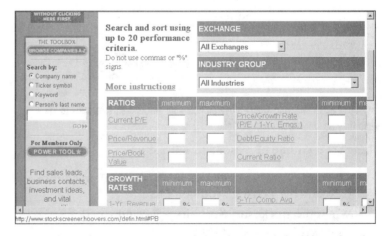

Figure 10-13. The same criteria you used to purchase a stock should be evaluated when selling a stock: Are the financials still appealing? Are expected earnings and growth still promising?

After you study these ratios, if you believe your stock is fully valued and that profits and earnings and growth don't support a higher price, get rid of the stock before the bottom falls out. Even if the company is profitable but not meeting the levels you found attractive, and not growing earnings over two or three quarters, and not growing sales if it has no earnings, get out. If the numbers tell you the stock is not headed up, sell and be done with it. Even the best ballplayers lose now and again.

If profits are stagnant, find out why. Maybe it's because the company is putting money into aggressive marketing and product development in a particular, promising area. If successful, this could ultimately generate new business and is no reason for you to flee. But if earnings don't pick up over a few quarters, admit that your stock is a loser, suck it up and sell.

But if all your research still tells you your stock is still strong — even if the market is kicking it around — hang in there. The worst thing to do is to sell a stock you believe is strong, only to see highs a couple of months down the road that prove your hunches were right, after all.

By the same token, even if you think your stock is a strong one, just as you believed last year and the year before, but the stock isn't moving the way you hoped it would, and it hasn't for years now, get out. Every month your dollars sit and stagnate is a month you could be getting closer to your goals with the right investment. Sell the yawner, and take the proceeds and put them into something that will perform for you.

Taxing consequences

Bear in mind the tax consequences of your sales. There's a huge difference between short- and long-term capital gains tax, which might warrant waiting a bit to sell.

If you own your stock for a year or less, you have to pay the short-term capital gains tax rate, which is your normal income tax rate.

If you hold it longer than a year, you pay the long-term capital gains tax rate of 20 percent (unless your are in the 15 percent tax bracket, in which case you pay 10 percent long-term capital gains).

Cross-Reference

For a refresher on all these terms, turn to Chapter 9.

Find It Online

To evaluate how a stock has performed over time, go to Keyword: **Market Guide**, enter the company's name or ticker symbol, and press Enter. Select Stock Reports for a full profile of the company and its numbers.

The report includes a chart of the company's performance for the past 12 months. If you'd like to fine tune this chart—to change the time frame, for example, or add a comparative value, click the chart itself to open up the Stock Point site. Add the criteria you wish to view to create a tailor-made performance chart.

10

Strategies to Put Stock In

Find It Online

Looking for the latest interpretation of those seemingly-ever-changing capital gains tax rules? Find one at Keyword: **Fool** and click Tax FAQs under the heading Personal Finance in the Quick Find box. Choose Investment Issues from the Tax FAQ Index. Scroll down and click Capital Gains Tax Changes for a quick summary of the latest changes to the tax law.

If you need more help, you can review the IRS publications 544 (Sales and Other Dispositions of Assets) and 550 (Investment Income and Expenses), available online at Keyword: **http://www.irs.ustreas.gov**.

Even with this in mind, don't let the tax consequences alone dictate whether to buy or sell.

When you sell your shares, you have to pay taxes on the difference between the amount you sold the shares for, less the amount you paid, including commissions. That sounds easy enough, but if you bought the shares at different prices, or you bought them through DRIPs, or you only want to sell some of your shares, the tax consequences can get very confusing.

And don't try to pull one over on Uncle Sam by dumping your stock for a loss, then picking it back up a short time later. Your uncle's on to you. According to a part of the tax code dubbed *The Wash Sale Rule*, if you sell your stock for a loss, that loss is disallowed if you buy shares in the same company 30 days before or after your loss sale. Sit down with your accountant and make sure you explore all the tax consequences of your sales before you unload your shares. The money you save making tax-prudent transactions is often a lot more than you would spend trying to fix your tax foibles after you make the trade. For a brief article on Wash Sales, go to Keyword: **Fool**. Choose Tax FAQs from the Quick Find pull-down menu. Next, select Investment Issues from the Tax FAQ Index on the right. Scroll down and click the link to the "Wash Sales" article, shown in Figure 10-14.

Figure 10-14. Uncle Sam keeps you honest: If you sell a stock for a loss and buy it back within 30 days, your loss is disallowed on that year's tax return.

Shorting Stocks

So much for selling shares you own. Now for selling shares you *don't* own. Many stock strategists pride themselves on figuring out not only when stock prices will rise, but when they will fall. And they put their money on it. This is the essence of *shorting* a stock.

To sell a stock short, you first have to "borrow" the shares from your broker and promise to give them back. As soon as you get these borrowed shares, you immediately sell them. If you're trading the stock on the New York Stock Exchange or the American Stock exchange, you can only sell short on an *uptick*, which means when the stock price is on the move up. If your stock trades on the NASDAQ, you can short sell at any time.

When the stock price falls to whatever level you think is the bottom, you buy the shares back and return them to the broker. You pocket the difference between the price you first sold them for, and what you paid to buy them back.

For a complete online guide to shorting stocks, as shown in figure 10-15, go to Keyword: **Fool** again. Select Fool's School, and go to the Step 12: Advanced Investing Issues.

But here's the hitch: There's a limit to what you can earn from shorting a stock, but there's no limit to your loss. If you buy the stock for $35 and it drops to $1, you make $34 a share. But if the stock climbs higher and higher, you lose more and more money with each increase. Why? Because if the stock *rises* after you short it, you have to pay a higher price to buy back the shares you must return to the broker.

Suppose you want to short Widgets 'R' Us stock. You have to tell your broker you want to put in a short order so she can borrow these shares from investors with a margin account and can give them to whoever buys them from you. If she can't find the shares to borrow, which is not uncommon with some small caps with little liquidity, you can't short the stock. Suppose she can find them. You order 100 shares at the price of $35. The cost to you is $3,500 plus commission plus the fees you'll read about in a minute.

Caution

With most stock trades, your loss is limited to the amount you invest. When you short stocks, though, your losses can be limitless.

10

Strategies to Put Stock In

Tip

Want to know what your fellow investors have to say about shorting stocks? Find out at Keyword: **Fool**. Select the Messages tab, and then select Investors" Roundtable. Scroll down to the search feature, and type in Shorting Stocks by the board name.

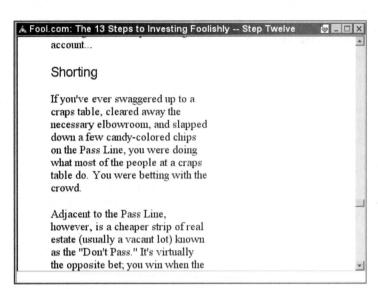

Figure 10-15. Shorting stocks is a strategy that requires a bit of bravado: If a stock's price falls, you may make a tidy profit, but if the price goes up, you'll be forced to pay the price.

All of a sudden, Widgets 'R' Us announces it has canned its CEO and replaced him with Steve Case. Next thing you know, the stock's rocketing to $75, and there's no landing in sight. Now you have to come up with $7,500 to buy back the stocks to return to the broker. Even if the stock isn't on the move, your broker might demand them back before you're ready to return them because she needs to return them to their rightful owner.

When you short a stock, you must be prepared to cut your losses before you get in over your head. This is one of the few times you should make a price target. Then, if the price reaches that target, sell and be done with it.

Keep the fees in mind, too. You have to pay two commissions — to sell the stock and then to buy it. You have to pay any dividends the stock earns, because the investor you borrowed the shares from is expecting them. You have to pay the broker a bit of interest on the stocks you borrowed to sell because it's like taking a loan. And you have to pay regular income tax on your profits, regardless of how long you hold the short.

The strategy behind finding the right stocks to sell short is the same as it is for finding those you want to buy long (for the long-term). In the previous chapter you unearthed stocks primed for growth based on different valuation methods. You invert this process to find stocks that are over-valued. These are the best prospects for stock shorting. You sell short what you think is overpriced and going down — whether earnings aren't as strong as predicted, or products aren't as splendid as they seemed, stock has been run up too high, or the numbers don't add up to a good buy and you believe other investors will soon realize this.

Selling a stock short is a way to make money when the market is on the decline. But it works in bull markets, too, as long as you find a stock you think is overpriced and the market agrees with you.

Some investors use shorting as a way to hedge their long investments. Maybe you're long on Chocolate Chips Corp. in the computer chip sector because you think it's the greatest company in a growing sector. Then you short Fishin Chips Inc. in that same sector because you believe the company is the weakest of the sector's lot. If that sector sinks, at least you can cushion your fall with your short.

Summary

Now you understand the difference between active and passive investing. You've explored a number of popular passive investing strategies such as using index funds and the Dow Dividend Approach, and you know which active strategies are more apt to succeed than others.

You understand the basics of IPOs and DRIPs, and you know when it's time to unload a stock. You also learned what short-selling is all about.

That's the long, and the short, of stock strategies. Now, use your newfound knowledge to start building those portfolios, up next in Chapter 11.

Find It Online

To review online how to value stocks, turn to the Motley Fool. Go to Keyword: **Fool**, click Fool's School, then select How To . . . Value Stocks. Click Valuation: Principles and Practice for a series of articles on how to find the relative worth of a publicly traded company. The series covers how to understand earnings, revenues, cash-flow, equity, and dividend yield to figure out how much a company is worth.

The Fools warn that trying to buy and sell stock without understanding these principles leaves the hapless investor "adrift in a sea of random short-term price movements and gut feelings," an unhappy picture at best.

The section also offers formulas for using a company's current financial figures and historical data to develop a rating for its overall worth. Learn how to calculate Return on Invested Capital and Return on Equity, both numbers that can help illuminate a company's economic prospects. Or call up the Fool's formula, known as the Fool Ratio, to value growth stocks.

10

Strategies to Put Stock In

CHAPTER

11

BUILDING YOUR PORTFOLIO

A Quick Look

▶ **Slicing Your Pie**   **page 290**

Asset allocation, diversification, stock strategies, passive vs. active investing . . .
Don't let all these decisions — which you need to make in order to build a
good portfolio — make you reconsider the under-the-mattress plan.

Fortunately, there is expert guidance available. Check out Standard & Poor's
interactive portfolio builder for help. Go to Keyword: **Personal Wealth**, and
click Financial Planner. To use this tool, you must be a registered user. Simply
fill out a short form and take advantage of this free and easy planner.

▶ **Getting Your Balance**   **page 294**

For an online primer on balancing your portfolio, try the University at Smart-
Money.com. Go to Keyword: **http://www.smartmoney.com** and click
SmartMoney University. Under Departments, click Taking Action to read the
articles on Asset Allocation, including worksheets to determine net worth and
an interactive planner that allows you to map out the makeup of your portfolio by changing such variables as age, economic outlook, annual income, and
your stomach for risk.

▶ **Know Thyself**   **page 297**

Your portfolio reflects not only your goals and timeline, but the kind of
investor you are. If you crave security and loathe surprises, conservative
investments should be your mainstay. If you live for quick results and don't
fear the bumps and knocks along the way, your portfolio might tolerate
high-risk investments quite well.

For a light-hearted look at your money personality, check out the quiz at
Keyword: **Whiz**. Click Investing, and scroll down to MoneyWhiz Investing
News. Select Your Money Profile to open Just Who Are You — Financially
Speaking. Answer the questions, keeping track of the letters you choose, to
find out if you are a conservative, moderate, or aggressive investor.

Chapter 11

Building Your Portfolio

Congratulations, your hard labor is nearly over! You have laid the groundwork to build your portfolio. You know what your goals are; how much they cost; how much you can save toward them; how much more you need to pay for them; what the return on your investments must be to make up the difference between what you can save and the amount you need; and how much you have already saved and invested, and where it is.

In addition to these inventories, you've learned how stocks, bonds, and mutual funds work; which types of stocks, bonds and mutual funds will best meet your needs; and how to search for and find the investment vehicles you seek.

Now comes the fun part: actually constructing your portfolio.

Asset allocation

A portfolio is simply a collection of assets — your stocks and your bonds and your bank accounts and your mutual funds and your real estate and any other vehicles in which you invest. To build the strongest portfolio you can't be chintzy with your construction materials. You must search for the strongest assets that work best for your needs — and that work well together — and then invest in those assets.

As you build your portfolio you must be faithful to a general design that reflects

- ▶ The type of investor you are
- ▶ The kinds of results you seek
- ▶ The amount of time you are willing to devote to research
- ▶ The assets you feel most comfortable with
- ▶ How you feel about risk
- ▶ How you react when the market gyrates

To make sure your portfolio keeps with this general design, you draw up and follow an *asset allocation* plan. Asset allocation — how you divide assets within your portfolio — is one of the most important investing decisions you will make. It's not something you have to do often, but it has long-lasting ramifications.

To read about it online, look to the article "How to divide your investment pie," shown in Figure 11-1, at Keyword: **Whiz.** Then select Investing, then scroll down to Investing Basics and click Divide Your Investment Pie.

First, you must decide how much of what *types* of assets you will carry in your portfolio — what balance of stocks and bonds and cash is *your* ideal. The percentage will apply to your entire portfolio, including your retirement plans, and will include assets you've purchased separately as well as through mutual funds.

Once you outline the asset types, you need to slice them into more finely tuned subcategories. If you're talking about stocks, for example, you must subdivide into large-, mid-, or small-caps, and then again by objective and characteristics. Are you targeting capital appreciation or income? Do you want growth or value?

Cross-Reference

For a refresher on many of these items, turn to your investment blueprint in Chapter 5.

Find It Online

Looking for suggestions on what makes for good asset allocation? Go to Keyword: **Sage Models** to see what the Sage experts have to say about different portfolio strategies.

11

Building Your Portfolio

Cross-Reference

You learned about these different types of stocks and objectives in Chapters 6 and 9.

Find It Online

As the article shown in Figure 11-2 confirms, there is no arguing that proper asset allocation improves risk-adjusted return. To read the full text, go to Keyword: **Moneymag**, click the Investing tab, scroll down and select Money 101: Investing in Stocks, and then click Article 15, Asset Allocation.

Figure 11-1. Building a portfolio is something you know you need to do. But what are you going to put in it?

For bonds, what industries, if any, will be represented? Will they be government or corporate? What maturities? Will you invest in your stocks and bonds separately or through mutual funds or both? When you put your assets and their subcategories together, what risks will your portfolio carry as a whole? What are its potential returns? What will be the tax implications? This chapter will help you build wisely.

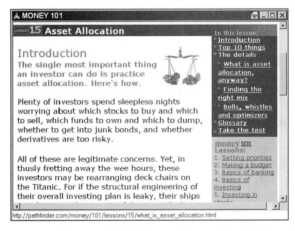

Figure 11-2. It may lack the glamour of a get-rich-quick scheme, but asset allocation is the most basic strategy for success.

Finding the Right Mix for You

Many different assets can contribute to a great portfolio. Stocks, bonds, cash, real estate, a combination of all — inside or independent of mutual funds. But how much of which asset makes for the perfect portfolio for you? That is the essence of asset allocation. You learned in Chapter 5 that the types of assets you select to meet your goals depends on your investment profile: your risk tolerance, your timeline, and your return needs.

For an online primer on what investment vehicles work for short-, medium-, and long-term goals, go to Keyword: **Whiz**, click the Investing category, then scroll down and choose Selecting Your Investment Objectives. Scroll to the end to review the chart pictured in Figure 11-3.

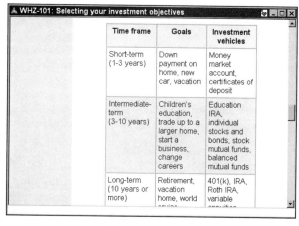

▲ WHZ-101: Selecting your investment objectives

Time frame	Goals	Investment vehicles
Short-term (1-3 years)	Down payment on home, new car, vacation	Money market account, certificates of deposit
Intermediate-term (3-10 years)	Children's education, trade up to a larger home, start a business, change careers	Education IRA, individual stocks and bonds, stock mutual funds, balanced mutual funds
Long-term (10 years or more)	Retirement, vacation home, world cruise	401(k), IRA, Roth IRA, variable annuities

Figure 11-3. If you're aiming for a short-term goal, you'll pack your portfolio with different investment vehicles than you would for a goal 20 years down the road.

Age and allocation

Your age figures heavily into the mix, too. Typically, the younger you are, the more you look to assets that generate high growth. When your expenses and your liquidity needs are limited, your investment possibilities seem limitless. Young investors typically look to large-cap growth stocks, small-cap growth stocks, aggressive growth funds, and some junk-bond funds or emerging markets sprinkled in for fun and daring.

Find It Online

To read more online about asset allocations for different stages of life, go to Keyword: **Personal Wealth** to open the S&P homepage. Click The Learning Center, under Departments. Select the Basics of Smart Investing, shown in Figure 11-4. Choose Getting Started, from the table of contents on the left, and then select Topic 4: Asset Allocations.

Find It Online

Are you at least 45 years old and working on your portfolio? Check for age-related portfolio pointers at Keyword: **ThirdAge**, then, under ThirdAge Money, choose Investment Center. Once there, choose Tips for a Positively Perfect Portfolio.

As investors age, expenses come charging like the bulls at Pamplona. A home, college tuition, impending retirement. Middle-aged investors slip out of harm's way, moving from high-risk investments toward more moderate ones. The growth stocks and funds gradually get replaced by blue-chip or value stocks or funds. (If the investors started when they were young, though, and now have loads of extra money then they can keep their risk level up.)

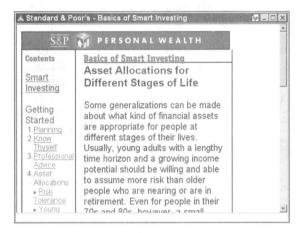

Figure 11-4. Your stage in life determines what you should have in your portfolio. Investments that are hot to a young investor may be unsuitable for a retired investor.

Older investors often depend on their assets for income. So they opt for low-risk, fixed-income vehicles, which have inherently lower returns but are more dependable. These include stocks with high dividends, and bonds. All investors, including older ones, should hang onto some growth stocks to avoid losing their nest egg to inflation.

What's the perfect asset mix? There is no formula. But here are some general guidelines you can consider. The guidelines assume all investors, regardless of age, keep about 10 percent of their portfolio in cash (in a money market or a CD).

Investors below age 30   Allocate at least 80 percent of your portfolio to stocks or stock funds, and 10 percent to fixed-income assets.

Investors 30 to 40 years old

Trim the equities to 75 percent, and up the fixed income a bit to 15 percent, unless you have more flexibility due to a high income, fewer bills or lots of money already working for you.

Investors 40 to 50 years old

Reduce dependence on equities, with around 65 to 70 percent in your portfolio, and increase fixed-income investments, to about 20 or 25 percent.

Investors over age 60

Shrink the equities allocation in your portfolio to about 40 to 50 percent, and hike fixed-income assets to about 40 to 50 percent.

Find It Online

Suggestions shown in Figure 11-5 are based on the changing needs in various stages in life. To read more, go to Keyword: **Family Money** and select How-To, under Investing. Click Investing for Life for tips on financial strategies as your life unfolds.

The suggested guidelines depend, of course, on how much money you have already accumulated and what your needs are.

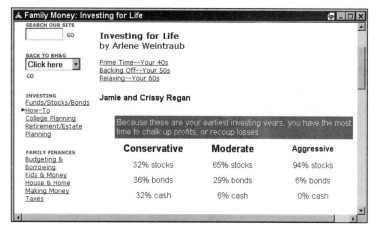

Figure 11-5. AOL offers many guidelines to help you develop your asset allocation plan.

11

Building Your Portfolio

Take allocation to the next level

Find It Online

Your portfolio should evolve as your life evolves. For a look at what should be in your portfolio over the years, check out Keyword: **Family Money**, then select How To under Investing, then scroll down to Investing for Life.

Once you've nailed down the asset categories you want, you have to subdivide these categories. The key to a sound portfolio lies in the subcategories, because they zero in on exactly what you're looking for. Select subcategories that work for your goals and for who you are as an investor. And make sure you're not overreliant on one subcategory or another, so that they all weave together nicely into a solid basket for your eggs.

The subtleties of how you subdivide your categories are addressed later in the chapter. For now, paint with broad strokes. You know how much you need for your goals. Match your needs to subcategories that can generate those returns.

For example, suppose you sit in the second scenario depicted in the guidelines, 30 to 40 years old, aiming for the following asset allocation in your portfolio: 75 percent in stocks, 15 percent in bonds, 10 percent in cash.

Let's say you have $15,000 a year to invest. Your subcategory possibilities are practically limitless. Pull out the investment blueprint you drew up in Chapter 5, which outlines what you need and by when, how much you anticipate saving and what kind of return you need to make up the difference. Then hand-pick the specific subcategory within the asset type that will generate the return you need to arrive at your goal. Then formulate a plan that directly addresses your asset preferences, your subcategories, and your goals.

Remember, as hammered home by the article in Figure 11-6 from the Whiz.com, you must have established goals to formulate a good strategy. To find the article, follow the Investment link from the Whiz homepage. Then click WHZ 101: Selecting Your Investment Objectives.

Tip

If you need help figuring the return you need in the time you have, call up that handy calculator at Keyword: **http://quicken.aol.com /saving/**.

Figure 11-6. Remember: A truly successful portfolio is one that is built around predetermined goals.

Your plan might end up looking something like Table 11-1.

Table 11-1. Mapping Out Your Agenda

Goal	Cost	Have	Need	Time
College	$250,000	$21,000	$229,000	15 years

(You need a 12% return to make these numbers.)

Action: *S&P index fund* at $250 per month; estimated return = 12%; annual investment = $3,000.

Goal	Cost	Have	Need	Time
Retirement	$3 million	$24,000	A lot!	30 years

Action: *growth funds* at $500 per month (plus $125 match from employer); estimated return = 12%; annual investment = $6,000.

Goal	Cost	Have	Need	Time
Cruise for parents	$10,000	$2,500	$7,500	5 years

Action: *bond fund* at $100 per month; estimated return = 6%; annual investment = $1,200.

Goal	Cost	Have	Need	Time
Rainy Day Funds	??	$12,000	??	ongoing

Action: *bond fund* at $75 per month, *money market* at $125 per month; *individual growth or value stocks* at $200 per month; annual cost = $4,800.

Double-check the subcategories

When you incorporate subcategories into your plan you need to make sure they all fit together with your overall asset allocation, as these do. Instead of just the 75 percent equities, 15 percent fixed income, and 10 percent cash parameters, now your asset allocation plan looks like this:

75% equities ($11,250)	20% index fund ($3,000); 40% aggressive growth funds ($6,000); 15% individual growth or value stocks ($2,250)
15% fixed income ($2,250)	15% bond fund ($2,250)
10% cash ($1,500)	10% money market

Voila! You now have an asset allocation plan.

But implementing it, well, that can be another story.

Advice from AOL partners

Here are a few asset allocation models developed by AOL partners. The models target long-term goals. Remember to tailor your own portfolio to your risk tolerance and your personal needs.

Personal Wealth Portfolios

Standard & Poor's Personal Wealth (Keyword: **PW**) offers a sample asset allocation table based on age. The table shows how investors change their allocations over time. The model assumes rising income until investors turn 65.

Age Range	Type of Investment
20–35	Aggressive growth stocks (international and small companies) 40%; total return stocks (large, blue-chip companies) 40%; bonds 10%; cash equivalents (money market, CDs) 10%.

35–50	Aggressive growth stocks (international and small companies) 30%; total return stocks (large, blue-chip companies) 40%; bonds 20%; cash equivalents (money market, CDs) 10%.
50–65	Aggressive growth stocks (international and small companies) 20%; total return stocks (large, blue-chip companies) 30%; bonds 30%; cash equivalents (money market, CDs) 20%.
65+	Aggressive growth stocks (international and small companies) 10%; total return stocks (large, blue-chip companies) 25%; bonds 40%; cash equivalents (money market, CDs) 25%.

Note that an investor's tax bracket will determine the extent of her involvement in municipal bonds.

Online Investor's sample

The second table, from the Online Investor's Ted Allrich (Keyword: **OI**) offers a different take on asset allocation over time.

Below age 30	Consider 80% in stocks or mutual funds, 10% in cash and 10% in fixed income.
Age 30 to 40	Pare back the equities portion a little to 70%, keep 10% in cash, and up fixed income to 20%.
Age 40 to 50	Consider 60% equities, keep cash at 10%, and raise fixed income investments to 30%.
Age 50 to 60	Pull back a bit more in stocks, to 50%, keep 10% in cash, and increase fixed income to 40%.

Continued

11

Building Your Portfolio

"Put your portfolio together like a puzzle," Allrich says, "adding a piece at a time, each one a little different from the other but achieving a uniform whole once the portfolio is complete."

Advice from AOL partners *(continued)*

If you're over 60	Slim down some more in stocks, to 40%, keep 10% in cash, and raise fixed income investments to 50% of the portfolio.
Retired	Reduce stocks even more and raise fixed income to meet your needs. Keep cash at 10%.

Keep in mind, notes Allrich, that your risk tolerance and investing style might call for more or less of each asset. He also recommends diversifying the fixed-income setion of the portfolio by buying bonds with at least five different maturities to spread out inflation risk.

Implementing Your Plan

You probably already have assets invested somewhere. First you have to make these fit into your new plan. Take the list of investments or savings you already have (which you drew up in Chapter 5) and divide it by asset category: stocks and bonds (or equity and debt, your preference). Then render it a step further and divide it into subcategories. For your 401(k), you might have to call the plan administrator to tell you exactly which assets you are invested in.

For example, maybe you already have $60,000 in your 401 (k); $50,000 in a hodgepodge of individual stocks; $25,000 in an index fund for the college tuition; $40,000 in a collection of a mutual funds you arranged through your bank; a collection of U.S. Savings Bonds, zero-coupon bonds, Treasuries, or other bonds worth about $25,000; and $33,000 in a money market. Again, get out the magnifying glass and subcategorize these assets into types, maturities and objectives of these stocks and bonds.

For some of your mutual funds these subcategories will be difficult to nail down. Do the best you can, but don't get stuck in minutiae. You will not be graded. You're simply formulating a plan. The object is to match the assets and subcategories you already have with the ideal asset allocation plan you created. You can be more particular when you assemble a portfolio with a new chunk of money, but it might take some maneuvering to get where you're headed with investments you already have.

Review your 401(k)

To get started on your new plan, first look to your 401(k) or retirement plan to lay the foundation.

The easiest, least expensive way to change your portfolio orientation or build it from scratch is to redirect the holdings in your 401(k). If you have the type of 401(k) or retirement plan that lets you choose any assets to invest in, direct most of your contributions toward either:

▶ The asset you want to have the most of according to your asset allocation plan

▶ The asset likely to generate the most taxes (which may very well be the same asset), because this asset will be tax-deferred in the plan.

Then use your savings outside your 401(k) or retirement plan to fund the rest of your portfolio according to your plan. You might need to redistribute your assets over time according to your goals' timetables.

To review online how your retirement plan can shape your portfolio, go to Keyword: **Money.com** and click the Retirement tab. Then select Step 2, Asset Mix, shown in Figure 11-7.

You don't need to implement an asset allocation plan immediately. (You might need to start out slowly and build piece by piece.) But you should have it in mind as you build your portfolio. Otherwise, your portfolio will end up looking like a house built without a plan: a couple of country kitchens here, a few contemporary living rooms there, several Victorian front porches — and not enough bathrooms or bedrooms to meet your needs.

Once you map out your portfolio, staying the course is the best plan of action. You won't get the adrenaline rush you might get on an investment roller coaster — buy one day, sell the next —

Find It Online

Want to discuss what's in your portfolio? Go to Keyword: **Sage Models**, then select Message Boards, then Portfolio Strategies

11

Building Your Portfolio

and you'll lose the opportunity to brag about your huge gains while hobnobbing with Dobbs at the Jones' cocktail party. But you will rest more easily knowing what to expect and when to expect it.

Find It Online

To find the best money market for stashing your money while you decide how to invest it, go to Keyword: **Bankrate**, click Checking, then click Money Markets. You can search by account type or state to find the best rates.

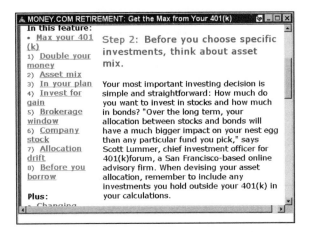

Figure 11-7. Don't forget to consider the makeup of your retirement plan as you build a balanced portfolio.

Asset allocation online

Want to design your asset allocation online? Check out Standard & Poor's Personal Wealth's interactive financial planner. Once you've registered for the free service, this tool can help you customize your dream portfolio.

Go to Keyword: **Personal Wealth**, and click the Financial Plan tab. If you are not a registered member, a pop-up box will ask you to subscribe; don't worry, it's fast and free. Just click Register Me Now for Free S&P Services to sign up.

After registering, you can access the interactive financial planner to help you set up a custom-fit portfolio. From the homepage, the financial planner tab brings you to an introduction on building your plan. Questions about your financial status, investing profile, and goals help the planner create a portfolio that suits your individual needs. Click Create a Plan to begin filling in the blanks. As you answer the five-part series, a red-flag will pop up to warn you if there are areas in your financial life that need tending to before considering investing. You can ignore these warnings for now and continue with the financial plan.

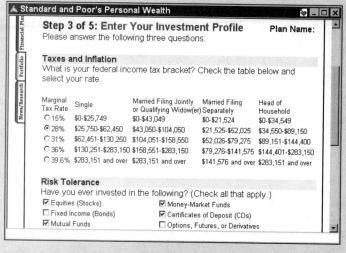

You can map out your asset allocation online using Standard & Poor's interactive financial planner.

After completing the questions, a tailored financial plan will give you specifics on how much you need to save each month to reach your goals, how your portfolio should be allocated among different types of investments and which specific investments you should choose to achieve that allocation.

Stocks, Bonds, or Funds?

Whether you turn to individual assets or to mutual funds to fill your portfolio can be tricky. Many investors find success with a patchwork of assets, subcategories, and approaches. Among them:

▶ Some use passive investments like index funds or the Dow Dividend Approach for parts of their portfolio, and actively choose those investments that reflect their interests or expertise for the rest.

Find It Online

As shown in Figure 11-8, a passive approach like the Motley Fool's Foolish Four strategy has turned in robust returns over the years. To review this strategy go to Keyword: **Fool** and select Foolish Four under the Strategies heading in the Quick Find box.)

Find It Online

TheStreet.com's Jim Cramer spent years perfecting his asset allocation model. You can try an interactive version at Keyword: **TheStreet**, then click Full TSC site, then click Basics, then scroll down to Jim Cramer's Asset Allocation Adventure.

Figure 11-8. There are dozens of investing strategies to choose from. You can pick an active strategy or a passive approach, such as the Motley Fool's Foolish Four, or a combination of both.

▶ Some rely on a handful to a dozen mutual funds to fill their entire portfolio.

▶ Some individually select each and every vehicle in the portfolio.

▶ Some assemble mutual funds at first, then wean themselves off the funds and turn to individual stocks and bonds once they become comfortable with the market's machinations and motivations, and have more money to work with.

▶ Most investors rely on a combination of funds and individual holdings.

If you're building a portfolio from scratch, it's easier to start with mutual funds because you can pick out exactly the materials you're looking for — funds carrying the subcategories or the objectives you want — with minimal effort and cost. As outlined by the experts at Sage, shown in Figure 11-9, mutual funds can combine a basketful of stocks and bonds with one investment. You can even start with just one fund — a balanced fund whose sole purpose is to spread out its investments among assets so you don't have to. Reach the Sage advice at Keyword: **Sage School**, then select Sage's Eight-Step Program.

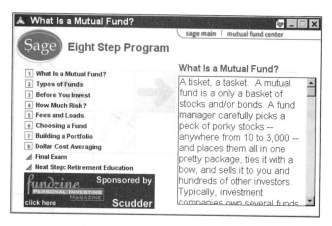

Figure 11-9. Why are mutual funds a first choice of many investors? As Sage's experts point out, a mutual fund is a neat package of assets conveniently selected by a financial manager.

If you want to buy all the stocks and bonds for your portfolio separately, you'll need a lot more time to do the research, and lots of money to buy enough for a good balance.

Mutual fund considerations

Using mutual funds as your cornerstones can be a bit slippery at the beginning. Suppose you want to end up with 80 percent of your entire portfolio in stocks, 10 percent in fixed income for stability, and 10 percent in cash. Say you want to dedicate 40 percent to large-caps, 20 percent to small-caps, and 20 percent to international stocks. Mutual fund minimums can throw a wrench in your plans. Suppose you have saved $6,500 to start investing. You put your first $2,600, or 40 percent of $6,500, into a large-cap fund, and add to it regularly. No problem yet.

For your next step, you want to put 20 percent of your investment into small-caps. But 20 percent of $6,500 is $1,300, and most mutual funds require an initial investment greater than $1,300 (although some are beginning to waive that minimum if you commit to a monthly deposit). Now what? Do you hunt for a mutual fund with a low minimum? No, not if that's the only reason you would go with it. You should invest in a fund that fits your strategy or your needs. To stay true to your asset allocation plan, hold off putting your money anywhere else until you have enough to reach the appropriate percentage in your plan.

Caution

Some mutual funds that call themselves "asset allocation" funds are really market-timers. They pull money in and out of the market according to somebody's best guess of which way the market's heading. You can flip a coin and figure that out just as readily. If you invest in an asset allocation fund, make sure it truly does spread itself among assets and doesn't simply bounce in and out of the market.

11

Building Your Portfolio

To find the best large-cap and small-cap funds, review Chapter 8.

What are the best balanced funds? Go to Keyword: **Mutual Funds**, then click Top Funds List. Funds are listed by category.

Here's one way to do that: You could continue to add slowly to the large-cap fund while you save up for the small-caps. Another option is to devote all your savings to the small-cap fund until you reach the minimum you need, then save up for the international fund. Once you start that last one, you would add to all three funds until you reach the percentage of assets in the stock portion of your portfolio that your plan calls for. Then you save for the fixed-income percentage.

The danger in building your portfolio in this way is that for a while you are fully exposed to stocks. If you're young, have a strong stomach, are less concerned about risk, and have fewer liquidity needs, this might not be a huge worry.

Building a balanced portfolio

But if, like many investors, you don't want this enormous exposure to stocks, you can start building with one balanced mutual fund.

Using a balanced mutual fund to fill your portfolio is like having a studio apartment. You have everything you need in one place. You can slowly add to this balanced fund until you accumulate enough money in it to spread out among other assets, then you disperse the money according to your plan. Keep adding to each category on a regular basis, and don't worry if you don't have the exact percentage in each subcategory that your asset allocation plan calls for. Use your plan as a rough guide.

Mix it up

For an online primer on how to obtain the right balance in your portfolio, read Finding the Right Mix, at SmartMoney.com, as pictured in the Figure below.

Go to Keyword: **http://www.smartmoney.com** and click SmartMoney University. Under Departments, click Taking Action, then select Building a Portfolio, to open A Matter of Style, a discussion on how to find the right portfolio mix.

Then, under Asset Allocation, choose SmartMoney One Asset Allocation System. This opens an interactive worksheet that lets you play with eight different variables —

age, portfolio, yearly savings, ten-year spending, income needed, federal tax bracket, volatility tolerance, and economic outlook — to see how they affect your portfolio design. Raise or lower the value of each variable and the pie chart adjusts itself according to how the changes affect your asset allocation.

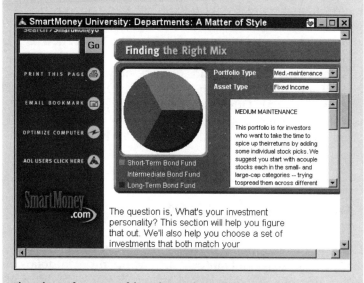

The right mix for your portfolio is the one that works for you.

If you have questions about a variable, click its name and an explanatory paragraph appears to the left of the pie chart.

There's no standard formula for how many stocks, bonds, or funds you should own. It's like making a stew. You work with the ingredients you have or can afford and try to make sure they all blend together for your tastes. With a portfolio (and a stew), make sure you are not duplicating your efforts. You don't need two dozen blue-chip company stocks, as well as an S&P 500 index fund, and shares in a large-cap fund. In your effort to diversify, you have ended up with vehicles that, although different, essentially do the same thing — they return the same as the market returns.

Buying half a dozen up-and-coming Internet stocks to augment your small-caps fund doesn't necessarily do the trick,

Find It Online

If you're considering Internet stocks, versus funds that carry them, find out what AOL's mutual funds experts think of the selections at Keyword: **Sage Models**. Click Portfolio Focus Archive in the features box, and scroll down to the article Internet Stocks or Mutual Funds? for insight into the volatile, roller-coaster world of cyberstocks.

Find It Online

Which industries can you invest in to best balance your career? Find out at Money.com (Keyword: **Money.com**), then scroll down under to Diversify Your Portfolio, under Tools, and plug in the numbers.

either, because you've selected different investments that behave in the same way. Make sure your vehicles actually target separate holdings in unrelated industries with different risks and characteristics.

If you're working only with individual stocks, buy at least a dozen or so from companies small and large, American and multi-national, representing at least half a dozen industries with different volatilities. Try to make sure each stock totals about the same amount of money in its specific section of your plan so it doesn't overshadow the rest. And make sure you don't have the same kinds of stocks in your 401(k), especially if your retirement plan is heavily weighted in the company you work for. Otherwise, if the industry you work and invest in suddenly falls on tough times, your portfolio will sink like a typewriter . . . or an Edsel . . . or an ice box . . .

Portfolio preferences

Here are a few examples of how some investors might allocate stocks, bonds, and mutual funds within their portfolios. These are not recommendations, merely examples of different investing preferences. They aim to show how different people with different investment profiles can use different materials to construct sound portfolios.

Lucy

Lucy is looking for long-term growth. She just turned 28, her salary more than takes care of her bills, and she's trying to build ostrich-size nest eggs. She knows those banner years in the stock market should outshine the bad ones over the long haul, so she is heaping her money into aggressive-growth stock funds in her 401(k) to complement the blue-chip company stock she gets from her employer each year. She is willing to wait patiently as her nest builds. Outside of her 401(k) she picks up individual stocks, mostly those she thinks are good values or are about to rocket. When she reaches a tidy sum in her Future Fund, she buys another Treasury.

Lucy's plan

80% stocks	Large-cap stocks and funds: 15%; Small
10% bonds	cap stocks and funds: 50%; International-
10%	cashstock fund: 15%; Treasury notes: 10%;
	Money market: 10%

Ethel

Her twin sister, Ethel, is leery of Lucy's reliance on stocks. Ethel is going to have a baby soon, and she and her husband are saving for a downpayment on a house, which they hope to buy in three years. Their stock money is in their retirement plans, mostly in an S&P 500 index fund, some in a growth fund. They're putting the house money into less risky Treasuries and a money market.

Ethel's plan

60% stocks	Large-cap-stock funds: 45%; Small-cap-
20% bonds	stock funds: 15%; T-notes, T-bills: 20%;
20% cash	Money market: 20%.

Ricky

Ricky is 52, paying for two kids in college and plying his portfolio with what's left over. Visions of a retirement home in the Colorado mountains, to be paid for with his nest egg, are spurring him on. He's counting on pension checks and Social Security (he has his fingers crossed on that one) to pay for his lift tickets. He has built a solid nest, with enough to cover college, a couple of weddings and a good deal more. He loves growth stocks, many of which he finds, researches, and trades online. He continues to aim for capital appreciation as the years pass.

Ricky's plan

70% stocks	Large-cap growth stocks and funds: 50%;
20% bonds	Small-cap growth stocks and funds: 20%;
10% cash	Municipal bonds: 10%; T-notes and T-bills:
	10%; Money market: 10%.

June

June is a 72-year-old widow. As a 10-year-old, she ran errands for the elderly folks on the block, who often rewarded her with a nickel. She would always insist on five pennies — a

Find It Online

Who you are and the kinds of risks you're comfortable with shape what to put in your portfolio. Do you seek security and reliability in your portfolio, dreading the thought of a sudden loss or disappointed expectations? Or do you thrive on the thrill of the long shot, viewing near-misses and bad eggs along the way as part of the overall adventure? Or are you somewhere in the middle, able to endure a moderate amount of uncertainty but unwilling to risk everything?

If you know which category best describes you, you can better decide how to allocate your assets. To get an objective take on your Money Personality, try the online quiz at Keyword: **Whiz**. Click Investing, and scroll down to MoneyWhiz Investing News. Select Your Money Profile to open the feature Just Who Are You, Financially-Speaking. Answer the questions, keeping track of the letters you choose, to find if you are a conservative, moderate, or aggressive investor.

11

Building Your Portfolio

Cross-Reference

To learn how to invest the best for your golden years, turn to the retirement planning section of Chapter 12.

penny for some licorice for her and her friends, two cents for that doll she was saving for, and two cents into the bank. She never made gads of money at Widgets 'R' Us, but she always made a point of saving a chunk of every week's check.

After her husband died years ago, she started spending one lunch break a week at the library, catching up on financial events and tweaking her portfolio accordingly. She's got about $4.3 million now, which no one would suspect, given her simple living. From her condo, next door to the three-family brownstone she owns, she reviews her statements each quarter and makes a few adjustments every now and then, happy knowing her family will be taken care of when she's gone.

June's plan

50% stocks	Large-cap stocks and funds: 35%; Small-
20% real estate	cap stocks and funds: 15%; Real estate:
20% bonds	20%; Muni-bond fund: 20%; Money
10% cash	market: 10%.

All these investors will change their portfolios over time. How will they know when to make adjustments? The tune-up will tell them.

Annual Tune-Up

Regardless of how you fill your portfolio, it needs an annual tune-up, just like any vehicle you own. Perform this examination in addition to the quarterly or more frequent monitoring of your individual holdings. For a little motivation, read the article "Is Your Portfolio Due for a Checkup," shown in Figure 11-10. Go to Keyword: **Family Money**, click Funds, Stocks & Bonds, under Investing, then click the article.

The point of the annual review is to ensure that all parts of your portfolio are working for you. Are you on target to meet your goals? If not, can you increase your savings or lengthen the amount of time you have to reach your goals? Or do you need to readjust your target and prepare for a lower result?

Figure 11-10. Like a garden, you must tend your portfolio, even if you think you've found a perfect mix. Make sure to review your holdings at least annually.

Find It Online

How might a wedding, a birth, college, or other life change force you to amend your portfolio? Find out at Keyword: **Your Money**, and click the topic you need — from Marriage & Money, to Diapers & Dollars, to Saving & School, to Retire in Style.

Scrutinize the assets in your subcategories. Look at their year-end results and compare their performance to benchmarks set by indexes or mutual funds in the same class. If your holdings are inferior, figure out why. Evaluate their prospects for the future (instead of lamenting the past), and if you are confident the scenario will change, stay the course. Otherwise, take the time to find a similar type of investment that fits well into your mix, and gradually replace your low performers with better choices.

Rebalancing your portfolio

In and out of your tune-up there are a number of scenarios that should trigger a change in your asset allocation plan:

▶ Components of your portfolio have been so successful that they tip the scales of your current mix. (For example, two of your favorite tech stocks now account for 50 percent of your small-cap holdings.)

▶ Parts of your portfolio have lagged behind their benchmarks and need to be sold.

▶ Your goal is close and you need to scale back on your riskier holdings and redirect new investments into more stable vehicles.

▶ Your profile as an investor has changed. Your risk-tolerance is different or you have a new or amended lifestyle, goals or means. Maybe there has been or you anticipate a marriage, a death, the end of tuition, the birth of a child, a lump-sum distribution, a job change or retirement.

11

Building Your Portfolio

For online tips on rebalancing your portfolio, try the article shown in Figure 11-11. Go to Keyword: **TSC**, click Full TSC site, and then click Basics. Scroll down to "How to Begin Investing in Mutual Funds" and click "Getting Your Rebalancing Act Together."

If you need to rebalance, try not to do it by selling solid performers, even if your asset allocation strays. You risk heavy tax consequences and transaction fees and put the brakes on a fun ride. Instead, try to use new savings — dividends, interest income, new investments, or a windfall — to slowly step up your investments in other areas. Recognize that you might need to save more, increase your risk or adjust your goal to meet your target.

If you're retired and drawing on your investments for income (and you don't have any deposits you can reallocate to rebalance your portfolio), simply draw from the category you have too much money in to reduce it to the level outlined in your portfolio plan.

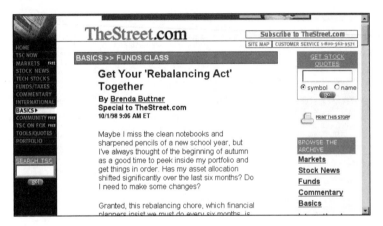

Figure 11-11. Rebalancing your portfolio should include looking at changes in your income, tax rate, and investments.

Summary

Construction has begun! You know the smart way to mix your assets when you build your portfolio and you understand how your age and timetable affect this mix. You've studied sample portfolios and you know which might work for you. You've mapped out a construction plan and you know how to implement that plan.

You know whether to pursue stocks, bonds or mutual funds for your particular needs, and you know that regardless of which you choose, your portfolio will need an annual tune-up. If you need to make changes, you know how to rebalance your portfolio without veering in one direction or another.

Next you'll see how your portfolio figures into your quest to reach your goals, coming up in Chapter 12.

CHAPTER

12

REACHING YOUR GOALS

A Quick Look

▶ **The Bottom Line**   **page 308**

When you imagine your retirement, does it involve travel, recreation, a beach
house, a boat? With some help you can establish how much your retirement
lifestyle will cost. AOL's *SmartCalc* (Keyword: **Calculator**) can help you
crunch the numbers. To figure how much you will need in order to cover
expenses in your golden years, look under Personal Finance and click
Retirement. Then select "What will my expenses be after I retire?" Fill in the
blanks, and up will come an estimation tailored to your needs.

▶ **Pay Now, Play Later**   **page 317**

After you establish how much you will need when you retire, you can start
working on making those fantasies come true. Turn to Quicken.com for help.
Start at Keyword: **Quicken**, click Quicken.com, and select Retirement. Click
Retirement Planner to open an interactive tool that will help you build a savings plan to fund your dream retirement.

▶ **Planning the Perfect Portfolio**   **page 319**

Maybe you've been saving for retirement since you earned your first paycheck.
More than likely you didn't give it much thought until you saw it rising over
the horizon. Whichever the case, your timetable plays a crucial role in shaping
how you invest for retirement. You can find age-specific investment strategies
at Keyword: **Retire**. Click *The* Plan for Four Strategies to open the Sage guide
to creating a retirement portfolio appropriate to your life stage — whether
you're just starting out or you're at retirement's doorstep.

▶ **School Daze**   **page 334**

In order to map out a strategy to pay for tuition, you need to know how much
of the tuition bill your family will be expected to foot, as well as how much (if
any) financial aid you will receive. AOL users can maneuver through the calculations with help from the College Board's financial aid calculator. Go to
Keyword: **College Board**, select Students and Parents, and scroll down to
Financial Aid Calculators, under Paying for College. Click Expected Family
Contribution to open the EFC Calculator.

Chapter 12

Reaching Your Goals

Now you have all the tools you need to find the right investments and to construct a solid portfolio. Does this mean an automatic ticket to reaching your goals?

Well, not exactly.

The fact is reaching your goals takes certain skills that a book like this can't teach. Things that you need to learn with practice. Things like circus skills:

▶ *Juggling*. You must be able to juggle many goals simultaneously. Some new goals get tossed in, others you discard. But you'll almost always have several in the air at the same time.

▶ *Timing*. Let go of that trapeze bar too soon and you hurl into empty space. Release the swing at its apex and you end up in the catcher's arms. So it is with investing. You might fall a few times, but after some practice you know instinctively when to make your moves.

▶ *Bravery*. If there's one maxim of investing, it's this: No risk, no rewards. You need to take chances to gain the highest returns. Bravery, however, is not foolishness. The lion tamer is well aware of the dangers before he steps into the ring, and he knows ahead of time how he will respond to those dangers. So too should you thoroughly understand the dangers of any investment before you make it.

▶ *Commitment*. It takes a lot of work to keep a top performer in shape. With the exception of a bottle of wine, nothing improves year after year without practice and fine-tuning the trouble spots. So it goes for your portfolio.

Note

Make sure the overall mix of your investments fits into the asset allocation you came up with a chapter ago.

Pursuing your financial goals even feels like a circus sometimes, with so many varied and challenging things happening concurrently. After you get a good grip on the tools and the knowledge you acquire in this book, your experiences can prove as exhilarating and entertaining as the Big Top.

Here's a look at two common goals that could very well be happening in your own arena right now. College and retirement. How do you get your act together to reach them?

Retirement Planning

You have to start with retirement first. Fully fund every retirement plan you can because, as you'll see later in this chapter, retirement plans multiply money unlike anything else, due to their tax-deductible and tax-deferred features. After you get retirement funding underway, then you can start stuffing the college fund.

The best launching point on AOL for all things retirement is Keyword: **Retire** (Figure 12-1). Follow the links to discover every facet of retirement, from getting the most from your

401(k), to retirement investing for all ages, to exploring annuities and understanding IRAs. Begin by clicking Money 101: Planning for Retirement to review Money Magazine's primer Roadmap to Retirement.

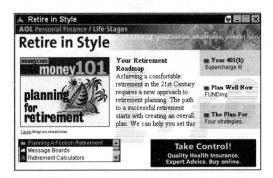

Figure 12-1. Retirement: whether it's around the corner or 30 years away, you can't begin preparing to enjoy those golden years too soon.

Plan to retire at 65? You'll likely need 20 or 25 more years of living expenses after you leave Widgets 'R' Us. What will your standard of living be? That hinges on your nest egg. Start building it now, or shore it up if building is already underway. To truly achieve the goal of a retirement that's free of financial worries, you have to do your work early, long before you have that retirement party and walk into the sunset, Golden Widget in hand.

Hopefully, you have been shoveling the most you can into your retirement account since you were a wee Widgeter. If you haven't, put this book down and start up that retirement account right now! If you have, congratulations. Pat yourself on the back and continue planning for the milestone.

How much will you need?

The first step in your planning is easy: Pick your magic year. Then, figure out how much money you'll need to live off after you retire.

In Chapter 2 you designed your budget, so you know what your expenses are. Some (like paying for college or the mortgage on your house) might increase, decrease, or disappear come retirement. But chances are most will continue.

The interactive worksheets at Keyword: **http://www. SmartMoney.com** can help you outline how much you'll need. (See Figure 12-2.) Click SmartMoney University, and select Retirement/401(k). Under the Retirement Savings title, select the article "How Much Should You Save?" to help determine what your retirement expenses will be, and to learn how much you need to save now to prepare.

Figure 12-2. A solid plan for the future must take into account how you expect your income and expenses to change after you retire.

To figure your retirement costs, increase your current expenses by 4 percent a year, from now until retirement, to account for inflation. (Okay, the rest of the book says 3 percent, but you're better off erring on the side of safety.) This gives you a basic idea of how much you can expect to spend your first year of retirement. (Remember, this amount is not set in stone. You might incur additional expenses when you retire, like paying for care for your elderly parents, or paying for your own health care, or paying for your own tuition.) Now, multiply this figure by 25 years, adding 4 percent a year again for inflation. Save yourself from math madness by calculating online.

Research shows you'll need about 70 percent of your current income to cover your annual expenses in retirement. This could swing dramatically depending on your retirement lifestyle. If you have no mortgage when you retire, or you sell your house and move to a smaller place and live off the proceeds, your expenses will decline significantly. If you buy a summer home, you'll add the expenses associated with living in two places. If you travel or play golf, where before you biked to work each day and had no social life, your expenses will climb. Whatever. Seventy percent of your current income times 25 years adds up to a whole lot of money.

Calculate retirement expenses

Don't feel like doing the math to figure your post-retirement costs? There's no need to. AOL's SmartCalc (Keyword: **Calculator**) will do it for you. Under Personal Finance, click Retirement, then select What will my expenses be after I retire?

First, enter the current and expected amount for expenses that should *decrease*. (Typically, after you retire, your housing costs decrease, as the average mortgage gets paid off. Other expenses such as clothing and transportation, also tend to decline.) Next, enter expenses that may increase. (Certain expenditures, such as health care, tend to increase. Often, with the gift of time, recreational costs increase significantly as well.)

Finally, enter the number of years until your expected retirement, and the annual inflation rate (4 percent is a good figure). Click the Results tab to see a breakdown of your projected monthly expenses, listed with and without inflation for direct comparison to your current expenses.

Keep in mind that this scenario does not take the tax bite into account. For a projection that accommodates the tax man in your future, click Am I Saving Enough? What Can I Change?, also in the Retirement Category, and fill out the blanks accordingly.

Where Will the Money Come From?

Now that you know how much you'll need, where will you get this money? Generally, retirement income comes from a combination of sources, including

- ▶ Social Security
- ▶ Pension plans
- ▶ Tax-deferred investments
- ▶ Taxable investments
- ▶ Part-time job

Social security

Since you earned your first paycheck from Burger Buddies, Uncle Sam has collected a percentage of your earnings — your first savings plan, so to speak — and put it aside for you. When you retire, you get to draw on this savings. Your benefits are based on the number of years you worked and your wages during that time.

But what you put in will not necessarily equal what you get out. In fact, the average Social Security payment is less than $10,000 a year. To find out how much you might receive based on your employment history, request an earnings and benefits statement online at the Social Security site. Go to Keyword: **Social Security**, shown in Figure 12-3, and click the Get Earnings Statement link in the column on the right. Or call the Social Security Administration at 800-772-1213. Then cross your fingers and hope Social Security exists when the big day comes. (Better yet, don't count on it at all; if federal benefits come your way, you'll have something extra to give to your grandchildren or your favorite charity.)

Find It Online

Check out Keyword: **Social Security** for the latest news and changes concerning Social Security.

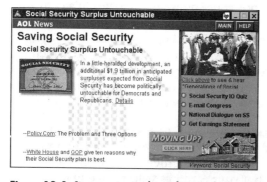

Figure 12-3. Since you received your first paycheck, you've been contributing money toward your Social Security income.

That big amount you came up with for your retirement costs will shrink a bit when you figure in annual Social Security income plus your anticipated pension income (if you have any). You will most probably still be short of what you need, though. This is where tax-deferred and taxable investments come in.

Tax-deferred plans

Hopefully, many of your assets are already accumulating in some sort of retirement account. These tax-deferred accounts protect your money, enabling it to compound without Uncle Sam grabbing a handful each year. When you eventually withdraw from these accounts after you retire, you have to pay taxes. But your dollar can work hard for you between now and then without taxes siphoning your growth.

Tax-deferred plans include the following:

Individual retirement account

An IRA is your personal retirement account. You and your spouse can each deposit up to $2,000 into this tax-deferred fund, even if only one of you works. You open an IRA with your bank or broker or credit union, and you invest the money inside it whichever way you please. (For the best choices, refer to Investing in Your Retirement Plan, later in this chapter.)

The amount you contribute to your IRA is tax-deductible so long as neither you nor your spouse participates in a company retirement plan, or you fall within certain income limitations (up to $31,000 if you're single and up to $51,000 for a couple). The money compounds each year tax-deferred, which means when you withdraw money from your IRA, you pay taxes on your contributions and your earnings. If you withdraw early, you have to pay a 10 percent penalty.

Even if your company contributes to a retirement plan for you, or you exceed the income limits, you can still deposit money into an IRA. You won't get the tax write-off from your contribution, but your earnings will still accumulate tax-deferred.

Roth IRA

You can't deduct your contributions to this type of IRA from your taxes, but that hardly matters when you consider the perks. Foremost among them — earnings in this special IRA grow *tax-free*, which means you never have to pay taxes on them.

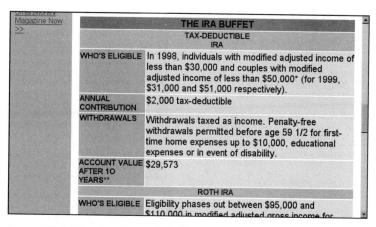

THE IRA BUFFET	
TAX-DEDUCTIBLE IRA	
WHO'S ELIGIBLE	In 1998, individuals with modified adjusted income of less than $30,000 and couples with modified adjusted income of less than $50,000* (for 1999, $31,000 and $51,000 respectively).
ANNUAL CONTRIBUTION	$2,000 tax-deductible
WITHDRAWALS	Withdrawals taxed as income. Penalty-free withdrawals permitted before age 59 1/2 for first-time home expenses up to $10,000, educational expenses or in event of disability.
ACCOUNT VALUE AFTER 1O YEARS**	$29,573
ROTH IRA	
WHO'S ELIGIBLE	Eligibility phases out between $95,000 and $110,000 in modified adjusted gross income for

Figure 12-4. IRA options have multiplied in recent years. Make sure you select the type that fits your income and goals.

If you don't participate in a company retirement plan, you and your spouse can contribute $4,000 a year combined, minus any deductible IRA contributions, to your Roth IRA.

Even if you participate in a company retirement plan, you and your spouse can contribute to a Roth IRA if your income is no more than $160,000 and you file jointly. If you're single you need to make less than $110,000 to contribute.

You can withdraw from your Roth with no penalty upon retirement. You may also withdraw money to buy a first house, to pay for college, or for certain medical emergencies. Unlike with most other retirement vehicles, you don't ever have to take money out of your Roth IRA.

401(k), 403(b), 457

If your company runs a 401(k), 403(b), or 457 plan, and you're not enrolled in it, stop reading and go call your employer to find out what you have to do to get in. As you learned in Chapter 5, between the tax savings and the matching contributions, 401(k)s and their ilk are like profits on a platter. No risks, ands or buts. There is no other place to get this instant return on your investment.

Find It Online

For an online comparison of the various IRAs, check out Keyword: **http://www. SmartMoney.com** and click SmartMoney University. Select IRA Corner, and choose Which IRA is Best? for the easy-to-read chart shown in Figure 12-4.

Find It Online

Which IRA is best for you? Find out at Keyword: **Retire**, then scroll down in the box on the left to Roth IRA Planner and double-click that. Now you're at Quicken.com's interactive planner. Click Launch Planner and fill in the blanks to find out which IRAs will best meet your needs.

12

Reaching Your Goals

Find It Online

To learn more online about this bounty, go to Keyword: **Money.com**, and scroll down to Money 101. Select Planning for Retirement, and click Tax-advantaged Savings Plans to the Rescue, as shown in Figure 12-5.

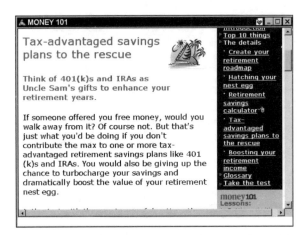

Figure 12-5. For retirement planning, the best place to start is with your company's 401(k) plan.

Many employers offer this type of retirement plan. Typically, for-profit companies offer 401(k)s, non-profit companies offer 403(b)s, and municipal governments have 457s. You contribute a percentage of your salary before taxes, and the company matches all or part of what you contribute in cash or in stock, and your combined contributions grow tax-free until you withdraw them, when you have to pay taxes. The most an employee can contribute to a 401(k) each year is $10,000, or a percentage of your salary that ranges from 12 to 20 percent.

Contributions, income limits, and funding options for the 403(b) and 457 plan vary according to a number of factors. Check with your plan administrator. Typically with all these plans, the company withdraws your contribution before you ever get your paycheck, so you're never tempted to spend it! You slice that contribution amount right off your reported income, erasing the taxes you would have paid on it.

The money you contribute is invested in the vehicles you choose, typically selections from the mutual fund company that administers the plan. You tell the company which funds you choose, and how much you want to put into each fund. Money in your 401(k) grows tax-free until you withdraw it.

These types of plans are the best way to invest for retirement. The Motley Fool's Retire in Style guide (see Figure 12-6) concurs. Learn why and find other retirement advice at Keyword: **Retire**, then in the box on the left, double-click Planning a

Foolish Retirement. Select Step 3, Free Money, and scroll down to read the pictured article.

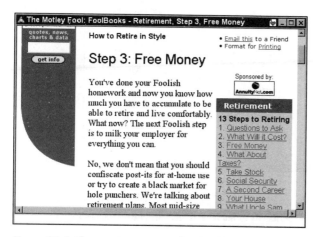

Figure 12-6. The tax advantages, combined with matching employer contributions, make your 401(k) a foolproof investment.

Before you know it, your contributions and the returns they earn compound into a great big tax-deferred heap. You can start withdrawing money from your 401(k) at age 59½ without penalty, and you must begin withdrawing the April after you turn age 70½.

Pension plans

Some employers offer a pension plan (also known as a *defined-benefit plan*). This guarantees you'll be paid a set amount of money each year of your retirement until you die. The amount is based on your salary at retirement, your years of service and a percentage rate determined by both. The check is reduced if you draw on your pension before age 65.

With a pension plan, you don't contribute money. Instead, the company sets it aside on your behalf. You become eligible for a pension — you are *vested* — after you work for a minimum amount of time, typically five or seven years. You don't get a say in where the money gets invested — the administrator whom the company hired to direct the plan decides where to invest the money. If you leave your job, the pension stays with the company until you're 65. Then you can start receiving benefits.

Find It Online

AOL partner Money Magazine (Keyword: **MoneyMag**) explains how the returns in a 401(k) add up.

"You can easily double your money the first year — while taking minimal risks. Here's how: Let's say you contribute 10 percent of a $70,000 salary to your account and earn an average annual return of 10 percent. Also assume that your company kicks in a 50 percent match on the first 6 percent you invest. For someone in a combined federal/state tax bracket of 31 percent, stashing away $7,000 in your plan saves you $2,170. That reduces the real cost of your $7,000 stake to just $4,830.

Meanwhile, you receive a matching contribution of $2,100 and your money grows tax-deferred. By the end of the first year, your $4,830 investment will have swelled to $9,529, for a gain of 97 percent."

Find It Online

For a quick online comparison of pension plans to 401(k)s, you can read the article pictured in Figure 12-7 at **Quicken**, then click Quicken.com and select Retirement. Under More to Explore, select Pension Plans, then click What It Isn't.

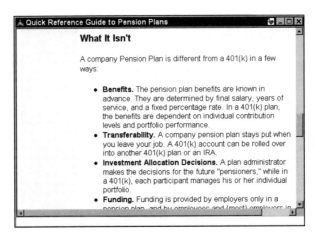

Figure 12-7. The traditional pension plan is still available with some companies, but it will not offer the portability or the types of benefits of a 401(k) plan.

When you're self-employed

If you're self-employed you can pick one of two options for your retirement plan. (You can't pick both.) To review your options online, refer to the article in Figure 12-8. Go to Keyword: **Sage Retirement**, and click Retirement Education in the subject box. Then select the title Self-Employed Plans.

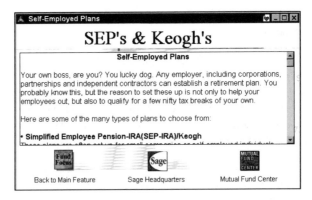

Figure 12-8. Even entrepreneurs can take advantage of tax-deferred retirement plans.

Stay put

Don't cash out your retirement plan when you change jobs. You will end up paying hefty tax penalties. Instead try the following:

▶ Keep your 401(k) plan where it is.

▶ Have your former employer directly roll the money in the plan over into a *conduit* IRA (which just holds it under the IRA umbrella), or directly into your new 401(k) plan.

▶ Whatever you do, don't let the plan administrator send the money to you first, or you will pay heavy penalties! For further advice, go to Keyword: **Whiz**, then click Money Whiz. Next, click Family Finances, and select You Can Take it With You, as in the Figure.

Find It Online

Want to talk about all these retirement options with your AOL brethren? Go to Keyword: **TheWhiz**, then select Messages, then Retirement Planning.

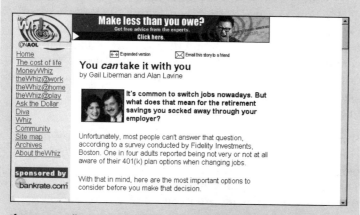

Make less than you owe?
Get free advice from the experts.
Click here.

WHIZ
©NAOL
Home
The cost of life
MoneyWhiz
theWhiz@work
theWhiz@home
theWhiz@play
Ask the Dollar
Diva
Whiz
Community
Site map
Archives
About theWhiz

sponsored by
bankrate.com

↔ Expanded version   ✉ Email this story to a friend

You *can* take it with you
by Gail Liberman and Alan Lavine

It's common to switch jobs nowadays. But what does that mean for the retirement savings you socked away through your employer?

Unfortunately, most people can't answer that question, according to a survey conducted by Fidelity Investments, Boston. One in four adults reported being not very or not at all aware of their 401(k) plan options when changing jobs.

With that in mind, here are the most important options to consider before you make that decision.

If you say goodbye to your employer, you don't have to say goodbye to your retirement plan.

▶ The *Keogh*, a retirement plan in which you can either contribute up to 20 percent of your income before taxes (no more than $30,000 a year), or set up a profit-sharing plan whose contributions vary according to your company's profits. You choose how it's invested, and the earnings accumulate tax-deferred. Whichever you do for yourself, you must do for your employees.

12

Reaching Your Goals

▶ The *Simplified Employee Pension*, a form of IRA but with no income guidelines. It's best for people who have few or no employees, like independent contractors, partners, sole proprietors, owner-operators. You can contribute 15 percent of your income before taxes, up to $30,000, to your SEP-IRA. You pick the way the money is invested and your investments accumulate tax-deferred.

Sit down with your accountant to decide which plan is best for you and your business.

How to Invest in Your Retirement Plan

After you figure out which plan is right for you, you have to decide how to invest your money within the framework of the plan. You don't need to do anything extraordinary here. Just follow the asset allocation plan you drew up in the last chapter. To refresh you, if your retirement is at least ten years down the road, invest the bulk of the retirement money into growth or aggressive growth vehicles, depending on your investment style.

Some investors mistakenly believe they are better off having *conservative* investments in their long-term retirement fund, because when they retire they'll be living off of this money. The theory is half right. While you will rely on more conservative investment vehicles *after* you retire, you should take the growth-producing route *to get there*. In fact, long-term retirement investments are the ideal place for *aggressive* vehicles, because, as you learned in Chapter 5, risk dissipates over a long timeframe. In addition, your big gains won't be impeded by taxes. Instead, your retirement plan will grow protected from taxes, until you withdraw from it years down the road, at which time your gains will be taxed.

A Quicken tool

How should you plan your investing and saving for retirement? To figure it out online, go to Quicken's interactive retirement planner at Keyword: **Quicken**, then click Quicken.com, and select Retirement. Click Retirement Planner to begin building a retirement plan based on your projected pension earnings, Social Security, tax-deferred and taxable savings.

The plan takes about ten minutes to complete. While Quicken recommends you submit a free registration, this isn't necessary to use the planner.

First plug in personal information like salary, economic expectations, assets, and retirement benefits. If you have questions about any of the information, click Help On This Page in the upper right corner for assistance. If you're up in the air on some questions, such as Estimated Life Expectancy, you can defer to the default value, which you get by clicking the Estimate button.

After you've entered all the information, the planner tabulates results and provides an action plan, outlining how your retirement will look based on your current financial picture, and what kind of savings and investments you need to retire in comfort.

 **Cross-Reference**

To evaluate the funds in the plan, follow the same strategy you pursued in Chapter 8.

Many retirement plans offer at least half a dozen mutual funds to choose from. But you don't need to invest in them all, and you don't have to pick the ones Mary in the next cubicle picked. Instead, find out from the plan administrator or your benefits officer exactly what's in the funds, then select a handful of funds that reflect *your* needs, as you dictated in your asset allocation plan in the last chapter.

As you know, your needs will change as your goals change — that's why the plans offer so many different funds. Not because one is any better than the next, but because different funds meet different needs. You transfer from one fund to the next as your needs change over time.

12

Reaching Your Goals

Find It Online

How do your funds compare? Find out at Keyword: **Morningstar,** AOL's partner for mutual fund reports. Type in the ticker symbol or name of your mutual fund and hit enter, and select Mutual Fund Report. Scroll down to the table Performance: Annual Return percent to see how your mutual fund compares to the returns of its respective index.

Caution

If you're given lots of company stock through an Employee Stock Ownership Plan, make sure to diversify your retirement plan with either complementary or less aggressive investments. It is safest to limit your company's stock to 10 percent of your whole portfolio.

Compare the funds with their benchmark. For example, if you're trying to gauge the performance of a large-cap stock fund, compare its 1-, 3-, and 5-year returns to the S&P 500 index. Size up the small-caps with the Russell 2000 index, or with whatever category the fund is in.

Things can get a little tricky if your funds don't perform as well as the norm. You want to take advantage of the tax protection of your retirement plan, and you want to maintain your asset allocation, but you don't want to feed your money into laggards. If a few quarters pass, and your fund continues to lag behind other funds with similar holdings, it might be time to make a change.

Chances are, all the plan's stock funds won't be dogs. Find the good ones, then do a little rearranging. Try your best to keep high performing equities in your retirement plan (to protect them from being eaten by taxes). Continue to put the maximum into your retirement plan, but put it in the better performing vehicles. Then pick up what you need outside of your retirement plan to maintain your ideal asset allocation.

You will most likely be moving your assets into less aggressive vehicles as you get older. In fact, just as you rebalance your overall portfolio on a regular basis, you should also routinely rebalance your retirement plan holdings. For example, if you set up your retirement plan five years ago according to your asset allocation and you haven't changed it, chances are you are too stock-heavy, as stocks have soared in the past couple of years. Bonds haven't kept pace. That would result in a heavier stock orientation than you were looking for when you set up the plan.

This could also mean a change within stock subcategories. Review your asset allocation in your retirement plan each year. If you've strayed about 5 percent, transfer your investments accordingly, or redirect your current contributions toward the assets you're short on to catch up to your desired mix.

Find a plan yourself

What do mutual fund experts Sage (Keyword: **Sage**) recommend you invest in to reach your retirement goals? As with any goal, the answer depends on your timetable. You can glean Sage's age-specific advice at Keyword: **Retire**. Click The Plan for You ... Four Strategies to open the site pictured in the following Figure. Sage offers four archetypal profiles as well as advice for retirement planning for the young, the middle-aged, the mature, and the already retired. Select the appropriate picture to open the following profiles. More specific recommendations follow at the end of the retirement section of this chapter.

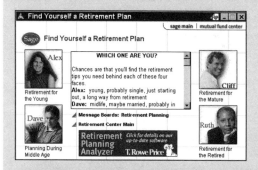

How you allocate your money for your retirement will depend on your timeline and your goals.

20–45 years old	25% Large cap; 25% Mid cap; 30% Small cap; 20% International stock.
45–55 years old	35% Large cap; 25% Mid cap; 25% Small cap; 15% International stock.
55–65 years old	55% Large cap; 10% Mid cap; 10% Small cap; 10% International stock; 15% Intermediate bond.
65+ years old	50% Short term bonds; 35% Large growth; 15% International stock.

Find It Online

Exactly what should you put in *your* 401(k)? To help you figure this out, try out the interactive planner at Keyword: **Retire**, then scroll down to Making the Most of Your 401(k) for an asset allocation planner from SmartMoney.com.

Note

About five years before you retire, redirect your contributions into the asset mix you want to end up with upon retirement.

After You Retire

After an eternity of saving, come retirement, it will be time to crack the eggs. When you retire, how much can you gobble each month without worrying you'll run out? For help finding out, go to Keyword: **Quicken**, click Quicken.com, and select Retirement. Under Retire in Style, select How Much Can You Safely Withdraw for Retirement?, as in Figure 12-9.

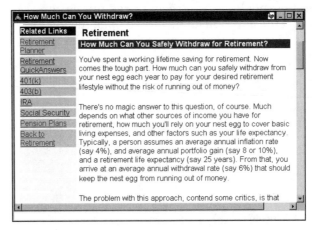

Figure 12-9. After you retire, you must determine how much you can withdraw every year without going through your savings too quickly.

To figure out how much to withdraw from your egg, take the total you've amassed at retirement, then assume your expenses will grow at an inflation rate of 4 percent a year; your portfolio will return 8 percent a year; and you will live 25 more years.

Then you come up with an average annual amount, maybe 4 percent, that you can withdraw from your nest egg and still be able to stay afloat if the market takes subterranean dips or inflation soars cloud-bound.

After you determine how much to withdraw each year, you have to choose where to take it from. Know those monthly, automatic deposits you make into your mutual fund account? You can withdraw money in the same way after you retire. (This helps you avoid removing a big chunk of cash when the market is down.) While you wile away the weeks watching the sunset in Key West, direct your broker to sell shares of your funds each month, quarter or year, and deposit the proceeds into a money market account if you're living off the money. (If you're not living off the money, follow the upcoming suggestions on how to maintain your balance in the most tax-prudent way.)

Withdrawing wisely

During retirement more than ever you need to make sure to keep your portfolio in check, especially as you draw from it. In order to maintain the allocation you want among stocks, bonds and cash, pay yourself from dividends, interest payments or capital gains, depending on where your portfolio is over-committed and needs balancing.

After you retire, with 25-plus years ahead of you, it is important not to let your investments stagnate. Otherwise, you will outlive your money, which is not a comfortable thought. While you could lump all your money into bonds and depend solely on that for your income, this won't allow for growth. In fact, over 20 plus years it will erode your nest egg.

Even as you retire, when your focus is on stability and reliable returns, keep some money in stocks. Granted, you probably won't be looking at international stocks and small-caps. But at least 20 percent of your portfolio should be in the S&P 500 — in equity-income funds, or growth and income funds, or in blue chips — in addition to your fixed-income vehicles, so you can generate enough growth to cover your expenses down the road.

Retirement portfolios

To take a look online at what specific funds Sage recommends for your retirement portfolio at different stages in life, go to Keyword: **Sage Retirement**, click Living in Retirement and then choose Retirement Portfolios of the Sages, or see the sample portfolios here. (Note that the first two suggestions are identical. What you select depends on your risk tolerance and your investment preferences.)

Continued

Note

If you're concerned about maintaining your asset allocation in your portfolio after those big retirement plan dollars start rolling in, simply move the money you withdraw into mutual funds that carry the same kinds of investments you had under your retirement umbrella.

Find It Online

For help in sorting out which retirement funds to draw from first, go to Keyword: **Quicken**, then select Quicken.com, then click Retirement. Under the Quick Answers section, select Which Savings Should You Spend First in Retirement?

Cross-Reference

Make sure your estate plan is in place. Adept planning can mean the difference of many, many dollars in taxes paid on the hard-won assets in your portfolio. For the ins and outs of estate planning, see Chapter 17.

Retirement portfolios *(continued)*

Just Starting Out: Younger Investors

Base portfolio	50% Vanguard Index 500; 30% Vanguard Small-Cap Index; 20% Schwab International Index.
Something less risky	60% Vanguard Index 500; 25% Vanguard Small-Cap Index; 15% Schwab International Index
Something more risky	40% Vanguard Index 500; 40% Vanguard Small-Cap Index; 20% Schwab International Index.

Planning During Middle Age: Mid-Life Investors

Base portfolio	50% Vanguard Index 500; 30% Vanguard Small-Cap Index; 20% Schwab International Index.
Something less risky	60% Vanguard Index 500; 25% Vanguard Small-Cap Index; 15% Schwab International Index.
Something more risky	40% Vanguard Index 500; 40% Vanguard Small-Cap Index; 20% Schwab International Index.

Retirement Planning for the Mature: Age 55-65, Within Five Years of Retirement

Base portfolio	40% Vanguard Index 500; 25% Vanguard Total Bond Market Index; 15% Vanguard Small Cap Index; 10% Schwab International Index; 10% Money Market Fund.

Something less risky | 30% Vanguard Total Bond Market Index; 25% Money Market Fund; 25% Vanguard Index 500; 10% Schwab International Index; 10% Vanguard Small Cap Index.

Something more risky | 40% Vanguard Index 500; 25% Vanguard Small Cap Index; 20% Schwab International Index; 10% Vanguard Total Bond Market Index; 5% Money Market Fund.

Retirement for the Retired: Over 65

Base portfolio | 25% Vanguard Index 500; 25% Vanguard Total Bond Market Index; 25% Money Market Fund; 15% Vanguard Small Cap Index; 10% Schwab International Index.

Something less risky | 40% Vanguard Total Bond Market Index; 25% Money Market Fund; 20% Vanguard Index 500; 10% Vanguard Small Cap Index; 5% Schwab International Index.

Something more risky | 35% Vanguard Index 500; 20% Vanguard Small Cap Index; 20% Vanguard Total Bond Market Index; 15% Money Market Fund; 10% Schwab International Index.

College Planning

 **Find It Online**

For an online primer on how to save for college, go to Keyword: **Money.com,** scroll down to Money 101, and click Lesson 11: Saving for College, as pictured in Figure 12-10.

Whew! You've taken care of retirement. Now for that other seemingly elusive goal: College.

Planning on higher education for little Sweet Pea? Better to assume she's going than to ignore the possibility until it's too late to do anything about tuition. Ideally, she's in the cradle now, giving you plenty of time to save. If Sweet Pea is a baby, four years at State U. will run about $200,000 by the time she is 18, estimates the College Board (Keyword: **College Board**). Ivy U. will run you at least $300,000.

How on Earth are you supposed to come up with this money? Gifts or an inheritance from Aunt Sofie? Loans from Mom and Dad? Your investments? Financial aid? What if Aunt Sofie ends up in a money-draining nursing home or decides she'd rather spend her remaining years in a beachfront villa in Barbados than pay your little tyke's tuition? As for financial aid, only about a third of students who apply actually get anything. And the majority of those get just a fraction of their total bill.

The fact is students and their parents usually end up paying the bulk of college costs.

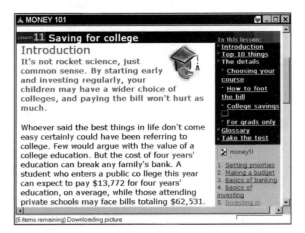

Figure 12-10. Don't put it off a moment longer. The earlier you begin saving for your children's education, the less painful the final bill will be.

AOL's pencil box

If you haven't started saving for college, now is the time to begin. AOL can help. Go straight to Keyword: **Saving for School** to find out how much you'll need, what it will take to get there and tips for enduring the process.

You can also take care of much of the college application process online. To apply for college, go to Keyword: **College**, then select Applications Online.

Check out Keyword: **Parent Soup** and select Experts, then click The Education Expert for information on college costs, financial aid Web sites, ways to budget for school and finding the aid you need (see the Figure below). Get tips from parents facing tuition turmoil on the site's very active message board.

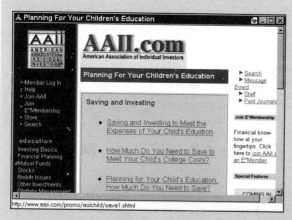

When facing a task as monumental as paying for college it helps to get advice from willing and experienced parents and professionals, ingredients you'll find in Parent Soup.

Being able to pay for college is a typical goal of many investors. The effort spent just trying to figure out how to do it can seem like a huge drain. But, as with many investments, when you consider the potential returns, your motivation to save might change.

Here, the investment is for your children's future. College grads earn, on average, twice as much as high school grads, notes AOL partner Motley Fool (Keyword: **Fool**). The average household income of two working college grads is about $80,000, the Fools say. Compare that to the average household income of two working high school grads, which hovers around $40,000. Now look at how two high school dropouts fare: about $25,000 a year for their *combined* household income.

So you see the ultimate return on your investment. But how much will you be able to save? Based on the asset allocation plan you drew up in the last chapter, or the investment blueprint you put together in Chapter 5, you know how much your college fund should generate between now and graduation day. If you haven't gotten around to working out the calculations, repeat this ten times:"I will complete my investment blueprint, I will complete my investment blueprint...."

Then go back to those calculators (Keyword: **Calculator**), choose Savings under Personal Finance, then select How Much Will My Savings Be Worth to figure out what your savings and returns should total in 10 or 15, or however many years till Sweet Pea dons a cap and gown.

Getting the Most from Your Money

Don't assume financial aid will bail you out if you haven't saved for tuition. Financial-aid officers take no mercy on parents who make a healthy chunk of money but never get around to saving any of it. So start that college fund now, and make sure you deposit money into it regularly. Think of the deposits as payments toward the tuition bill, so by the time the real, six-figure bill comes, you will have already paid it. (What's the worst-case scenario? If your little one doesn't end up going to college, you will have a huge nest egg at your disposal!)

If Sweet Pea is a baby and you put $200 a month for the next 18 years in a savings account that pays 2 percent, you end up with about $52,000. That's enough to make a big dent in your college bills but probably not enough to cover them. Savings accounts, savings bonds, CDs, zero-coupon bonds — these are all used to pay for college, but they're not the best way to build the amount you need.

So what is? You know this, but it bears repeating: *based on historic averages, stocks are the only investment to outpace inflation and generate double-digit returns.* If Sweet Pea is in the cradle, her college fund should be doing what she's doing: growing fast and furious. For this kind of performance, turn to small-cap or growth stocks, or to growth or aggressive-growth mutual funds (see Chapters 6 and 8 for information on these), depending on your investment style.

If you're averse to risky small caps, even with the long time-frame, don't rule out stocks altogether. Instead, put your college fund in an S&P 500 index fund, which holds large, less risky, blue-chips. Or choose a large-cap or blue-chip fund. After you find a fund you like, set up an automatic investment plan that withdraws a set amount from your checking account each month and deposits it into the fund. Putting $200 a month in a fund that returns 12 percent (the stock market average over the last 40 years), nets you $151,572 in 18 years.

Now you're talking!

Climbing for ivy

To reach the $200,000 you'll need for State U., you have to save $264 a month at 12 percent for 18 years. For Ivy, that climbs to $396 a month.

How much will you have to save in your timeframe? Go to Keyword: **Quicken**, and select the Investing tab. Click the Basics link, under the heading Departments along the left-hand side. Then click College Planner under Tools. Select the College Planner to open the interactive tool (shown in Figure 12-11) that helps you measure your savings to college costs, and helps you plan how to make up the difference.

Note

Saving this amount actually gets easier as time goes on, as your wages will probably go up significantly in 18 years' time. Establish your automatic investment plan now and hike it every year you get a raise. Then you might finish ahead of time!

12

Reaching Your Goals

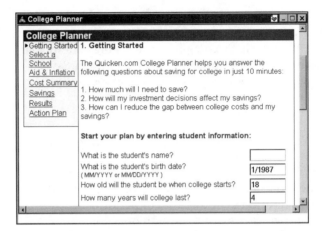

Figure 12-11. Interactive planners such as this one from Quicken can help you make a realistic savings plan based on anticipated college costs and your timeframe.

Investing for college

What? Sweet Pea is already 12? (Where did the time go?) And Junior is 9? You haven't accumulated anywhere near what you'll need? You're not alone. A study by Sallie Mae, the Student Loan Marketing Association, found that most parents of college-bound high-schoolers don't have even half of what their kids need for college. And one in five hasn't saved a penny!

Don't do anything foolish, like dumping all your hard-earned money into commodities to try to make up for lost time. You risk losing it all. Just take the maximum you can spare each week and deposit it into a college fund you promise not to touch until the day Sweet Pea signs her letter of acceptance.

How you invest that money in the college fund depends on your kids' ages and the strength of your other assets. For an online primer on this subject, read Investing for College: Piecing Together a Plan, shown in Figure 12-12. Go to Keyword: **Quicken**, select Quicken.com, click Retirement, then click the Planning tab. Under College, select Don't Wait to Save, and then click Smart Investing: Tailor Your Investments to Your Child's Age.

As you'll see in the following sample college fund portfolios, the bulk of your college fund should be in aggressive stocks until your child is about 8 or so (although the types of stocks you pick depends on your risk tolerance and investing preference). When your darlings turn 9, put new money into less aggressive vehicles, such as blue-chip or large-cap stocks.

When the kids' ages hit double digits, slowly move their college funds into more stable investments such as balanced or income funds. When Sweet Pea or Junior turns 14, move a quarter of the tuition money into money markets or Treasury bills or notes, and move an equal proportion more each year. If you have two college-bound children, adjust your portfolio to reflect the ages of each.

Caution

If the stock market is booming, it's tempting to let all the college money multiply in stocks. But if stocks suddenly nosedive, like they did in the summer of 1998, four years' worth of tuition money could suddenly be reduced to three. As the children get closer to college age, gradually move their tuition money to safer havens, like CDs, money markets or Treasuries. And, by all means, don't invest the college fund money in stocks when Sweet Pea is in college!

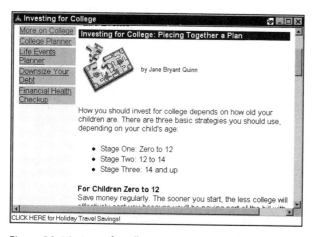

Figure 12-12. Saving for college tuition is a dynamic process: As your children's ages change, so should the content of your college portfolio.

Sample allocations

There is no "perfect" portfolio for college but here are some great suggestions from AOL's partners. All of these recommendations assume that your asset allocation will change as your child ages.

The Motley Fool (Keyword: Fool)

Age	Assets
Birth to 5	100% growth stocks. Say the Fools, "You have more time, you can take more risk."

Continued

Sample allocations *(continued)*

6 to 13	70% stocks, 30% bonds. "You might want to think about making a few more 'prudent' selections," they suggest.
14 to 18	30% bonds, 20% stocks, 50% money market funds. "You want things to continue to grow," they say, "but you also want to protect yourself from market volatility."
College age	100% money market, so the money is safe, liquid and interest-bearing.

Here's another set of suggestions, this one from AOL's Advice and Planning section. Go to Keyword: **http://www.aaii.com/promo/aolchild**, shown in the Figure, then select Saving and Investing to Meet the Expenses of Your Child's Education.

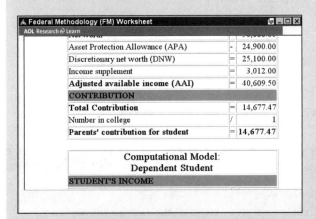

The American Association of Individual Investors can help you map out a long-term investment strategy for meeting college expenses.

American Association of Individual Investors

Age	Portfolio/Purpose
Early years	Large-cap stocks/funds: Initial investments serve as a core.

Middle years	Large-caps/funds: Keep at least 50% as core. Aggressive growth stocks/funds: Add as you can for diversification and growth. International stocks/funds: The amount depends on your risk tolerance.
Approaching college age	Large-cap stock core: At least 50%. Aggressive growth stocks/funds: Varies (depending on what you have and your comfort level). International stocks/funds: Varies (as above). Short-term bond fund or Money market fund: Withdraw the tuition money from the stock investments in equal amounts each quarter over several years. Take this money and put it in the bond fund or the money market fund, from which you will pay the tuition.

School selection strategies

There's more to reaching your goals than figuring out how to invest your savings. Often, you have to put together very different pieces in order to assemble the puzzle. Such is the case with paying for college, for which the best financial strategies often have less to do with how much financial aid you get from a school and how your investments fare than with the school you're targeting.

First off, figure out if Sweet Pea really wants to go to college, and if she wants to go full time. (Remember, if she's too young to tell you one way or the other, assume she will go.) Then, when college time rolls around, make sure she is willing to work hard to stay there.

Come your child's freshman year in high school, start comparison shopping. There are *huge* differences in costs of schools, even those with similar programs. For an example, go to Keyword: **College Board**, then click Search, type in Tuition and Fees and Introduction. Then click Introduction. Now, click a state. Take a look at the disparity in prices among private, public, and community colleges, shown in Figure 12-13. Some cost ten times as much as others. Whatever the amount, tack on about 5 percent per year from now till college time (historically, college costs have risen higher per year than inflation) to come up with a total.

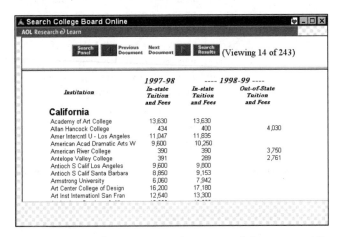

Figure 12-13. Send your mouse on a hunt to unearth the enormous differences in the costs of colleges.

If paying for the full four years looks like it's going to be impossible or a stretch at best, you can reduce the total tab by a huge chunk and still end up with the same college name on Sweet Pea's resume. Enrolling in night, weekend or summer classes at the local (and inexpensive) community college can trim a semester or two off of the four-year total. So can taking classes online. Some accredited colleges offer discounts to AOL members. Keyword: **Courses** goes directly to AOL's online campus, as shown in Figure 12-14. Your child can always take the first two years' worth of credits at a less expensive school, then transfer to a prestigious (read more expensive) school for the diploma.

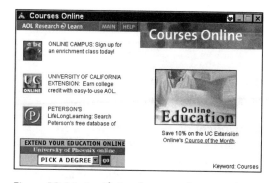

Figure 12-14. Considering alternative plans — such as attending courses online — can slash the amount you need to save.

Figuring Out Financial Aid

Saving for college is a big Catch-22. If you don't save a dime, you won't be able to pay come tuition time. If you save regularly and prudently, and amass a huge pile of money, you'll have to turn it over to State U. — and you might still fall short of the amount you need. That's where financial aid comes in.

To find financial aid information online, start at Keyword: **Financial Aid,** as pictured in Figure 12-15, for links to information from schools, states and the federal government, to lists of available loans and scholarships, as well as success stories from AOL members who untangled the financial aid labyrinth.

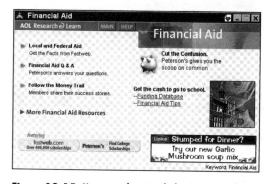

Figure 12-15. No matter how much they've set aside, most families hope for some kind of financial assistance.

Billions of dollars in scholarships are awarded every year. You can review an extensive list of rewards at Keyword: **Financial Aid**. Click Funding Database to open the RSP Funding Focus site. Select Money Database for an index of available scholarships. Search the entire database, or search by category, such as Military or Minority scholarships. Awards are listed in alphabetical order, as shown in Figure 12-16. To find more information about a particular scholarship, double-click the name for a brief summary, eligibility requirements, and contact information.

Looking for answers to your financial aid questions? Go to Keyword: **Financial Aid** and click Financial Aid Q&A.

Financial aid typically includes:

▶ grants, scholarships, loans, or employment from the school

▶ loans or grants from the government

▶ scholarships or grants from civic groups

Most financial aid is dependent on financial need. Merit aid is the only assistance that isn't need-based, and there's not much of it around. Colleges use merit aid to lure students who are exceptional at something — academics, athletics, or an extraordinary skill.

If your child applies to a school where her test scores and grades put her in the top 25 percent of the class profile, she stands a better chance of getting aid. While Sweet Pea's grades might be good enough to get her into Ivy U., State U. might appreciate your little genius so much it will pay a scholarship to get her. If you're looking for a substantial aid package, look within your state first.

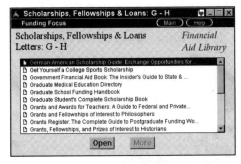

Figure 12-16. There's a scholarship for just about any special interest. Small, unique awards can make a big dent in your college bill.

Calculate your contribution

For a ballpark figure of how much you might be expected to contribute toward tuition, call up the College Board's EFC calculator. Go to Keyword: **College Board**, then select Students and Parents, and scroll down to Financial Aid Calculators, under Paying for College. Then click Expected Family Contribution, then EFC Calculator.

After answering a few yes or no questions, select which worksheet you prefer to fill out. The *Federal Methodology* (shown in the Figure) worksheet determines eligibility for federal financial aid programs, and the *Institutional Methodology* is a more extensive worksheet used by many colleges and private scholarship programs to determine students' eligibility for non-federal sources of aid. You may also select to fill out both simultaneously by clicking Both FM & IM.

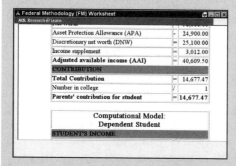

Federal Methodology (FM) Worksheet		
AOL Research & Learn		
Asset Protection Allowance (APA)	-	24,900.00
Discretionary net worth (DNW)	=	25,100.00
Income supplement	=	3,012.00
Adjusted available income (AAI)	=	40,609.50
CONTRIBUTION		
Total Contribution	=	14,677.47
Number in college	/	1
Parents' contribution for student	=	14,677.47
Computational Model: Dependent Student		
STUDENT'S INCOME		

Ignorance is not bliss when it comes to planning for college. Better to face the bad news early and design a plan to meet the expected costs.

Fill in the numbers. Be sure to click Help for terms you don't understand, such as what to include under Untaxed Income/Benefits. Then brace yourself. You could very well see a great big chunk of money that seems impossible to produce.

The bulk of your contribution level on the EFC is determined by your income. (It accounts for about 25 percent of your expected contribution.) Your assets (including the equity on your home!) account for about 5 percent of the contribution. Children are expected to contribute about 35 percent of their assets and about half of their income as freshmen, and about a quarter after that.

Click Return to Data Input to play with the numbers a bit, seeing what you can change here and there to affect your EFC. (The biggest change comes when you have two people in college, even if one is a parent. Then the expected contribution shrinks. Also, taking your assets out of Cash/Savings and into home equity or another asset will change things a little bit.) Going through the EFC calculations will give you a good idea of what you can expect to pay come college time.

How much will you get

Be sure to apply for financial aid as close as possible to January 1 of your child's senior year in high school, the earliest date schools will accept applications for aid. Don't wait until your child is admitted, and don't wait until you file your tax return! (Use an estimate based on the most recent return you have.) After financial aid is distributed, it's gone, regardless of how much you would have qualified for.

The amount of aid you will qualify for each year depends on your income and your assets. Most schools use a federal formula called the *Expected Family Contribution* to come up with the amount of financial assistance for which you qualify. The EFC measures parents' and students' incomes, investments, assets, and other factors. If your EFC equals or exceeds the cost of the college, Sweet Pea doesn't get financial aid. If the school's cost exceeds your Expected Family Contribution, Sweet Pea qualifies for aid. After you apply, the school's financial-aid officers figure out how much you qualify for, then they go out and get the money (typically, loans or work-study money) for you.

Now, for an interesting twist. Don't rule out applying to Ivy U. just because you think you can't afford it. The Estimated Family Contribution is always the same, regardless of the cost of the school. If Ivy U. costs $35,000 a year, versus $15,000 for State U., and your EFC says you can ante up $5,000 a year, you could end up getting a lot more money from Ivy U., because the school is much more expensive.

Types of aid

The federal government offers need-based and non-need-based loans to students and parents. Web sites such as Keyword: **http://www.finaid.org** (see Figure 12-17) can outline the various loans.

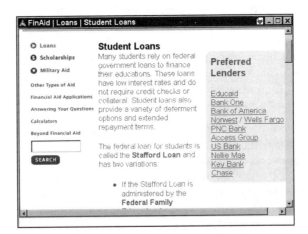

Figure 12-17. Even after years of saving, many people must turn to federal government loans to help defray college costs.

Here are some of the more common offerings:

The Stafford Loan

There are two versions of this federally guaranteed loan. One is the *subsidized* version, which is need-based, and the other is the *unsubsidized* version, which is non-need-based. Both types defer payments until Junior graduates.

PLUS

PLUS stands for Parent Loans for Undergraduate Students. This non-need-based loan lets you borrow up to the annual cost of college, less any financial aid Junior gets. You have to start repaying the loan 60 days after you get it, but you have up to ten years to repay it. The variable interest rate is tied to the Treasury bill rate.

Perkins

Perkins loans are made directly to students in need, who can obtain the loans without parents or co-signers. Repayment starts after the student graduates, leaves school or attends less than half time. These loans charge about 5 percent interest and the interest doesn't accrue while Junior is in college.

Uncle Sam recently pitched in to help his nieces and nephews pay for school with special IRAs and tax credits.

Education IRAs

Education IRAs allow families to contribute up to $500 a year per child in an E-IRA earmarked for college. You don't get to deduct the contribution from your taxes, but the earnings generated in the E-IRA are *tax-free* as long as you use them to pay for college. There are income limits — up to $160,000 for joint filers, and up to $110,000 for single filers — but these are for the contributor. A relative who qualifies might be happy to set up an E-IRA for Junior.

You can contribute to an E-IRA in addition to your other IRAs. And if you have money left over from the E-IRA after you pay tuition (hey, you never know), or if Sweet Pea changes her mind about college, or if she turns 30 (when she becomes too old for the E-IRA), you can roll it over into an Education IRA for your other children or for your grandchildren, nieces and

Find It Online

For the finer points of federal loans, refer to the federal government's Student Guide for Federal Aid at **http:// www.ed.gov/prog_info/ SFA/StudentGuide/.**

12

Reaching Your Goals

You can withdraw from a regular IRA for higher-education expenses without incurring the 10 percent penalty tax that you normally pay for payouts before age 59½. But you'll still owe income tax.

You can set up most IRAs online. E-mail the brokers at Keyword: **Broker** for information.

To compare the various government sponsored tax benefits for higher education, as pictured in Figure 12-18, go to Keyword: **http://www. irs.gov,** scroll to the bottom of the page and click Forms and Publications. Then click Search for a Form or a Publication, and enter Pub 970 to open the IRS guide Tax Benefits for Higher Education.

nephews, or siblings. If you don't use the E-IRA money for college for a qualified family member, you will owe income tax, plus a 10 percent penalty on your withdrawals.

Roth IRAs

Again, as you read in the retirement section of this chapter, couples can contribute up to $4,000 a year (minus their deductible IRA contributions) to these special IRAs. The contributions aren't tax-deductible, but the earnings accumulate *tax-free*. There's no penalty, either, if you cash them out early to pay for college. The Roth IRA has the same income limits as the E-IRA.

HOPE and lifetime learning credits

Two relatively new tax credits for higher education allow you to take deductions on your tax return for a portion of your college costs. The HOPE Scholarship Credit allows you to deduct up to $1,500 per year per student for the first two years of college. You can slash off your taxes 100 percent of the first $1,000 you pay in tuition and 50 percent of the next $1,000 for the first year, and the same for the second year.

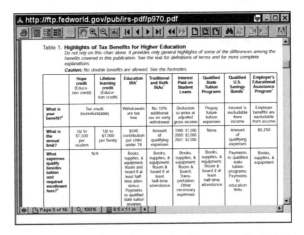

Figure 12-18. Uncle Sam has introduced new tax credits for higher education, hoping to encourage parents to begin saving early and to offer everyone the opportunity for a higher education.

The Lifetime Learning credit equals 20 percent of the tuition you pay each year (up to $5,000 of tuition, to rise to $10,000 after 2002). This equals a maximum credit of $1,000 now and $2,000 after 2002. You can take this tax credit any year you don't take the HOPE credit. And neither credit applies in a year you take distributions from an Educational IRA.

State prepayment plans

More than a dozen states and institutions offer college prepayment programs, in which you prepay Junior's tuition at State U. and the amount you contribute is guaranteed to increase in value at the same rate as tuition. But if Junior doesn't end up at State U. your principal is returned to you with a tiny fraction of what you would have earned had you put the money in a stock fund.

If you have the money to prepay tuition, and you have a long timeframe, you might as well invest the money in a vehicle like a good stock fund which, based on history, should generate a lot more interest than the prepayment plan will. To discuss the pros and cons of pre-payment plans, go to Keyword: **Family Money,** click College Planning, and select Pay Now, Learn Later to read the article in Figure 12-19.

Note

If you cash in your U.S. Savings Bonds to pay for college, and you and your spouse earn less than $79,650 to $105,650 filing jointly (or you earn $53,100 to $68,000 for single filing), a portion of the interest on the bonds is tax-exempt.

Caution

You can't put money toward an E-IRA and a state prepayment plan for the same student.

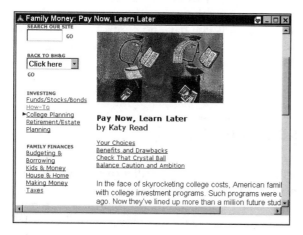

Figure 12-19. You might consider state-run college prepayment plans, but keep in mind they earn little interest.

E-mail the financial aid office in your state university system to find out if the university offers a prepayment program.

529 plan

A second prepayment plan that recently debuted might be more worthy of consideration, especially to people whose incomes are too high for all these other plans. It's called the 529 plan, based on the IRS tax code from which it was derived. This trust plan allows you to invest money on a tax-deferred basis in certain mutual funds, many of which contain equities. The most you can invest is $150,000 in total, or a maximum of $50,000 a year, without paying gift tax.

When the money is withdrawn for college, it's taxed at your child's tax rate, not yours. (If it's not used for college, the money gets taxed at *your* rate, plus you have to pay a penalty. The penalties are waived, though, if the 529 money gets transferred to another qualified beneficiary.) The 529 money can be used anywhere the child goes to college, which is another big advantage over other prepayment plans. Ask your broker or your mutual fund company if they offer this type of fund, or e-mail the brokers at Keyword: **Broker**.

You can't take the HOPE credit or Lifetime Learning credit in the same year you use money from the 529 plan, but you probably make too much for these, anyway, if you have a 529. The only other drawback is you have no control over how the money gets invested. You have to leave that up to the fund manager.

Tax Consequences

Parents, especially those with a hefty wallet (more than about $150,000 in income and $500,000 in assets, not counting your home) should talk with their accountant about these different plans and credits before they make any moves with their college fund investments. Sometimes, a few prudent adjustments in timing and planning can help you avoid unfavorable consequences.

For example, in an effort to maximize the amount of aid they can qualify for, some parents consider putting assets in their children's names. But this approach can backfire. As a student, Sweet Pea will be expected to shell out a much greater chunk of her money than her parents. And if the money is in her name, it legally belongs to Sweet Pea. If she decides she'd rather buy a red Corvette than pay for school, that's her choice.

If you don't qualify for aid, you might consider giving your child less than $10,000 in appreciated securities (in other words, things like stocks that you bought for $2,000 that are now worth $9,022) and have her use it toward tuition. It has to be less than $10,000 or Sweet Pea will have to pay taxes on the gift. She then sells the shares, pays a 10 percent capital gains tax and helps pay the tuition. That's better than the 20 percent capital gains tax you would pay if you sold the stocks.

Similarly, be mindful of the capital gains implications when you move from one investment to the next. When you apply for financial aid you have to submit your previous year's tax return; the financial aid formula is more dependent on income than assets. You don't want to cash in your accounts and have all those gains you generated from years of saving for college to show up as investment income on the most important year's tax return.

At this critical time, it's important to *reduce* your income, not *increase* it. If possible, don't sell any securities for a profit the year before you apply for aid, and don't take any lump-sum distributions. In other words, try to cash in your investments with capital gains before the January of Sweet Pea's junior year in high school, or after her junior year in college.

Other strategies

Still don't think you'll get there? Don't give up! Millions of dollars in scholarships are not based on need. These are most often provided by civic, ethnic or religious groups to students who meet the organization's criteria, as well as by corporations for children of their employees. To find out if Sweet Pea qualifies for any, check out these options:

▶ AOL partner FastWeb (Keyword: **FastWeb**) is a free service that culls through 400,000 scholarships to turn up any that might be applicable to you.

Continued

12

Reaching Your Goals

Tip

About a dozen books from AOL partner Barnes & Noble.com (Keyword: **BN**) can connect you to scholarship information.

Other strategies *(continued)*

▶ AOL members can search at no charge Reference Service Press' database of literally billions of dollars in scholarships for education, research, creative activities and personal development, from undergraduate through professional levels. Go to Keyword: **RSP**, shown in the Figure below, or reach it via AOL's Research and Learning Channel (Keyword: Research & Learn). To create a list personalized to your needs, click Money Database and then select Search for Money. Check the appropriate boxes under Funding Level, Characteristics, and Disabilities. You may also enter in key words, such as a profession, ethnic group, or a religious affiliation to search for scholarships within that category.

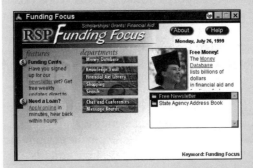

Sifting through the financial aid process is easier than ever. The Internet gives you hundreds of options and opportunities to help ease the burden of paying for college.

▶ Consider having your child sign up for the National Service. Volunteers to this federal program not only help the disadvantaged, they often get college aid in return for their community service. Find out the details at Keyword: **http://www.cns.gov**. Military service is another option to investigate. Find out about Military Aid at Keyword: **http://www.finaid.org**.

Summary

Wow, two giant goals taken care of. You learned how to plan for retirement: how to save, invest and allocate your money. You learned all about taking advantage of retirement plans. You know a Roth IRA from a 401(k) and you know which is appropriate to your needs. You examined sample retirement portfolios and you know which will work best at this point in your life. You also learned what to do if your nest egg falls short of your requirements, and you know how to maintain the right balance of your investments upon retirement.

At the same time, you conquered college costs. You know what to put in Sweet Pea's college fund portfolio and when to move the funds to stay on track.

You know the ins and outs of financial aid, including where to look to estimate your college costs, and how to find out how much you'll be expected to contribute. You know the tax consequences of moving your investments around in your college and retirement fund portfolios and how to make those moves prudent.

Now you can take all this knowledge and go and fill your portfolio, coming up next in Chapter 13.

A Quick Look

▶ **Measuring the Money Mongers** **page 347**

Granted, all those brokers look so smart and trustworthy in the TV commercials. Their pitches make you want to dump your dollars into duffel bags and deposit them on the brokers' desks. But upon closer scrutiny, all brokers are not alike. At Quicken.com you can compare them side by side to see how they measure up against each other.

Start at Keyword: **Quicken**, select Quicken.com, click Investments (under Departments), and then choose Finding a Broker. Scroll down to Brokerage Listings for all kinds of tips and tools and advice on how to separate the winners from the wannabes.

▶ **Finding the Right Stockbroker for You** **page 354**

Choice is good, right? Well, maybe not if there are so many choices that the whole act of choosing becomes overwhelming. When it comes to picking a broker, the vast array of brokerage services can make the entire matter dizzying. But you don't need to be intimidated by the selections — *MONEY Magazine's* online brokerage-screening tool is ready to help.

The interactive tool breaks out the best brokerages in cyberland, and helps you track down the ones that will fill your needs. Launch it at Keyword: **MoneyMag**, click the Investing Department at the top of the page, and then scroll down and click Online Brokerage Screener.

▶ **Which is the Best Horse in a Tight Race?** **page 356**

After you've narrowed your brokerage choices, it makes good sense to scrutinize their features. Does one offer more services or easier access? Or better customer service? How do the prices compare?

To see how your finalists measure up, check out AOL partner Gomez's independent ratings at Keyword: **Gomez**. Under Scorecards, select Internet Broker Scorecard to review ratings and features for Gomez's top 20 brokerages.

Chapter 13

Trading Online

Finally! You've figured your goals, finished your research, and outlined your asset allocation. You know what you need to buy to get on track toward reaching those goals.

But how do you *actually do it*?

Sure, you can pick up the phone and call your Uncle Ned, the stockbroker. But after all your research, you probably know what you need better than Uncle Ned does. Why pay for somebody's notebook when you've already done the homework?

You do need a broker, but not to tell you what to buy. You need her because only licensed brokers can *execute* your trades.

Screening Brokers

Brokers are salespeople for *brokerage houses*, entities that have purchased the right to execute trades on the stock exchanges. They make their money on commissions from your trades, whether or not you turn a profit.

To get an idea of what different brokerages offer, start at Keyword: **Broker** and click any of the brokerages to learn more about what they offer. Then hop over to Keyword: **Quicken**, and click Quicken.com. Click the Investing tab. At the Investments page, look again under Departments and click Find A Broker.

Scroll all the way down to Brokerage Listings at the lower right. Click Invest-o-rama's Brokerage Directory for a list of brokerages by category, including full, discount, online, and international. If you just want to check out the firms that do business online, or you want practical tips and advice for finding the trustworthy ones, click InvestorGuide's List of Online Brokers. Under Brokerage Resources, click Which type of broker do you need? for advice and rankings according to service, costs and public opinion. (see Figure 13-1).

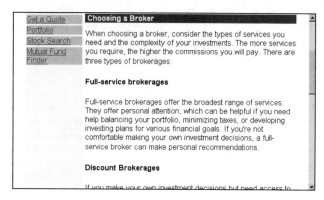

Figure 13-1. Although more expensive, a full-service brokerage offers a level of personal attention and service you can't expect from a discount firm.

Full-service versus discount brokers

Find It Online

Looking for a stockbroker near home? Find one through the AOL Yellow Pages. Go to Keyword: **Yellow Pages**, type in **Stock and Bond Brokers**, then your city and state, and up will appear a complete list of those in your area.

Full-service brokers offer you advice, exercise your trades, give you tips, and hold your hand. And you pay a fat commission for this service. Buying 100 shares of a $55 stock may cost you $300 in commission at a full-service broker. Don't even bother calling if you only want to buy or sell a handful of stocks. The commission will wipe out much of your future gains.

And then there are *discount brokers*. They don't come knocking for your business; they trade at your direction, and they don't tell you what to or what not to buy. Most will take your orders online or on the phone. They usually offer different degrees of research and customer service online or on the phone. Discount brokers charge you in the neighborhood of $10 to $30 a trade, regardless of the number of shares you want to buy or sell.

If all you're looking for is administration, *no-frills* traders (also referred to as *deep-discounters*) execute your trades electronically, but seldom offer more. They charge from pennies to $10 a trade, and trade whatever number of shares you have in mind.

The difference between discount and full-service

Should you opt for a full-service or a discount broker? It depends on "who you are as an investor," says Ted Allrich, finance expert and AOL partner since 1996. Allrich runs The Online Investor (Keyword: **Online Investor** or **OLI**; see the Figure below) and authored a book of the same name. Do you want your hand held or do you want to do your own homework? If you want someone to tell you what to do, go with full service. If you pick a discount broker, he says, "You are really responsible for your own research. You need to be comfortable with researching, gathering data, and making decisions on your own. The biggest distinction between this and a full-service brokerage is that no discount broker will call with a tip of the day."

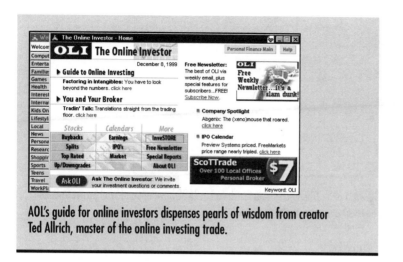

AOL's guide for online investors dispenses pearls of wisdom from creator Ted Allrich, master of the online investing trade.

All licensed brokerages offer the same minimum Securities Investor Protection Corporation insurance (up to $100,000 cash and $400,000 other assets), and many brokerages augment that with private insurance protection into the millions of dollars. All brokers execute your trades at the same rate of speed.

Beginning to Trade Online

If you need lots of advice and someone to do your research, and you don't mind paying a bundle for it, opt for full service. But, hey, you've gotten this far. Why spend money you could otherwise invest? Promise yourself to invest wisely, pick a discount broker online, and heap the savings into your piggy bank.

You will be in good company. Investors are flocking online like seagulls to French fries. More than 5 million people will invest online in 1999. Online brokers execute about 10 percent of all trading in the United States each day, and that number is skyrocketing. Cyberspace trading is surging at least 25 percent a month. One look at discount broker E*TRADE's business is an indication of how the numbers are growing. The brokerage had about 20,000 online *customers* in all of 1995. In 1998, the brokerage executed about 80,600 *trades a day*.

Find It Online

To try E*TRADE, go to Keyword: **ETRADE** (see Figure 13-2). To explore the site, click E*TRADE info. To open an account, click SIGN UP NOW! and download the application forms, which you will need to sign and return to E*TRADE.

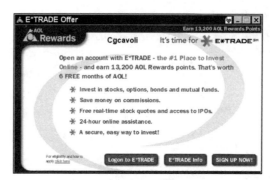

Figure 13-2. Discount brokers such as E*TRADE have opened Wall Street to online traders of every pocketbook size.

Benefits

Why do people invest online? Convenience. Consider the following benefits:

- ▶ You can order a trade at any hour of the day or night.
- ▶ You can tap into massive amounts of research and information for free.
- ▶ You can access your accounts any time you want and shift accounts instantly.
- ▶ You can get stock quotes at real or close to real time.
- ▶ You reap tremendous savings of time and money.

And there's a psychological benefit. Trading online levels the playing field for individual investors. They don't have to think twice about the share minimums to which previous generations of investors were beholden. Today, anyone with a pocketful of dollars can buy a stock as easily as someone with a pocketbook-full. Nobody looks sideways if you want to buy 15 shares of a stock as opposed to 150.

Precautions

But along with the benefits, online brokers have risks. Trading online is so darn easy it makes moving $10,000 seem like child's play. And if the money disappears in a week, all it takes is a few stroked keys to "invest" another $10,000 to try to make up for it. A couple of blunders or a little bad luck and that money is long gone, with you in serious trouble.

In the old days — when an investor had to use a full-service broker — the broker played Big Brother. Most of the time, Big Brother was smart enough to drag you out of the schoolyard when you were outmatched. But when you trade online, there is no one watching your back. You have to have that sense yourself. For your own protection, don't venture into uncharted territory without taking precautions for your safety.

IPOs, or It's Potentially Ominous

Take trading in IPOs, for example. On numerous occasions over the past couple of years many investors have been scorched trying to get hold of these hot stocks. Typically, the scenario goes like this:

▶ You read about HotStock.com in the paper and see it's going public. Initial offering price: $12 a share. You like what the company does, you figure it'll skyrocket, and you want in.

▶ That night, you go home and order up on your computer 500 shares at the market price, figuring it will cost you $6,000.

▶ The next day the stock goes public. The institutional buyers and insiders get first dibs, buy everything up, and then start releasing the stock back into the market. By the time your order comes up, the stock's price has soared to $82 a share. What you thought would cost you $6,000 actually costs you $41,000.

▶ Alas, the morning's sizzle turns to afternoon fizzle. By the end of the trading day, HotStock.com cools to an even $22 a share. Now you're stuck with $11,000 worth of stock for which you paid $41,000.

The example underscores the importance of being prepared when you trade online. Know *exactly* how much something costs before you buy or sell it. (All brokers offer real-time quotes, although many brokers make you pay for them.)

Find It Online

Interested in the latest news in online investing and brokerages? Go to AOL's search engine, Keyword: **Search**, and enter **online brokers** for the latest relevant stories and AOL links.

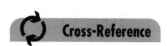

Cross-Reference

For a refresher on IPOs, see Chapter 10.

Choosing an Online Broker

Note

"If you are very comfortable with a computer and you trade a lot, then go for the lowest commission because all you want is to save the most money," says Ted Allrich. "But you may be a long-term investor. If what you want is research, if you want to talk to people and you don't trade much, the commission doesn't matter as much. What's important is that the firm has capital, it has customer support and all the help you need to make good decisions. It offers a high comfort level."

Definition

zero-coupon bond: A bond that doesn't pay you fixed interest. Instead, you buy the bond at a discount from its face value, and when the bond matures, you're paid the face value. These can be municipal, corporate, or government bonds.

Online brokers are lining up to get your business. There are at least 110 online brokers operating today. But be forewarned: All online discount brokers are not alike. Price does not necessarily equal best value. Service and research are free flowing at some brokerages, nonexistent at others. Phone help is courteous and prevalent at some, unavailable at others. While human contact might not seem necessary (you're doing it all online, after all), it's crucial when your "traditional" methods of electronic trading are failing, and the phone is the only way you can operate. The last thing you need is a broker whose phone lines are jammed when you can't get through online! That's just one risk of investing online that reminds you to make sure to choose wisely up front.

The characteristics of online brokers can be as varied as the investments they trade. How do you know who's best? The one who's best for you. Put those research skills to use once again, determine what services you want or need and which you can live without, and then find the broker whose offerings and costs fit your needs.

Questions to ask a prospective broker

Ted Allrich and Gary B. Smith, contributing editor of AOL partner TheStreet.Com (Keyword: **TheStreet**), helped put together the following checklist:

Before you sign on with a brokerage, ask

- ▶ What's the commission or cost per transaction for stocks? Mutual funds (load and no-load)? With/without broker assistance? How do I pay?
- ▶ Do I have to deposit a minimum amount in order to open an account? Do I have to pay a monthly fee in order to maintain an account?
- ▶ How do you confirm my trades — e-, snail, or voice mail, or real voice contact? Will you send me immediate confirmation when my order is received or my trade is executed?

▶ Do you supply me with instant/daily/monthly statements? Will you provide a history of my trading activities for free?

▶ Can I access my account online or by phone at all hours? Does it cost more to order my trade through a person? Do you provide person-to-person customer service? What are the hours and days? Is there a charge? What's your customer/service representative ratio?

▶ In which vehicles can I invest or trade online with your service? Stocks, penny stocks, foreign stocks, options, municipal bonds, Treasury securities, CDs, money markets, IRAs, metals, commodities, mutual funds, trusts, corporate bonds, zero-coupon bonds?

▶ Does the cash in my account earn interest, and how much interest is it? Do I get to choose where to put the money in my account? Can I write checks against my balance?

▶ Can I deposit money into my account directly and regularly from my bank? Can I transfer funds within my accounts? Will you collect or reinvest my dividends at my direction?

▶ How many accounts can I set up within my umbrella? (An equities account, bond account, and cash account, for example.) Can I set up a trust, joint account, or custodial account? Can I set up a retirement account? What is the interest rate on margin accounts? (The lower the better.)

▶ What research-oriented services do you provide? Real-time quotes online or via phone? Industry forecasts? Company news? Earnings predictions? Stock screens and charts? Reports on insider-trading activity? E-mail upon news of my holdings? Cost of these?

▶ How much insurance is offered for free?

▶ Do I need proprietary software? What do I do if you have technical difficulties and I can't get through?

▶ What violations and complaints have been lodged against you? What is your method for resolving a dispute?

When you're comparing services, bear in mind that you don't necessarily have to rule anybody out if some of their research

Definition

insider trading: Sales of securities by corporate insiders — people who are officers or directors of a corporation, or any person owning 10 percent or more of the company's stock.

Find It Online

To check whether complaints or violations have been lodged against specific brokerages, turn to **www. nasd.com** for securities traded on the NASDAQ, **www.nyse.com** for securities traded on the New York Stock Exchange, or **www. sec.gov** for the Securities and Exchange Commission.

Note

If the brokerage is reluctant to answer these simple marketing questions, forget about a sympathetic ear when the systems are crashing and you can't make a trade. Even though discount brokers don't give you investing advice, they—by all means—are supposed to provide customer service. With so many discount brokers available today there is no reason to settle for one that does not make customer service a priority.

Tip

Have a question about finding the right broker for you? Ted Allrich provides answers in The Online Investor's "You and Your Broker" column at Keyword: **OI**.

tools are lacking. AOL provides dozens of investing tools and resources for free, including research services such as charting, screening, and tracking tools; real quotes (delayed up to 15 minutes); and breaking, company, and market news. Review them all in Chapter 9.

Find a broker online

To find out which discount brokers best suit your needs go to Keyword: **MoneyMag.** Then, choose Investing, and then, under Stock Tools, click Online Brokerage Screener. This opens up an interactive tool (see the Figure below) to help you find a brokerage with services that are the most important to you.

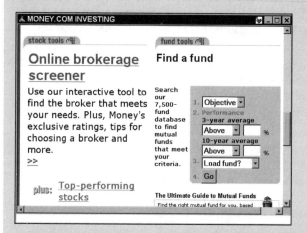

How do you choose from the dizzying array of brokerages? Screening tools allow investors to sift through all the information to find the best fit.

First, answer the questions to help define your profile. Do you want 24-hour-a-day service? Are you interested in trading options? Do you want to buy Treasuries? Answer Doesn't Matter if a question asks something unimportant for your current needs.

After you answer the questions, up comes a list of brokers appropriate to your needs. This might still represent a large group, but the online screener provides a way to further refine your choices by ranking the brokerages according to the criteria you select.

For example, if good customer service is most important to you, scroll down to Question 5, "How important is customer service?" and select Extremely Important. Then click Rank Brokers at the bottom of the page for a revised listing. Up next comes a new list with the firms offering the best service listed first. You can rank them according to one criteria or several, including price, service, research, and ease of use.

From this list, click the brokerage name and up pops a scorecard listing how the brokerage fared on your most important criteria. It's also assigned an overall *MONEY Magazine* rating.

For help, click Find the Broker That's Right for You, located to the left of the interactive questions. *MONEY Magazine* picks brokerages according to your investment style: Mainstream Investor, Frequent Trader, Beginner, or Wealthy Investor. The three best brokerages for each profile are given, along with the firms' strengths and weaknesses. The ratings are updated annually.

What Type of Investor Are You?

When you have your questions in hand, look in the mirror to determine the type of investor you are. Now you can better match up with a broker. AOL partner Gomez slots investors into three main categories: "hyperactive traders, serious investors, and life-goal planners." *Hyperactive traders* need a trading fix several times a day. If you're a hyperactive trader, look for cheap commissions, low margin rates, how fast screens load, quick or real-time account turnaround, and real-time quotes.

 Note

One question most online investors never ask is the brokerage's commitment to the "quality of the fill," as Smith calls it. How well the broker *fills*—or executes—your order. He says some brokers will "work your order," which means they will try to execute it for a tiny bit higher or lower price to your advantage, rather than just put it in the computer queue and execute it automatically.

Smith offers this example. Say you go to one of those $8-a-trade brokers who executes your order electronically, but doesn't do anything else. You buy 1,000 shares of IBM at $125, and you pay $125,008 for the transaction. Another broker, one who will try to "work your order," might be able to buy the shares for a slightly lower price, say $124 ⅞. "They save me $125, so that $8 becomes a joke," says Smith. "It's more important that the broker get a good fill, which is something 99 percent of the people trading online don't think about."

Scoring the brokers

How does your broker measure up to others? Check out AOL partner Gomez's independent ratings at Keyword: **Gomez**, then, under Scorecards, select Internet Broker Scorecard (see the Figure below).

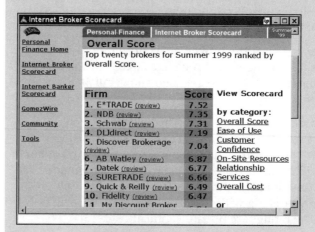

Different brokerages meet different needs. Make sure you review the laundry list of what each brokerage has to offer before making your choice.

Based on direct examination, questionnaires, and telephone interviews with customer service representatives and brokers, Gomez rates each brokerage, giving it a score from zero to ten. Then Gomez lists the top 20 performers.

In addition to an overall score, the brokers get separate ratings in several categories: ease of use, customer confidence, on-site resources, relationship services, and overall cost. To view scores by category, click the category and the list will be revised according to the scores.

Gomez also rates the brokerages according to how well they serve a certain investment profile: hyperactive trader, serious investor, life-goal planner, or one-stop shopper. Click the profile that best describes you to see which brokerages should meet your needs. Then, to learn exactly how the brokerage scored, click Review, next to the brokerage's name. Gomez sums up key benefits and shortfalls, and then lists the brokerage's score in each category. You can also follow the link to the brokerage.

Serious investors make half a dozen to a dozen trades per month. If this is you, price per trade matters, but not as much as the service, research, tips, and tools available to you.

If you're a *life-goal planner*, you probably want a little more service and comprehensive planning than your fast-food-mentality investing brethren. Search for brokers who provide a personal touch, such as attentive customer service, comprehensive trading possibilities, and the ability to move fluidly between accounts.

Do your homework

With your mirror in one hand and checklist in the other, hop over to AOL's Brokerage Center (Keyword: **Broker**, see Figure 13-3), a hub for reliable, legitimate brokers who service online traders.

Find It Online

Save research time by going directly to brokers' keywords for answers to your preliminary questions at Keywords: **Ameritrade, DLJ, E-Trade,** and **Waterhouse**.

Figure 13-3. Clicking AOL's Brokerage Center brings you to some of the best names in the online brokerage business.

From the brokerage center you can travel directly to brokers' sites. Thumb through the pages of information, select a group of finalists, then call them up or e-mail them and ask them the questions on your list. Call customer service (the phone numbers are listed in the sites) and see how long you sit on hold. Can you talk to a real human being if you need account help? Technical help? If you want to make a trade?

Ask the customer-service representative how a customer proceeds on a day the market plunges 500 points and you can't get through. Does the company have backup support in the event its systems go down or the power goes out? Send a couple of questions via e-mail, too, and see how long it takes to

Exercising your trades via AOL doubles your security protection. You need a password to get on the service, and another to access your brokerage account. Remember, no employee of an online brokerage or America Online will ever ask you for your password. To ensure secure transactions, do not reveal your passwords to anyone.

get a reply. If you can't get a human to answer these simple marketing questions, forget finding one who will actually help you when there's trouble.

Don't rely on a brokerage's marketing pitch on the phone, or in ads, which are designed to lure you into thinking the advertiser offers the cheapest/smartest/quickest deal. To determine who really has what you're looking for, check out broker ratings and rankings by industry experts at AOL's Brokerage Center. The independent rankings are updated quarterly and rate brokerages in categories such as ease of use, on-site resources, available services, and customer support.

Also, be sure to learn what fellow AOL members have to say about your finalists. Start with the Message Boards (Keyword: **Stock Talk**), then scroll down to Broker Discussions, shown in Figure 13-4. The board focuses on individual brokers, brokerage firms, and their transaction tactics. Want to know how other investors have fared with a particular brokerage? Look for the name on the alphabetized list of topics, highlight it, and click List All. Up comes a list of available comments. Click Read Post to learn what's been said. If you want to respond to the post, click Reply and then write your comment.

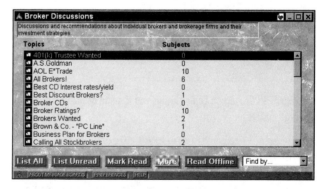

Figure 13-4. Nothing recommends a brokerage as much as a satisfied customer. For comments from your fellow online investors, check out AOL's message boards.

If you don't see your broker's name as a separate subject listing, or you want to make sure you find all comments related to a certain brokerage, try searching for relevant comments. In the lower-right corner, click the Find By box. Search by date, word, or phrase, or create a custom search. For example, to search out posts concerning E*TRADE, click Find by Word or Phrase, and type **E*TRADE** in the search box. You have the option of restricting your search to the Brokerage Message Board, or of searching all AOL message boards.

Also, check out Motley Fool's Consumer Rap Board of Best and Worst Experiences at Keyword: **Fool**. Click the Messages tab, then click Investors' Roundtable, and select from the Consumer Rap choices. Next, see The Street.com's message board at Keyword: **TheStreet**, then Forums, then Finding the Right Online Broker. Or, if you're an active trader, try Shark Attack's message boards at Keyword: **Shark Attack.** Click Message Boards and then scroll down to Brokers: Good, Bad & the Ugly.

Time to Trade

The hard part is done. You know what you want to buy and you've chosen a broker. The next thing you have to do is open an account. To expedite the process, you can apply online via the individual brokerage. Uncle Sam insists on having your signature, though, so you'll have to send in a paper application as well, or risk rejection. Your application will look pretty much like one you complete to open a bank account. It can take a couple of days or a couple of weeks to process, depending on the company you choose. When your application is accepted, your broker will assign you a PIN number and you'll have to pick a password. You will most likely need to deposit money to open your account. This could range from $1,000 to $10,000, depending on the brokerage.

Language lessons

You might as well be in a foreign country when it comes to trying to understand the machinations of actual trading. The process is immersed in a culture, language, and customs of its own. Within that culture exist subcultures, defined by the exchange on which a particular stock trades. These include the New York Stock Exchange, the American Stock Exchange, and the NASDAQ (formerly the National Association for Securities Dealers Automatic Quotations, now the NASDAQ Stock Market, Inc.).

Over-the-Counter Markets, like the NASDAQ, don't have an actual trading floor. All transactions are conducted electronically.

To learn about shorting a stock, turn to Chapter 10.

As you learned in Chapter 6, on the NYSE and the ASE, "specialists" match the orders of people who want to buy with those of people who want to sell. These specialists work for brokerage firms and, as the name implies, specialize in the trading of a particular stock. They match blocks of stock available with blocks of stock sought. For this brokering service, they charge the buyer either 6¼ or 12½ cents a share, depending on the price of the stock.

The NASDAQ, NASDAQ SmallCap, and OTC Bulletin Board are known as Over-the-Counter markets. With OTC markets, brokerages make deals via computers managed by the NASDAQ. A brokerage working on behalf of the seller offers an *ask* price and a brokerage working on behalf of the buyer offers a *bid* price. The difference between the ask and the bid price — *the spread* — is paid by the buyer and split by the two brokerages that make the deal.

Types of accounts

Your online broker will most likely offer three kinds of accounts. One is a *cash* account, in which you settle everything in cash. When you buy a stock you'll have three days to pay for it, either by sending in a check or by having the broker withdraw cash from your account. If you sell a stock, the broker will deposit the proceeds into your account, unless you ask to have a check sent to you.

Another type of account is a *margin* account. Using a margin account can be dangerous and is better left to high rollers. With a margin account, you can borrow money from the brokerage firm for your personal use or to buy stocks. Your holdings are used as collateral. For example, if you have $25,000 worth of stocks in your margin account, you can borrow against it to buy more stocks or you can borrow half in cash. Granted, this is a great way to buy securities if you don't have the money. But if the market tumbles, you'll owe money fast. Buying on margin is a gamble and is not for the undisciplined investor.

A *short account* is one in which you sell stocks you don't really own, in anticipation that the stock's price will fall. Shorting stocks is not to be fooled with unless you've mastered the concept of shorting.

Types of orders

You will need to send your broker an *order* to execute a trade. When the order form comes up you will have to fill in the blanks accordingly. Order types include

▶ *Buy order* — This is your directive to buy shares. You will have to tell the broker how many shares you want to buy. You must also tell her how much you are willing to pay. To do this, you have to select either:

   Buy at market — You will pay the prevailing market price. When you buy a stock at market, you buy at the *ask* price, the price sought by the seller. This is the fastest way to buy stock, the most common, and it's perfectly appropriate for the majority of trades. That said, NEVER put in a market order for an IPO without knowing the likely consequences — buy at limit, instead.

   Buy at limit — You will pay a specific price or less for your transaction. For example, you might direct the broker to buy 200 shares of Disney at a limit of $40, which means you want to buy the shares only if you can do so for $40 a share or less. This is a *buy limit order* of $40. The downside is, if your stock trades on the NASDAQ and is never offered for exactly $40 (even if it is offered for less), you will not get to fill your order.

▶ *Sell order* — This order directs the broker to sell your shares. You need to tell the broker how many shares you want to sell, and at what price. Your choices are:

   Sell at market — which means sell at the prevailing price. (When you sell a stock at market you sell at the *bid* price. The bid price and ask price are always different. The difference between them is the *spread*, and the brokers split the difference.) Or,

   Sell at limit — Shares are sold for a specific price or higher. Just like with the buy limit order, if your stock trades on the NASDAQ and is never offered for exactly the price you have specified (even if it is offered for more), you will not get to sell your order.

▶ *All or None* — Often it is investors with large orders who select this directive. If you select this option, you are telling your broker that if she can't sell all your

If you're willing to do your homework, to get all the information you need to make an investment decision, "you can use the computer to open a whole new world. You can use your computer like a miner uses a shovel to find gold," says trading expert Ted Allrich.

shares at once, or can't buy the total amount you want all at once, not to sell or buy anything at all. The downside is you might not be able to get the trade executed, but the upside is your specific orders will be guaranteed if the trade can be made. Similarly, *Fill or Kill* means to fill the entire order at this price now or take the order away.

▶ *Stop Order* — A directive to your broker to automatically sell your stock if it falls below a certain price. For example, you tell your broker to sell your Disney stock the second it reaches $35. (If it does not hit $35 exactly, it will be sold at the next lowest bid.) This ensures that you limit your loss on the stock. If you really want to be particular, you can request a *Stop Limit Order*, which means you want to sell the stock at an exact price. But if the stock is never actually bid at this price, you might lose your opportunity to sell it in the ballpark of the price you specify.

▶ *Buy Stops* — A directive to your broker to automatically buy a stock if the price moves to a certain price or higher, much like an effort to jump onto a moving train.

▶ *Price* — You need to enter an amount in the price box only if you are specifying a buy or sell at limit order (see above). The price you enter can be above or below the prevailing market price. Keep in mind that you might not be able to exercise your trade if the price you mandate isn't met. If you are buying or selling at market, you leave the price box blank.

▶ *Quantity* — How many shares do you want to buy or sell? In the old days, brokers encouraged investors to buy or sell in *round lots* (usually 100 shares), as opposed to *odd lots* (orders not in even hundreds). But most of today's trades can be executed in any quantity.

▶ *Duration* — What if the trade cannot be executed the day of your order? Would you like it to remain valid in the future? There are generally two options:

> *Day Order*, which means you want the trade to stand only on the day of your order, and if the order cannot be executed on that day it is canceled; or

Good Til Canceled, which means your order stands for 90 days or until the broker can execute it. Beware of GTC orders, however, as breaking news can drastically affect the value of the security you want to buy. If you have such an order pending, stay on top of your targets.

Anatomy of a Trade

All brokers are not created equal, but their procedures are close enough! Here's an example of what you need to do in order to trade online. This is from AOL partner DLJ Direct. You can find it at Keyword: **DLJ**, then click Quick and Easy Demo. For other trading samples, go to Keyword: **Broker** and explore the sites.

Open an account

First you need to open an account. You can fill in all the questions online but you won't be ready to trade yet. Uncle Sam requires that your signature be on file with the broker, so you'll have to wait for a form, then sign it and send it back.

It takes more than paperwork to apply. As Figure 13-5 indicates, it takes some decision-making about what kind of account you want to open. Will you want to trade on margin? Do you want your money to accrue in a money market? Will you be selling short? (All these features are explored earlier in this chapter.) Once you set up your account accordingly, you'll also need to send in a check. Most brokerages require a minimum deposit before they'll do any trading for you.

Once your account is set up, you can begin trading. You log on to the brokerage by typing in its keyword. For example, if you're trading with DLJ you go to Keyword: **DLJ**, then you activate your account from there. You'll need to use a password to access your brokerage account. As an added safety measure, invent a different password for your brokerage account than you use for AOL.

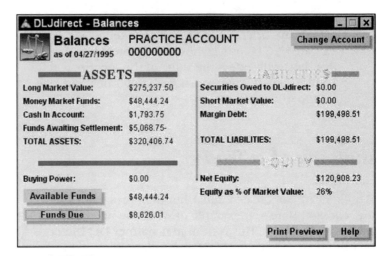

Figure 13-5. Your online account can include selling on margin and shorting stocks.

Buy a stock

You can follow along with this anatomy of a trade at Keyword:
DLJ, then select Quick and Easy Demo, then select Practice
Account. Once you log on with your brokerage, you click the
Trading icon to begin your order. The first screen you'll proba-
bly see, like the one in Figure 13-6, is one that asks what you
want to do — buy or sell.

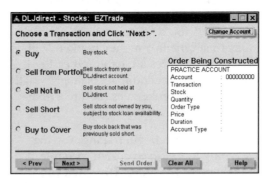

Figure 13-6. After researching potential investments, you are ready to purchase
a stock.

What stock do you want to trade? Type in the ticker symbol
and the company's name appears. It's easy to make a mistake
when you type in the symbol, so make sure the name is right.
Once you confirm that you're making the right transaction,

you need to enter the number of shares you want to trade.
You don't have to trade in round lots. Any number is fine. Fill
in the number in the Enter Quantity box.

Next you have to tell the broker what kind of buy order you
seek — Market, Limit, or Stop. (All these terms are explained
earlier in this chapter.) Pick one, as shown in Figure 13-7.

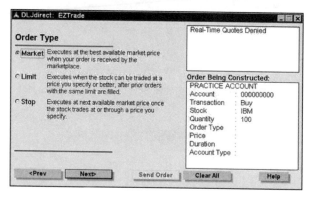

Figure 13-7. The order type tells the brokerage how you wish to purchase stock: at
the going price or at a specific price you select.

Then tell the brokerage how you'll be paying for your transaction,
whether in cash (which means you have to pay within
three days) or on margin (which means you're borrowing
from your account and using your holdings as collateral).

Next you get a confirmation screen (see Figure 13-8). Review
this closely. You don't want your intended 100-share transaction
to turn into an outrageously expensive 1000 shares, just
because your finger paused a second too long on the keyboard
when you leaned over to pet the cat. After you scrutinize
the order, send it.

Sell a stock

When your order is to sell, you again must tell the broker
what kind of price you seek — Market, Limit, or Stop. If
you specify Limit or Stop you need to enter a price (see
Figure 13-9). Then you have to tell the broker if your order
is only for the day on which you're making it or, if the price
you seek can't be met, if the order should stand until you
cancel it.

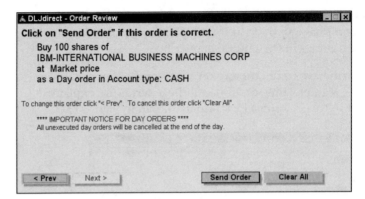

Figure 13-8. After completing the order form, your order is ready to be filled by the brokerage.

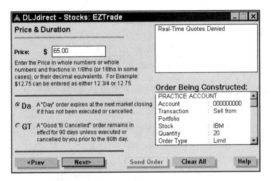

Figure 13-9. Sometimes stocks sell quickly, sometimes not. You must indicate on your sell order whether you want the broker to try to sell your shares for one day only or for up to 90 days (a GTC order).

Up will come that confirmation screen. Again, check it thoroughly first before you click Send Order. Once you dispatch the order there's no turning back, as most trades are executed seemingly instantly.

Check the status of your order

If you order up a trade at night or on the weekend, or you run up a number of pending trades, you'll be able to check their status instantly, as in Figure 13-10. You can change or cancel the orders that have not been executed.

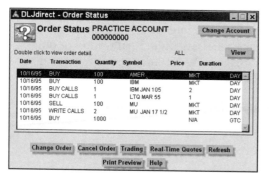

Caution

Not all brokers offer this feature. Make sure you know what your broker is willing to trade before you sign up.

Figure 13-10. With an online account, you have constant access to the status of your orders. It is even possible to change or cancel an order, if sale has not been executed.

Trading online isn't limited to stocks. With many online brokerages you can also redeem or add to your mutual funds.

Now for a tremendous time-saver that was probably the last thing you thought about when deciding to trade online: easy record-keeping. To track money in, money out and your transactions, call up your History (Figure 13-11) and get a chronology of the details.

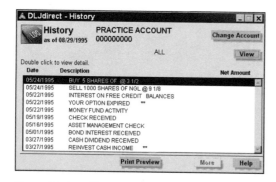

Figure 13-11. All account activity is kept on file, allowing investors to keep track of their portfolio.

Summary

There. You've learned the difference between full-service and discount and no-frills brokers, you've been forewarned about the dangers of trading online and you know how to choose a broker.

You know that finding the broker who's right for you has more to do with how you trade and what's important to you than with the brokerage's fee schedule. Finally, you not only learned the secret language of Wall Street, you can order up a trade like a pro.

Next up, tracking the portfolio you've so carefully assembled.

TRACKING YOUR

PORTFOLIO

A Quick Look

▶ **Keeping Up with the Joneses**   **page 375**

The real benchmark for your investments is not how they compare with your neighbor's, but how they compare with the market at large. Is your money marooned in a dud while the rest of the economy gallops full speed ahead? Or have you found a real diamond that outshines everything in sight?

You can add indexes to your tracking portfolio to provide a side-by-side comparison when you check your holdings. To do this, go to Keyword: **Portfolio**, open the portfolio you want to add to, and click Add. Then type in the symbol of the index you wish to enter. (A list of common indexes is provided later in this chapter; or, to find one online, click Help from the Portfolio screen and select Index Quotes.)

▶ **Time to Split**   **page 384**

It's easy to modify your portfolio as your assets change. At Keyword: **Portfolio** you can delete, add, increase, decrease, or change a holding by opening the portfolio and clicking the appropriate button.

If your stock splits, you don't need to master math in order to figure out your new cost basis, how much you own, or how much you've made or have lost. Just click Edit, and select the Split Item tab.

▶ **The Art of the Chart**   **page 386**

If you're looking at your portfolio and you want a quick appraisal of how your holding has fared historically, you can find out with a couple of keystrokes.

From Keyword: **Portfolio** select the holding you want to view, then click the Details button, then choose Select A Chart. You can custom-create a chart to your own specifications to help you depict holdings over time.

Chapter 14

Tracking Your Portfolio

Do you long to know how your investments are faring each day? Do you wish you could easily follow your investments even after you sell them? Is there a certain investment, analyst or investing strategy you're sweet on but want to check out for a while? Do you want to track the stocks or funds your online brethren are worked up about?

Yes, yes, yes, and yes?

There is one solution to all these wishes, and it's a simple one: online portfolios.

With AOL's *My Portfolios* (Keyword: **Portfolio**) you can create up to 20 different portfolio registers that will track up to

100 items each. You can use this tool to chronicle your current investments, to track investments targeting a particular goal of yours and to track stocks that you've sold, among many other uses.

Why you need to track your portfolios

Why bother? For plenty of reasons. Online portfolios are a scorecard of how your investments are performing, not only on a given day but from the time you started tracking them. The portfolios provide at a glance a running total of your gains and losses and are a direct window into your investments' market activity (see Figure 14-1).

Figure 14-1. Setting up portfolios — both real and imagined — allows investors a chance to test various investment strategies without risking real cash.

Portfolio registers are useful even if you don't own the investments you're tracking. Many investing approaches and individual stocks appear very promising at first. But you know by now to investigate all recommendations. When you track targets, you can learn how formulas, analyst recommendations and your own gut instincts would fare in the real marketplace.

Shadow portfolios

Do you tend to buy too late? Sell too soon? Do you accurately judge how the economy affects your holdings? Setting up shadow portfolios can show you. A shadow portfolio tracks your potential targets' behavior before you even buy, so you won't be shocked at how they perform once they become yours (see Figure 14-2). How do they compare with holdings in their sector? How do they respond to news events? Are these reactions what you anticipated? You can also set up shadow portfolios after you sell, to learn if the moves you make tend to be on the mark.

Tip

If you have a question during the process of creating your portfolio, click the Help button for detailed information. Click the data points in the contents box for more information on the feature.

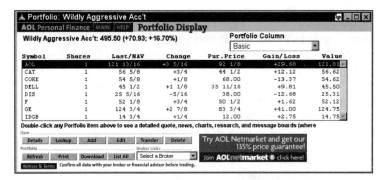

Figure 14-2. Why create shadow portfolios? They are a good way to track a stock without any risk. Pretend you have one share of each and list the share price when you begin tracking.

Setting Up Online Portfolios

Whether you want to set up portfolios to track your holdings, your targets or your has-beens, the process is the same. To create a portfolio, go to Keyword: **Portfolio** or click the $ Quotes icon on the AOL toolbar. Once at My Portfolios, click the Create button, enter a name for your portfolio, such as "Buddy's College Fund," and click Next (see Figure 14-3).

Figure 14-3. Different portfolios can reflect your various investment goals — from planning for retirement to buying that dream house.

Voila! You have a portfolio. Now it's time to add the items you want to track.

Entering stocks

Maybe you want to start with all the Widgets 'R' Us stock you own. If you know the ticker symbol, enter it into the box next to Symbol. If you don't know the stock symbol, click the Symbol Lookup link and search for the symbol by typing in the company's name (see Figure 14-4), clicking on Name, then pressing Lookup again.

Tip

Even if you were busy passing notes to your friends during math class you probably remember that 4½ is the same as 4.5. But what if you buy a stock at 68⅜? Or 42¹¹⁄₁₆? Don't worry — the portfolio feature forgives more easily than a math teacher. Enter your purchase price with fractions or decimals, whichever you find easier. Either will work. Just remember when you enter a fraction to leave a space between the whole number and the fraction.

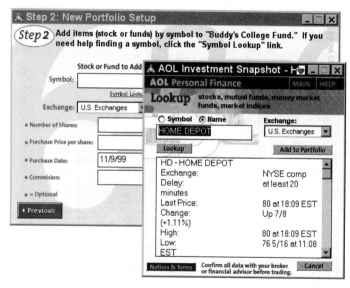

Figure 14-4. Don't know the symbol for that stock you're considering? Click Lookup to find it.

Click the correct item, and press Select. Then press the Add to Portfolio button. Next, fill in the vitals. You can include the number of shares you own, the date you bought them, the purchase price and the commission, if applicable. Click Add Item and the stock will be added to the portfolio.

You can add as many as items in the portfolio. If you want to include cash from this initial setting up point, click Next. In the box next to Enter a Dollar Amount, do just that: enter the amount you want to include. From this point you can also select more than half a dozen popular indexes. (There's more about tracking indexes later in this chapter.)

Tip

If you're just following the stock, you can leave blank items such as price and date. If you want to see how the stock price moves from the time you begin tracking it, enter 1 for number of shares and the price on the day you start your search. That way each time you look at the portfolio you can see at a glance how much you would have gained or lost per share.

Add mutual funds and cash

Cross-Reference

See Chapter 5 to review the needs you outlined in your investment blueprint.

Add your mutual funds the same way. If you don't know the symbol for a mutual fund, go to Keyword: **Morningstar** to search AOL partner Morningstar's database (see Figure 14-5). First, select Name, then type in the exact name of the fund. (If you don't know the exact name of the fund type in the name of the fund company, and a screen will appear of all the company's funds. Find the right one and get its symbol to the right.)

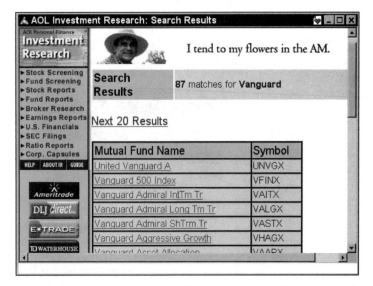

Figure 14-5. You can track your mutual funds on AOL, too. Look up mutual fund symbols with Morningstar.

You might also want to "track" your cash. Maybe you've sold some stock and the money is sitting in your account at the brokerage awaiting your next move. All you have to do is click the Add button in the portfolio, then click the Cash tab. Enter the dollar amount in the amount field and click OK.

Create, delete, rename portfolios

When you track investments, it makes sense to group them in portfolios according to the goal you are trying to attain. Maybe you put your retirement holdings in one portfolio, the kids' college fund in another, the money to buy the apartment building in another. The purpose is not to micromanage each pick, but to track with ease the progress toward your goals.

To create another portfolio, go to My Portfolios again (Keyword: **Portfolio**) and press the Create button. Then enter a name for your new portfolio, click Next, and then follow the same steps as above.

If you want to delete an entire portfolio, highlight the one you want to get rid of on the My Portfolios page and press the Delete button. To rename a portfolio, highlight it, press Rename and change the name as shown in Figure 14-6).

14

Tracking Your Portfolio

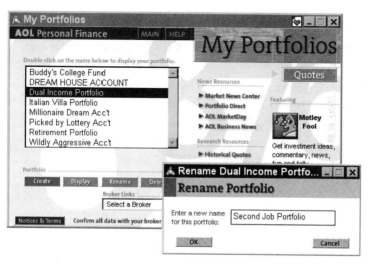

Figure 14-6. AOL's My Portfolios makes it a snap to change, delete, add, and rename portfolios.

If you get stuck during any of this, Keyword: **Portfolioguide**, shown in Figure 14-7, takes you through the process step by step. First, click the list of portfolios. You can refer to detailed instructions to help you create, modify, and track your portfolios. Read through the guide or click the page containing the information you seek. Page 4 of the Guide provides useful links to related AOL features for stocks and mutual funds, such as Morningstar, Sage, and Online Investor.

Now your portfolios are set up, and your holdings are chronicled. Not only can you see in an instant how much money your investments have gained or lost, which helps you keep track of the march toward your goals, but you can also learn the motivation behind the movement. You can check the news, learn the volume and get the day's highs and lows at a glance, which you'll learn to do in a minute.

Tip

To return to your own list of portfolios while using Portfolio Guide, click View Your Portfolio Summary Page.

Figure 14-7. Portfolioguide can help answer your questions about fine-tuning and tracking your portfolios online.

And once your targeted stock or mutual fund has reached your price point, you can trade immediately, right from the page. The Portfolio Display screen includes direct links to online brokerages E*TRADE, AmeriTrade, Waterhouse Securities, and DLJ Direct.

How to Navigate Your Portfolios

This is how the portfolios work: Double-click the portfolio you want to open. Your list of holdings will appear, as well as the current value of your portfolio and how much it has gained or lost. By default, your holdings will be displayed in the basic format, showing standard information as displayed in Figure 14-8. Here's what you'll see:

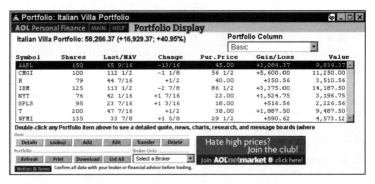

Figure 14-8. Setting up your portfolios in the basic format shows you number of shares, latest trading price, change from the previous day's close, how much you've gained or lost, and total value of the holding.

▶ Symbol — The trading abbreviation for the stock or holding.

▶ Shares — The number of shares you own.

▶ Last/NAV — The most recent price quoted. Quotes on AOL are delayed about 20 minutes. In the case of a mutual fund, which is updated once daily based on the day's trades, the NAV, or Net Asset Value, is calculated at the close of the trading day and is the price of one share of the fund.

▶ Change — Whether the current price is up or down from the previous day's close.

▶ Purchase Price — What you paid for the stock or fund, a number you inserted when you set up the portfolio.

▶ Gain/Loss — How much you're up or down based on the current quote.

▶ Value — How much the investment is currently worth.

The default Basic View is just one of the available ways to monitor information in your portfolio. You can select other views by clicking the box under Portfolio Column Views, and choosing from the list shown in Figure 14-9.

Tip

If you buy more of the same stock for a different purchase price, you can best track it by setting up two different entries for it.

14

Tracking Your Portfolio

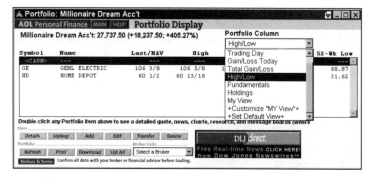

Figure 14-9. You can view information in your portfolio in several ways, from the status of the current trading day to the highs and lows for the last year.

Options include

▶ Trading Day — A reflection of the current business day's activity

▶ Gain/Loss Today — A quick look at the day's impact on your portfolio

▶ Total Gain/Loss — The total increase or decrease of your portfolio over time

Note

AMEX and NYSE stock quotes are delayed at least 20 minutes on AOL's portfolio feature, while NASDAQ quotes are delayed at least 15 minutes. Index quotes are real-time. Daily updates on mutual funds are generally provided by 7 p.m. eastern time. Money market funds are updated each Wednesday by 7 p.m. eastern time.

▶ High/Low — Depicts the highest and lowest prices for the holding during the business day and over the past 52 weeks

▶ Fundamentals — An overview of the holding's principal financial ratios

▶ Holdings — A look at your overall portfolio, including purchase dates

▶ My View — A view you customize

Customizing Your Portfolio Display

If you would prefer any one of these views to the Basic view, you can select the one you prefer as your default view. On the drop-down list, select Default View, and choose the view you prefer from the drop down list. After your selection, you have two options: set this view as the default for all of your portfolios, or for the current portfolio only.

If the pre-set views still don't offer the information you'd like to see, you can customize a view with the exact information you want, in the order you select. Your customized view can also be set as the default view for a particular portfolio or for all of your portfolios, or simply included as one of the viewing choices.

You can list up to seven columns in all, including the following:

▶ % Change — How much your stock or fund price has moved since the close of the previous day

▶ Commission — How much you paid to make the trade

▶ Cost Basis — How much the price plus commission totaled

▶ Currency — Dollars or other

▶ Exchange — On which exchange the holding trades

▶ % Gain/Loss — How much you have gained or lost since you bought the stock

▶ Gain/Loss Today — How much your stock price has risen or fallen since the close of trading the previous day

▶ Name — Name of the stock or fund

▶ Previous Close — The price of the stock or fund at the end of the previous trading day

▶ Purchase Date — When you bought the stock or fund

▶ Time — The time the latest quote was pulled

Additionally, for stocks, you can select 30-Day Average Volume, 52-Week Low, 52-Week High, Beta, Earnings per share, High, Low, Market Cap, Open, P/E Ratio, Shares Outstanding, Volume, and Yield.

For mutual funds you can also include the 52-Week High, 52-Week Low, and Yield. For money markets you can also include Seven-Day Yield, Assets, and Average Maturity. For indexes you can also include High, Low, and Open.

Cross-Reference

Refer to Chapters 9 and 6 for more information on beta, EPS, P/E, yield, and market capitalization.

Two looks in one

There is no "best" way to look at your portfolios. In fact, you might like to have more than one customized view for the same portfolio — so you can see the information you want instantly. Create a duplicate portfolio, and change the defaults on the second portfolio. To add a column, highlight it in the Column Choices list, then click Add to Display (see Figure 14-10).

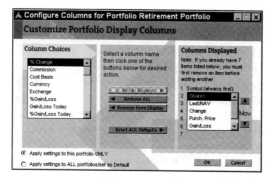

Figure 14-10. AOL allows you to set up your portfolio to display as much or as little information as you need.

If you want to remove a column, highlight it in the Columns Displayed list, then click Remove from Display. If you want to change the columns' order, highlight one and move it up or down with the arrows in the Columns Displayed area.

Editing Your Portfolio

The contents of your portfolios will change over time. You might buy or sell stocks, put more money into your mutual funds, transfer funds from one portfolio to another or merge several holdings together in a new portfolio.

To edit and monitor your portfolio, turn to these buttons at the bottom of the portfolio for help:

- ▶ Lookup — Finds the ticker symbol
- ▶ Add — Adds an item
- ▶ Edit — Changes the values for the item
- ▶ Transfer — Moves the holding from one portfolio to the next
- ▶ Delete — Deletes the item from the portfolio
- ▶ Refresh — Updates the numbers on the screen
- ▶ Print — Prints the portfolio
- ▶ Download — Retains the information from the portfolio offline
- ▶ List All — Lists all your portfolios
- ▶ Details — Takes you to the Snapshot

Snapshots

Details directs you right to the Investment Snapshot screen (see Figure 14-11). The stock is listed at the top, as is the exchange it trades on and the amount of time the quote has been delayed. The snapshot reveals whether the price is up or down from the previous day's close, the high and low price of the day, the price at which trading opened, the previous day's close, current trading volume, the past month's trading average, the number of shares outstanding, the market cap, the year's high and low, the beta, the dividend yield, the stock's P/E ratio, earnings per share, and the currency in which the stock trades. Mutual funds also include the Net Asset Value, or NAV, of each share.

To view a snapshot, select in the portfolio the holding you wish to see and click Details (or double click the holding). The Investment Snapshot appears, offering the latest financial activity of the selected holding. Look in the News section for recent articles and press releases concerning the holding.

Click any titles you wish to read to view the text. To find out what's happening in the business world, click the links to the Market News Center or the Business News Center. To view a different snapshot, type in the company's symbol or name and click Get Quote. Then, if you wish to add the company to your portfolio, click Add.

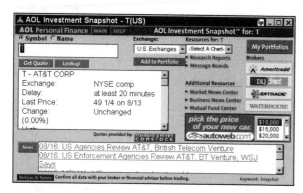

Figure 14-11. The Snapshot offers up the stock's vitals — from its highs and lows to volume and news stories.

Many of the items in the snapshot provide clues about the stock's health. Is volume higher than usual? Did the stock open at a price significantly higher or lower than the previous day's close? If so, you don't need to snoop too far to find out why. Look below the stock's snapshot for headlines of current news stories that mention your stock (see Figure 14-12 for an example). Or click Message Boards to jump to the forum directly related to the stock to find out what your fellow investors think is moving the stock.

Figure 14-12. When your portfolio indicates positive movement, you can probably trace the reason through news stories.

While you're scouting around the portfolios area, the stock price will probably change. If you want to know the latest price, click Refresh to update the quote.

Mutual funds usually trade just once a day and their price is updated in the evening. Market index quotes are real-time.

Perhaps during your exploring you come across yet another intriguing investment possibility. To add the target to your portfolio so you can follow it while you do the rest of your research press the Add button on the portfolio screen and insert the symbol. After a while, if you actually buy it, click the Edit button to amend information in the portfolio such as purchase price and number of shares. If you don't want to follow the target anymore or you sell the stock, get rid of it with the Remove button. To move it from one portfolio to another, click Transfer.

If your stock splits, press the Edit button and select the key that reflects the split ratio (as in 2-for-1 or 3-for-2). Then choose Calculate New Values (see Figure 14-13). Your portfolio automatically changes the number of holdings and purchase price.

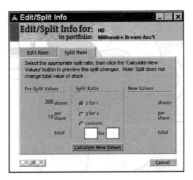

Figure 14-13. A stock split affects the numbers in your portfolio. You can update your portfolio automatically using the Edit/Split Item feature.

Adding indexes

If you track mutual funds in your portfolio, it is helpful to add market indexes of similar holdings to see how your funds fare compared to their market peers. You add the symbol of the index (see Tables 14-1 and 14-2) the same way you add a stock symbol to the portfolio. Say you have a blue chip mutual fund. You might want to add the symbol for the Dow Jones

Industrial Average ($INDU) to your portfolio to see how the funds compare (see Figure 14-14). If another mutual fund of yours concentrates on the transportation sector, for example, include in your portfolio the symbol $TRAN to see how your fund compares with the Dow Jones Transportation Index.

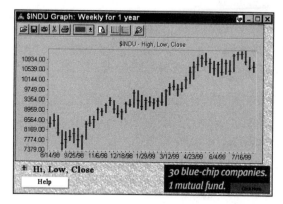

Figure 14-14. Adding an index such as the Dow Jones Industrial Average to your portfolio allows you to see how your investments are faring compared with the overall market.

Table 14-1. Symbols for Common Indexes

Symbol	Index
$INDU	Dow Jones Industrial Average
$COMP	Dow Jones Composite Average
$TRAN	Dow Jones Transportation Index
$UTIL	Dow Jones Utilities Index
$COMPX	NASDAQ Composite Index
$INX	S&P 500 Index
$MID.X	S&P 400 Midcap Index
$IUX	Russell 2000 Stock Price Index
$SOX.X	Semiconductor Sector Index
$MMX	Major Market Index
$NDX.X	NASDAQ 100 Index
$ADR.X	International Market Index
$IIX.X	Inter@ctive Week Internet Index

Cross-Reference

For more options on how to use this charting feature, see Chapter 9 under the section "A Look at History."

Table 14-2. *Sector Indexes*

Symbol	Index
$DRG.X	Pharmaceutical Index
$NF.X	Financial Index
$PSE.X	High Technology Index
$RMS.X	MS REIT Index
$BTK.X	Biotechnology Index
$UTY.X	Utility Index
$XOI.X	Oil Index
$SOX.X	Semiconductor Index
$XAU.X	Gold and Silver Index
$NV.X	Transportation Index

Charting success

In the course of your tracking, you might want to see how a stock has fared historically. To get a quick look at a stock's past performance, open your portfolio, select the holding you wish to view, then click the Details button. From the Investment Snapshot, click the pull-down box reading Select-a-Chart to view a chart with the holding's high, low and closing price from the most recent business day, the past month, the past year, or the past three years.

For further options, click More Charts. This opens the Historical Quotes feature. (This feature may also be accessed by going to Keyword: **Portfolio** and clicking Historical Quotes under Investment Research.)

Enter the name or symbol of a company. Click the Custom option, then click Graph. You may choose the frequency of the quote (daily, weekly, or monthly) and specify the exact date range you would like to see graphed. When you're finished, click continue to see the graph.

Summary

You learned why it's important to track your portfolios and you know how to set up many variations of them online.

You also know how to navigate the numbers behind the pictures, how to customize those displays to show exactly what you're looking for and how to add indexes to see how your holdings compare to their peers.

Now that you know how to keep on top of your portfolios, learn how to do the same for your holdings, coming up in Chapter 15.

CHAPTER

15

STAYING ON TOP

A Quick Look

▶ **Home Delivery**   **page 393**

Instead of tracking down the business news that affects you, let it track
you down. AOL's Portfolio Direct delivers the news to your desktop. Go to
Keyword: **Portfolio Direct**, enter the ticker symbols of the stocks you're
interested in, and click Subscribe; e-mail delivery starts that day.

You receive updates on closing quote data for each investment, as well as
market news and company news summaries at the end of each business day.

▶ **Keep an Eye on the Merchandise**   **page 397**

Even with your thorough research before you bought that stock or fund, there
are no guarantees that these assets won't take a nosedive after you're already
in deep.

Be prepared. Don't just watch the ticker tape parade when you can get inside
the floats. Go to Keyword: **Quotes** to pull up an AOL Investment Snapshot.

Enter the symbol of your fund or stock, and press Enter; an overview of the
latest financials will pop up in the window. A list of relevant current news articles appears at the bottom of the snapshot. Click a title to read the text. For
more in-depth information, click Research Reports to access all the information that's fit to print about your investment.

Chapter 15

Staying On Top

Y ou know by now that investing in the right stocks, bonds, and mutual funds takes hard work — saving your money, designing your blueprint, figuring your asset allocation, researching investments, finding a broker, making your trades. You've spent so much energy on all that you might be tempted to sit back and relax, stopping only to count your dollars every now and again.

But take note: It is one thing to buy and hold intelligently. It's another altogether to let your investments stagnate.

Smart investors stay on top of their investments. They know all their hard work (as well as that Colorado retirement getaway) is on the line. To keep your portfolio in tiptop shape,

you have to stay on top of what's happening with your investments. Then you'll be able to jump out of harm's way when
big news barrels in like a bulldozer.

The news and you

Company news, business news, market news, sector news,
political news, economic news — they can all crack your nest
egg. If, let's say, an analyst predicts a paucity of earnings for a
company that's in the same line of business as your favorite
holding, your stock can rock. You need to uncover what's
behind the shortfall. Is the industry depressed, which means
your company's earnings also might not be up to snuff? Or is
your company doing such a great job outselling the competi-
tion that it's time to boost your number of shares?

A hurricane rips through the southeast. Gas prices tumble
in South America. There is a labor strike in Britain, and beef
imports have been banned in most European countries.

So, what does that have to do with you? Plenty.

As you're stuffing your mutual funds in order to afford that
country house when you retire, your funds could begin to
belch a bit in response to events halfway across the globe.
An earthquake can shake your international funds. Labor
problems can rattle your equity funds. Gas prices can roll
your transportation shares.

Current events trickle down to affect every holding. You don't
need to dedicate your free time glued to the newspaper to
keep on top of things. Keyword: **Business News** takes you
to the latest news and events throughout the business world.
Scan the headlines or click one of the Departments for specialized information: Consumer Briefs, International,
Technology, or Economic news.

Looking for more details? Click Business Newsstand for the
latest news from magazines such as Business Week, the Financial Times, and Time.Com. If you just want the down-and-dirty
summary of what's happening, click Business News Summary
for quick, bite-sized news chunks from the wire services. If
you want to know what your investments have been up to,
type in a company or fund name and click Search. A list of relevant news articles will appear. To read an article, double-click
its name, as shown in Figure 15-1.

Figure 15-1. Current events, new legislation, international affairs — how will they affect your investments? Online news sources help you stay in the loop.

Reading one news item about one entity — granted, more than some investors do — isn't enough to get you the information you need to make sound decisions. You need to dig through everything you can find to understand — and prepare for — how this news will affect you.

Keeping Up with the News

Staying on top can seem daunting. Sometimes it's impossible even to get through the local paper each day, never mind the newsletters, press releases, magazine pieces, online chronicles, and breaking news that ultimately affect your holdings. But you don't need to sneak your Thermos by the librarian and hunker down in the reference room to study it all. With a few electronic tools on AOL, keeping up with your investments can take less time and energy than taking a long shower.

What the heck — take a shower while the tools work *for* you. Portfolio Direct (Keyword: **Portfolio Direct**) is a great tool to start with. The free, e-mail–based news summary delivers daily and weekly news reports on up to 20 American ticker symbols or specific industries. You request the industry or symbols you're interested in when you subscribe, and about an hour after the market closes you get a summary of your stock's activity, comparable index quotes, market news, company news, and hyperlinks to relevant AOL content such as full news stories.

News services

Tired of waiting for information to download, or feel like you've already done enough pointing and clicking to last a lifetime? AOL's Portfolio Direct could be just what you need.

Instead of seeking out information, you can have the latest news and price quotes e-mailed to you. To get the free service, go to Keyword: **Portfolio Direct**. Enter up to 20 stocks or funds you want to keep track of, as shown in Figure 15-2. If you don't know the symbol, click Lookup to help find it. Type in the company or fund's name and press Enter. Click the name you want and choose Select. An investment snapshot will appear, giving an overview of the company's financials. If this is the correct company, click Cancel, and enter the company or fund's symbol into one of the blank spaces at Portfolio Direct.

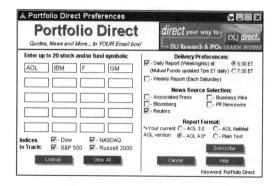

Figure 15-2. How did your investments react to the day's events? Portfolio Direct keeps you posted with updates on the companies you select.

After you pick the investments to track, choose a Daily Report, delivered at either 5:30 p.m. or 7:30 p.m., or a Weekly Delivery, e-mailed every Saturday. Then click Subscribe. Closing quote data, a market news summary, and current news from Reuters, Bloomberg, The Associated Press, the PR Newswire, and the Business Wire, as well as your portfolio updates, will be delivered to your AOL e-mail account.

To make changes in the portfolio makeup, return to Keyword: **Portfolio Direct,** delete or add to your investments in the 20 slots provided, and then click Save Changes.

While that's working for you, you can tackle the day's news and business happenings.

Find It Online

Want to know what's new on the Exchanges? Keyword: **Exchange Center** tells you. It's a supermarket of information on the nine U.S. exchanges, offering everything from options trading on the Philadelphia Stock Exchange to the latest in cattle futures.

Be informed

To get a grip on the news, start with Keyword: **Business News** (see the Figure below). Scan the top business stories of the day, which often dictate what moves the markets and why. Then follow the links: to news in the markets, technology, the economy, consumer briefs, international news, and industry news (which also links to earnings reports).

Keeping abreast of financial news helps you anticipate how your investments will perform.

News Searches

If you're in the mood for browsing, a little-known newsstand of sorts might help. From the Business News page you can search for business news by subject, under the Business News Search heading at the left side of the page. Say you're snooping around for information on health-care companies. Select By Subject, type **Healthcare** in the box, then click Go. Suppose you're interested in earnings. Type **Earnings** in the Subject box, then click Go. Chances are there will be dozens of stories of the day on the subject, and thousands in the search. They come from a newsstand's worth of sources, including Bloomberg, Reuters, The Associated Press, and the Business Wire (see Figure 15-3).

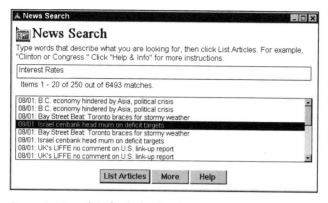

Figure 15-3. Looking for the lowdown on a particular subject? Find the latest news with AOL's Business News Search.

Market News Center (Keyword: **MNC**) is another option. Active traders turn to it regularly. The site drops you on Wall Street, key ring in hand. MNC is a live chronicle of the day's market activity, summing up the movement, listing the most active stocks and pointing out the biggest gainers and losers. You can call up all the news, charts and trading updates. The site highlights activity of the Dow Jones Industrial Average, the NASDAQ, Treasury bonds, and the yen.

If you don't need to know every detail of the day but you want to keep up with the investment chatter by the water cooler, hop over to Keyword: **Business Summary** (see Figure 15-4). This gives you the hour's business news and offers a quick feature on the hot topic of the day, like why tech stocks are taking a beating, why car sales are in a slump or why the Brazilian economy is wreaking havoc on mutual funds.

Figure 15-4. News summary services feed you short, easy-to-digest news chunks, which are great for keeping up with news events without expending a lot of your time.

For the fastest way to get news about your favorite holdings, go to Keyword: **Company News**, type in the ticker symbol, and press Enter.

Which are the day's most active stocks? Go to Keyword: **Market News Center** and then scroll down to Most Active Stocks.

15

Staying On Top

News analysis

Next, you need to tap into "analytical" or "value-added" journalism — stories that pull together disparate trends and news events, and make sense of them so you don't have to do all the spadework yourself. Here's the challenge: Sometimes it's difficult to determine which writers have a bias and which don't. Does the writer own the stock he's touting? Is the "trend" really an attempt to jack up a stock so the writer can unload it?

This is why it's in your best interest to explore the credentials of the "experts" before taking their word. Explore the sites on which the news appears and figure out who's behind the information. Is it a news organization with objective information? Or an outfit or individual that benefits if you buy something based on the advice. You need to understand the point of view, determine whether or not there is a vested interest, and examine the site's or the expert's track record before you heed their advice.

Company News

After you get the journalists' take on what's happening in the markets and why, go and find out what the company you own stock in has to say.

In the old days investors had to rely on that slick, rah-rah annual report for news from the company. Anything beyond that was slim pickings. But today's investor can find out what the company has to say via the PR Newswire, at Keyword: **Quotes**.

This inside information can be crucial to your investment's health. The news that a couple of top executives have "resigned" with no reasons cited could have underpinnings in a management move. New plans for plants overseas could mean the company is expanding globally — or is having labor troubles at home. A story on higher prices for raw materials could mean reduced profits at year's end.

Although the "news" comes straight from the public relations experts the company employs to make it look good (so the articles are tailored to ease harsh reports and polish good news), it's worth a look. Keeping apprised of company news gives you a glimpse of what's to come, helping you decide whether to board the investing train before your fellow passengers, or disembark before it careens off the track.

Company snapshots

The quickest way to get news directly from the company is via Keyword: **Quote**. Plug in the stock's ticker symbol and select Get Quote. Up will come the snapshot (see Figure 15-5), which you examined in Chapter 14.

Cross-Reference

For a close-up of the numbers in the Stock Snapshots, see the legend in Chapter 5. For a look at the components, see Chapter 14.

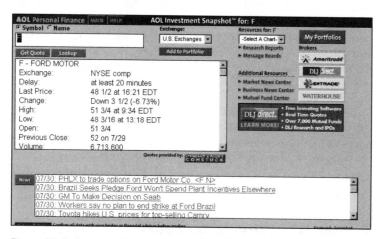

Figure 15-5. A company's investment snapshot offers a couple of tools useful in assessing financial prospects — news stories on the company and its industry, as well as press releases from the company.

At the bottom of the snapshot, you'll find a list of headlines where it says News. The company's public relations news is mixed in with other news. Click a headline. You can tell if the story that comes up was generated by company spokespeople if it says Business Wire in the dateline or Corporate News Release on the strip over the box of the story.

The snapshot is a springboard to all things news-related. You can hop off of here to the Market News, Business News and Mutual Fund centers. You can call up a chart that chronicles the stock's activity by day, month, or over the years. You can

Looking for a live chart on your stock's activity of the day? How about the market's activity? Decision Point has both at Keyword: **DP.**

click Research Reports and blast off to Investment research, or you can go directly to the Message Boards.

If something you've come across is so powerful it leads you to want to trade, you can link right to the brokers from the Snapshot page.

Stock news

So now you're up on business news, company news, and news analysis. Next is some detective work. If you are an active trader, you'll want to examine your stock snapshots during the trading day to see if anything peculiar is going on. First, call up Keyword: **Portfolio** for your holdings at a glance. Any unanticipated activity here? If you have the time, scroll down holding by holding and double-click each to open a snapshot of your stock's market activity. Is trading volume about average? Did the stock open at about the same level as the previous day's close? Has the price remained relatively constant throughout the day?

If the answer to any of these questions is no, chances are you can probably link the volume and the price with the day's news. While you're reviewing your portfolio, get into the habit of checking Company News at the bottom of the snapshot screen. AOL culls stories that mention your stock and lists them chronologically for your review.

A peek at partners' pickings

The Online Investor's (Keyword: **OI**) analysis of the news is targeted at people who, as the name indicates, invest online. Does it seem like all you keep hearing about lately is Gigantic Conglomerate, Inc.? Haven't gotten around — in spite of your best intentions — to figuring out the hullabaloo? OI's Company Spotlight feature focuses on what's causing the buzz (see Figure 15-6). Maybe it's the company's new products, management changes or earnings reports. If something piques your interest there, the page links to related stories as well as the company's financials and Web site. Online Investor archives a month's worth of reports.

Figure 15-6. Hearing a buzz — good or bad — about a particular company? Find out what's causing it before you decide whether you want in or out.

OI's info grid chronicles analyst upgrades and downgrades, IPOs and splits and buybacks. The site reports what economic news is slated for release that day and how that news might impact the market. After the numbers are out, Market Calendar interprets the fallout. The Earnings Calendar spells out which company is expected to report earnings on which day.

Hoover's Online is another partner with daily news offerings for online investors. Keyword: **Hoover's** features daily updates to IPO Central, and adds to your prospecting possibilities with a Company of the Day spotlight.

Business Week Online offers a magazine's worth of analysis. To get the weekly version of the magazine, start with Keyword: **BW**, then select Contents. BW Online also offers daily fare. Click BW Daily for the Streetwise column to zero in on one component of the day's activity (see Figure 15-7). Select Barker.Online for mutual fund analysis. Click Washington Watch for analysis on how Washington's activities affect your investments.

Each day Multex clues you in on the analysts' analysis at Keyword: **Multex**. After you're done with the analysts, meander over to Talk, to discuss this new information.

Find It Online

You've spent so much time gathering solid strands with which to weave a healthy, profitable portfolio. And now you're supposed to keep up with international, national and local, financial and economic events? All in the hopes of keeping your portfolio on even ground in this unsteady, ever-changing world?

Never fear. Scores of experts await you at Bloomberg.com with news and analysis to help you stay on top of the day's events. Keyword: **Bloomberg** runs breaking news headlines on the front page, and links to business, world, technology, and sports news by clicking your choice under Departments.

After a long day, if you're just too tired to read one more thing, Bloomberg offers a fresh alternative: news slideshows with audio and video, including interviews. To see up-to-the minute slideshows, go to Keyword: **Bloomberg Slideshows** for a list of current events, and double-click any title you'd like to see and hear. To access older titles, click Recent Slideshows.

15

Staying On Top

Tip

On AOL, the majority of investing and personal finance partners admit any interest or bias they might have up front. For a sketch of partners referred to in this book, see Appendix A.

Note

Other investors and analysts will not always share your opinion. Remember, each time you buy a stock, somebody else thinks it's worth dumping.

Figure 15-7. OK, you've read the latest headlines. But what do they really mean? *Business Week*'s Street Wise Columns analyze them for you, helping to explain why a tax hike in Indonesia could mean lower profits in your portfolio.

Talking It Over

After examining all this news, you might feel like talking about what it all means. Where to start? It's not like you can go out in the driveway and talk to your neighbor about the latest eBay deal and expect him to have a clue about what you're saying. But, in an instant online, you can find investors who share your interest or passion.

Chats, message boards and forums are the ticket. Here you'll find investors and analysts who are never short on opinions.

A good part of successful investing is dialogue. Talking with somebody else about your motives helps you weigh the advantages and disadvantages of your anticipated moves before you ever execute them. In addition, if you keep in constant touch with investors and Wall Streeters, you shouldn't be surprised by how they react to different news and scenarios. Eventually, you'll be able to anticipate the reaction when the events occur again.

Talk to the experts

If you simply must know what's motivating the market movers on a given day, you can ask an investment expert, right on the spot. Sage runs AOL's daily market chat at Keyword: **Market Talk** each day from 9 a.m. to 7 p.m. EST, with industry insiders each hour. In the evenings, they bring on mutual fund managers and fund experts. Unlike the TV people, these experts will answer *your* questions — real time — about the likely fallout on *your* stock (see Figure 15-8). Go to Keyword: **Market Talk** and then click Go to the Event. If you want to ask a question or make a comment, click Participate in Event, type in your comment, and press Enter. An emcee from Sage inserts market updates periodically during the chats and keeps things running without spammers or salespeople getting in the way.

Figure 15-8. Whether you seek an alternative viewpoint or a variety of opinions, online discussion groups and chat rooms can be just what you need.

You might as well listen in on other experts' running commentary, too. MarketDay (Keyword: **Market Day**) runs live assessments of what's happening in the market, including earnings reports, analysts' upgrades and downgrades, and movement in the sectors, including tech stocks (see Figure 15-9). The analysts also evaluate what's driving the markets and assess the implications for trading stocks, bonds, or currency.

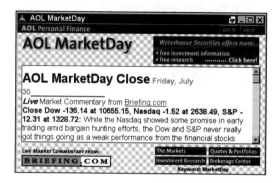

Figure 15-9. MarketDay provides market commentary and analysis from the start to finish of every trading day.

15

Staying On Top

Find It Online

If you just need to vent about the day's activities with your investing brethren, find them in the Market News Chat (Keyword: **MNC**) and then scroll down to Market News Chat: Investor to Investor.

Tip

You can get to your stock's message board right from your stock snapshot at Keyword: **Quote**.

Then take a walk down TheStreet.com (Keyword: **The Street**) for candid opinions and analysis on how the day's disparate stories are shaking down on Wall Street. There's no need to guess where these folks are coming from. Their holdings and opinions are included with each post.

Business Week Online corrals two experts a week: an analyst from Standard & Poor's each Tuesday afternoon and various investment experts every Thursday night. Keyword: **BW**, then select Conferences. The transcriptions are archived and downloadable from the library.

If you want to stay on top of financial planning news, ask and hear the latest on credit and debt from the experts theWhiz.com pulls in. Talk with them live each night at Keyword: **thewhiz**.

Chat with fellow investors

After you've heard from the experts, go and mull things over with your fellow investors.

To talk about your stock, go to Keyword: **InvestingForums**. Then scroll down to the letter your stock begins with, and double-click it. Another screen will open up asking you to further refine your choice. Double-click the appropriate letters for your stock. A list of stocks will pop up. To read what people are saying about a particular stock, click List All. Another list pops up, giving the subjects of the different messages about the stock. To read a message, click Read Post (see Figure 15-10). Do other investors believe you have a gem, or does their sentiment dull the shine? If you want to respond to a message, click Reply and enter your opinions.

Newsstand in a Suitcase

AOL delivers enough news to make a paper boy cry "Uncle." Check these out in addition to the others already mentioned in this chapter.

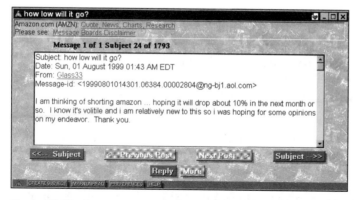

Figure 15-10. Chat rooms are great place to solicit advice, comments and experiences from other investors. But remember to rely on your own formal assessments of performance before making any moves.

On tap daily

Business Week's Street Wise column is a market intelligence column that goes live at about midnight. It takes a close look at trends affecting a particular company or industry. Enter Keyword: **BW** and then click Street Wise.

Want to know today what will play in the papers tomorrow? Sign up for Bloomberg's News to Go, a composite of top business and finance news stories. Bloomberg e-mails it to you each day at 5 p.m. EST. Sign up at Keyword: **Bloomberg** and then scroll down to Bloomberg News to Go (see Figure 15-11).

Caution

Keep in mind that on many message boards you'll find cheerleaders as well as naysayers. You get people who claim to be insiders bullying the stock because they plan to short it. You get CEOs masquerading as commoners. So you need to take the postings in stride. As Business Week's Arnold points out: "It can be very slippery, or you can have some very intellectual discussions. You have to gather as much information as you can, then you have to make up your own mind."

15

Staying On Top

Figure 15-11. For an e-mail summary of the top business and finance stories each weekday, sign up for Bloomberg News to Go.

What's on tap for the day that could move the market? What numbers, reports, or trends? Check Business Week Online's Meetings of Note and Numbers Coming Out Today at Keyword: **BW**, then click BW Plus, then Investors Central. Or see Online Investor's Calendar at Keyword: **OI** and TheStreet.com's predictions at Keyword: **The Street.**

Looking for a briefing on the day's market activity and earnings reports? Check out Business Week's daily version at Keyword: **BW Daily**. Or try Online Investor's earnings section at Keyword: **OI**; look under Calendars, then click Earnings.

Need your fix three times a day? The Motley Fool will supply it. At Keyword: **Fool**, check the news before the market opens by selecting Breakfast News in the Quick Find pull-down menu under the heading News. Then check in during the day by picking Fool Plate Special at 12:30 p.m. EST. For the Fool's take on the motivation behind the day's movers, select News and scroll down to Quick News for the day.

Do charts and technical analysis get you giddy with pleasure? If so, you need to check out Decision Point's chart madness at Keyword: **DP** for daily and live chart action.

Want to know what's happening in the market but don't have time to go looking for it? Standard & Poor's will e-mail you market news during the day, featuring a look at what's moving and why. Sign up at Keyword: **Personal Wealth**

Weekly

The entire *Business Week* magazine goes up Thursday night, a full day earlier than a postal-dependent investor gets it. Of particular note to investors — the magazine's Inside Wall Street column, and about 100 stories that all have something to say about a particular company. Keyword: **BW**

For a weekly roundup of the best features, news summaries and market stories on AOL, sign up for *The Investor* (Keyword: **The Investor**), a free newsletter delivered to your desktop (see Figure 15-12). It comes out every Friday after the market closes.

OK, so this one's not weekly, but it's worth looking at anyway. Business Week Online runs Sector Scope, a biweekly examina-

tion of a particular sector. Go to Keyword: **BW**, then click BW
Daily and pick Sector Scope.

Figure 15-12. Wrap up the week with an e-mail delivery of *The Investor,* a recap of
events and trends following the close of business every Friday.

Summary

You learned why it's important to stay on top of the news, and
you learned how to do that with minimal effort. Now you can
recognize trends and feel the pulse of Wall Street without having to travel to Manhattan.

- ▶ You know to check an "expert's" bias before considering her advice, and you know where to turn for objective news and information.

- ▶ You learned where to find people who share a passion
  for investing news and issues — experts and investors
  alike.

- ▶ Finally, you found a newsstand's worth of information
  at your fingertips.

Now that you've mastered the Research and Execution phase
of investing, you can wrap up this tidy financial package by
turning to Part IV: Managing Your Money Online.

15

Staying On Top

A Quick Look

▶ **Assessing Your Coverage** **page 413**

There's not much point spending your time amassing a fortune if it could all get swept away in a moment due to an accident or unforeseen event. Are you adequately protected against sudden loss?

To make sure you have enough coverage, spend a few minutes with Quicken's Insurance Planner. Go to Keyword: **Quicken**, click Quicken.com, and select the Insurance tab. Then click Insurance Planner under Tools. Click Begin the Insurance Planner to open the tool.

▶ **Insurance, Insurance Everywhere** **page 415**

Why spend hours on the phone shopping around for the best insurance deals when the Internet can do it for you? Save time and hassle and enter your information only once to get the best rates on all types of insurance online — and avoid sales pitches and pressure to buy as well.

Go to Keyword: **Quicken.com**, click the Insurance tab. You can get insurance quotes in the Instant Quote Comparisons box. To begin, enter your ZIP code under Life Insurance or Auto Insurance and press Enter.

▶ **Preparing for the Worst** **page 427**

No one likes to think about a debilitating accident or injury, but unfortunately, life can deal out unexpected and difficult cards. Prepare ahead: determine what you and your family will need if a catastrophe should occur.

For assistance, go to Keyword: **http://www.smartmoney.com**, and click the Planning tab. Select Insurance under the Planning header on the left. Choose the Disability tab. Scroll all the way down to the bottom and click How Much Do You Need? to open an interactive worksheet.

Chapter 16

Insurance

You may think that flood insurance is unnecessary, But if your basement turned into a swimming pool during Hurricane Floyd, damaged your washer and dryer, caused the circuit breaker to catch on fire, and broke your year-old water heater, you might think otherwise. That's why you have insurance — to cover those unexpected — and expected — risks.

The fact that you'll die is certain, you just don't know when. You might get some form of life insurance to assist your loved ones when the day comes. You or your family might get sick and need a doctor's care or hospitalization, so you need some form of health insurance. You'll probably own a home or a car at some point, so you'll probably need homeowner's and auto insurance.

What is insurance?

Simply put, insurance is a way to protect your assets and your financial stability against any kind of loss from weather, accidents, the passing of a loved one, or a debilitating illness.

AOL can help you understand insurance and how to best prepare yourself for the ups and downs that are a part of life. You may own a dozen or so policies covering all aspects of your life, or you may think your car insurance is more than enough to protect your interests. But sharpening your insurance acumen will help you decide on the best and most cost-efficient way to protect yourself and your family. Begin by going to Keyword: **Insurance** to access the AOL Insurance Center, shown in Figure 16-1. Click the type of insurance you are interested in to open that portion of the Insurance Center, or browse the links for insurance quotes, information, and education.

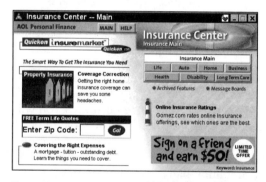

Figure 16-1. For every stage of life, there are different insurance needs. AOL's Insurance Center can help you find the policies for your specific needs.

How Insurance Is Priced

Insurance is priced according to the risk it's protecting against. The bigger the risk the more you have to pay for protection. Whatever your lifestyle, it's important to make sure you'll be protected, no matter what kind of curve balls life pitches in your direction.

Find It Online

Need further convincing? Check out the article pictured in Figure 16-2. Go to Keyword: **Whiz**, select Insurance, and then select Protect Thyself.

Figure 16-2. Think insurance is just for people who own a home or have a house full of kids? Everyone needs to protect themselves with the appropriate insurance.

Basically, you pay an insurance premium for the coverage specified in the policy. The insurance coverage is what is paid out in the event of a claim. If you have a $100,000-life-insurance policy and you die, then your beneficiary is paid $100,000, the face amount of coverage.

The premium is priced according to the coverage and the risk associated with the possibility of loss. With life insurance, for example, if you are 35 years old and smoke cigarettes, you will pay a higher premium for insurance than a 35-year-old non-smoker, because of the risks associated with smoking. For auto insurance, if you've had a lot of car accidents or speeding tickets you pay a higher premium than someone who has flawless driving record. You may even be denied coverage. If the insurance company believes it will pay out money often or sooner than average for the policy, it will charge you a higher premium.

Most insurance policies have a deductible, which is what you pay out of pocket before your insurance kicks in. The insurance company will pay you for the damages or loss that exceeds the amount of the deductible for each claim. Deductibles are a way for you to share the risk with the insurance company. If you take on more of the risk with a higher deductible, then the insurance will charge a lower premium. Basically, the higher the deductible, the lower your premium payments will be.

For example, if someone steals your daughter's $300 bicycle, and your deductible on your homeowners insurance is $500, then the insurance would not pay because the loss is less than the deductible. If your house were burglarized and you lost your $600 VCR and $800 television, then you would file a claim with your homeowner's policy. The total loss would be $1400. The insurance would pay $900, which is the difference between the value of the stolen goods and the deductible.

Note

Usually, the deductible must be met for each claim; it is not cumulative throughout the year. Also, the deductible is an out of pocket expense that you won't get reimbursed for and that you cannot deduct from your taxes.

Are you adequately covered?

Turn to the Quicken InsuranceMarket's Insurance Planner to help you assess your current insurance coverage. Based on your information, the planner develops an action plan that includes a prioritized list of insurance and quick access to policy quotes and information. Go to Keyword: **Quicken.com**, and select the Insurance tab. Under Tools, click Insurance Planner, and then click Begin the Insurance Planner to open the tool.

The first step is to create a Personal Insurance portfolio that will be used in developing your action plan and saved for future reference. Type in your information and press Enter. Once a portfolio in your name has been established, you can begin the planner.

The first section requests personal data and information about your health, job, and insurance in order to develop your profile. Once you've entered all the information, an action plan is created outlining the areas in which your coverage is weakest, and explaining why it is important to address those areas and how to find the coverage that will suit you, as pictured in the Figure below. Links to more information and tools for every step of the plan are available as well.

Continued

16

Insurance

Note

If you're trying to decide between using an agent or a broker, keep in mind that a broker has access to more insurance providers than an agent does, and may offer greater objectivity. This is handy when you need competitive homeowners insurance right away to close on a house, or auto insurance to buy a car.

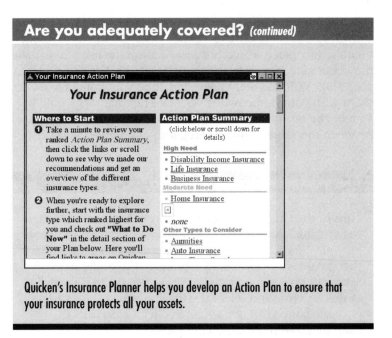

Quicken's Insurance Planner helps you develop an Action Plan to ensure that your insurance protects all your assets.

Keep in mind that every time you file a claim and the insurance company pays, your insurance premium may be raised. If you file too many claims, the insurance company will begin to look at you as a higher risk and will increase your premiums at renewal or possibly deny you future coverage. There is no specified number of claims that determines when and how much to raise premiums. The insurance company expects to pay out a certain percentage for each individual and class, and if it pays out more than expected, premiums will probably increase.

Insurance companies measure risk by demographic class and decide how much to charge as a result. For example, it is more likely that a teenage male will speed and get into accidents than an older parent, so risks will be higher for the teenager than for the parent. That's why the 19- to 25-year-old class of drivers pays higher premiums than the 40- to 45-year-old class of drivers.

Buying insurance

Insurance is often sold through agents or brokers, who earn commissions on the sale of all insurance products. Agents generally represent one insurance company, while brokers may represent many different insurance companies.

You may not see the commission you pay to an insurance broker or agent when you buy a policy. The insurance provider may pay the broker or agent directly for getting new business. This fee is then built into the total cost of the insurance, making the premium slightly higher.

 **Find It Online**

For a review on buying insurance through a broker, go to Keyword: **Edelman** and select The Truth About Money Online from the subject box. Click Part 10, Insurance, and select Chapter 70 – Should You Buy from an Insurance Agent?

Comparison shopping

Forget about calling a dozen companies and sitting through agent after agent giving you their spiel. Comparing insurance rates and coverage is much easier and faster online. For fast results, go to Keyword: **Quicken.com**. Click the Insurance tab, and under the Get Quotes header on the left click either Life, Auto, or Medical Insurance. Scroll down to the bottom, under the header Compare Quotes from America's Top Providers, and enter your ZIP code.

In order to provide you with the correct insurance quotes, you will need to answer several questions. Answer as fully as possible, keeping in mind that all the information is entered anonymously, for quote purposes only.

Once you've filled in all the necessary information, a list of quotes is provided. You can contact these companies by e-mail or telephone if you wish to learn more. It is recommended that you click Save Your Information, as new insurance quotes are added all the time. In the future, if you wish to compare quotes again and your status has not changed, you will not need to re-enter all of your information.

16

Insurance

Life Insurance

beneficiary: The person or persons designated by the policyholder to receive the proceeds of an insurance policy upon the death of the insured. The policyholder can name both a primary and secondary beneficiary.

Life insurance is a way to protect the financial security of your loved ones. When you die, the face amount or coverage of the policy is paid to the beneficiaries that you have designated.

If the insurance contract is for $100,000, then your loved ones will receive that amount plus accrued cash value, if any.

There are many kinds of life insurance, but the most common are term, whole-life, universal, and variable universal insurance. The main difference between these kinds of policies is that while all are considered permanent insurance, term, universal, and variable universal insurance have flexible premiums. Term insurance provides pure protection based on the cost of insurance for a specified period of time. The other policies offer permanent life insurance protection that begins with the first premium payment and does not end until death (as long as you do not default on the premium payments). These others also offer the ability to build a cash value.

Life insurance can play a significant role in your financial planning. To help you understand why, check out the series of articles pictured in Figure 16-3. Go to Keyword: **Family Money**, select Insurance from the category Smart Spending, and click the title.

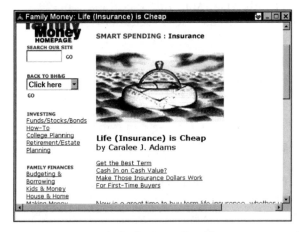

Figure 16-3. Can you afford to live without life insurance? It may be a vital part of your financial plan.

Term insurance

Unlike whole-life and other forms, term insurance is temporary. You are only covered during the term of the policy. The term can be one year, five years, ten years, or up to thirty years. The premium is based on your age and your health at the time the policy is purchased as well as the specified time period. You are buying pure life insurance, with no opportunity to build cash value. Your beneficiaries only receive payment if you die within the term of the policy. Nothing is paid if you survive the policy's term. However, you may have the option to purchase a new term policy, which would require another medical evaluation and would be based on your age at the time of underwriting.

Term insurance is an optimal choice for those who have minimum available resources (cash flow is tight) to pay premiums or are middle-aged. Term is also used for individuals who are accumulating wealth and want to be self-insured later in life. This is the cheapest way to have the most coverage.

Whole life

Whole life is a permanent life insurance policy that offers a fixed premium for a fixed coverage amount. This premium will remain the same throughout the term of the policy. Throughout the life of the insured, there is an opportunity to build cash value. The total benefit paid to the beneficiaries is the life insurance coverage, or face amount, plus any accumulated cash value.

You can borrow money against the amount of the cash value in your insurance policy. There is no legal obligation to repay this loan. However, if you don't repay the borrowed sum back into your policy, the benefits paid to the beneficiaries will reflect the difference. After death, beneficiaries will receive the face amount of the policy plus the cash value, minus any outstanding loans.

Whole life premiums are usually a lot higher than premiums for a term policy. Once whole life is purchased, no change in medical condition will affect the coverage.

Don't let the various types of life insurance confuse you. Refer to the Quicken table shown in Figure 16-4, for a quick review of what means what when it comes to selecting your policy. Go to Keyword: **Quicken**, then click Quicken.com. Select the Insurance tab. Under Quick Answers, select "How much life insurance do you need?" Select "Life Insurance Basics" under the "Want to know more?" heading. Then scroll down to

cash value: How much money you would be paid at any given time if you cancel your whole life policy. It's also the amount you can borrow from the policy, or its loan value.

The Internal Revenue Service treats the amount paid to the beneficiary as non-taxable. Also, any interest or other income earned on the excess premiums, called the cash value (total payment less the total cost of insurance) of the policy is not taxed.

For a discussion on how much life insurance you should have, go to Keyword: **Insurance,** and click the Covering the Right Expenses to read a series of articles sponsored by Quicken's InsureMarket.

16

Insurance

"Which type do you need?" and click The 60-Second Selector. Click Quicken's Look at Life to review the table.

Find It Online

Do you feel pretty certain that you found a good insurance deal online? See how your company stacks up compared to other providers by going to Keyword: **Gomez** for a comparative guide. Click Internet Insur-ance Scorecard to see the top ten online insurance companies. Each company is given a score based on ease of use, on-site resources, customer confidence, and relationship services. You can read more about each firm by clicking Review by the firm's name. If the company you're looking for didn't make the top ten, click View All Firms... to find the name you want.

Quicken's Look at Life™

The table below summarizes the generic forms of life insurance, describing the basic features of each policy. For a more detailed description select **"More about"** from the last row of the table.

	Term Life	Whole Life	Variable Life	Universal Life	Universal Variable Life
Cost	least expensive policy; premiums start low, gradually increase as you age	premiums stay level	premiums stay level	premiums are flexible	premiums are flexible
Coverage	in many cases, renewable	permanent, but without face amount	permanent, but without face amount	permanent, with face amount	permanent, with face amount

Figure 16-4. There is a type of life insurance to fit every need.

Universal life

Unlike whole-life, where you have fixed premiums, universal life has flexible premiums and includes a provision allowing you from time to time to increase the death benefits. The premiums paid are credited to the cost of the insurance within the policy, with the excess being invested into a fixed investment account earning a minimum guaranteed interest rate. The interest rate may fluctuate according to changes in the economy and other variables. The excess premiums and the interest earned on them will increase your cash value. The cash value can be used as a savings program, or to pay future premiums.

Universal life insurance is an optimal choice if you have erratic income (using your bonus to pay the premium), if you would like to earn a higher interest rate than whole life, or if you would like to use the cash value to pay the premiums in the future.

Variable universal life insurance

Like universal life, variable universal insurance has flexible premiums. Variable universal life insurance also has variable investment options. Universal life insurance is limited to fixed investment options, with a guaranteed minimum interest rate.

Variable universal insurance, however, allows you to invest in a more diverse manner.

Variable universal primarily invests in accounts run by institutional portfolio managers. These portfolio managers invest the excess premiums (after the cost of insurance is paid and administrative fees are collected) in sub-accounts that pursue specified strategies. The insured can choose from many different strategies (aggressive growth, value, small cap, international, balanced, and so on). The cash value in the variable universal policy grows from the excess premiums paid and the rate of return each sub-account generates throughout the year. The face amount and cash value fluctuate according to the returns or losses from the underlying investments in each sub-account, which are made up of stocks, bonds, fixed investments or a combination. The sub-accounts run almost exactly like mutual funds and usually mirror a retail mutual fund. There are some subtle differences, because they are run as separate accounts.

Variable universal life insurance is an optimal choice when you have a good steady cash flow and sufficient available resources to pay the target premium or more. This product is best used when you are looking for a vehicle that will provide a tax-efficient way to invest in addition to the needed life insurance. If used properly, this product would provide tax-free cash value that can be used for loans to pay for college, vacation homes, and other investments or be used as a tax-free pension during your retirement years. Due to the costs associated with this type of policy, it is best used when you can exceed the target premium and invest the maximum allowed by law. Like all other insurance policies, it is best to purchase this type earlier rather than later in life to receive the maximum benefit.

Even after you've chosen the type of insurance that best suits your needs, you need to make sure your plan covers your assets and protects your family. Your financial plan demands that you pay exactly the right amount for insurance: not too much, and not too little. For help in assessing exactly how much life insurance is right for you, turn to the article pictured in figure 16-5. Go to Keyword: **TSC**, click Full TSC site, and select Basics. Click "A Primer on Buying Insurance," and then choose "Calculating Your Life Insurance Needs."

Find It Online

Looking for quick answers to all of your life insurance questions? *SmartMoney's* got a wealth of wisdom for all your needs. Go to Keyword: **Money.Com**, and select Insurance to read the series "Solve The Mysteries of Life," a primer on unraveling the complexities of life insurance.

16

Insurance

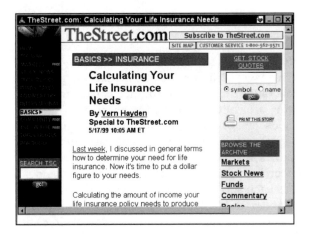

Figure 16-5. How much should you insure yourself for? Make sure you know your family's needs when determining the right policy for you.

Death benefits

The cash value for each type of insurance policy, other than term insurance, will fluctuate according to how the underlying investments perform. At the time of payout, the cash value will be added to the death benefit. If, for example, the policy's investment performance, in the sub-accounts in the variable universal policy you chose, exceeded your expectation, or the interest rate in the universal policy was more than the guaranteed minimum (usually 4 percent), then your cash value would be more than the illustration provided at purchase. You would then receive the excess as part of the death benefit. The death benefits (coverage or face amount plus the cash value) of all insurance policies are still qualified as tax-exempt (tax-free income to the beneficiaries).

Annuities

Annuities are to insurance companies what fish are to fishermen: the bread and butter product that keeps them in business. There are several types, including fixed and variable annuities.

Fixed annuities

In a nutshell, fixed annuities pay a specified sum of money each month for a specific period of time (or a life span) based on a specified amount of money, the age of the annuitant, and the interest rates at the time the annuity is established. Fixed annuities are invested in fixed income instruments like Treasury notes and bonds.

Generally, annuities outlive the holder. When this happens, the balance is paid out as a death benefit to a beneficiary or to your estate. Fixed annuities are an optimal choice when the annuitant is looking for an immediate payout and needs a specified sum of money each month that can be provided based on the current interest rate.

Find It Online

For a list of key benefits of annuities, see the table shown in Figure 16-6. For further information, go to Keyword: **Quicken**, click Quicken.com, select the Insurance tab, and click Annuities.

Find It Online

To compare the rates offered by different insurance companies offering annuities, go to Keyword: **http://www.smartmoney.com**, and click the Planning tab. Choose Insurance under the In Planning header. Then select Quotessmith.com. Scroll down and click Instant Annuity Quotes.

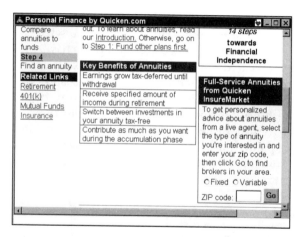

Figure 16-6. Annuities have become a more attractive investment option as annuity providers have introduced low-cost products with a variety of investment options.

Variable annuities

The trouble with receiving a fixed amount every year from an annuity is that market conditions change. If inflation goes up, the dollars you receive buy less. As a result, the largest pension fund in the world, Teachers Insurance Annuities Association College Retirement Education Fund (TIAA-CREF) devised variable annuities, which invest in equities and fluctuate with market conditions. The money that you deposit into annuities before your retirement, for example, is invested in equity sub-accounts offered by different investment strategies (aggressive growth, value, international, small cap, balanced, bonds, and so forth).

You can buy variable annuities while you continue to deposit additional monies and then switch to a fixed annuity during retirement, or vice versa.

Personal Insurance

Maybe you just got a new job with health benefits. Congratulations! Now you have to decide if you want traditional health insurance or a health maintenance organization plan (HMO).

Even if you're young and healthy, trying to figure you what you want and what you need isn't easy; health plans have become very complicated, and it may often seem like the family doctor is a relic of the past. With so many options and variables to choose from, deciphering the fine print of your health plan can be a health risk in and of itself. Don't despair, there are many places to turn for help, such as the primer on health insurance basics pictured in Figure 16-7. Go to Keyword: **Whiz**, select Insurance, then select Health Insurance Basics to read the full text.

Figure 16-7. Health insurance basics from the Whiz.com helps explain confusing health insurance issues.

Fee-for-service

Traditional fee-for-service healthcare insurance is divided into four classes:

- ▶ Hospital expense coverage
- ▶ Surgical expense coverage
- ▶ Physician expense coverage
- ▶ Major medical expense coverage

Your basic coverage in any healthcare insurance policy is the hospital expense. Generally, the insurance company will pay for room and board in a hospital for a set number of days. There is also coverage for other necessities, such as X-rays, drugs, operating room costs, laboratory charges, and, in some cases, anesthesia.

General surgery may be covered by the policy if it pertains to routine procedures, such as appendectomy or repair of a heart valve. Any specialized surgery would have to be approved on a case by case basis by contacting the insurance company.

Most people have family coverage with coverage of the physician's fee. You submit a record to the insurance company of the visit to the doctor's office with a diagnosis and fee. Generally, the insurance company may pay 80 percent of the amount, while you may have to pay 20 percent out of pocket.

Coverage of major medical expenses protects you from incurring large fees for service that would wipe out all your income and assets. They usually cover $500,000 to $1,000,000 in expenses and go into effect when you have an accident or serious illness. They may last a lifetime also. If the policy is a group plan — say a benefit that you get from work — there may be no limit in terms of how much the insurance company covers.

 Find It Online

Been turned down for a procedure you or a family member has to have? Don't give up — find help with the Whiz. Go to Keyword: **Whiz**, and select Insurance from among the links at the bottom. Select "WHZ-101: Coverage Denied! Medical procedures not covered by insurance." Read the article "Coverage Denied: What To Do When Your Insurance Company Says 'No.'"

Choose a plan

Given the endless variables and complicated subject matter, it's never easy to choose a health plan. To help you make a sound, informed decision, *MONEY Magazine* has developed an interactive tool called The Health Plan Navigator, designed to enable you to select the kinds of treatment that are important to you, and then to compare how different health plans stack up to meet your needs.

Go to Keyword: **Money.com**, and select Insurance. Scroll down and click Health Plan Navigator (shown in the following figure). Begin by reviewing the list of treatment categories, and indicating how important they are to your needs. For example, if you have young children, pediatric care is important, while if you are retired, you might be more concerned about other areas.

THE HEALTH Plan NAVIGATOR

Choosing a health plan is never easy, but the Health Plan Navigator, developed in conjunction with John Connolly, author of *The ABCs of HMOs*, will help complete the task.

Use the Health Plan Navigator to select the kinds of treatment that are important to you, and then to compare the level of benefits for three plans of your choosing.

To get started, read through the list of treatment categories below, setting a priority for each according to your needs. For example, parents of young children probably want full well-baby care and easy access to emergency care. When you're done, hit "Submit."

CATEGORY	Score the importance
Alternative care (acupuncture, etc.)	○ Important ○ Somewhat ○ Not important

Feel like you're comparing apples to oranges? The Health Plan Navigator can help you compare various health plans to select the one best suited for your needs.

Up to three different health plans may be compared at one time. For each category listed in the first screen, assign the plan a score, based on how well it meets your needs. References are given to help you determine what is ample coverage and what might be insufficient.

The final screen tallies the score for each plan and ranks them accordingly.

HMO

Unlike traditional fee-for-service health care, an HMO offers comprehensive health care services in return for a fixed premium and a co-payment. The co-payment can be from $5 to $20 for each visit to your doctor. Usually, you select a primary physician from a network of doctors who participate in the HMO. You also choose from a network of pharmacies. You must use members of these networks or your care will not be covered.

Before you select an HMO option, make sure the HMO can provide the services you need. For a take on what you should demand to know before signing on with any health care plan, check out the article pictured in 16-8. Go to Keyword: **Family Money**, and select Insurance from the category Smart Spending. Click Survive Your HMO, and then choose Ten Questions You Should be Asking Your HMO.

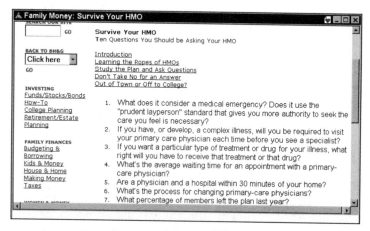

Figure 16-8. Start at AOL's Family Money site to help you determine how to choose an HMO.

The premiums may be higher than traditional fee-for-service health insurance, because the out-of-pocket expenses for medical treatment and illnesses are much lower. However, you can reduce a high premium by paying a higher co-payment for each doctor's visit and for prescriptions at the pharmacy. Generally, the $5 to $20 co-payment for each visit to the physician or for each prescription is a far cry from the $65-per-visit fee to the doctor and the average prices for prescriptions you'd pay under the traditional fee-for-service plan.

16

Insurance

If you're self-employed, you can deduct 60 percent of the amount you pay for health care insurance in 1999 (increasing to 100 percent in the year 2003) as a business expense.

The disadvantage of an HMO is that you can only use a doctor in the network. Once you go outside the network, you pay traditional fee-for-services charges, with less reimbursement (70 percent versus 80 percent). If you want to see a specialist outside the network, you may have no coverage, unless your primary care doctor from the HMO plan refers you to them. In the case of an emergency, you may be required to contact the HMO plan for approval (beforehand or very soon after) if you go to a hospital that is outside the network, or the HMO may not cover the expenses. Nevertheless, HMO plans are very popular, due to the co-pay and minimum out-of-pocket expenses.

Preferred provider organization

A Preferred Provider Organization (PPO) is a network of doctors and hospitals that an insurance company contracts with. In turn, the PPO offers discounted services, because the insurance company encourages you to use doctors in the PPO network. If you don't, you pay higher deductibles.

The company may have a cafeteria plan, which offers credits to employees to pay for benefits such as life insurance, dependent care, health insurance, even legal services, as well as other benefits. Employees can choose individually which benefits they want for themselves and their families.

Dental insurance

This covers regular dental care and damage care caused by accidents. Usually, there is a higher deductible, and it varies according to the treatment. Also, there is usually a limit of coverage paid each year, as well as a maximum lifetime coverage amount. Routine examinations and teeth cleanings (1 to 2 per year) are often covered, but braces and other non-necessities often aren't.

Disability

You receive disability payments if you are prevented from working by some mental or physical condition. Benefits won't be paid until an elimination period has passed and a doctor certifies your condition. If you are enrolled in a plan at work, then your salary and the length of time on the job are important criteria for determining how much disability you may receive. If you own a personal disability plan, the amount of disability paid is predetermined by the monthly premiums, as long as you meet the criteria of the specific plan.

Disabling dilemma

Do you need disability insurance? How much is enough? No matter how invincible you feel, an accident could leave you out of commission at any time. Disability coverage can ensure that you and your family get through any rough patch without major sacrifice or financial stress. To get a take on how much coverage you need, try the *Smart Money* interactive worksheet. Go to Keyword: **http:// www.smartmoney.com**, and click the Planning tab. Select Insurance, and scroll all the way down to the last section, Disability Insurance, and click Worksheet: How Much Do You Need?

The worksheet is divided into two parts, as pictured in the Figure below. The first section tallies how much money you will need each month, and the second section calculates how many months you can get by with your current coverage and savings without purchasing extra insurance. As you enter the data, the numbers are totaled immediately, so try changing your variables to see how they affect the bottom line. For example, if a spouse could bring home a greater salary, or if must-pay expenses could be decreased, then the necessary coverage might be somewhat lessened.

Note

Personal health insurance premiums and expenses can be deducted on your taxes if you itemize deductions. However, the only deductions allowed on your taxes are the premiums and expenses that exceed 7.5 percent of your adjusted gross income (AGI).

Preparing for the unexpected, such as a debilitating accident, can be easier than you think, using worksheets such as this one, offered by SmartMoney.

16

Insurance

Insurance for Elders

 **Cross-Reference**

See Chapter 17 for more information on ensuring your affairs get settled as you wish.

Once you reach a certain age, you're eligible for certain government insurance benefits.

Medicare

The most common form of insurance that you qualify for as a senior citizen is Medicare. Depending on when you were born, you qualify to begin receiving full Medicare benefits as early as when you become 65 years old. You have the option of taking Medicare earlier, at a discounted rate.

There are two forms of Medicare. One covers hospital care, rehabilitation costs, hospice care, and medical home visits. The other is supplemental emergency insurance and covers doctors' fees and other costs. The monies come out of Social Security and have eligibility guidelines. You have to be old enough to be eligible for full benefits. If you aren't you must pay a premium to Medicare.

Medicaid

This is government aid for families who can't afford private insurance benefits. It's administered by each state. There are some limitations that pertain to emergency services.

The Medicaid program is designed only to supplement Medicare insurance for poorer people. The government will check into your financial status and make sure you have depleted your own assets before granting you Medicaid benefits. Prior planning is essential to protect your assets — especially if your spouse also relies on them. Prudent estate planning techniques include protecting your assets in living trusts to avoid having to deplete your assets for expensive medical coverage in your elderly years. You should consult an estate-planning lawyer for more information.

Long-term insurance

Another way to avoid depleting your assets through the costs of incapacitation or an extended illness is to buy Long-Term Care Insurance prior to experiencing any medical problems.

As illustrated in Figure 16-9, the staggering costs of long-term health care can eat through savings in a dismayingly short amount of time. Go to Keyword: **Insurance,** click Long-Term Care, and select Keep Your Savings: $1000 Now Will Cost You $50,000 Later in Nursing Home Costs.

Tip

You may need to consider long-term care for an aging parent long before you begin preparing for your own future needs. For a discussion on the ups and downs of caring for an elderly family member, go to Keyword: **Insurance**, click Long Term Care, and select Thinking of Caring for Your Parent?

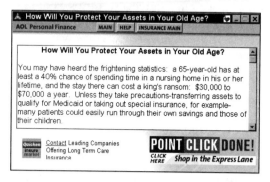

Figure 16-9. Long-term care insurance can prevent financial loss during an incapacitating health care situation.

Americans are living longer, and many of them are spending their final days in nursing homes. There is a need for long-term care insurance to cover the hefty costs associated with nursing home care. Long-term care insurance is aimed at those who are old and frail and need help in their daily living. Nursing homes can cost between $5,000 and $9,000 per month! Ten years of paying long-term care insurance premiums (example $3,500 per year) would still be a bargain, even if you are forced into a nursing home only for four to seven months. You may hope you never have to use the insurance for nursing home care, the same way you hope your home never burns down and you never get into an auto accident.

Long-term care insurance is a relatively new kind of plan for meeting the costs of continuous care, whether in your own home or a nursing home. This pays for the everyday care that is needed and not provided by Medicare or your gap insurance (for example, AARP) coverage. You should consider purchasing this type of insurance in your fifties and sixties, based on your medical history. This is the best type of insurance to keep you in your home longer and out of a nursing home. Also, it will give you peace of mind that you will not be a burden to your children or other family members. The long-term care benefits provide a daily living allowance and are not taxable as income.

16

Insurance

Homeowner's Insurance

Tip

Your home is your castle, but no one wants to overpay for that moat protecting it, right? So why pay too much for homeowner's insurance? The experts at Third Age can help you save on your insurance. Go to Keyword: **Insurance**, then select Home under Insurance Main. Click Savings on the House for a list of ten factors that can affect your home insurance rate.

This falls under the category of property and casualty insurance. Because properties and houses are different depending on their location, homeowner's insurance also varies. People living in Florida normally don't have to worry about damage caused by pipes freezing. Those living in Texas may want coverage for sandstorms and tornadoes.

Make sure you understand exactly what your homeowner's insurance will do for you and how it will protect your home: Are you protected against theft? Storm damage? Don't wait until an accident happens to find out the details of your coverage. For a primer on understanding homeowner's insurance, read the article pictured in Figure 16-10. Go to Keyword: **TSC**, click Full TSC site, and select Basics. Click A Primer on Buying Insurance, and then choose the link Reading the Fine Print on Your Homeowner's Policy.

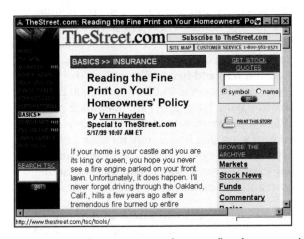

Figure 16-10. The Street.com provides an excellent discussion on the ins and outs of homeowner's insurance.

You need homeowners insurance in order to buy a house. An insurance appraiser will inspect the property first to appraise the cost to rebuild the home, which determines the minimum necessary insurance coverage. Before buying the house, make sure there are no hazards or dangerous conditions affecting the property that your insurance company will not protect against. The insurance company should also be notified of any improvements to the property that increase the value of the home. The insurance company may not send an appraiser every time you make an improvement to the property. They usually allow you to increase the coverage based on the description or the cost of the improvement.

Your premium will increase as the amount of coverage increases. But making sure your home has the proper coverage will pay off if there is ever any loss. If you lose your house in a fire, for example, you want the insurance company to reimburse you for its replacement value at the time of the loss. This includes any improvements recently made to your home.

What is covered?

Homeowner's insurance covers damage to or loss of personal property. Damage to property falls under 16 categories including everything from fire and lightning, to windstorm or hail, to falling objects, to civil commotion.

Figure 16-11. Homeowner's Insurance: Why bother? What can go wrong? Plenty! To be best prepared is to prepare for the worst.

What may not be covered

Homeowner's insurance covers most theft, but there are exceptions. The exceptions include theft in a house or building under construction and theft in a rental property that you, the policyholder, may own but not reside in.

Tip

Do you know what to do in an emergency? Preparing ahead of time can save you time, money, and help you weather unexpected events more easily. As pictured in Figure 16-11, Quicken's InsureMarket offers advice on what to do in almost any unexpected situation, from floods and earthquakes to confronting a thief. To read the advice, go to Keyword: **Insurance**, click the picture for Property Insurance.

Tip

Homeowner's insurance premiums are usually included in your monthly mortgage payments. Also, the annual premium amount is tax deductible.

16

Insurance

You need to check whether your homeowner's policy covers external structures, such as detached garages, patios or sheds. Many policies do cover these. However they may not cover property that is used for business purposes, such the old guesthouse you made into an office.

Homeowner's insurance won't cover damage from earthquakes or floods or damage resulting from a power failure. Also, if you have neglected something and it breaks, or if you intentionally lost something, there is, of course, no coverage.

If you file a claim for damages to your property or for stolen items, you need proof of each occurrence. Otherwise, the insurance company won't reimburse you. If something is stolen, you need to file a police report and contact your insurance company within a reasonable timeframe. If you file a claim for damages to your house, such as frozen pipes, you may need to have a plumber or appraiser inspect the damages and estimate the cost to fix it. Most insurance companies will accept multiple repair cost quotes instead of sending an appraiser, as long as the cost remains under a certain dollar amount (which is different for each insurance company).

If you have some jewelry, a mink coat, or other valuable personal belongings, it's a good idea to itemize them on a rider or addendum to the insurance policy. It costs a little more, but it allows you to replace these items. The additional cost depends on the total value of the insurable items covered. For a rough idea of how much insuring valuable items will add to your premiums, read the article pictured in Figure 16-12. Go to Keyword: **Family Money**, and select Insurance from the category Smart Spending. Click Take Coverage and choose The Limits of Plain-Jane Policies.

Personal property insurance

This is part of your homeowner's insurance. Generally, you're reimbursed for your personal property up to a specified limit. Even if you don't own your home, purchasing renter's insurance can provide protection for your belongings for a relatively small investment. Check out the table pictured in Figure 16-13 by going to Keyword: **Whiz.** Select Insurance. Then select **WHZ-101:** Renter's Insurance and scroll down to review the table.

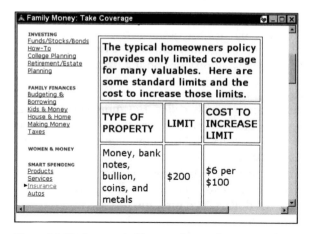

Figure 16-12. Certain valuable items of personal property, such as jewelry, need additional insurance protection. Find out how much at Keyword: **Family Money**.

Your home computer: you've come to rely on it for almost everything you do, but what happens if it gets damaged in a flood or tornado? Or gets stolen, gets broken, or gets vandalized? Protecting your computer falls into a special insurance category. To make sure you're covered, go to Keyword: **Insurance**, and click Home. Select Is Your PC Covered? to learn more about how to protect your computer.

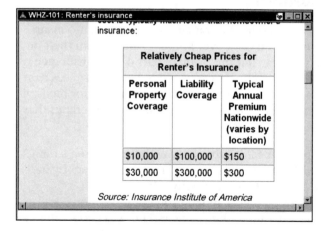

Figure 16-13. Protecting your property and your peace of mind can be done at a fairly low annual rate.

Liability Insurance

You may drive to the market and get into a car accident. Your babysitter may take your car to the market and get into an accident. A neighbor may trip and fall on your property. Or a child may use your swing set and get hurt. All these can result in lawsuits.

16

Insurance

Find It Online

Don't let car insurance lingo discourage you from understanding exactly what you are buying. For a primer on the basics of auto insurance, go to Keyword: **TSC**, click Full TSC site, and select Investing Basics. Click A Primer on Buying Insurance, and then choose the link Crash Course on Auto Insurance Coverage.

Personal liability coverage protects against any civil legal action that can occur when someone gets hurt on your property — if they trip on the doormat and fall, for example. Forget the fact that they may be clumsy or coming back from a late-night party.

This type of insurance is usually called an Umbrella policy. An umbrella policy is needed to cover claims that are not covered or that exceed the monetary limits of coverage in your homeowner's and auto insurance. Most homeowner's and auto insurance is limited to $300,000 of coverage for personal and medical injury. A liability insurance policy extends that coverage up to millions of dollars. The premium is based on the coverage amount. You can buy separate liability insurance, but usually it's included in your homeowner's policy.

Auto insurance

Another form of liability insurance is included in auto insurance. Auto insurance can cover losses resulting from theft or damages to your car. But the primary part of auto insurance covers your legal liability in cases where your car causes damage to another person or to their property. It pays for medical expenses from accidents as well as for dents and scrapes that you caused on other cars.

In many states, you can't drive a car without carrying a minimum amount of liability insurance. The amount is set by individual states. Understanding exactly what your state's requirements are and how much protection you need is an important safeguard for your finances. The Whiz.com offers a good tutorial to guide you through the basics of understanding your insurance policy. Go to Keyword: **Whiz**, and select Insurance from the links at the bottom of the page. Then select WHZ-101: Car Insurance Basics, as pictured in Figure 16-14.

The most important thing to remember about the cost of the different types of liability insurance is that your premium will be affected by the amount of deductible you are willing to pay. The higher the deductible, the lower the annual premium. You may want a higher deductible, so that you can afford the premium when your cash flow is tight. If you own your own business, you may elect a lower premium, because it is partially deductible from your taxes and means you will have less out-of-pocket expenses. You need to select your deductible based on your current financial situation.

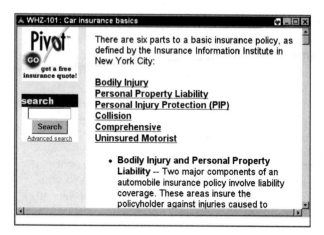

Want to lower your auto premiums? Check out the advice from Keyword: **Thirdage**. Scroll down and click More on Thirdage: Money, and go down to Features: Must-Read Articles on Money. Select A Road Map to Lower Auto Insurance under the Spend heading for a list of ten factors that can lower your rates.

Figure 16-14. Bone up on the basics of automobile insurance with this primer from the Whiz.com.

For a quick look at some tips on maximizing your auto insurance dollar, go to Keyword: **Family Money**, and select Insurance from the category Smart Spending. Click Savvy Shopping Can Cut Your Car Insurance Tab, as pictured in Figure 16-15.

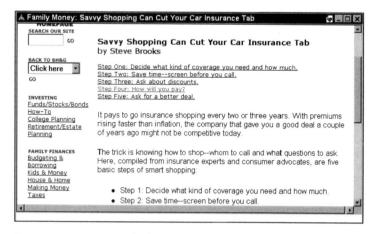

Figure 16-15. Everyone who drives a car must have insurance, but there are ways to save and get the most for the money you put into premiums.

Summary

In this chapter, you learned all you need to know about various types of insurance and how they protect the financial stability you built throughout earlier chapters. It's up to you to decide whether the costs of insurance are worth the protection they offer from a variety of risks. Some may keep you from losing your hard-earned savings and property. Others are designed to provide money to your heirs and beneficiaries, in the event that you die unexpectedly.

The next and final chapter, Estate Planning, will present various plans you can follow to limit taxes and pass on to your loved ones more of your accumulated wealth and assets after your die (hopefully after a long and rich life).

A Quick Look

▶ **Getting Ahead of the Tax Man**   **page 444**

It is painful to consider that all of your careful investments may go to the tax collector instead of to your loved ones. Planning is essential to avoiding such a fate. To get an idea of what kinds of taxes your estate will face, check out the Money.com interactive inheritance tax worksheet. Go to Keyword: **Estate Planning.** Scroll down and click Calculate Your Estate Taxes.

▶ **Online Lawyer**   **page 445**

Do you ever wish you had a lawyer in the family? The Internet can provide the next best thing with legal information, education, and advice from Nolo.com: Law for All. The site includes detailed information on all aspects of estate planning, from making a will to living trusts and gift taxes. Go to Keyword: **Estate Planning.** Scroll down and click Nolo: Wills & Estate Planning in the subject box.

Chapter 17

Estate Planning

Don't skip this chapter! Granted, you may be tempted to do so, as few people want to face the fact that someday, inevitably, they will breathe their last. It might be even harder to bring up the subject with your parents, spouse, or children. And if you do have to talk about death, it seems downright heartless to discuss subjects like wills and inheritances.

But estate planning is one type of financial arrangement that can't wait until the last minute. Believe it or not, property you have legally acquired over the years does not automatically belong to your loved ones when you're no longer alive. If you haven't prepared a will in advance, your property could go to Uncle Sam.

Where there's a will, there's a way

Interstate laws determine who will inherit your assets — which could rule out people you thought would be getting your assets. Without a will, your assets go through probate, where the court decides how to distribute them among immediate family; no charities, workers, or close friends get anything. Making a will is vital if you want your wishes to be carried out. To find out why, read "10 Good Reasons Why You Should Have a Will" by ThirdAge, pictured in Figure 17-1. Go to Keyword: **Estate Planning** and click Write a Will.

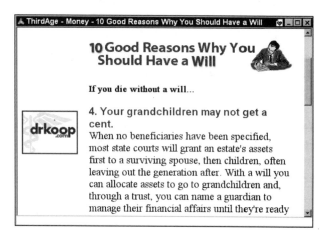

Figure 17-1. Allowing the law to decide how your estate is divided could leave out people you wished to include.

A will, however, enables you to give the property to whomever you want — spouse, children, other relatives, friends, charities, or any combination of these. If you care about your loved ones, you need to make sure they're cared for after you're gone. As noted by *SmartMoney* in Figure 17-2, the days when your children took over the estate by moving into the master bedroom are gone. If you want to leave a legacy behind, you have to plan ahead. To read this article, go to Keyword: **http://www.smartmoney.com**, click the PLANNING tab, select Estate Planning from the left, and select Passing Your Home to Heirs from the drop-down list.

Find It Online

Old age creeps up faster than you might think. AOL offers many articles on how to save for retirement. Go to Keyword: **Estate Planning** and you'll see a box on the left that says Foolish Uncle Sam. Double-click that and you find a 13-step process for saving for retirement while enjoying your current lifestyle.

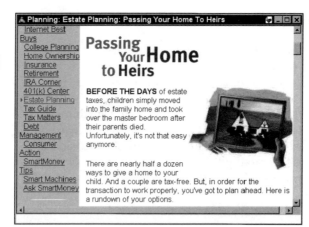

Figure 17-2. Don't let a lifetime of work and savings disappear when you die. Plan ahead to make sure your assets are passed on according to your wishes.

Yet, many people are not looking ahead. In fact, Americans spend more time planning their vacations than they do planning their estates. Fewer than one third of Americans 45 and over have set up an estate, reports Merrill Lynch in a 1998 survey. And half of the respondents surveyed had estates worth between $300,000 and $600,000.

What Is Property?

Before you decide who will inherit your property, you need to know what you have to bequeath. You may have enough to keep your spouse and children comfortable, give something to your nieces, nephews, and grandchildren, and help your favorite charities. Or maybe you were already more generous than you really could afford.

Property isn't just what many people think of as solid goods — your house, car, furniture, and jewelry. It also includes all your financial assets, including stocks, mutual funds and savings accounts. Also, don't forget the nonready cash — for instance, life insurance and retirement plans.

Basically anything you own, tangible or intangible, is property, including your time-share in Jamaica, your daughter's bike rusting in the garage, and your season tickets to the Pittsburgh Pirates.

Knowing What You're Worth

Now that you're thinking about writing a will, there are some important steps to follow. First off, you have to figure out how much you're worth. To do this, you have to figure out how much you have. Here is a short list of assets and liabilities for calculating your estate value.

Assets (these should include property and accounts held jointly by you and your spouse):

- ▶ Portfolio assets — Stocks, bonds, mutual funds, and cash.
- ▶ Retirement assets — 401(k), Defined benefit plans, and IRAs.
- ▶ Proceeds from life insurance policies.
- ▶ Personal property — Cars, boats, art, and jewelry.
- ▶ Real estate — Your primary home, vacation home, and farm.
- ▶ Other assets — Interest from limited partnerships or business interests.

Liabilities:

- ▶ Mortgages — Primary mortgage and home equity loan.
- ▶ Personal loans — Car loans, credit card balances.
- ▶ Estate settlement costs — These vary according to estate size and include future expenses, attorney, accountant and executor's fees as well as estate administration costs.

Basically, you subtract the liabilities from the assets to determine your net worth. This assumes you have more assets than liabilities. If the liabilities are greater, your family must pay for them when you die.

Tip

If you feel that estate planning is a difficult topic to manage, you're not alone. So if misery loves company, why not turn to the experienced and sympathetic ears of your fellow online investors? Check out the message boards at Keyword: **Quicken**. Click Quicken.com, and choose the Retirement tab. Then, click Wills & Estates, and scroll down to find the Discussions.

Definition

estate: The total property owned by an individual prior to the distribution of that property under the terms of a will, trust, or the inheritance laws in the state of legal residence of a deceased estate owner. An individual's estate includes all assets and liabilities, and all property.

Death and taxes

So you think you know how much you are worth — but did you remember to include the value of your car? Your profit-sharing plan? Your savings bonds? To help you get a realistic picture of what you are worth, get a little assistance from *SmartMoney*'s Net Worth Calculator.

Go to **http://www. smartmoney.com** and click the TOOLS tab, scroll to the bottom of the page to the Calculators section, and select Net Worth Calculator. This interactive tool provides a worksheet that helps you remember all of your assets and liabilities. A running total is calculated of your overall net worth as you enter the items.

When you know what your assets are worth, you can figure out your inheritance tax bill. Your beneficiaries may pay nothing or they may pay a lot. If you die in 1999 and your estate is worth $650,000 or more, your estate has to pay inheritance tax, which is 55 percent. Your estate only pays taxes, however, on the amount that is higher than $650,000. So if the estate is worth $800,000, then Uncle Sam takes out 55 percent on $150,000 ($800,000 minus $650,000). If the estate is less than $650,000, no inheritance tax is owed. That amount will increase gradually to $1 million by 2006. Then, if your estate is $1 million or more, your estate will pay taxes only on the amount that exceeds $1 million.

Estate taxes

To get an idea of what kinds of taxes your estate will face, check out the Money.com interactive inheritance tax worksheet pictured in Figure 17-3. Go to Keyword: **Estate Planning,** and click Calculate Your Estate Taxes in the subject box. Then click Worksheet: Estate Tax Calculator to open the site. This tool takes into account all of your assets and liabilities, including funeral expenses and any exempt bequests, such as gifts to charity or a surviving spouse. After you enter the appropriate figures, click Calculate.

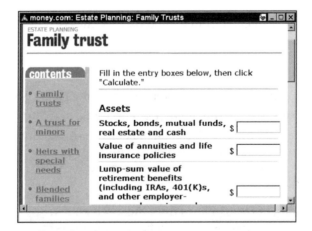

Figure 17-3. Knowing the amount of inheritance tax your estate will face can help you determine how to protect your assets.

The worksheet will return a figure for your gross estate and your taxable estate. If you owe any estate tax, that will be shown as well. After these totals have been calculated, the worksheet is again available with your original figures. You can change some of the numbers, such as gifts to charity, to see how they affect your totals.

Try to keep your estate value below the threshold where it's taxed. You can do this by giving property away to your family or spending the money that exceeds the threshold.

Putting a Pen to Paper

Okay, you've decided to write a will. Now you have some decisions to make. You have to figure out carefully how much to give away. Here are some things to consider:

- ▶ To whom are you going to leave the estate? Will you leave it all to your spouse? If so, are both estates coordinated in case you die before your spouse?

- ▶ Is your spouse comfortable managing the assets or should you set up a trust, whereby a trustee has certain powers over trust assets? What happens if your spouse dies before you do?

- ▶ Who will be your minor children's guardian if you and your spouse die?

- ▶ Do you want to leave the assets to charity, like your place of worship, or an organization where you volunteered when you retired?

Remember, also, that the will can be and in certain circumstances should be changed. You may divorce, and your spouse may remarry. You can opt to give everything to your children. The easiest way to change your will is to write a new one. Adding a legal addendum such as a codicil is expensive and troublesome. For more information on preparing for changes to your will, check out the article in Figure 17-4, offered by Nolo's Legal Encyclopedia. Go to Keyword: **Estate Planning,** and click Nolo: Wills and Estate Planning in the subject box. Scroll down and click Wills from the Table of Contents, and scroll all the way down to Is It Time to Change Your Will?

Find It Online

To keep up with the latest changes in inheritance tax, go straight to the horse's mouth, Keyword: **http://www.irs.gov**. This official IRS Web site offers forms and publications, which are available for download. Click Forms and Publications to download Publication 950: Introduction to Estate and Gift Taxes.

Caution

There are limits to how much you can give away before being subjected to gift taxes. Talk to your accountant as you formulate your giving plans.

Definition

codicil: A supplement or addition to a will. A codicil may explain, modify, add to, subtract from, qualify, alter, or revoke existing provisions in a will. Because a codicil changes a will, it must be signed in front of witnesses, just like a will.

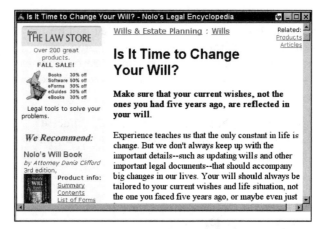

Figure 17-4. When the circumstances of your life change, you need to consider updating or rewriting your will.

Inevitable expenses

Next you have to hire a lawyer to write up the will. The fees for hiring a lawyer range from $2,000 to $2,500.

You also have to choose an *executor.* This is the person who executes the will. Read the article pictured in Figure 17-5 offered by Nolo's Legal Encyclopedia, for answers to frequently asked questions about choosing an executor. Go to Keyword: **Estate Planning**, and select Nolo: Wills and Estate Planning from the subject box. Click Probate and Executors and scroll down to Executors FAQ.

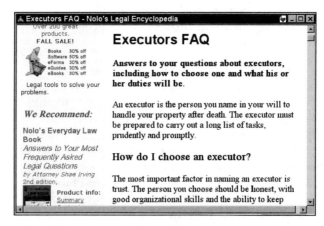

Figure 17-5. Choosing an executor wisely ensures that your will's intentions will be carried out smoothly.

Executors pay any bills and taxes that you have left before they transfer your property to the beneficiary. The bills must be paid in cash and may include funeral expenses, medical expenses, mortgages, pledges to charities, and others. If the estate is large or complicated, there may be court costs too.

Administering the estate can be a hefty expense — up to half of what it's worth, depending on the size and complexity of the estate. Fees for administration are taken from the estate and used to pay a broker to appraise the primary residence and/or vacation home, maintain the property, and sell stocks, bonds, and other securities.

Cutting Out Uncle Sam—Legally

Normally you wouldn't try to reduce the value of what you own. But estate planning is different. After all, this whole exercise is about how to give away everything you own eventually. So if you start giving assets away sooner, you can shrink the size of your estate and thus cut your tax bill. As financial planning guru Rick Edelman advocates in the chapter shown in Figure 17-6, sometimes you make money by giving it away. To read this article, go to Keyword: **Edelman,** and select The Truth About Money Online from the subject box. Click Chapter 11, Estate Planning, and select Chapter 75 – How to Make Money by Giving it Away.

Figure 17-6. It may seem backwards, but sometimes the best way to protect your assets is to give them away.

Find It Online

For a review of gift tax strategies, go to Keyword: **http://www. smartmoney.com**, and click the PLANNING tab. Click Estate Planning, and read the article "Start Giving It Away Early" for details on the ins and outs of the gift tax.

Find It Online

SmartMoney offers helpful advice and worksheets for figuring out what taxes you will owe if you sell your house. Go to Keyword: **http://www.smart money.com**, click the Planning tab, and select Home Ownership. From the list of advice articles, select Taxes When You Sell Your Home. Scroll down to the topic Death and Taxes for advice on estate planning matters.

You can consider several strategies. First, every year both you and your spouse each can give your children up to $10,000 without paying a gift tax. This is $10,000 per child. It is a way to reduce the size of your estate. In fact, these gifts are the best estate-planning tools. You can give larger gifts, but you may have to pay a gift tax.

You should know about a few things before passing a home on to your children or someone you care about. First, you need to appraise it to find out the *fair market value*. Fair market value is what the house is worth if you sell it today, and will determine the size of the gift you are passing along. Any broker can appraise your home. They typically charge a fee of $300 to $400, depending on the size of the home.

Another way to reduce your tax bite — on your regular tax bill as well as in your estate — is to give money to charity. The organization receiving the contribution must be a corporation, association, or fraternal society organized for religious, scientific, literary, or educational purposes. For more information about charitable contributions, check out the SmartMoney article in Figure 17-7. Go to Keyword: **http://www.smartmoney.com**, and select the Planning tab. Click Estate Planning, and select the article "Charitable Trusts."

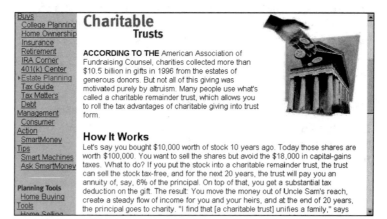

Figure 17-7. Many investors prefer to give their assets to charitable causes during their lifetimes.

Should You Trust a Trust?

You can also establish a trust. If you are successful in your investing and financial planning, or if you have been fortu nate enough to land stock options in a successful company, chances are you have accumulated enough money to warrant starting a trust.

Trusts fall into two categories: a *living trust* or a *testamentary trust*. Living trusts are trusts that you set up and are effective when you're alive. A testamentary trust goes into effect only when you die.

There are two forms of living trusts: revocable and irrevoca- ble. You may set up a revocable trust to avoid probate and to have a trustee manage the assets in case you become disabled. You can end your revocable trust any time while you're alive and competent.

The advantage of a revocable trust is that you can administer the plan, watch how it operates, and make any adjustments while you're alive. Also, if you can afford it, you can give a life- time gift of up to $10,000 per year on an ongoing basis to each of your children. Moreover, the property in the trust is not subject to probate court or distribution under intestacy laws or under a will. Finally, it's more immune to legal attacks by someone who is not a beneficiary but feels entitled to receive part of your estate.

Of course nothing is perfect. A revocable trust is included in your estate for estate tax purposes. And paying trustees to administer the trust and manage the property offsets any tax savings.

So how about an irrevocable trust? Well, it's a lot less flexible. You lose your rights to any property that you give to a benefi- ciary. Once you've made this decision, it's set in stone and you can't change anything. With an irrevocable trust you cannot modify or revoke the trust, change beneficiaries or what they will inherit, change any enjoyment that the beneficiary may get from the property, or manage or direct the investments.

Definition

intestate: The condition of dying without a valid will. The probate court then appoints an administrator to distribute the deceased person's property according to state law.

Find It Online

The legalities of setting up a trust may seem formidable, but don't let the legalese intimidate you. There are online sites available to help you untangle the Web of legal jargon and decide if a living trust is the best way to settle your estate.

Go to Keyword: **Estate Planning** and click Nolo: Wills & Estate Planning to open up Nolo.com's Legal Encyclopedia. Click the topic Living Trusts for a series of articles that will help you decide whether this sort of legal arrangement is suitable for your needs. The series starts with the Living Trust FAQ, a series of answers to common questions that provides a good starting point for your research. This series also provides helpful information on choosing a lawyer to assist you in establishing a living trust, and offers guidelines as to how much such a service should cost.

Tip

AOL can value your stock portfolio in the blink of an eye. Go to Keyword: **Quote** to arrive at AOL's portfolio center.

The upside of this type of trust, however, is the sizable tax savings — because, in this case, you truly have reduced the value of the assets over which you exercise control.

Trust investments

Relax: the trustee isn't going to blow all your hard-earned money on a hot stock tip from his brother-in-law. There are laws to protect against that, such as the so-called prudent man rule. The trustee has fiduciary responsibility when it comes to protecting trust assets. As fiduciary, he or she must invest the way any prudent, knowledgeable person would.

In practice, the prudent investor standard has generally meant that trusts invest in a diversified mix of fairly low-risk, big-name stocks, bonds, and even real estate (depending on the size of the trust). Indeed many states spell out exactly what the trust may invest in (typically short-term U.S. Treasury notes, bonds, and public utility bonds). The trouble is that low risk usually produces low returns.

However, these laws are changing as more Americans are growing wealthy and the need to have a trust has never been greater. Stock market returns have created huge wealth over the last 15 years. In fact it's estimated that $20 trillion in assets can be transferred over the next 25 years.

Summary

In this chapter, you learned about the risks your beneficiaries face if you do not plan how your assets will be dispersed upon your death. The government may take all the wealth you have accumulated unless you devise specific plans to give the money and property to your heirs or to your favorite charity. There are a number of tools an AOL keyword away to help you prepare an adequate will or establish a trust. This final chapter should be the last step for you to establish a secure financial foundation.

The following appendices give you a list of AOL partners and keywords to explore the full range of financial planning tools available.

Appendix A
Who's Who?

J ust because you're an individual investor doesn't mean you have to go it alone. AOL has lined up the best partners in the business to help you. Here's a sampling.

Armchair Millionaire (Keyword: Armchair Millionaire)

These AOL partners capitalize on commonsense tools and advice for saving and investing, as opposed to hot tips or get-rich schemes. Based on the belief that it is possible for anyone to become a millionaire in 20 or 30 years through regular saving and investing, Armchair Millionaire offers a variety of tools for investors, particularly those interested in investment clubs. Pointers include the ABCs of investment clubs, forums to discuss finding other club members, model portfolios, stock suggestions, and the Millionaires' "Five Steps to Financial Freedom" — a long-term plan that helps investors reach their financial goals.

Bloomberg Online (Keyword: Bloomberg)

This financial news service reports world and business news all day, every day. In addition to market, technical, and workplace updates, Bloomberg offers portfolio trackers, calculators for mortgages and retirements, charts, quotes, news videos, and other resources for the personal investor looking for up-to-the-minute news and information.

Business Week Online (Keyword: BW)

An electronic version of the world's largest business magazine offers current and archived issues, live conferences with editors and newsmakers, and an electronic bookstore.

Decision Point (Keyword: DP)

Partners with AOL since 1992, Decision Point features daily analysis from industry leaders, teaches investors the basics of technical analysis, and tracks the relative strength of 102 industry groups. TraderNick gives his top choices on the weekly Nick's Picks. This site features a wide variety of indicators for the chart-watchers.

Edelman Financial Services (Keyword: Edelman)

Ric Edelman's AOL site offers financial advice on everyday issues such as planning for retirement, buying and selling a house, and getting out of debt. Edelman, a Georgetown University faculty member and founder of Edelman Financial Services, was named "arguably the most successful financial advisor in the nation" by Dow Jones Investment Advisor. He hosts two weekly syndicated radio shows and is the author of *The Truth About Money* and *The New Rules of Money.*

Hoover's Online (Keyword: Hoover's)

Hoover's Online offers AOL users free snapshots on more than 13,500 companies, as well as in-depth company profiles. Besides providing industry reports and current financial data, Hoover's has features like Company of the Day, which profiles businesses in the news, and IPO Central, which teaches users how the IPO process works; and gives timetables for new company ventures. Tools like Stock Spotlight, which identifies stocks poised for big future gains, and Today's EPS Surprises, which notes unexpected market gainers and losers, teach investors how to select stocks that are right for them.

Intuit Inc. (Keyword: Intuit)

This financial software maker sells products such as Quicken, TurboTax Online, QuickenMortgage, and Quicken InsureMarket, and, through its Web site, offers content to augment these products. Message boards address questions about Intuit products and financial issues, while interactive areas offer online banking, tax-preparation, insurance, investing, personal finance, and technical support needs.

Investor's Business Daily (Keyword: http://www.investors.com)

Investor's Business Daily newspaper covers business, financial, economic, and national news. Drawing from its sister company, research services firm William O'Neil & Co., the paper offers evaluative tables, screens, and graphs in each issue.

AOL members follow founder O'Neil's course "26 Weeks to Investment Success." Members can also talk over the day's market news on the IBD message boards or join the monthly IBD stock challenge, which awards free months of AOL membership to the member who identifies the stock with the most growth potential.

Market Guide (Keyword: Market Guide)

A provider of investment information to the professional investment community for more than 15 years, Market Guide's comprehensive financial databases and screening tools are now available to AOL subscribers. Individual investors have access to a wide variety of charts, histories, and statistics on more than 10,000 publicly traded companies. The Market Guide Stock Report offers investors a comprehensive basis for comparing stocks, Investor's Corner keeps members on top of daily market action, and What's Hot reports daily on the hottest sectors, industries and stocks.

Money Whiz (Keyword: Money Whiz)

The mission of the MoneyWhiz, owned by Bank Rate Monitor, is to educate and inspire people to make positive changes in their financial lives. Through a community-oriented, interactive, personal finance forum, Money Whiz offers AOL members non-intimidating features such as nightly chats on standing up to creditors and evaluating insurance coverage. Today's Money Story enables AOL members to question experts on pressing financial troubles. Message boards cover areas from "Diapers & Dollars" to retirement planning, while experts offers columns on family finances, life planning, and reducing taxes.

Motley Fool Inc. (Keyword: Fool)

The Motley Fool, founded by brothers David and Tom Gardner in 1994, educates, amuses and enriches investors. The site is dedicated to helping investors create wealth by investing in stocks. The group's flagship Fool Portfolio routinely doubles the returns of the S&P 500. On AOL, members learn the 13 Steps to Investing Foolishly, how to invest in the Fool Four stocks and how to value stocks via the Fool Ratio. Members meet other Fools through chats and message boards with topics like the Fool Top 25 and Investment Strategies. Follow the brothers' investment ideas with the Fool, Boring, DRIP, and Cash-King model portfolios.

Multex Investor Network (Keyword: Multex)

Multex Investor Network offers online access to more than 650,000 analyst reports, plus content such as Highs & Lows, about the peaks and valleys of stock trading; Tech Beat, which tracks technology stocks; and New Buys — recent "buy" recommendations from various brokerage firms. Multex provides multimedia and rich-text research reports, advanced searching features, customizable delivery options and viewing, printing, faxing, and e-mail options.

The Online Investor on America Online (Keyword: Online Investor)

The Online Investor guides investors to financial sites and then explains them. Partners Ted Allrich and James Hale oversee features like Guides to Company Research and Mutual

Funds, Market Watch, Company Spotlight, and Ingredients of Investment Success. AOL members get market news and alerts in Market Watch and can focus on specific firms in Company Spotlight. Special features include weekly IPO and Earnings Calendars; columns like You and Your Broker, which demystifies brokerage accounts; and a variety of message boards, including one on market rumors — what investors are hearing and whether it's true.

Sage Online (Keyword: Sage)

Founded in 1996 by brothers Stephen and Alan Cohn, Sage Online's goal is to help individuals make better mutual fund and other investment decisions. Besides checking on daily mutual fund news, AOL members can go to Sage School to learn the eight lessons every beginning mutual fund investor should know; participate in Sage Voices, where investment experts chat and answer postings on mutual fund questions; and build investment portfolios from Sage models based on the different stages of a person's life. Members can also find other mutual fund investors at the 24-Hour Chat Café and say what's on their mind at the Sage Soapbox.

Shark Attack (Keyword: Shark Attack)

Shark Attack is dedicated to the idea that money can be made by aggressively trading stocks, and provides the arena where beginners and experts alike learn about day trading. AOL members visit the Shark Tank, where day traders chat, review top market news and charts, and check out the Rev. Shark's current portfolio holdings. Get day-trading tips from the Trading Methods Q&A message board.

SmartCalc (Keyword: Calculator)

Need a calculator tailored to a specific investment need? SmartCalc offers more than 100 financial calculators in 11 different categories, as well as tools to explore specific financial decisions, compare alternatives, and test future scenarios. SmartCalc's computational programs include graphs and pie charts to illustrate computed results and potential scenarios.

Standard & Poor's Personal Wealth (Keyword: Personal Wealth)

S&P's Personal Wealth offers investment recommendations and analyses on more than 9,500 publicly traded stocks and 8,500 mutual funds, drawing not only from Standard & Poor's, but other McGraw-Hill companies such as Business Week, MarketScope, and MMS International. Market Snapshots offers real-time news and commentary on the day's stock, commodities, and bonds markets; Technical Market Insight offers an analyst's technical view of the equities market; and in the Plans and Advice section, S&P advisors help investors understand and create realistic ways to meet financial goals.

TheStreet.com (Keyword: The Street)

TheStreet offers news from financial journalists around the world to assess the performance of investment vehicles, as well as the performance of those who manage them. AOL members read James Cramer's daily columns, along with a host of others, post in forums like Home Traders Trade Secrets and Finding the Right Online Broker, or visit Options, Mutual Funds and Company News where TheStreet reporters explain how things really work.

TaxLogic Online (Keyword: TaxLogic)

TaxLogic provides easy-to-understand tax information that helps readers reduce taxes. AOL members keep up to date on changes in tax laws, find out the effect of rate changes, chat regularly with tax experts about personal issues, and get answers from a comprehensive FAQ with answers developed by experienced tax accountants. TaxLogic also guides members on how to file taxes online and make sense of IRS forms.

Zacks Investment Research (Keyword: Zacks)

Zacks provides all facets of quantitative research for analysts, corporate investors, brokers and individual investors. Zacks summarizes current stock recommendations of 3,000 analysts employed by 230 U.S. brokerage firms to give complete analyses of 6,000 companies. Special features include Timely Monthly Buys, the Stock Pick of the Month, and Earnings Surprises — daily reports on over- or underperforming stocks.

Keywords

Keywords for financial resources

Keywords for banks online

Keywords for stock trading online

This book is littered with **Keywords**! Where do they take you? Here's the treasure map.

Active Trader	A direct line to quotes, news, and information on your investments, as well as key indices. Special departments feature commentary on equities, Internet stocks, IPOs, options, futures, and more.
Advice & Planning (also **Budget** or **Your Money**)	Financial advice and links on how to prepare for the different events in your life, such as getting married, having kids, planning for retirement, and facing health problems.

Armchair Millionaire	For investment club information, including how to start and run a club, and keep it running smoothly. Interactive tool offered helps create a personalized, five-step financial plan to becoming a millionaire.
Auto Buying Guide	For how-to tips and guidance on buying or selling a car, the latest loan rates, car ratings, and more.
BW Daily	Daily columns and articles from Business Week's online version, as well as daily market updates.
Banking (also **Bank**)	To bank online, or to shop for online banking services in the AOL Banking Center.
BankNOW	To bank directly with more than a dozen institutions. Transactions are secured by encryption, PIN, and password.
Bank Rate Monitor (also **BRM** or **BankRate**)	Tracks interest rates on car loans, credit cards, mortgages, certificates of deposit, and the like.
Bloomberg	For comprehensive coverage of financial markets in the United States and around the world. Includes the day's top business and world news, and the latest market figures.
Broker	Takes you to the AOL Brokerage Center, from which you can invest and trade online via DLJ Direct, E*TRADE, AmeriTrade, and Waterhouse Securities.
Business News (also **BusNewsCenter**)	Brings you the latest business, economic, and industry news, along with the day's top stocks, searchable databases, press releases, and market news.
Business Summary	Hourly headlines and summaries keep you updated with the latest news and events.

Business Week (also **BW**)	Accesses Business Week Online, the online version of the weekly business publication, plus an archive of every issue back to 1991.
Calculator	SmartCalc's calculators provide members an easy way to calculate everything from how much house they can afford, to how much it will take to retire, and more.
Chartomatic	Chart-O-Matic follows the ups and downs of the stock market with charts showing stock market indices, as well as stocks from the S&P 500, updated every few minutes.
Charts (also **Historical quotes**)	Historical quotes and graphs help chart the performance of stocks and mutual funds over time. Create your own charts, or download data in the format of your choice.
College (also **College Prep**)	Information about how to find and get into the college of your choice, as well as how to go about paying for it.
College Board	Starting points for college applications and entrance examinations, as well as beginning the financial aid process.
Company News	Type in a ticker symbol to search the latest news for stories related to your investments.
Company Research (also **Investment Research**)	Everything you need to research potential investments. The searchable database includes company profiles, historical quotes, earnings data, SEC filings, and mutual fund reports.
Credit Alert	Provides access to your own credit report, as well as other personal records for review, with an annual subscription fee.

Credit&Debt	A launching pad for information on how to gain control of your finances and get out of debt, including links to credit and debt calculators, the best interest rates, and how to repair a damaged credit report.
DP (Also **TAC** and **Decision Point**)	Decision Point Timing & Charts provides technical analysis tools to help you weigh investing factors. Includes daily reports more than 150 stocks and 160 mutual funds.
Disclosure (also **Financials**)	Disclosure provides information on public companies, including 10K and 10Q filings with the Securities and Exchange Commission. Also links to other searchable databases.
Edelman (also **Money U**)	Easy-to-follow financial planning advice from *The Truth About Money* author Ric Edelman.
Edgar	Electronic Data Gathering, Analysis and Retrieval from the SEC. The site features a search engine, and also shows investors how to use the information reported in two primary SEC reports: the 10K and 10Q.
Exchange Center	Springboard to a half-dozen exchanges, including the NASDAQ Stock Market and the Chicago Mercantile Exchange.
Family Money	The Better Homes & Gardens site for financial education and advice on everything from insurance and college funds to bonds and stock trading, geared toward families.
FastWeb	A free scholarship and college search program that allows users to enter personalized information.

Finance (also **Personal Finance** or **PF**)	AOL's Personal Finance area offers everything from quotes to market snapshots, and provides direct links to investing and marketing departments and financial centers.
Financial Aid	Complete guide to finding both federal and private financial aid for college, including tutorials and links to a scholarship database.
Financial Independence	Tips and tools for people looking to get out of debt and begin investing, includes a valuation guide of your own current net worth.
Fool (also **Motley Fool** or **MF**)	To The Motley Fool, a great place to hone your investing skills with humor, helping you laugh all the way to the bank. Includes tools and advice on financial information, as well as forums for discussing investment and personal financial decisions.
401(k) (also **401K**)	Everything you need to maximize the earnings potential of your current 401(k) plan, or to set up a new one.
Fund Companies	Gets you direct access to some of the top mutual fund company Web sites. Also provides links to Morningstar's fund reports and Sage's fund message boards.
Fund Screening	A guide to fund definitions and fund family names and explains how to screen funds. The screening tool allows you to input variables to find funds that match your needs.
Gomez	The arbiter of online commerce, Gomez offers impartial ratings for online brokers and bankers, as well as help on how to find and use the best of the best online.

B

Keywords

HomeFair (also **HomeBuyer'sFair**)

HomeFair will help you with all your relocation needs: Salary comparisons, school reports, lifestyle optimizer, and more.

HomePriceCheck

Home Price Check helps you locate all homes that sold on a particular street, find the sales history of a specific address, and find all homes sold within a certain price range in one city.

Hoovers (also **Company Profiles**)

Hoover's Business Resources offers detailed profiles on more than 2500 companies and basic statistics on more than 10,000 others.

IPO Central (also **IPO**)

Hoover's provides the latest IPO filings, offerings, news, and more.

IVillage

Among many other features, gives women debt-management and investment advice in the Money department. Includes a financial health checkup.

Insurance Center (also **Insurance**)

The Insurance Center offers advice on insuring your health and protecting your wealth, as well as rates and quotes.

InsureMarket

Provides tools to figure your insurance needs, as well as instant quotes. From Quicken's InsureMarket.

Interest Rates

The latest headlines, news, and commentary regarding interest rates.

Investing Basics (also **PF Basics**)

Eight easy steps to becoming an investor; including basic investing concepts; information on stocks, mutual funds, and bonds; and tips to finding good investments and a good broker.

InvestingForums (also **PF Forums** or **Investors** or **StockTalk**)	AOL's community center for discussing stocks, mutual funds, and the like with fellow investors via the message boards, including those on Online Investor, Sage, Armchair Millionaire, Sage, Decision Point, The Street.com, Motley Fool, and others.
INVESTools	The Web-based section publishes daily advisories from independent analysts at investment newsletters, focusing on individual stocks, sectors, and trends.
Market Day	A pulse reading of current market activity, including live reports on active stocks and what's driving them and the day's hot and weak sectors.
Market Guide	Provides Market Guide's comprehensive fundamental financial information on more than 10,000 public companies. Includes searchable databases, earnings estimates, stock reports, and company overviews.
Market News Center (also **MNC**)	Market News Center provides the latest market news and data. Includes access to Dow Jones and NASDAQ composites, the Long Bond and yen, constantly updated. Also includes searchable databases.
Market Talk	Live chats with market experts and industry insiders, hosted by Sage. Ask questions and get answers weekdays from 9 a.m. to 7 p.m. EST.
Money.com (also **MoneyMag**)	Money Magazine's online equivalent offers resources like tutorials, tools, financial makeovers, and tips addressing financial and investing topics.

B

Keywords

Morningstar
(also **Mstar**)

Morningstar provides the latest in mutual fund information to determine how your mutual funds are performing, or to evaluate potential investments.

Multex

Multex Investor Network provides a place for serious investors to read and discuss investment research. Includes more than 200,000 investment research reports from more than 200 brokerage houses, investment banks, and independent research providers.

Mutual Funds

The Mutual Funds Center is a one-stop shop for links to every bit of mutual fund information on AOL.

Nightly Business Report (also **NBR**)

Site of the television program The Nightly Business Report. Includes transcripts and investment information.

Online Investor
(also **OLI**)

The Online Investor offers tips, news, and information for anyone currently investing online, or exploring the possibility.

PF Live

Personal Finance Live is the center for live events and community information in the Personal Finance Channel. Hosts daily live events and chats related to investment and finance.

PF Newsletter

Brings you a newsstand worth of newsletters, such as Checks and Balances, the AOL newsletter full of advice about managing your money. Can be delivered weekly to your e-mailbox.

PF Search

The search engine examines AOL's entire personal finance section to find the information you're looking for.

PS Money	A forum from Parent Soup that allows you to ask your specific financial questions and receive answers from the experts.
Parent Soup	Links to advice and information for parents on the costs of raising a family, from affording a newborn to paying for college.
Personal Wealth (also **S&PPW** or **S&Ppersonalwealth**)	Standard & Poor's Personal Wealth section provides comprehensive investment planning and advice. Premium services also available for a monthly subscription fee.
Portfolio	To the portfolios section, which enables you to set up online portfolios to track your holdings. You can refresh them constantly and follow their progress during the market day.
Portfolio Direct	A free AOL subscription service that delivers personalized stock market quotes, news, and other information to your e-mail box each day.
PortfolioGuide	Online help manual for setting up and tracking your portfolios, both real and imaginary, using AOL's Portfolio tool.
Quicken	Links to Quicken.com's investing and personal finance site. Includes advice, tools, and tutorials that help you make the most of your money. Also features current news, interactive savings calculators, financial quizzes, and an insurance center.
Quicken Mortgage	Helps you comparison shop for mortgages and find the best loans for what you need.

Quotes (also **Snapshot** or **Stocks**)
Provides a snapshot of your stock's current activity, from price to volume to highs and lows. Also includes annual and monthly averages.

Real Estate
A guide to helping you look for real estate; finance, sell, or rent it; or move.

REC Looking (also **Looking**)
More than a million current real estate listings from Realtor.com.

REC Renting (also **Renting**)
More than 6.5 million rentals available from SpringStreet.com, as well as available apartments from Apartments.com, among other renting-related content.

REC Mortgage (also **Mortgage**)
Tools and advice to help you determine the best loans for what you need, and comparison shop for mortgages.

REC Moving (also **Moving**)
Thinking of moving? These tools help with all your relocation needs, from salary comparisons, to free school reports, to helping you compare costs and find a moving company.

RSP (also **Research** or **Funding Focus**)
Guide to scholarships, grants, and financial aid for higher education, including links for applying online for loans.

Retirement (also **Retire**)
The AOL gateway to retiring in style, full of articles, tools, tips, and links on how to make the most of your golden years.

Shark Attack (also **Traders**)
The place for active traders who want to talk with their fast-buying and selling brethren. Also features sample portfolios and advice on how to swim with investing's elite.

Sage
Comprehensive information, research, and advice on examining and investing in mutual funds.

Sage Models	Portfolio strategies from the mutual fund experts at Sage to help you maximize your earnings potential, including lists of top funds and sample portfolios.
Sage School	A primer for mutual funds and other areas of investing, including bonds.
Saving for School	Advice on how to plan and budget for a college education, whether you are aiming for 20 years or 2 years down the road.
Social Security	Get the latest on how current legislation is affecting the future of Social Security, as well as links to estimating your retirement earnings and to contacting your Congressman.
Stock Screening	A guide to screening for stocks. The screening tool allows you to input variables to find stocks that match your particular needs.
Tax	For tax-planning advice, news, forms, schedules, chats, software, and IRA information, as well as the U.S. Tax Code.
TaxLogic	While taxes might not always seem logical, TaxLogic provides information to help take the mystery out of this American staple.
Telescan	A launching pad to Telescan, the analytical investment tool that enables you to select and evaluate securities according to criteria you select.
TheStreet.com (also **TSC** and **TheStreet**)	Daily analysis of the day's market movements, forums, research and chats from Jim Cramer and colleagues.
TheWhiz (also **MoneyWhiz** and **Whiz**)	Provides real-life solutions to personal financial quandaries, in a user-friendly format.

B

Keywords

ThirdAge	ThirdAge provides folks in their 40s, 50s, and 60s financial advice targeted to needs of this stage in life.
Vault	Opens the door to the mutual fund archives.
Worldly Investor	Provides a gateway to global investing and research, including daily regional reports, portfolios, and tips.
Yellow Pages	Resources to help you find local businesses by business category and city or state.
Zacks (also **Earnings**)	Links to Zacks Investment Research, which includes databases on earnings estimates and reports, as well as financial statements, SEC filings, company overviews, and stock reports.

Bank Online

To bank online directly, use any of the following keywords:

Bank of America

BankOne

Chase Manhattan

Citibank

FirstBank

First Union

Mellon Bank

PNC Bank

Republic National Bank

U.S. Bank

Wells Fargo

Or go to **Keyword: Banking**, and scroll down to your state under State Banking Centers

Trade Online

To trade directly with a broker use Keywords:

Ameritrade

DLJdirect

Etrade

Waterhouse

To access mutual fund companies directly use Keywords:

Scudder

Kaufmann

T.Rowe Price

B

Keywords

Index

(Continued)

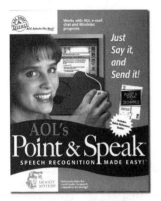

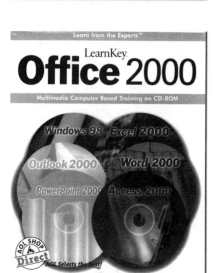

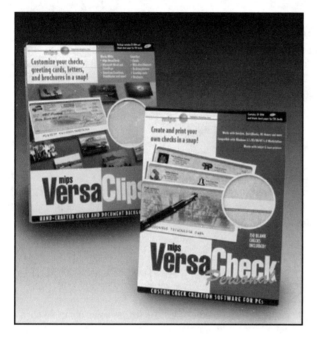

AOL Selects the Best

Send and receive email anywhere, anytime!

Go to
AOL Keyword:
Anywhere

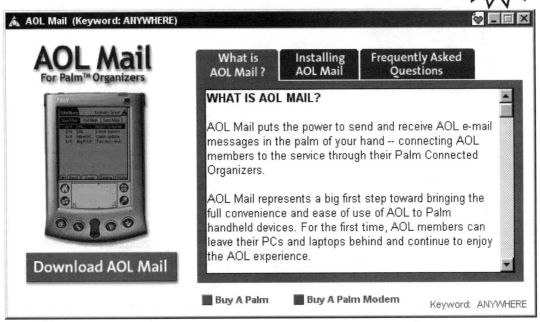

AOL Mail For Palm™ Organizers

AOL Mail represents a significant first step toward bringing the full convenience and ease of use of AOL to Palm™ handheld devices. For the first time, AOL members can leave their PCs and laptops behind and continue to enjoy the AOL experience. All you need to get going is a compatible Palm™ device*, a Palm™ snap-on modem, and an AOL account. AOL Mail connects members directly to AOL using their regular screen names and passwords. Leveraging AOL's global network of access numbers, AOL Mail allows members to connect with the service from just about anywhere. AOL Mail requires a Palm III, IIIe, IIIx, V, VII, or an earlier Palm that has been upgraded to Palm III compatibility, and 425K of free RAM.

AMERICA
Online.

Coming Soon... AOL Mail for Windows CE Palm-Size PCs

*So easy to use,
no wonder it's #1*

AOL Selects the Best

Visit the Great Shops at AOL Shop Direct!

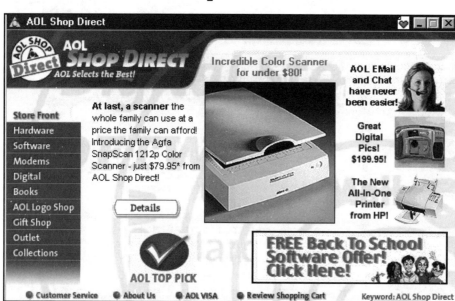

AOL Shop Direct's goal is to simplify your online and computing needs by selecting the best quality and value products available and presenting them to you in an informative easy to use store. The products in AOL Shop Direct have been pre-tested to not only ensure your 100% satisfaction, but to specifically enhance your computing and America Online experience.

Visit us today and check out our:

> Daily Specials
> Easy to use computer and Internet guides
> New Releases
> Top Picks
> And our Clearance Outlet!

All this and more is available at AOL Keyword: AOL Shop Direct

AMERICA Online.

So easy to use, no wonder it's #1

250 Hour Free Trial for One Month

Try AOL 5.0 Now!

CD-ROM Installation Instructions for Windows

1. Insert the AOL CD-ROM into your CD-ROM drive.
2. If installation does not begin automatically, click **Start** on the task bar (Windows 3.1 users click on the **File** menu of your Windows Program Manager) then select **Run**.
3. Type **D:\SETUP** (or **E:\SETUP**) and press OK. Follow the easy instructions and you'll be online in minutes!

CD-ROM Installation Instructions for MacIntosh

1. For AOL 4.0 for Mac, **insert** the AOL CD into your CD-ROM drive.
2. Double-click on the **Install** icon.
3. Follow the easy instructions and you'll be online in minutes!

FREE 250 HOUR TRIAL MUST BE USED WITHIN ONE MONTH OF INITIAL SIGN-ON. TO AVOID BEING CHARGED A MONTHLY FEE, SIMPLY CANCEL BEFORE TRIAL PERIOD ENDS. Premium services carry surcharges, and communication surcharges may apply in AK, even during trial time. Members may incur telephone charges on their phone bill, depending on their location and calling plan, even during trial time. Offer is available to new members in the US, age 18 or older, and a major credit card or checking account is required. 56K access available in many areas: actual connection speeds may vary. For information, go to Keyword: **High Speed**. America Online, AOL, and the Triangle Logo are registered service marks of America Online, Inc. Windows and Internet Explorer are registered trademarks of Microsoft Corp. Other names are property of their respective holders. Copyright ©1999 America Online, Inc. All rights reserved.

Availability may be limited, especially during peak times.

Use the unique registration number and password below for your FREE trial.

4A-3642-7681

COEVAL-LANCET

Need Help? Call us toll-free at **1-800-827-6364**